Canadian
**Culinary
Imaginations**

Edited by **Shelley Boyd**
and **Dorothy Barenscott**

Canadian Culinary Imaginations

McGill-Queen's University Press
Montreal & Kingston · London · Chicago

© McGill-Queen's University Press 2020

ISBN 978-0-2280-0086-0 (cloth)
ISBN 978-0-2280-0087-7 (paper)

Legal deposit third quarter 2020
Bibliothèque nationale du Québec

Printed in Canada on acid-free paper

This book has been published with the help of a grant from the Canadian Federation for the Humanities and Social Sciences, through the Awards to Scholarly Publications Program, using funds provided by the Social Sciences and Humanities Research Council of Canada. Funding was also received from the Faculty of Arts Excellence and Advancement Fund, Kwantlen Polytechnic University.

We acknowledge the support of the Canada Council for the Arts.

Nous remercions le Conseil des arts du Canada de son soutien.

Library and Archives Canada Cataloguing in Publication
Title: Canadian culinary imaginations / edited by Shelley Boyd
   and Dorothy Barenscott.
Names: Boyd, Shelley, 1974- editor. | Barenscott, Dorothy, editor.
Description: Includes bibliographical references and index.
Identifiers: Canadiana 20200203835 | ISBN 9780228000877 (paper) | ISBN
   9780228000860 (cloth)
Subjects: LCSH: Food—Social aspects—Canada. | LCSH: Food in art. |
   LCSH: Food in literature.
Classification: LCC GT2853.C3 C36 2020 | DDC 641.3/00971—dc23

Contents

Acknowledgments | ix

Introduction | 3
Shelley Boyd and Dorothy Barenscott

Part One
Indigeneity and Foodways: Stories from Home and Abroad | 29

1 *Foodland Security*: Access to Country Food by Inuit in an Urban Setting | 31
   Barry Pottle

2 What Can We Learn from Dining with Bears? Indigenous Stories, Worldviews, and the Environment | 37
   Margery Fee

3 Changing Tides: Indigenous Chefs at the Culinary Olympics and the Gastronomic Professionalization of Aboriginal Cooking | 57
   Sebastian Schellhaas

4 *Terra Nullius* on the Plate: Colonial Blindness, Restaurant Discourse, and Indigenous Cuisines | 77
   Zoe Tennant

5 From Meat to Metaphor: Beavers and Conflicting Imaginations of the Edible | 93
   L. Sasha Gora

CONTENTS

Part Two
(Sub)Urban/Rural Imaginations: Producing and Representing Foodscapes | 115

6 Montreal in the Culinary Imagination | 117
Nathalie Cooke

7 Creating Contemporary Canadian Agri-Art: Learning from Practice, Responding to Place, Working with Immateriality | 146
Sylvia Grace Borda

8 Food, Place, and Power in Timothy Taylor's *Stanley Park* | 162
Wendy Roy

9 PLOT: An Interview with Cora and Don Li-Leger (The People's Food Security Bureau) | 183
Cora and Don Li-Leger (interviewed by Dorothy Barenscott)

10 A Case Study on Ghost River Theatre's Food Performance | 200
Angela Ferreira

Part Three
Culinary Lineages: Collective and Personal Reflections | 211

11 Chewed a Book Lately? Douglas Coupland's *Souvenir of Canada* Coffee-Table Books | 213
Shelley Boyd

12 Phototextual Remembering in Janice Wong's *Chow: From China to Canada: Memories of Food + Family* | 241
Glenn Deer

13 The Royal Cafe Experience | 263
Elyse Bouvier

14 Writing beyond "Currybooks": Construction of Racialized and Gendered Diasporic Identities in Anita Rau Badami's *Can You Hear the Nightbird Call?* | 277
Asma Sayed

15 Playing with Food | 295
Jason Wright

Part Four
Subverting Categories: Critical-Creative Re-interpretations of Food | 309

16 Breaking Bread: Queer Foodways and the Non-human | 311
Jes Battis

17 A Taste for the Abject: Food in the Relational Artworks of Sandee Moore | 333
Sandee Moore

18 "Viciousness in the Kitchen": Women and Food in Alice Munro's Fiction and Mary Pratt's Visual Art | 348
Heidi Tiedemann Darroch

19 Table of Contents: Reading, Cooking, Eating Canadian Literature | 364
Alexia Moyer

20 A ~~MEAT~~/MEETing in the Park: Ursula Johnson's *(re)al-location* and The Festival of Stewards | 376
David Diviney and Melinda Spooner (in conversation with Ursula Johnson)

Figures | 391
Contributors | 397
Index | 403

Acknowledgments

Canadian Culinary Imaginations developed from an undergraduate course project and teaching innovation, followed by an interdisciplinary symposium and art exhibition that took place at Kwantlen Polytechnic University (KPU) in February 2016. Partnering with a group of scholars researching food in literature, Shelley Boyd looked to build a community of interest at her home institution of KPU in the fall of 2015 by initiating a teaching collaboration with art historian Dorothy Barenscott and several studio instructors in the Department of Fine Arts. Working closely with these instructors in this first-ever interdepartmental collaboration, Boyd paired students from English and Fine Arts to create interrelated written and visual art projects interpreting food-related poems assigned in her English 2301: Canadian Literature in English course. Fine Arts faculty participants included Nancy Duff (Painting), Sibeal Foyle (Painting), Ying-Yueh Chuang (Ceramics), Kitty Leung (Printmaking), Paulo Majano (Photography), Emily Geen (Photography), and Matilda Aslizadeh (Digital Media). Funded through a Faculty of Arts Excellence and Advancement Fund, the symposium, co-organized by Boyd and Barenscott, drew on the energy generated from the teaching collaboration and the students' cross-disciplinary projects. The vibrant two-day event assembled literary scholars; creative writers; art historians; food journalists and historians; performance, mixed-media, and visual artists; anthropologists; community activists; and members of the public. An art exhibition, *Artful Fare: Conversations about Food*, emerging from the students' course projects, featured textual and visual exchanges between English and Fine Arts students at KPU; it was on display at the symposium and welcomed a younger generation to be part of the conversation. During the symposium's presentations and discussions, what became clear was a common interest in enacting food – in exploring food's potential to challenge perceptions and societal norms; to transform ideas and narratives about individual experience, community, and nation; and to be experienced as a living material to be shaped, altered, consumed, or shared in unfamiliar ways. Following the symposium, presenters were invited to submit proposals and papers for consideration in this collection of essays. From 2017 to 2018, additional submissions were solicited from scholars and artists whose areas of interest are food-related.

We are grateful for the dedication and patience of the contributors who worked tirelessly in researching, writing, compiling, and revising their chapters. We would also like to thank KPU for supporting this project through our back-to-back sabbaticals, which allowed us to move this book forward during time-intensive stages.

In addition to the hard work of our contributors, this collection has been made possible through the encouragement and practical support of many people. Special thanks are due to our KPU colleague Wendy Smith (Department of English) for her generosity in volunteering to copyedit several chapters of the manuscript. Wendy, your thoroughness and attention to detail are simply amazing. We also appreciate the printing support provided by KPU's Department of Fine Arts. As a department, you are always ready to lend a much-needed hand. Shelley would like to thank Marilyn and Keith Boyd for their love and encouragement (and especially Marilyn for her proofreading assistance); Paul Ohler for his editorial advice and emergency technical support; Nathalie Cooke for her friendship and for first inspiring my interest in food as a graduate student; and Dorothy Barenscott for her knowledge and talent in art history that brought this book to fruition. Dorothy would like to thank Brian Barenscott for his constant support, love, and patience; and Shelley Boyd for her drive and vision in seeing the potential for this cross-disciplinary project from its earliest stages.

We save our final words of thanks for McGill-Queen's University Press for their skill and professionalism; for the anonymous reviewers who provided constructive and encouraging reports; for Eleanor Gasparik's skilful and attentive copyediting; and for our editor, Khadija Coxon. Khadija, your enthusiasm, guidance, and insightful suggestions throughout this process have been invaluable. We could not have asked for a better fellow "cook" in the kitchen.

This book has been published with the assistance of a grant from the Federation for the Humanities and Social Sciences, through the Awards to Scholarly Publications Program, using funds provided by the Social Sciences and Humanities Research Council of Canada. We are also deeply grateful to Kwantlen Polytechnic University and the Faculty of Arts Excellence and Advancement Fund for their generous support.

Canadian
Culinary
Imaginations

Introduction

"Add food and *stir*."[1]

In the twenty-first century's global economy and "global village," a term first popularized by Canadian philosopher and public intellectual Marshall McLuhan, food cultures and their expressions hinge on the connections and tensions between the local, national, and transnational – relationships that creative thinkers and producers are primed to explore.[2] Within these contexts, the imagination harnesses food's critical and aesthetic potential for unpredictable results, something that McLuhan indirectly suggests when reflecting on information media: "Food for the mind is like food for the body; the inputs are never the same as the outputs."[3] For McLuhan, the media environment shapes people as they inhabit and incorporate it. Manipulated and assimilated daily, food similarly constitutes our environments and extends our perceptions. Indeed, on the Chicago School of Media Theory's website, the entry for "food" states that while "speech and print ... fit more comfortably with the Oxford English Dictionary or McLuhan-esque definitions of mediums, food also occupies such an everyday role ... Its significance as a medium is overwhelmed not only by the smartphones and computer monitors that occupy much of our attention, but also by some of its own characteristics, such as its fleeting, distracting, and most noticeable traits of taste and smell."[4]

Food not only imparts a world of information and meaning but also connects the larger world. When commenting on the mediated environment, McLuhan's use of food metaphors is striking, even though his argument is for the mechanical and electronic transformation of society. "'We have become like the most primitive Paleolithic man,' argues McLuhan, 'once more global wanderers, but information gatherers rather than food gatherers. From now on the source of food, wealth and life itself will be information."⁵ This strategic use of aphorisms is, as B.W. Powe argues, how McLuhan creates "counter-environments, or counter-readings" so that his readers may be alerted to their everyday mediated world.⁶

For McLuhan, routine perceptions, or fixed points of view, are the main obstacles as society becomes habituated in and through the media it consumes.⁷ One aim of this collection is to approach food critically and creatively so that counter-environments may reactivate normative or non-perceivable Canadian food environments. How might we flip some of McLuhan's aphorisms and analogies in order to see food as information media that is continually remade and reimagined over time, just as it reinvents us? Understanding food not solely as an expressive medium (in the singular) but as multimodal media (in the plural) means that food sits at the intersections of material and popular cultures, languages, literary and artistic forms, screen cultures, local traditions, and the global market. McLuhan and graphic artist Quentin Fiore's collaborative edition *The Medium Is the Massage* opens with the greeting "Good Morning!" in juxtaposition with a provocative and arguably dystopic black-and-white photograph of a simple plate and raw egg, its yolk partially covered with a trademark created by "a no-contact, no-pressure printing technique."⁸ This merging of technologies – print (text) and print (image) – with food evokes the notion of food not only as media but also as manipulated and represented through further distinct media channels. Animating Claude Lévi-Strauss's theory of the raw and the cooked, the untouched egg has been "cooked" through its multimodal representation, which includes mass-market food rituals and the brand environment. The egg suggests (or warns) that food is a highly consumable technological environment that surrounds and enters us.

McLuhan's reflections on how distance is bridged through mass media have inspired food journalists to speak more recently of a "global *food* village."⁹ At the same time, Sandra M. Gilbert's directive, "Add food and *stir*," from her landmark book *The Culinary Imagination: From Myth to Modernity* highlights food's indelible connection to lived experience – to emotions, memories, and dreams. Food is a significant mode of thinking and imagining, Gilbert contends, having assumed an unparalleled place in popular culture and the arts in the "gastronomically obsessed twenty-first century"; "when we add food," we stir emotions, reminding others "of their places at the complicated buffet of self, family, culture."¹⁰ We also potentially *stir the pot* by provoking the unexpected through ideas and conversations that disrupt the status quo. Gilbert's book invites reflections that scale outward from the individual and the community, to the nation and the globe. The intrigue of this

Figure 0.1
"Good Morning!" reprinted in Marshall McLuhan and Quentin Fiore, *The Medium Is the Massage*, 2001.

metaphorical buffet is certainly in Bee Wilson's mind in her review of Gilbert's book. Noting the "allure" of imagined food, Wilson observes that it allows one to "borrow someone else's mouth" and experience the world viscerally from another point of view.[11]

Taking its initial inspiration from McLuhan and Gilbert, *Canadian Culinary Imaginations* is an interdisciplinary collection that strategically brings together academics, creative writers, food journalists, artists, and curators who revel in this kind of exchange, inviting conversations about food that have shaped creative thinking within a range of contexts both at home and in the world. What culinary imaginings stir Canadians? What is it like to experience the nation and the world through someone else's mouth and food-related memories, concepts, and emotions? How has food entered into our literatures, restaurants, galleries, screens, studios, popular cultures, kitchens, and public spaces? And why is the topic of food potentially more relevant today than ever before? These are just a few of the questions pursued by the contributors in this collection as they traverse the boundaries of their respective disciplines and exploratory frameworks. Together, they reveal that Canadian culinary imaginations are pluralistic in their articulations of diverse historical and contemporary contexts, cultural and spatial geographies, and personal and artistic sensibilities. These imaginations are also transformational: they not only reflect but also produce the diverse bodies, places, communities, and larger environments that we inhabit. In the hands, minds, and mouths of creative thinkers and producers, food has the power to defamiliarize the everyday, to facilitate novel interactions with others and the surrounding environment, and to provoke conversations.

In light of the fact that no book focuses exclusively on food-related creative expressions in the Canadian context, *Canadian Culinary Imaginations* looks to broach a more in-depth conversation. Until recently, edited collections in Canadian food studies have been guided primarily by historical objectives.[12] But as communications scholar Charlene Elliott acknowledges in *How Canadians Communicate VI: Food Promotion, Consumption, and Controversy*, "much more talking needs to be done" when it comes to exploring how food conveys meaning and circulates within various media so that Canadians can become more discerning about what they consume (both literally and figuratively).[13] In the closing comments of their introduction to *Edible Histories Cultural Politics*, Franca Iacovetta, Valerie J. Korinek, and Marlene Epp beckon readers to explore "the history of what Canadians eat" and its significance.[14] This statement resonates with Jean Anthelme Brillat-Savarin's aphorism, "Tell me what you eat, and I shall tell you what you are."[15] But as Gilbert suggests through her amendments to Brillat-Savarin, there are other directives that merit consideration: "*Tell me what you read and write about what you eat … Tell me how you envision food in stories and poems, memoirs and biographies, films and pictures and fantasies, and we shall begin to understand how you* think *about your life.*"[16] Imagined food – what McLuhan identified and linked to the mediated environment of the global village and economy decades earlier, food that is not necessarily tangible or edible but can be, and that is shaped by storytellers, poets, novelists, journalists, photographers, conceptual and mix-media artists, chefs, cookbook authors, and creators of screen culture – inevitably furnishes multifarious and complicated Canadian buffets.

Food across Canada: Connecting Local, National, and Global Imaginaries

Within local communities and the global village, food has become the language of choice. Circulating in many guises and contexts and across an ever-transforming media and digital landscape, imagined food proliferates, assuming what has always been part of its daily material and cultural functions: to connect, challenge, divide, and transform society. In Canada, a resource-rich country spatially divided across a vast and challenging geography and with a contested national history of just over one hundred and fifty years, the extraction, production, and distribution of food have shaped many of the nation's most compelling narratives and representations. Today, these legacies of Canadian foodways, as our collection reveals, are made manifest in both familiar and unexpected places and expressive forms, offering glimpses of paradigms of imagination.

Consider *The Great Canadian Baking Show*, a television series that premiered in 2017 on the national Canadian Broadcasting Corporation (CBC) network. Based on the highly popular British series, the show's producers select amateur bakers from across the country to take part in weekly competitions set around a particular theme. Key to the series' success are the individual contestants, who are not only directed to embrace their particular regional traditions but also encouraged to celebrate their personal, cultural, and ethnic backgrounds, leading to interesting and sometimes contradictory creations that reflect the unstable, imagined understandings of "Canadian" culinary identity. During the episode "Canada Week," bakers were asked to interpret tourtière (an iconic Quebec tart adapted from French cooking traditions) and to create unique condiments to make their creations "pop." Sabrina, the only contestant from Quebec, opted to make a traditional dish and explained to the camera her distaste for the tart and worries about letting down her home province. Linda from the West showcased Alberta beef and had a hard time pronouncing the French word *tourtière*. Julian paid homage to a "Halifax donair" with a matching condiment and noted how the late-night Maritime snack has probably never been prepared in this style. James made a vegetarian tourtière, alluding to his laid-back West Coast roots, while Vandana also created a vegetarian dish that played on her South Asian heritage, using chickpeas and cashews with a yogurt-based condiment. Later, for the technical round, the bakers were asked to make "iconic maple leaf cookies." Several of the contestants, including the winner of the round, had never heard of, let alone made and eaten, the confection. Even so, one of the co-hosts stated, "the only thing more Canadian" than the maple leaf cookie "would be if Celine Dion rode in on a moose drinking a brewsky."[17]

In our increasingly urbanized nation with its often-superficial shorthand for diverse food cultures, finding ways to reconnect citizens with food producers and food-producing landscapes seems an essential task for culinary imaginations. At the same time, the global economy brings to the foreground the fact that nations' foodways are interconnected and dependent. The global popularity of cooking shows based on national and regional specialties is strong evidence of this impulse. On an episode of *Parts Unknown*, world-renowned chef Anthony Bourdain profiled Newfoundland and the resurrection of the local fishery along with traditional food cultures. Set within the broader historical context of the 1992 moratorium on the cod fishery, which nearly devastated the island's economy, the narrative arc of the episode follows Bourdain as he sets out with two "outsider chefs" (David McMillan and Frédéric Morin from Montreal's Joe Beef) to learn about how local chefs are reintroducing the rest of Canada and the world to the forgotten and often stereotyped foodways of Newfoundland.[18] Importantly, Bourdain chose to narrate the opening scene of the show, featuring striking cinematic shots of the island's natural beauty, not with his usual monologue, but through the spoken words of local chef Jeremy Charles: "For a long time, we were forgotten about. We were the joke of the country. Now we are the ones having the last laugh. It's a magical place to live, and we are surrounded by amazing things. You can go outside and jig a fish or shoot a moose or go out and pick some berries … and bring that to the table and create a sense of place where people, when they look out the window, know they are in Newfoundland."[19] Later, at a critical moment in the episode, Bourdain interviews the province's intangible cultural heritage development officer, Dale Jarvis, who explains how Newfoundlanders have come to value themselves differently through the safeguarding of sustainable, traditional food cultures. Unlike most provinces, locals can acquire permits not only to buy wild game from resident hunters but also to hunt and sell the game themselves, giving Newfoundlanders and visitors a taste of terroir that most Canadians can only imagine.[20] And as Bourdain discovers, many Newfoundland chefs proudly do their own hunting. "Food security is an issue here," begins Jarvis, explaining that while Newfoundlanders will continue to import food, recognizing the realities of global trade, there will be shifts in how things are done to accommodate the transforming pace of the times: "tradition is not static – it changes to the conditions of the environment."[21]

What does it mean to observe, represent, or produce the spaces and environments of Canada's foodways – past, present, and future – in today's culture of speed?[22] This is a critical question that animates many of the pieces in our collection. In response to moments of conflict like this, the call has been to *slow* the system and interrogate perception, resulting in various slow movements that have sought to bring renewed attention to acts of socio-cultural reflection. Within Canada, protests that begin locally and then spread to the nation's capital or across the country have united various communities around the right to maintain access to locally controlled resources and country food (harvested from land, air, or water in the wild). In 2016, Indigenous and non-Indigenous communities united in Labrador to challenge the construction of the Muskrat Falls hydroelectric dam, a project that would flood and potentially poison the fish supply.[23] Sparking demonstrations and hunger strikes, at first locally and then across Canada, the protesters converged around these issues. As journalist Justin Brake observed, "this is the first time in the history of Labrador that all four groups (members of three First Nation groups and settler Labradorians) have united over something they have historically been divided about."[24] With respect to safeguarding and promoting local foods through activists' culinary imaginations, it is also important to note that the popular 100-mile diet originated in British Columbia.[25] This lifestyle principle of daily food choices extols the virtues of reconnecting with the immediate surroundings, eating seasonally, and protecting the shared environment by curtailing reliance on transported goods, foreign investment, and fossil fuels. Canadian journalist Carl Honoré, whose international best-selling book and manifesto *In Praise of Slow* helped to introduce mainstream audiences to the concept, put it in its simplest (and most "Canadian") of terms: "Slow activists are not out to destroy the capitalist system. Rather, they seek to give it a human face."[26]

Food as Multimodal Media: Diverse Language(s) and Representation(s)

In Canadian culinary imaginaries, food is multimodal media: it may be edible, textual, sensorial, simulated, visually represented, digital, or any combination of these. Therefore, foundational to this collection is food's semiotic role – how it functions, according to French linguist and semiotician Roland Barthes, as "a system of communication, a body of images, a protocol of usages, situations, and behavior" within a given society.[27] Like McLuhan, Barthes held a profound interest in popular culture – the daily objects and modes of consumption – and has even been referred to as the "French McLuhan."[28] Barthes once noted "that an entire 'world' (social environment) is present in and signified by food," and today, it seems more than ever before as though culinary imaginations are expanding and on the move in their material, textual, visual, and digital forms.[29] Culturally specific meanings are reiterated and circulated through everyday culinary practices and multimodal expressions. Food's "semantic algebra," as Lévi-Strauss conceptualizes it, points to the fact that cultural categories and modes of preparation are not arbitrary, but rather part of a system of meaning.[30] These practices, traditions, and expressions are also vulnerable to external forces as different food languages can be imposed, enacted, and challenged when cultures interact or clash over time. In these contexts of cultural politics and power relations, then, creative thinkers and producers can innovate food's signification within a range of private or public spaces, their storied meals resulting in new meanings that enter the mouth, body, and mind.

Indeed, within the context of contemporary art – one of the many important subjects framing this collection – there has been a concerted move towards an expansive conceptual approach, resulting in the crisis of traditional forms and materials (painting, drawing, and sculpture, etc.). As art critic Lucy Lippard describes in her foundational study *Six Years: The Dematerialization of the Art Object from 1966 to 1972*, under these conditions art ceases to be defined in predictable ways: by what is tangible, readily categorized, or commoditized.[31] Instead, art embraces the conceptual, ephemeral, and non-traditional (such as performance, video, installation), while examining the tensions between high and low culture. In this context, food takes on unexpected formulations, especially because the critical function of these artistic works depends upon a transparent process, triggering a set of relations between audience and artist/performer.

Related examples come through the multimodal expressions of Canadian writer and artist Douglas Coupland and emerging Filipino-Canadian artist Jay Cabalu. Both artists work in the pop art idiom and intimate that communication technologies and food are comparable, but their respective self-portraiture projects facilitate very different and even competing stakes for possible Canadian identities – public and private. The broadcast era of television may have been designed for "communicating across wide distances," Coupland writes, but "the next version of

Figure 0.2
Douglas Coupland, *Gumhead*, 2014–15 (from the *everywhere is anywhere is anything is everything* public installations in Vancouver and Toronto).

Figure 0.3, 0.4 *Opposite detail*
Jay Cabalu, *De Los Reyes*, 2018.

the dream will be food-based."[32] Coupland's recent, highly publicized self-portrait public art installation bears out his predictions. Using techno-food as material, *Gumhead* (2014) is a project that Coupland has described as a "crowd-sourced, publically interactive, social-sculpture" that directly engages with the Canadian public and creates spaces of communal experience.[33] Gum as a temporary food is made for chewing, not swallowing, and is typically produced from synthetic materials; it is a form of entertainment difficult to fully digest and dispense with, and an ever-present nuisance or graffiti in the urban landscape with its bright primary-colour palette. With *Gumhead*, Coupland succeeds in taking a product that is often associated with sweetness, play, and childhood, and transforms it into a new form of sugar-coated grotesque, rendering it a successful work of conceptual and relational art. Coupland achieves his intended outcome via the spectacle of street art, engaging with and attracting a much broader audience. The distinction between Coupland's Vancouver and Toronto installations (in Vancouver, on the street outside the city's art gallery; and in Toronto, inside the entranceway of the city's largest luxury department store) also mirrors the long-standing rivalry between two of Canada's unmistakable urban and food cultures – one linked to stereotypes of the laid-back, left-leaning, farm-to-table West Coast; the other conjuring clichéd associations of old-money conservatives, fine dining, and Central Canadian privilege.

INTRODUCTION

Moving from shared spaces of public exchange to more intimate articulations of difference and outsider cultural cuisine, Jay Cabalu's collaged self-portraiture *De Los Reyes* (Of the kings) (2018) explores the world of privilege, access, and affirmed Canadian-ness in close connection to the class and status associations of immigrant food cultures. On its surface, the art work appears celebratory – aligned to Coupland's arguably nostalgic take on food and nationhood – and shows Cabalu proudly hoisting a mega-sized container of Spam over his head, a food associated with his Filipino heritage and the thin fried slices of the processed meat served with garlic fried rice and fried egg that is a staple meal in his family.[34] Indeed, this traditional dish called "Spam-si-log" signals Spam's rise to cultural prominence within the Philippines when this Southeast Asian country was an American territory. For example, during the Second World War, American soldiers based in the Philippines received Spam as part of their military rations, which they shared with the local population.³⁵ Upon closer examination, then, the collaged materials making up Cabalu's Spam, a food often stereotyped in North America as inexpensive and "low-brow," reveals something far more conflicted. We find a cut-up and collaged world of out-of-reach consumerism, laced with the promise of perfection and beauty – luxury handbags, expensive perfumes, exotic cars, and other embellishments from the pages of high-fashion and lifestyle magazines – that Cabalu strategically deploys to examine his experience of exclusion and desire while searching for a place in the popular culture. In the letter *S* on his tin of Spam, Cabalu includes a clipping of the Robin Hood flour label, an iconic Canadian brand (now owned by the American company Cargill). Coupland often represents this flour brand in his art and once described it as central to national identity: "'We have all grown up with Robin Hood flour. It's been so much a part of us, it's almost part of our DNA'"; for Cabalu, however, his experience of Canadian brands differs.³⁶ "When I started to do self-portraits entirely out of hand-cut collage," Cabalu explains, "my perspective became clear: there was a sentimentality attached to these materials that had excluded me, and a new desire to reframe it on my terms."³⁷ Like Coupland, Cabalu's search for Canadian identity operates in a rapidly shifting and globalized world (note that the Grizzlies jersey he wears, once connected to a Vancouver team, today signifies an American-identified city), but his materials suggest another kind of sugar-coated grotesque altogether, one tied to the superficial fantasy and masquerade of social inclusion through material culture and media communications. Critically, neither Coupland's nor Cabalu's vision of Canadian identity is entirely real, yet both offer quick shorthand through multimodal representations and their own unique means of representation that are immediately recognizable to divergent Canadian audiences.

Food as Counter-Environment and Unstable Category

If culinary imaginations are multimodal, then the immersive spaces activated by food as media and by food's reinterpretations within a range of expressive forms require closer critical reflection. As McLuhan famously explained, "environments are not just containers, but are processes that change the content totally. New media are new environments. That is why the media are the message."³⁸ As our collection reminds readers, communities and nations are constructed in different ways through different media. But more importantly, many of our contributors explore how imagined food creates counter-environments that reshape perceptions and consciousness at the levels of the individual and the collective. A food-saturated society will inevitably become "numb" to food's agency, but critical-creative acts can "open the door of perception."[39] How we grow, harvest, prepare, embody, write, represent, speak about, regulate, and share food necessarily impacts our memories, understandings, and experiences of the world and of each other.

One trail-blazing work of literary commentary on the mediated food world's numbing effects is Margaret Atwood's *The Edible Woman*, a novel written in 1965 shortly after a twenty-something Atwood had worked at the Toronto-based Canadian Facts Marketing "during the heyday of product testing, the era of Tang and Pop Tarts."[40] The protagonist, Marian MacAlpin, begins to perceive her environment and her relationship with her fiancé in disconcerting ways: superficial, prepackaged, and threatening since she herself is an object of consumption. Atwood's novel is, in Gilbert's view, a key "female-authored" work of "romantic nausea" that rejects gendered conventions.[41] In his study of literature's response to advertising media, Michael Ross highlights MacLuhan's direct influence on Atwood, arguing that *The Edible Woman* is a critique of marketing's power to distort individuals' desires through all-encompassing discourse and visual representation. "Marian must liberate her vision from promotional blinkers," Ross contends.[42] Unable to voice her thoughts and emotions in a consumer world that determines how women and men "ought" to behave and appear, Marian subconsciously rebels when her body refuses to eat. Food becomes sentient as Marian identifies with it: egg yolks stare up from the plate with accusing eyes; carrots scream when plucked from the earth and are later peeled. In many respects, Marian assumes what McLuhan calls the "antisocial" stance of someone who "cannot go along with currents and trends" and "sees environments as they really are."[43] Ultimately, her dwindling appetite and final symbolic act of baking a cake-effigy in her own image empower Marian to end her engagement and to participate in the consumer world on her own self-sustaining terms.

Just as food informs and takes shape on the written page by detailing either fictional or real experiences, its potentially subversive connotations enter into the sensory and visual languages of art movements, popular culture, and emerging technologies, all of which highlight food's interconnectedness with an array of semiotic

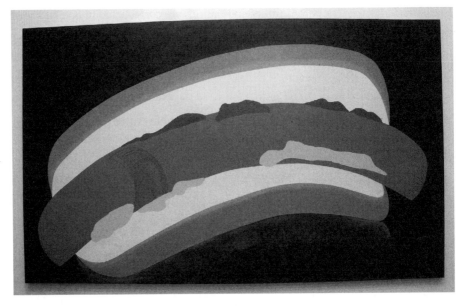

Figure 0.5
Lawrence Paul Yuxweluptun, *Haida Hot Dog*, 1984, acrylic on canvas.

frameworks. Often politically charged and inventive in its signification, multimodal food has the power to communicate diverse cultural and Indigenous worldviews. For instance, Lawrence Paul Yuxweluptun, a globally recognized contemporary artist of Coast Salish and Okanagan ancestry, has taken up themes of colonialism and capitalism in his paintings that unite Indigenous and modern art traditions. Yuxweluptun is especially interested in bringing attention to the Canadian resource environment, actively disrupting the notion of an untamed and boundless Canadian "wilderness" landscape pictured and popularized by the Group of Seven painting tradition of the early twentieth century – images that suggest free and infinite settler-colonial access to resources.[44] "How do you record 600 million salmon brought down to 40 million?" he asks. "I am living in a time when what happened to the buffalo has happened to the salmon."[45] Yuxweluptun's is an incendiary and avant-garde painting style, activating traditions of European surrealism (operating on the seemingly irrational juxtaposition of ideas and images) that speak literally and figuratively to audiences through brightly and beautifully painted canvases uniting Northwest Coast and modern European visual languages. In paintings ranging from *Haida Hot Dog* (1984) – a commentary on both the commercialization of First Nations art at the expense of specific political and social meanings and the playful undermining of settler expectations of Indigenous art[46] – to *Fish Farmers They Have Sea Lice* (2014) – an indictment of the mismanaged fish farming industry in British Columbia – Yuxweluptun raises important topics of conversation linking food, environmental concerns, and Indigenous rights. Indeed, one of the many lessons to be learned through the pages of this book is that culinary imaginations (textual, oral, visual, olfactory, digital, and otherwise) carry their influence, as Nathalie Cooke puts it, "through time, across space, and between cultural groups," even as communities evolve, demographics shift, and new foods enter the mix through Indigenous, colonial, diasporic, and global histories.[47]

Just as culinary practices are neither arbitrary nor fixed, food's intersections with other media, contexts, and national and global environments extend its sociocultural reach and unpredictability as a system of signification. Gilbert reminds us that storytelling and literary traditions, visual art and screen cultures, and performance are all part of the culinary imagination. In a similar fashion, literary theorist Terry Eagleton and food writer Betty Fussell contend that language and food are closely related as embodied forms of expression and "media of exchange."[48] Fussell explains: "Eating, like speaking, mediates between opposite worlds, forging a bridge over the natal chasm between mind and body, images and substances, symbols and things that reason works hard to keep apart."[49] Food (both real and imagined) is the twenty-first century's dream of instant, corporate communication,

Figure 0.6
Maddy Shaw, *#remain*, 2016, also commonly known as *Brexit, a Still Life*. Photograph first circulated via Facebook 23 June 2016 (accessed 14 December 2016).

and food's multimodal formulations offer shared yet particularized means of expression within and across wider publics. For example, the Brexit vote of June 2016 in Britain prompted an array of food-related responses. In an article written for *The New Yorker*, Bee Wilson noted that the European Union had "not only nourished the British but changed British palates" and that for "the first time since the Second World War, Britain's ability to feed itself" was now in question.[50] The tangible impact of Brexit's political machinations was made apparent by UK-based professional musician Maddy Shaw's *#remain* (2016), also commonly referred to as *Brexit, a Still Life*, a digital image that went viral in its representation of the future of British food as a "lonely can of beans," set apart from a delicious European buffet.[51] In the days following the outcome of the vote, Wilson's article and Shaw's widely circulated photograph communicated the changing political landscape in a "uniquely accessible way" – through food – capturing Britain's culinary landscape as one of immense cultural exchange, soon to be diminished by its withdrawal from the European Union.[52]

In the context of Canadian popular media, food similarly communicates in an instant through both political cartoons – a mass-distributed form combining artistic skill, hyperbole, and satire in order to question authority and raise awareness around corruption – and online memes – cultural symbols virally transmitted through mash-ups of appropriated images and/or text. In connection with Shaw's mourning of lost cultural exchange through *#remain*, Canadian cartoons and memes often signal a fragile and problematic national food culture. For example, the numerous cartoons that circulated in 2014 when American fast-food chain Burger King purchased Canadian-owned Tim Hortons express collective anxiety over economic imperialism within the national foodscape.[53] Caricatured politicians appear passive and indifferent, while symbols of Canadian identity in the form of "Johnny Canuck" or the beaver (in one example from *The Economist*, a beaver holds a hockey stick, referencing the Canadian NHL player that is Tim Hortons' namesake) are pictured under attack by the relentless American food-monster. A tenuous sense of nationhood as tied to food-related sovereignty is paradoxically embodied in and overtaken by commercial enterprises. As one commentator in *The Economist* acknowledged in response to the merger, Burger King had purchased not simply a company but also "a national symbol."[54] Graphic images evoking nostalgia through the minimal line and colour of the original Tim Hortons coffee cup (as drawn by Terry Mosher, or Aislin), as well as deliberately deskilled digital mash-ups of menu items (such as the *The Doburger* meme, which appeared in a 2014 online edition of

Figure 0.7
Aislin [Terry Mosher], "Canadian No More? Get Serious: A Double-Double and a Whopper? Tim Hortons Has Agreed to Be Bought by the Company that Owns Burger King," Editorial cartoon, 2014.

the *Toronto Sun*), emphasize the absurdity of Canadian-American fast-food fusion, sentimentalize the formerly Canadian-owned chain, and bemoan its transformation within the global economy. But cartoonists and meme-producers also satirize the nation's own late-capitalist, commodity-driven mentality that equates food culture solely with commercial exports. In these cases, Canadians' supposedly cherished necessities and pleasures of life – water, beer, wine, and double-doubles – often flow in bulk alongside other raw resources, relegated to the mass-market forces of supply and demand.

The Challenges and Pleasures of *Canadian Culinary Imaginations*

In culinary imaginaries, food communicates in provocative ways, challenging normative or unconscious ways of relating to food on a daily basis. Suddenly, food-related environments and narratives, which have previously gone undetected or have been taken for granted, are perceived anew. Food's intersections with an array of expressive modes and forms within a rapidly changing media environment suggest that its place and role have transformed in the twenty-first century. The contributors in this collection delineate how creative thinkers and producers in and outside Canada re-envision food so that which is *everywhere* suddenly becomes unfamiliar and potentially transformative. A guiding principle of this collection is to interpret what culinary imaginaries have to communicate about the past, present, and future through food's multimodal expressions. While no collection could claim to capture the totality of the nation's culinary imaginations, we have attempted to call into question the normative, traditional, and expected of our topic and to include perspectives and voices from diverse regions, generations, cultural backgrounds, and media channels. Guiding our editorial selection and arrangement has also been a desire to highlight the integral and ever-evolving relationship between creative thinking and production. Our contributors reflect the hybridity of individuals moving across and between academic, artistic, and disciplinary boundaries, while remaining necessarily self-reflexive and experimental in their examinations of what it is to think, write, and represent Canadian contexts. As such, we hope this collection provides a glimpse of the many possibilities of Canadian culinary imaginations and inspires future experimentations, studies, and critical-creative collaborations.

Most of our contributors have been challenged in one form or another by the instability and contingency posed by food as a category of meaning. Parentheses and scare quotations appear throughout the collection – rhetorical cues that evoke one meaning of a food term or practice, while still gesturing to other interpretations. Words such as "local," "cuisine," "foodie," "taste," "homemade," "cook," and of course "Canadian" challenge many of us with their denotations and connotations. Subject to ever-shifting affiliations and categorizations, supposedly generic foods, convenience foods, domestic cooking, and restaurant cuisine appear throughout the collection, often repurposed as potent modes of expression and political commentary. And totem foods – those tied to distinctions of culture and place stemming from the local and regional (West Coast salmon, Montreal smoked meat, Alberta's ginger beef, Nova Scotia's moose) to the national (Canadians' penchant for Kraft Dinner and Tim Hortons) – play significant roles in celebratory rituals, daily meals, and collective storytelling. These foods speak to, unite, but also exclude specific audiences. In other words, categorizations help to reveal the social and political agency derived from, or curtailed through, food. On this topic, the contributors provoke conversations by recasting expectations around Indigenous and settler cultures, class and social status, gender identities, sexual orientations, ethnic diversity, and cultural appropriation within Canada, just as Canada, itself, becomes the target of, and a player within, the larger forces of the global economy. Stereotyped foods are often readily dismissed as facile or suspicious when it comes to understanding cultural and national identities, but these foods, as some contributors reveal, can be used in creative ways to unpack difficult topics and social taboos. Similarly, the superficiality posed by junk food and mass-produced, branded food provides vital points of entry into debates concerning high and low culture, commercialization (of the arts, cultures, identities) and the current global conversation around populism. To be sure, an idea consistently explored across the collection is how food categories can be both enduring and mutable – depending on geographical and cultural contexts, time frames, producers and consumers, and the critical and artistic interventions that are brought to bear on these factors.

There is a growing appetite for substantive conversations about Canadian culinary imaginations because food spills into every area of our lives. At the same time, the place of food in our global culture is shifting and transforming, creating both fascination and anxiety. Our choice to focus on Canada – both at home and in the world – through the interconnected worlds of popular food culture, art, storytelling, literatures, and digital media is deliberate. Not only are we seeking to unpack ideas around what makes Canada unique in its many national tastes, food practices, and culinary cultures, we are seeking to do so through examinations of human creativity and the will to represent and remake the world in unexpected ways. Ours is also a collection in the spirit of the avant-garde that seeks to dismantle the expectations of disciplines, to play with traditional forms, and to question the boundaries that artificially separate ideas of "high" and "low" cultures. It is our hope that this book will shift culinary conversations towards the very best that imagination offers us – a chance to form new ideas, images, concepts, and experiences of the multimodal food world that surrounds and enters us. Although this world is not always present to our senses, there are ways of challenging the status quo. Pull up a chair, stir the pot, and prepare to feast.

Notes

1 Gilbert, *Culinary Imagination*, 8.
2 For further readings on McLuhan's theories concerning media and the "global village," see McLuhan, *The Gutenberg Galaxy* and *Understanding Media*.
3 The Marshall McLuhan Estate has published a collection of his most famous aphorisms, including many food-related examples, such as this one. See the website www.marshallmcluhan.com/mcluhanisms/.

4 Zhang, "Food."
5 Powe, *Marshall McLuhan and Northrop Frye*, 105. McLuhan's aphorism quoted by Powe is from *The Book of Probes* (edited by Eric McLuhan and William Kuhns, Hamburg, Germany: Gingko Press, 2003).
6 Ibid. In McLuhan and Fiore, *The Medium Is the Massage*, McLuhan explains what he means by counter-environments: "Environments are not passive wrappings, but are, rather active processes which are invisible … [and] elude easy perception. Anti-environments, or countersituations made by artists, provide means of direct attention and enable us to see and understand more clearly" (68).
7 McLuhan and Fiore, *The Medium*, 68.
8 Ibid., 158.
9 Editors, "Does Food Connect Us All?"
10 Gilbert, *Culinary Imagination*, xv, 8.
11 Wilson, "The Allure of Imagined Meals."
12 The first edited collections include Cooke's *What's to Eat? Entrées in Canadian Food History* (2009) followed by Iacovetta, Korinek, and Epp's *Edible Histories Cultural Politics: Towards a Canadian Food History*. Both collections acknowledge that prior to academic interest in the field, Canadian food studies was "pioneered by researchers from the worlds of museums and historical kitchens," public historians, cultural commentators, and home economists (Cooke, "Introduction," 7). These watershed books led the way in their respective examinations of domestic foodways, and the "'culinary turn'" in historical research. More recently, communications scholar Charlene Elliott has broken new ground with *How Canadians Communicate VI: Food Promotion, Consumption, and Controversy*. This collection approaches "food *as* communication, and also food *and* communication" within the specific contexts of the food industry and food regulation (public policy, discourses surrounding food controversies and public health crises, etc.) (Elliott, "Introduction," 6). While the emphases of these three collections differ, all are inspired by the fact that food allows for news ways of thinking, communicating, and understanding. For instance, Iacovetta, Korinek, and Epp describe food as enabling Canadian historians to discover original points of critical departure "not organized around wars, rulers, or exploration" ("Introduction," 7). Elliott similarly argues that a significant and mostly unexamined part of Canadians' larger food systems includes "food messaging" found in everything from food packaging to radio and television programing; from popular guidebooks to responses to food scares ("Introduction," 7).
13 Elliott, "Introduction," 16.

14 Iacovetta, Korinek, and Epp, "Introduction," 22.
15 Qtd. in ibid., 22.
16 Gilbert, *Culinary Imagination*, 6.
17 *The Great Canadian Baking Show*, Season 1, episode 4, "Canadian."
18 Bourdain's decision to bring two chefs from Quebec for an episode focused on "legitimatizing" Newfoundland's culinary scene did not go unnoticed by Canadians. Soon after the airing of the episode, a war of words broke out over social media between Bourdain and Newfoundlanders. On Twitter, Bourdain defended his choice, writing that it was the two chefs' "relentless advocacy for #Newfoundland" that encouraged him to visit the province. See "'Frenchies' Tweet Fuels Anthony Bourdain's Twitter Spat over Newfoundland Show." In the weeks following the airing of the episode, several articles also appeared in the Canadian press attempting to set the record straight and educate a broader public on issues raised on the show (i.e., from the proper pronunciation of the province's name to the history and ramifications of the fishing ban). See, for example, Coles, "5 Things Anthony Bourdain Will Teach You about Newfoundland." Such debate and exposure of political and social issues, on the heels of a show centred around culinary travel, highlight the powerful associations made between food and place-making.
19 *Parts Unknown*, "Newfoundland." Since this introduction was written, Anthony Bourdain tragically took his own life on 8 June 2018. In the immediate days following his passing, Bourdain's legacy as a chef, writer, and journalist was discussed by the media, the culinary community, and by his friends, colleagues, and the public, as one connected to promoting food and travel as a means to open-mindedness, cross-cultural understanding, and toleration of difference.
20 A 2016 article in the *Globe and Mail* highlights the unique regulatory circumstances of both Newfoundland and the North. According to one Toronto chef, his tasting of wild turkey for the first time was an "'a-ha moment'" that led him to question what is "real" when it comes to supermarket food (Sufrin). For further discussion of hunting and wild game regulations, see Gora, "From Meat to Metaphor," chapter 3 in this volume.
21 *Parts Unknown*, "Newfoundland."
22 Virilio's account in *Speed and Politics* in a time of capitalist expansion ends with an ominous conclusion: "the reduction of distances has become a strategic reality bearing incalculable economic and political consequences, since it corresponds to the negation of space" (149).
23 For a history of the Muskrat Falls project, as covered by Canada's national media, see Johnson, "Fight Against N.L.'s Muskrat Falls Project Comes to Toronto."
24 Justin Brake, award-winning Atlantic reporter for Canada's Aboriginal Peoples Television

Network, was interviewed by journalist Jesse Brown for his Canadaland podcast shortly after Brake was served with a court injunction for live-streaming and writing web stories about the peaceful protests at Muskrat Falls in 2016. See Brake, "The Occupation of Muskrat Falls."

25 Canadian writers Alisa Smith and J.B. Mackinnon published their best-selling book *The 100-Mile Diet: A Year of Eating Local* in 2007 (Toronto: Random House). See Tennant, "*Terra Nullius* on the Plate," chapter 4 in this volume, for her discussion of locavore diets and movements that were popularized in the twenty-first century.

26 Honoré, *In Praise of Slow*, 17.

27 Barthes, "Toward a Psychosociology," 21.

28 Willmott, "McLuhan's Message," 384. Willmott notes that both men explored "everyday culture" and showed "striking similarities in their consideration of objects and events of popular culture," such as advertisements, food products, fashion, print, and photographic images (384).

29 Barthes, "Toward a Psychosociology," 23.

30 Leach, "Oysters, Smoked Salmon, and Stilton Cheese," 33.

31 Lippard, *Six Years: The Dematerialization of the Art Object from 1966 to 1972*.

32 Coupland, *Souvenir of Canada*, 19.

33 Coupland quoted on the Vancouver Art Gallery website promoting exhibition of *Gum Head*. Accessed 27 November 2016. www.vanartgallery.bc.ca/the_exhibitions/exhibit_gumhead.html.

34 Jay Cabalu, interview by Dorothy Barenscott, 12 February 2019.

35 See Ke, "Why Filipinos Love Spam So Much," and Ong, "Spam: A Love Story of Love and Hate," for Spam's cultural significance and historical beginnings in the Philippines.

36 Goddard, "Coupland Maps."

37 "Jay Cabalu Artist Statement," Jay Cabalu, Pop Goes The Easel, Jay Cabalu. Accessed 12 February 2019. http://jaycabalu.com/statement.

38 McLuhan, "Technology and Environment," 48.

39 McLuhan, *Essential McLuhan*, 342.

40 Cooke, *Margaret Atwood*, 49.

41 Gilbert, *Culinary Imagination*, 254.

42 Ross, *Designing Fictions*, 110, 105.

43 McLuhan and Fiore, *The Medium*, 88.

44 For a discussion concerning Yuxweluptun's practice within the context of Canadian painting traditions, see Todd, "Yuxweluptun: A Philosophy of History."

45 Quoted in an interview with art critic Robin Lawrence. See Lawrence, "Artist Lawrence Paul Yuxweluptun Redraws and Redresses History."

46 In a conversation with Dorothy Barenscott, the artist described how the term "hot-dogging" was understood not only as both a food and popular culture object, referencing, for example, Andy Warhol's pop art aesthetic through the use of food products like soup cans, but also as a colloquialism referring to a strategic act of subverting expectation and showing off or showing up the competition. Lawrence Paul Yuxweluptun, telephone conversation with Dorothy Barenscott, 30 September, 2019.

47 See Cooke, "Montreal in the Culinary Imagination," chapter 6 in this volume.

48 Eagleton, "Edible Écriture," 448. For further discussion of Eagleton, see Boyd, "Chewed a Book Lately?," chapter 11 in this volume.

49 Fussell, "Eating My Words," 441.

50 Wilson, "What Brexit Means."

51 Cascone, "Who Is the Brilliant Mind behind the Brexit Still Life?" This image was shared over 300,000 times on Facebook (and at a similar rate on social media platforms Instagram and Twitter) in the immediate days following the Brexit vote. The identity of the photographer remained a mystery until *artnet news* confirmed Maddy Shaw, a British citizen and professional musician, had composed the digital photograph the morning of the vote results and circulated it publicly on Facebook. Interestingly, the image confused many people who believed that a professional artist had likely composed the photograph as a conceptual work of art, pointing to how the worlds of "high" and "low" culture become blurred through the mediation of screen culture. See Cascone, "Who Is the Brilliant Mind Behind the Brexit Still Life?"

52 Ibid.

53 The Canadian multinational holding company Restaurant Brands International (RBI) was formed when Burger King and Tim Hortons merged in 2014. The majority of RBI is owned by 3G Capital, a Brazilian-American investment company.

54 "Chomping Timbits." The article in *The Economist* further notes that Tim Hortons had long "aligned its brand with the twin Canadian passions of watching ice hockey and eating doughnuts (often at the same time). It has been the backdrop of choice for government politicians pandering to ordinary Canadians who frequent its 3,453 outlets" ("Chomping Timbits"). More recently, this now-global corporation has become the target of criticism through its seeming shift away from "Canadian" values when some franchise owners eliminated employees' coffee breaks and other benefits in response to an increased minimum wage. On this issue, see cartoonist MacKay's blog post "Tuesday."

Bibliography

Anthony Bourdain. Season 11, episode 91, "Newfoundland." Aired 13 May 2018, on CNN. https://explorepartsunknown.com/newfoundland/.

Atwood, Margaret. *The Edible Woman*. 1969. Toronto: McClelland & Stewart, 1989.

Barthes, Roland. "Toward a Psychosociology of Contemporary Food Consumption." In *Food and Culture: A Reader*, edited by Carole Counihan and Penny Van Esterik, 20–7. New York: Routledge, 1997.

Brake, Justin. "The Occupation of Muskrat Falls." Interview with Jesse Brown. Canadaland. Podcast Audio. 31 October 2016. www.canadalandshow.com/podcast/occupation-muskrat-falls/.

Cabalu, Jay. "Jay Cabalu Artist Statement." Jay Cabalu, Pop Goes The Easel. 2019. http://jaycabalu.com/statement.

Cascone, Sarah. "Who Is the Brilliant Mind behind the Brexit Still Life?" *artnet news*, 29 June 2016. https://news.artnet.com/art-world/brexit-still-life-meme-505757.

"Chomping Timbits." *The Economist*, 11 December 2014. www.economist.com/the-americas/2014/12/11/chomping-timbits.

Coles, Terri. "5 Things Anthony Bourdain Will Teach You about Newfoundland." CBC, 10 May 2018. www.cbc.ca/news/canada/newfoundland-labrador/newfoundland-anthony-bourdain-parts-unknown-1.4655654.

Cooke, Nathalie. "Introduction." In *What's to Eat? Entrées in Canadian Food History*, edited by Cooke, 3–17. Montreal and Kingston: McGill-Queen's University Press, 2009.

– *Margaret Atwood: A Critical Companion*. Westport, CT: Greenwood Press, 2004.

Coupland, Douglas. *Souvenir of Canada*. Vancouver: Douglas & McIntyre, 2002.

Eagleton, Terry. "Edible Écriture." In *Eating Words: A Norton Anthology of Food Writing*, edited by Sandra M. Gilbert and Roger J. Porter, 445–9. New York: W.W. Norton, 2015.

Editors. "Does Food Connect Us All?" *The Walrus*, 12 September 2012. http://thewalrus.ca/discussion-6/.

Elliott, Charlene. "Introduction." In *How Canadians Communicate VI: Food Promotion, Consumption, and Controversy*, edited by Elliott, 3–18. Edmonton: Athabasca University Press, 2016.

"Frenchies' Tweet Fuels Anthony Bourdain's Twitter Spat over Newfoundland Show." *Globe and Mail*, 15 May 2018. www.theglobeandmail.com/canada/article-frenchies-tweet-fuels-anthony-bourdains-twitter-spat-over/.

Fussell, Betty. "Eating My Words." In *Eating Words: A Norton Anthology of Food Writing*, edited by Sandra M. Gilbert and Roger J. Porter, 439–44. New York: W.W. Norton, 2015.

Gilbert, Sandra M. *The Culinary Imagination: From Myth to Modernity*. New York: W.W. Norton, 2014.

Goddard, Peter. "Coupland Maps Canada from the Rec Room Out." *Nanaimo Daily News*, 5 July 2002. Canadian Newsstream.

The Great Canadian Baking Show. Season 1, episode 4, "Canadian." Aired 22 November 2017, on CBC. www.cbc.ca/life/greatcanadianbakingshow/gcbs-episodes/episode-4-canada-week-1.4368091.

Honoré, Carl. *In Praise of Slow: How a Worldwide Movement Is Challenging the Cult of Speed*. Toronto: A.A. Knopf Canada, 2004.

Iacovetta, Franca, Valerie J. Korinek, and Marlene Epp. "Introduction." In *Edible Histories Cultural Politics: Towards a Canadian Food History*, edited by Iacovetta, Korinek, and Epp, 3–28. Toronto: University of Toronto Press, 2012.

– "Preface." In *Edible Histories Cultural Politics: Towards a Canadian Food History*, edited by Iacovetta, Korinek, and Epp, xi–xiv. Toronto: University of Toronto Press, 2012.

Johnson, Rhiannon. "Fight Against N.L.'s Muskrat Falls Project Comes to Toronto." *CBC*, 1 October 2017. www.cbc.ca/news/indigenous/battle-for-muskrat-falls-comes-to-toronto-1.4314563.

Ke, Bryan. "Why Filipinos Love Spam So Much." *Nextshark*, 12 December 2017. https://nextshark.com/filipinos-love-spam-much/.

Lawrence, Robin. "Artist Lawrence Paul Yuxweluptun Redraws and Redresses History." *Georgia Straight*, 24 March 2010. www.straight.com/article-299379/vancouver/history-redrawn-and-redressed.

Leach, Edmund. "Oysters, Smoked Salmon, and Stilton Cheese." In *Claude Lévi-Strauss*, 15–33. Revised ed. New York: Viking Press, 1974.

Lippard, Lucy R. *Six Years: The Dematerialization of the Art Object from 1966 to 1972: A Cross-reference Book of Information on Some Esthetic Boundaries*. New York: Praeger, 1973.

MacKay, Graeme. "Tuesday, January 9, 2018." *Mackay Cartoons*. https://mackaycartoons.net/2018/01/08/tuesday-january-9-2018/.

McLuhan, Marshall. *Essential McLuhan*, edited by Eric McLuhan and Frank Zingrone. Concord: Anansi, 1995.

– *The Gutenberg Galaxy: The Making of Typographic Man*. Toronto: University of Toronto Press, 1962.

– "Technology and Environment." In *Beyond Wilderness: The Group of Seven, Canadian Identity, and Contemporary Art*, edited by John O'Brian and Peter White, 344–7. Montreal and Kingston: McGill-Queen's University Press, 2007.

– *Understanding Media*. London: Sphere Books, 1973.

McLuhan, Marshall, and Quentin Fiore. *The Medium Is the Massage: An Inventory of Effects*, produced by Jerome Agel. Corte Madera, CA: Gingko Press, 2001.

Ong, Sherina. "Spam: A Story of Love and Hate." *Rappler*, 24 June 2014. www.rappler.com/move-ph/balikbayan/identity/60979-spam-love-hate.

Powe, B.W. *Marshall McLuhan and Northrop Frye: Apocalypse and Alchemy*. Toronto: University of Toronto Press, 2014.

Ross, Michael L. *Designing Fictions: Literature Confronts Advertising*. Montreal and Kingston: McGill-Queen's University Press, 2015.

Sufrin, Jon. "Hunted Game Is Mostly Illegal, But Chefs Argue for the Vibrant Taste Only Found Outside the Farm." *The Globe and Mail*, 19 April 2018. Updated 16 May 2018. www.theglobeandmail.com/life/food-and-wine/food-trends/wild-flavours-of-game-meat-wrapped-up-in-provincial-regulation/article29673827/.

Todd, Loretta. "Yuxweluptun: A Philosophy of History." In *Beyond Wilderness: The Group of Seven, Canadian Identity, and Contemporary Art*, edited by John O'Brian and Peter White, 344–7. Montreal and Kingston: McGill-Queen's University Press, 2007.

Virilio, Paul. *Speed and Politics: An Essay on Dromology*. Los Angeles: Semiotext(e), 2006.

Willmott, Glenn. "McLuhan's Message." In *Marshall McLuhan: Critical Evaluations in Cultural Theory*. Vol. 2, *Theoretical Elaborations*, edited by Gary Genosko, 376–92. London: Routledge, 2005.

Wilson, Bee. "The Allure of Imagined Meals." *The New Yorker*, 26 August 2014. www.newyorker.com.

– "What Brexit Means for British Food." *The New Yorker*, 28 June 2016. 2018. www.newyorker.com.

Zhang, Jessica. "Food." *The Chicago School of Media Theory*. Accessed 14 December 2016. https://lucian.uchicago.edu/blogs/mediatheory/keywords/food/.

PART ONE

Indigeneity and Foodways
Stories from Home and Abroad

The five essays in Part 1 explore dynamic histories and present-day expressions related to Indigenous foodways. These culinary imaginaries – in the forms of urban photography, storytelling, professional cooking, restaurant culture, cookbooks, screen culture, and national symbols – have the potential to reshape intercultural awareness and understanding both within and beyond Canada. Interrelated topics include environmental ethics and cultural connections to the land through food, foodie trends, and the visibility/invisibility of culinary practices in national and international contexts. Opening the discussion, Inuk artist Barry Pottle creates a photographic essay paired with Inuit voices promoting the visibility of these communities living in southern Ontario. Highlighting the challenges of obtaining country food in urban centres, Pottle's art practice is tied directly to his people's cultural identity, health, and land. Following Pottle, Margery Fee reads Indigenous stories that speak to human-bear relationships, examining the animals with whom we eat and share the earth (as well as the proverbial questions of what we eat and who we are), and reveals lessons of reciprocity that might serve as a model for addressing current environmental issues.

Shifting the discussion internationally, German scholar Sebastian Schellhaas examines Indigenous chefs who competed at the Culinary Olympics, one of the world's most prestigious professional cook-offs, leading to growing participation of Indigenous peoples in Canada's culinary scene. In dialogue with Schellhaas, journalist Zoe Tennant draws attention to the near-invisibility of Indigenous foods in Canadian restaurants and popular food culture by raising awareness around enduring "colonial blindness" and the politics of menu discourse. Concluding this section, L. Sasha Gora documents the complex transatlantic histories and transformations of the beaver from meat to national symbol, unpacking this animal's representations in popular pastries, edible art, Indigenous and non-Indigenous cookbooks, and television shows. Gora provides answers as to why this national animal is not widely consumed today.

1

Foodland Security
Access to Country Food by Inuit in an Urban Setting

Barry Pottle

My *Foodland Security* photographic project is twofold. First, it's based on the Inuit's close connection to and love for country food that comes from land, sea, or air – it's what Inuit hunt (caribou, seal, fish, birds, and whales) to feed their families and communities. This food also comes from plants that people gather. Food preparation includes the skinning and butchering of animals, cleaning of plants, and further preparation, such as boiling, drying, and other techniques. Inuit identify with it, even after leaving Inuit Nunangat (Inuit homeland). Second, the project is about what I call contemporary urban Inuit art photography. Photography has rarely been a viable genre within the realm of Inuit art (a market dominated by sculpture and prints/drawing), and so my goal in producing *Foodland Security* is to build a foundation towards an alternative Inuit art practice that also opens up the viability of an art market for Inuit photography.

Foodland Security is inspired by an original art project that I have been exploring over the past couple of years. The name is not only a play on words (the land, food, and security) but also about my knowledge and experiences of Inuit country food in an urban context. Living in Ottawa affords me an opportunity to explore our Inuit community. Through my camera, I am able to bring forth issues and imagery that speak to many topics, including access to country food by Inuit. To date, *Foodland Security* has been exhibited in the Allen Library at the University of Washington (Seattle), the Canadian Museum of Nature (Ottawa), and the Bonavista Biennale (Bonavista, Newfoundland). Country food is intertwined with Inuit culture. Once they are in urban centres, Inuit experience a great shift in diet from traditional or country food to store-bought, processed foods.

While growing up in Labrador, we had access to and hunted country food for both subsistence and family needs. Although we were introduced to store-bought food at a very early age, we did attempt to supplement our diets with country food whenever the opportunity arose. Now, living in southern Canada, we have to remember those times and to appreciate them more since it is not always easy to obtain food from home or other Inuit regions. The cost of shipping can get expensive; at times no one is able to bring country food with them, or we just don't have access. Now we rely on store-bought food, which at times is not very healthy.

> Country food means maintaining good health that I was brought up with from birth; country food means that I get to eat the freshest and purest forms of vitamins, minerals, and nutrition. If I don't eat it, I get weak and sick.
> – Pitsulala Lyta, Ottawa, Ontario

> I grew up on country food. What it means to me is strength, and healthy. It's also good for the spirit and eating my own country means healing. Eating my country food is less stressful, and it means I get less tired. I have lots of energy all the time. If you compare Inuit and the caribou or seals, both Inuit and the caribou are fast runners. When we eat the liver of the seal at minus 40 or 50, it means we are hot for the rest of the day. That is how the seal survives in the cold. – Piita Irniq, Ottawa, Ontario

In preparing for *Foodland Security*, I wanted to find out from my fellow Inuit residing in Ottawa and other urban centres what country food means to them, where they get country food, and how often. My fellow Inuit quoted here have been living in, or have recently moved to, various urban centres and, like me, at times crave and want easier access to country food.

> Country food means many things to me. It provides a nutrition that I don't get from store-bought foods. And I know that the food is not injected with hormones or any other chemical/pharmaceutical treatments. The satisfaction of eating country foods cannot be described. There is a spiritual and cultural charge that comes from eating country food – especially caribou. My children and I are smiling before, during, and after a meal of *quaq* or *tiqtitaq*. It means we are Inuit, and can continue to be Inuit even if we are not living in the Arctic. It also takes me to a time and place where my grandparents survived off of these foods –appreciation is always expressed to the hunter who harvested the catch, and to God when receiving country food, while eating, and after.
> – Melissa Irwin, Ottawa, Ontario

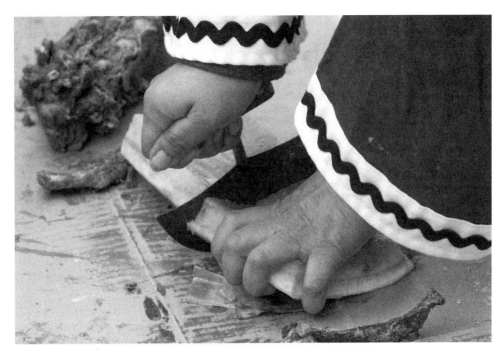

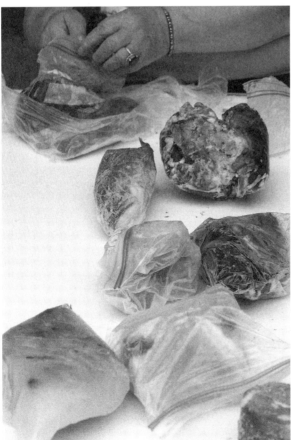

Figure 1.1 *Above*
Barry Pottle, *Starting the Feast*, 2012.

Figure 1.2 *Left*
Barry Pottle, *From the Community Freezer 1*, 2012.

Figure 1.3 *Top*
Barry Pottle, *Cutting Tuktu (Caribou)*, 2012.

Figure 1.4 *Bottom*
Barry Pottle, *Setting the Table*, 2012.

Figure 1.5 *Opposite*
Barry Pottle, *Mamaqtut (Delicious)*, 2012.

The late Elder Susanna Singoorie (from Nunavut and Ottawa) said: "We need our country foods to remain healthy and connected to our Lands. It is part of who we are." In juxtaposing the images with the quotations from my fellow Inuit, my objective was to depict or explain the importance of country food to Inuit (in their own voice) and to give voice to the photography as art.

To me, country food means food that someone killed in the wild. It is food that people hunt for, and they skin, clean, prepare the meat. It could also be berries or fish. I get country food from Labrador, from my dad. It's food that my family has hunted, gathered, or fished. I get country food a couple times a year when I go home or when my family comes here, and I get enough so that I can eat it a couple times a month. If I was in Labrador with my family I would be eating country food every day. – Tammy Hannaford, Scarborough, Ontario

We try to have ample amounts of country food for all our four main community events – graduation, Christmas party, Annual General Meeting, and Inuit Day. As you know, this is an important part of bringing the families together and fostering a sense of belonging and community. We have been

Figure 1.6
Barry Pottle, *Kanon-ized*, 2012.

successful at times connecting with a community hunter and having it shipped down that way or at times we have gotten it directly from Hunters and Trappers Association. It is always different and we try many different communities to be successful. It's definitely a challenge most times. – Karen Baker-Anderson, Ottawa Inuit Children's Centre, Ottawa, Ontario

Figure 1.6 depicts a traditional ulu, or woman's knife, and canned food. As access to traditional food becomes limited, alternative food sources must be found. *Kanonized* juxtaposes the traditional way of life and Inuit lifestyles in contemporary society. The photograph is a small *p* political/social comment on how I (and we Inuit) are living in southern Canada, and how we conform to new lifestyles and practices. The political and social commentary – more or less messaging through my photographic voice – is so closely tied to history, cultural and traditional issues, and new lifeways that it gets difficult to separate them. But I ask: "Do we need to separate them?"

2

What Can We Learn from Dining with Bears?

Indigenous Stories, Worldviews, and the Environment

Margery Fee

Introduction

Modern children know a lot about bears: in the English tradition, for example, bears and people like the same food ("Goldilocks and the Three Bears"); bears picnicking in the woods should not be disturbed ("Teddy Bears' Picnic"), and bears are good to eat (gummy bears). Finally, bears are like people. For many of us, a teddy bear was a constant childhood companion and conversational partner, a relationship exemplified by Winnie-the-Pooh and Christopher Robin in A.A. Milne's books for children. Among children at least, cultural connections to bears persist even in cities where there are no self-supporting bears. However, perhaps Goldilocks's assumption that she could use or take what she wanted from the bears, not to mention her choice to flee rather than to apologize, might serve as a message to avoid superficial or exploitative relationships with bears or other animals.

Ideas that connect food and reciprocity feature even in these random snippets from modern childhood. And these themes also pervade Indigenous[1] stories, stories intended for the whole community. Many stories focus on food, how to get it and how to share it; a worldview is produced from these connections, what philosophers might call an environmental ethic. As I hope to show, these stories are foundational for the traditional worldviews that enabled the peoples who told them to survive for millennia, even in deserts or in the Arctic.[2]

Understanding food in this worldview entails understanding food in a way that is, for the most part, unfamiliar to those of us who are not Indigenous. Perhaps thinking of the Roman Catholic Mass might help. In a highly sacred moment, the communicant eats the body and blood of Christ, as the food has been transubstantiated from ordinary food to convey Christ's sacrifice: "Take this, all of you, and eat of it, for this is my body, which will be given up for you."[3] Even at the secular level, we know that offering food – or not offering it – can signal important social connections. But the mainstream way of life has moved many of us away from situations where we engage with food in ritual ways, pray for food, or thank God for providing it; where we grow or gather our own food; or where we cook meals regularly for friends or even family. Food has been reduced to fuel for many people, although we see resistance to this reductionism in veganism, vegetarianism, and local and slow food movements. Many who shift to these ways of thinking and eating do so with more than personal health benefits in mind, often citing an ethic based on avoiding cruelty to animals and/or environmental impact. Indigenous worldviews go further still: they do not allow for thinking about food outside of the sacred and the relational in its broadest sense.

Bears, Stories, and the Nature/Culture Divide

Many Indigenous thinkers regard all life as embedded in and dependent on a web of relationships that require constant care, an animate world of "who" rather than of "what." In this perspective, the land itself is alive and has much to teach us. Such Indigenous worldviews are not marked by the Cartesian nature/culture divide. Indigenous scholars Marie Battiste and James Sa'ke'j Henderson state: "We reject the concept of culture for Indigenous knowledge, heritage, and consciousness, and instead connect each Indigenous manifestation as part of a particular ecological order."[4] They reject the dominant view of nature as a material object distinct from culture, as if we humans somehow were outside the earth's systems rather than originating from them and dependent on them.

Modern readers of transcribed oral stories often find it difficult to take them seriously, given their animal characters and apparently supernatural events. They, at best, move them into the category of fiction or "magic realism" and, at worst, deem them suitable only for children. As Susan Squier, a science and technology scholar, notes, "science and literature are the two pre-eminent technologies that the Enlightenment produced for constituting social subjects and the objects of knowledge."[5] Science took over the realm of the true, literature the realm of the untrue; however, in Indigenous cultures, the two were never separate. Our ideologies of literature and reading also interfere with our understanding the stories as sources of useful knowledge or valid ethics. For example, a central ethical concern of at least some Indigenous worldviews is how to deal with a huge problem. Animals preceded humans in creation, and many Indigenous people regard them as ancestors, family members, teachers and, indeed, as having more-than-human powers. These ideas derive from worldviews unfamiliar in the West, whether secular or religious.

From this perspective, bears feed, support, and teach humans. Anthropologist Franz Boas began his fieldwork with the Inuit; he recounts a story about a single woman who adopts a polar bear cub. When grown, the bear hunts for her, proving "the woman had not taught him in vain."[6] These relationships are reciprocal: the Inuit say that they learned to hunt seals from polar bears.[7] The Syilx/Okanagan storyteller Harry Robinson describes a starving man whose hunting partner refuses him food. Expecting death, he goes into a grizzly bear den, possibly to offer his body as food to the bear. To his surprise, the bear feeds him all winter, shows him the way home, and provides the means to punish the greedy fellow hunter.[8] Rather than spreading the message, "Watch out for the bears!" these stories teach that bears are quite like humans and have similar obligations to feed strangers. Hospitality is a paramount obligation in Indigenous cultures: "It was bad manners to imply one had control over food by even asking a visitor, 'Are you hungry?' One just brought out the food."[9] Notably, these stories focus on maintaining good relationships across a human-animal divide, a divide constructed differently from that of western humanism, which sees humans as superior to animals, and indeed in many cases deems some humans superior to others who are characterized, like animals, as uncivilized, wild, or savage. Indigenous studies scholar Kim Tallbear explains that "our traditional stories … portray nonhuman persons in ways that do not adhere to another meaningful modern category, the 'animal.'"[10]

Close relationships with animals and plants, all viewed as other-than-human persons, are taken for granted in Indigenous traditions, as ethnobotanist Nancy J. Turner outlines in *The Earth's Blanket: Traditional Teachings for Sustainable Living*. She quotes Helen Clifton, a Coast Tsimshian elder, who says that "all animals and plants, whether they are used for food or not, must be treated deferentially, with appreciation and reverence … you should never joke about them, because this is disrespectful."[11] Shirley Sterling tells a story about her grandmother harvesting roots; for every bulb she pulled, she put a spoonful of sugar into the hole that she left.[12] Obviously, the sugar is not traditional;[13] what comes from tradition is the attitude of respect, of demonstrating a reciprocal relationship with the plant world.

This respect was necessary because Indigenous worldviews do not position humans as masters of the universe: "Generally, Indians held that humans were spiritually less powerful than animals. Humans, in fact, were the only creatures born essentially powerless. To live well in the world, that is, to hunt or gather well enough to feed one's family, to avoid being killed in battle, and to contribute to the tribe, one had to gain power. This power usually came from an animal or a mythological being."[14] Anthropologist Catharine McClellan notes that "in their broadest extensions, the social systems of the southern Yukon Indians incorporate both humans and animals. For example, a man of the Crow moiety would address a wolf or a bear as 'brother-in-law' or perhaps, 'grandfather.' Indeed, the major philosophical concern of all the Yukon Indians is how they may best live in harmony with the animals who basically have so much more power than do humans, especially since the Indians continually have to confront and kill the animals if they are to stay alive themselves."[15] Of course, the nature of these relationships differs among nations, and often within them too: not everyone had the same attitudes and not everyone followed the laws conceptualized in the stories (or there would be little need for the stories!).

Bears and/as Food

Bears and humans are brought into proximity not only because humans hunt bears but also because they compete for many of the same foods: seals in the Arctic and, further south, berries, acorns and other nuts, roots, fish, mushrooms, kelp, honey, and small animal prey.[16] (They also like insects and grubs, which most humans are happy to leave to them.) Anyone who picks berries in Canada knows that bears are out picking too.[17] Generally speaking, however, humans are a far greater danger to bears than the other way around. Bears prefer smaller prey, although of course they may attack if confronted. Humans continue to hunt bears, although nowadays not usually for their meat. In the past, however, they were a staple for Indigenous people and settlers alike. Pierre-Jean De Smet, a Roman Catholic missionary, writes of a memorable feast provided by a French-Canadian host in 1845 in what is now British Columbia, where bear meat had pride of place: "I cannot leave my good Canadian without making an honorable mention of his royal cuisine à la sauvage. The first dish he presented me contained two paws of a bear ... A roast porcupine next made its appearance, accompanied by a moose muzzle which had been boiling all night. The latter I found delicious. Finally, the great kettle, containing a sort of hotch-potch, or salmagundi, was placed in the midst of the guests, and each one helped himself according to his taste; there was the choice back-fat of the buffalo cow, venison, cutlets, beavers' tails, quails, rabbits, dumplings and a substantial broth."[18] Apart from their similarly omnivorous tastes in food, bears share many abilities and behaviour with humans: they can easily stand up and walk on their hind legs, they are devoted to their cubs, and they use their paws like hands. Bears, then, more easily provide us with a subject for ethical reflection about human behaviour than do many other animals.

Stories about Bears: Tsimshian, Tahltan, Tlingit, Tuchone, and Inuit

Reading the commentary on many of the stories I focus on gives an idea of what literary scholar Ralph Maud calls the "transmission difficulties"[19] of language and situation and of the variety that can emerge from a single storyteller or storytelling community. Nonetheless, stories do provide us with some useful messages about bears and food. Here I look at two collections.

The twenty-four Tsimshian[20] stories written by Henry Wellington Tate between 1903 and 1913 for Franz Boas work the territory between the everyday need to eat and what we might call the supernatural. *The Porcupine Hunter and Other Stories* reflects a world where Tsimshian people were still managing to maintain many of their traditional ways of life in British Columbia, despite increasing colonial state and missionary regulation and epidemics that killed between sixty and ninety per cent of many communities between 1770 and 1863.[21] Tate was a Christian and wrote in charming, if non-standard, English. Nonetheless, it's clear he took these stories and the ethic they promoted seriously.

Of the eleven of Tate's stories that do not feature Raven, seven deal with those – hunters, grizzly bears, or others – who take more than they need to eat or who treat other people or animals improperly. The perpetrators are invariably punished, and sometimes their village is nearly wiped out. Three stories deal with the flip side of these failures: one explains how to treat bear remains respectfully; another features a prince who shares salmon with eagles and is rewarded with success in fishing; another recounts how a great shaman saves his people by dreaming of how to catch halibut. The only story that does not focus on food tells of the origins of the sun, moon, and fog. In the Raven tales, Raven begins as a shining boy who eats nothing who then transforms into a voracious being who eats all the food in the village.[22] Finally he has to be banished: "Then he went out not knowing which way to turn. / He was very hungry."[23] From this point on, Raven's nature leads him to desire good things, like rivers, light, and salmon, not to mention food, sex, and admiration. In going after them, he sometimes fails spectacularly, but sometimes, he transforms the world for the better.

Tate's collection includes a version of "The Girl Who Married a Bear," which can profitably be read with Catharine McClellan's eleven examples of "The Girl Who Married a Bear," collected from Tagish, Tuchone, and Tlingit[24] storytellers in the Yukon. Although much more is going on in these stories than eating, the girl is out picking berries when she is taken to live with a bear husband, and "nearly every day they hunted gophers and picked berries."[25] Events that modern readers find improbable are anchored in everyday activities of hunting, gathering, food preparation, and eating. In these stories, the relationship often begins when the girl treats bear scat with disrespect, in one story insulting bears by saying, "Big flappy foot always pooping where you can step on it."[26] A handsome man, who she eventually realizes is a bear, appears and invites her to go with him. She becomes his wife. The girl's bear-hunting brothers eventually track the couple to their den. The powerful bear husband, deciding that he will allow himself to be killed by his brothers-in-law, teaches his wife songs and special rituals to follow after his death. The bear's widow returns with her bear children to her human family, bringing new powers to use in the hunt. However, in some versions her brothers tease her into putting on a bearskin: she turns into a bear and kills them. These transformations from human to bear and back mark a permeable line between animal and human. As Kim Tallbear notes, "our stories avoid the hierarchical nature-culture and animal-human split that has enabled domineering human management, naming, controlling, and 'saving' of nature."[27] Seeing animals as autonomous, powerful, and even dangerous beings produces a different set of attitudes and a much wider social circle. Importantly, the need to respect animals leads to protocols around using all parts of the animal and preventing overhunting.

In *Stories in a New Skin: An Approach to Inuit Literature*, Keavy Martin retells an Inuit story about Angusugjuk and his polar bear wife.[28] Conflict between the hero's in-laws and the other polar bears erupts over whether to let Angusugjuk live; the conflict is only resolved when he wins a contest of strength by obeying his polar bear mother-in-law without question.

This story, like the stories about the girl who married the bear, can be seen not only as teachings about relationships with bears but also about family and marriage – all potential sources of conflict. Relations between humans and bears, like all social relations, are not necessarily easy; in fact, given the powers ascribed to the bear, they may be fraught with even more anxiety than relations between humans: "In the areas where bears were an important source of meat, many of the tribes believed that bears had control of the supply of other game."[29] Displeasing a bear could mean starvation.

Indigenous Food Science

Few modern readers have experienced near-starvation or have had to hunt for the next meal. Even those of us who obsessively read the microprint on food packaging are extremely ignorant about what we eat, an ignorance that is, in part, reflected in a wide array of books about special diets, such as the 100-mile diet or the Paleolithic diet, that focus attention on where our food comes from or on its history. This shift to thinking more seriously about food is also marked by the popularity of an ever-changing array of "superfoods" such as quinoa or blueberries or kale. However, the authors of the books and articles featuring these diets and foods rarely consider the epistemological framework that connected (and still connects) Indigenous cultures with the local foods that sustain them. This omission comes even though many supermarket staples, including quinoa, but also others such as avocado, beans, cassava, chocolate, corn, peanuts, peppers, pineapples, potatoes, pumpkins, squash, and tomatoes were developed from wild plants by Indigenous peoples.[30] The domestication, cultivation, and safe preparation of these foods required profound scientific knowledge of plants and growing conditions over long periods. We have seen how Indigenous epistemology rewrites the human-animal boundary. And the same was true for plants used for food or medicine. Given bears' dining habits, which include eating medicinal plants, they were often seen as healers with special knowledge, as the "bestower of the secrets and mysteries of plants."[31] The close observation of the behaviour of plants and animals combined with strong respect and admiration for them supported amazing advances in making unpromising plants into foods that now sustain millions.

One of the reasons that the worldviews of Indigenous people should be central to discussions of sustainability is that they live in the most ecologically diverse areas of the world and have worked to maintain that diversity. The non-profit organization Terralingua calls this phenomenon "biocultural diversity"; as their website explains: "Languages, cultures, and ecosystems are interdependent."[32] Why is this the case? In locations where human beings have survived over millennia in sometimes incredibly harsh conditions, they of necessity have learned an immense amount about their surroundings. Each ecosystem differs, presenting a vast array of natural possibility, and the languages of these Indigenous groups are marked by detailed knowledge of particular ecosystems and of the seasonal progression of life there, not just in vocabulary but even at the more stable level of grammar. For example, Ahtna, an Athabaskan language spoken in Alaska, contains directionals, that is, word segments that indicate one's location, and these are embedded in the grammar. When an elder tells a story set on the land (and they are all set on the land), listeners know exactly which way she is travelling, how high up on the mountain, and how far from the river.[33] This embedded GPS system was vital for finding one's way in a seasonal round governed by the ripening of berries, the migration of game animals, and the spawning of fish.

Okanagan/Syilx and Nuu-chah-nulth Worldviews

Jeannette Armstrong has spent a career writing about the Okanagan/Syilx perspectives in her fiction, poetry, and critical analysis. She sees language and story as central to the relationship between human beings and the land. In "Land Speaking," she writes, "All my elders say that it is land that holds all knowledge of life and death and is a constant teacher. It is said in Okanagan that the land constantly speaks ... Not to learn its language is to die. We survived and thrived by listening intently to its teachings – to its language – and then inventing human words to retell its stories to our succeeding generations."[34] And she points out that the people are, in fact, made up of the land: "The flesh that is our bodies is pieces of the land come to us through the things that the land is. The soil, the water, the air, and all the other life forms contributed parts for our flesh. We are our land/place."[35] And of course, this fact is true of all humans, although many of us rarely think of it. Nor, despite the centrality of science in our culture, do we really follow through on Darwin's finding that all organic life on the planet is related.

In the story that Armstrong discusses as the foundational origin story of her culture, the story of the four chiefs (or "How the Foods Were Given"), the chiefs rule the animals, fish, roots, and berries. The black bear is the chief of all. For a long time they discuss how to deal with the "ripped from the earth people to be," that is, humans – how will they live – and they decide to "lay down" their lives to become food for humans.³⁶ The bear leads the others. To return him to life, his body must be treated properly, with appropriate songs. The fly, the smallest, sings the most powerful song, and the bear returns to life, demonstrating that if human hunters and gatherers perform their duties with respect, the animals and plants will willingly return to feed them.

The basic question that the four chiefs are discussing is how can humans have a sustainable ethic if we eat our relatives? They don't depend on eating people to survive. What is it that humans have to offer the world, if it is not physical sustenance? Armstrong notes that this story takes place in a world before humans; it is an origin story in which four different perspectives enact a way to build consensus that is still practised in her culture today. She spends a great deal of time outlining this process, emphasizing that it is a form of governance that systematically ensures that diverse opinions held by different interest groups in the community are solicited and discussed, as in the discussion among the four chiefs. This study, as well as one of Armstrong's earliest publications, her collaborative *We Get Our Living Like Milk from the Land*, makes the point that the land is a sacred being, a respected elder who teaches those who listen carefully how to survive. The land speaks as a nursing mother, both forming and sustaining beings who become human only after a lifetime of listening and learning to speak and behave so as to continue the lives of all those around them, including their own descendants. Armstrong says: "The first concept is that the human is separate from other beings as a result of the human ability to use its unique survival mechanism of analytic ability and memory. From this perspective, to be human is to be a being with the unique ability to discern, categorize and remember things and that characteristic is what makes them separate."³⁷ What distinguishes humans from the rest of the beings on earth – reason and memory – allows them to fulfill their obligation to sustain the ecosystem that feeds them, a relationship characterized as that between a helpless infant and a mother, whereas all the other animal and plant people arrive already knowing how to survive. For Okanagan/Syilx people, this notion that the land is our mother is not simply the increasingly abstract metaphor of "Mother Earth" or "Mother Nature." In Okanagan/Syilx terms, if we wish to eat without being eaten, we are obligated to keep the whole ecosystem alive. If humans do not listen properly, they become what Armstrong describes as "people-eating monsters,"³⁸ which Coyote is tasked with destroying. Her account makes us think immediately of cannibalism. But we humans cannot survive without eating plant and animal people: in this system we are cannibals by nature, and the only way to balance out that negative designation is to keep the animals and the land living through care and respect, song and ceremony.[39]

E. Richard Atleo is the author of two books on Nuu-chah-nulth epistemology, *Tsawalk: A Nuu-chah-nulth Worldview* and *Principles of Tsawalk: An Indigenous Approach to Global Crisis*. He, like Armstrong, points out that the interactions between the animal and human worlds should be thoughtfully negotiated. For example, unable to steal the light from the chief, who keeps it hidden in a box, Raven devises a typically sneaky way to be born into that family and grow up within its knowledge system. In another story, this one about a bear, Atleo figures relationships in terms of diplomacy rather than familial affection. A man discovers that a bear is emptying his fish trap and then wrecking it. At this point, a non-Indigenous plot line would have him get out the gun, but the man simply asks the bear why he is taking the fish. The bear takes the man back to his village to show that he is feeding them to his people. After the man learns about the bears' way of life, he and the bear chief negotiate an agreement: "If the man was willing to share from the bounty of his fish trap, there would always be plenty of fish for both tribes, the man's tribe and the Bear's tribe … Part of the agreement was that the Bear would no longer wreck the trap so that equitable sharing might continue in perpetuity."[40] Atleo comments that both Raven and Bear learn "about the natural need to obtain consent by developing protocols with their neighbours."[41] This comment reverberates, given that the British and then the Canadian state have rarely engaged in proper diplomatic relations with Indigenous nations. It also reverberates with the many failures to inform or consult with Indigenous peoples when "development" projects threaten their territories or ways of life. For example, in recent history, British Columbia has faced (and often failed to resolve) conflicts over logging (Clayoquot Sound, 1993), dams (Site C, 2016, which will be the third dam on the Peace River), oil pipelines (the proposed Kinder Morgan Trans Mountain expansion), and mining (Mount Polley disaster, 2014). All such projects seriously impact the lives of Indigenous people who rely on fishing, hunting, and gathering berries and roots for food. After little or no consultation, they are often forced off the lands that in the past supported them. And, of course, this impact reverberates across the living ecosystem (and indeed around the globe as outsourcing of production also outsources environmental destruction and human exploitation; see Tsing). The diplomatic discussions of the four chiefs and of the fisherman and the bear allowed for multiple and conflicting perspectives to be articulated without presuming that solutions required everyone to assimilate to the same perspective. Negotiation was possible.[42] Anthropologist

Anna Lowenhaupt Tsing describes such a collaboration to support community-managed forests in Indonesia where "collaboration was not consensus making but rather an opening for productive confusion."[43] As we have seen, conflicts over resources are often thematized in stories. Perhaps current ways of dealing with such inevitable conflicts might be enhanced or even revolutionized by considering Indigenous thought on how to produce and manage good relationships, including our relationships with food.

Current State of Cultural Studies and Literary-Critical Studies

At the moment, despite the importance of stories in learning about these matters, cultural studies and literary-critical studies are belated in coming to terms with ecological issues in comparison with many other disciplines, especially anthropology, but also philosophy, history, geography, and the biological sciences, particularly applied sciences such as forestry, nutrition, and agriculture. In a useful overview of environmental ethics in the *Stanford Encyclopedia of Philosophy*, Andrew Brennan and Yeuk-Sze Lo note that "contemporary environmental ethics only emerged as an academic discipline in the 1970s."[44] Although they mention Indigenous ideas only in passing, they point out that "the *new animists* have been much inspired by the serious way in which some indigenous peoples placate and interact with animals, plants and inanimate things through ritual, ceremony and other practices. According to the new animists, the replacement of traditional animism (the view that personalized souls are found in animals, plants, and other material objects) by a form of disenchanting positivism directly leads to an anthropocentric perspective, which is accountable for much human destructiveness towards nature."[45] Graham Harvey's 2013 *Handbook of Contemporary Animism* begins with a chapter by Linda Hogan (Chickasaw) and brings together scholars, mainly anthropologists, who describe contemporary Indigenous worldviews in many parts of the world, including Canada. Harvey himself provides a chapter on contemporary Indigenous creative writing and animism intended to inspire future critical work. Indigenous worldviews, once conveyed only in oral story, now are often transmitted in contemporary creative writing, a fact that I hope my focus on traditional story and contemporary analytical texts does not obscure. Although scientists and social scientists are aware of the importance of Traditional Ecological Knowledge (TEK), the idea that contemporary literary works might transmit TEK is less common.

Both cultural studies scholars and literary critics have more to do. In the introduction to her edited collection *Animal Subjects: An Ethical Reader in a Posthuman World*, Jodey Castricano notes that cultural studies is still strongly tied to notions of the human as distinct from animals, despite the field's intense focus on forms of domination that impact human animals, such as sexism, racism, and homophobia, and forms of domination and discrimination that often use the category of animal, invariably seen as inferior, to characterize other humans. Castricano argues for a paradigm shift to including animals in "a new moral community based on reciprocity."[46] In 2011, Rob Nixon, author of *Slow Violence and the Environmentalism of the Poor*, argued that most environmentalists track only an American tradition grounded in figures such as Thoreau, and states that "for the most part, a broad silence has characterized environmentalists' stance toward postcolonial literature and theory while postcolonial critics have typically been no less silent on the subject of environmental literature."[47] However, along with the recent increase in public acceptance of global warming has come increased attention to the environmentalism of the poor, what has been called "empty-belly environmentalism."[48]

Dining with bears has led me rather deep into the intellectual forest here, since debates around the role of other-than-humans in the global north are both contentious and complex. Some philosophical arguments around the extension of consideration for non-humans focus on the ability to form a moral intention, while others consider the capacity to suffer.[49] Mainstream philosophy comes at the issue step by step, it seems, while some Indigenous notions of respect may extend even beyond those who are our relatives in a Darwinian sense (all organic life, including bacteria, some of whom live inside us) to include features of the landscape such as rivers and mountains, not to mention spiritual beings. I once had a brief discussion with a Cree elder about whether it was all right to kill mosquitos. Her answer was no, it was not. I doubt her answer was based on considerations of mosquitos' ability to form moral intentions or their capacity to suffer. However, I do not make this point to discount the ways that western philosophers are working towards an environmental ethic, since there is no one perfect way to do this. What is important is that these ideas can be articulated in forums where stakeholders are free to discuss them from the perspectives of their different worldviews.

Theorist Bruno Latour makes the case for a "symmetric anthropology" that turns its gaze equally on those of us who once thought we were modern as well as those Indigenous peoples once excluded from modernity. He argues this could lead to important diplomatic negotiations between those who have lost their lands through colonial land theft and resource extraction and those facing the prospect of homelessness as a result of climate change.[50] In a conversation with Chilean scholar Carolina Miranda, he, like Atleo, calls for more constructive and innovative forms of diplomacy: "Do we want someone representative of the entrenched categories of a culture, or do we want to seize the occasion given by rare diplomatic encounters to modify deeply what we hold to? That's where couching ethnography in a diplomatic instead of an epistemological mode makes a big difference. A diplomat is the one who finds degrees of liberty where none was visible before, when the parties at the negotiation table were simply stating their cases, their interests, and simply drawing, as the saying goes, red lines they don't want to trespass."[51] Although here Latour is talking about human diplomacy, in other places he has extended the realm of politics to include both western science and the other-than-human realm, showing how humans in fact form alliances with a range of beings, including animals, plants, and things (including human-made technologies, such as electron microscopes) to produce new relationships and politics.[52]

Ecological Indians vs Practical Ecological Philosophers

In this account I do not want to reproduce the stereotype of "the ecological Indian" exposed by historian Shepard Krech in his book of the same title as a version of the Noble Savage. To learn from Indigenous worldviews is not to adopt them without question. Although Krech has been criticized as "anti-Indian," Tallbear argues that his examination of Indigenous worldviews should raise interest in more study from Indigenous scholars along the same lines, implicitly to test and update the assumptions of the past: "Part of what is admirable about this book is the author's careful discussion of specific historical practices within a context of tribal spiritual belief about nature and how nature regenerates itself."[53] Certainly the stereotype of the ecological Indian has been used to undermine the perspectives and authenticity of any Indigenous people who use modern technology, from rifles to freezers to snowmobiles to word processors. If Indigenous people can live in the modern world while maintaining the belief that they should maintain good relationships with other-than-humans, and many obviously can and do, this persistence inspires hope that mainstream society can adapt its worldviews to the challenge of global warming and other dangers to planetary survival. But this will not be easy. As postcolonial literary theorist Gayatri Spivak says, "in our global emergency, 'learning from below' can only be an impatient vanguardism with a winning slogan. To achieve deep epistemic shift into an animist liberation theology is a task that would need a displacement of millennial history and deep language learning of lost languages at once. Our animism is tied to accountability for resources – a reckoning parasitical upon love."[54] Of course, the same might be said of the practical ecologies of Indigenous people, whose need for food was parasitical on love, too. We may not have the privilege of dining with bears (or, I hope, any need to dine *on* bears), but a major shift of perspective is required if we are to keep the planet living. Fortunately, in the process we can draw on worldviews that were developed by those who consistently faced such challenges over thousands of years.

Notes

1. For a variety of reasons, the word "Indigenous" is now preferred in Canadian academic and government circles to refer to the original peoples of what is now called Canada. Many earlier formulations, such as "Native," "Indian," or "Aboriginal," are to some degree pejorative or state-imposed. "First Nations" has come to equate to the state designation "Status Indian," which does not include Inuit and Métis people. Indigenous is very broad, however, gesturing to Indigenous worldviews derived from close interactions with the natural world around the globe, as well as to political alliances epitomized in the United Nations Declaration on the Rights of Indigenous Peoples. Suffice it to say that the stories I talk about are told on the west coast and in the nearby interior of northern North America, although some of the critics I quote generalize more widely. For more on terms, see Canada.
2. See Nabhan, *The Deserts Smells Like Rain*; see Gombay, *Making a Living*.
3. See "Order of Mass," 19. Here the priest is quoting Christ at the Last Supper, where he prophesies his own death.
4. Battiste and Henderson, *Protecting Indigenous Knowledge and Heritage*, 34.
5. Squier, *Liminal Lives*, 28.
6. Boas, *The Central Eskimos*, 230–1; for a more recent version and more commentary, see Bennett and Rowley, *Uqalurait: An Oral History of Nunavut*, 124–5.
7. Laugrand and Oosten, *Hunters, Predators and Prey*, 184–6.
8. Robinson, "Saved by a Grizzly Bear," 125–37.
9. Holden, "Restorying," n.p.
10. Tallbear, "Indigenous Reflection," 235.
11. Turner, *Earth's Blanket*, 82.

12 Sterling, "The Grandmother Stories," 138.
13 Many introduced foodstuffs such as flour, sugar, and apples as well as imported foods, like oranges, were eaten and distributed even at potlatches, proving that this ceremony has adapted to modern circumstances. In a description of one held in 1945, "then the people began coming in with huge piles of food, boxes of biscuits, soda crackers, loaves of bread, quarters of beef and boxes of apples or oranges." Beynon, *Potlatch at Gitsegukla*, 114.
14 Rockwell, *Giving Voice to Bear*, 95.
15 McClellan, *The Girl Who Married the Bear*, 6.
16 In "Saved by a Grizzly Bear," storyteller Harry Robinson remarks: "Then they [bears] get food / like the Indian food they use, / like the dry meat, deer meat, dry meat, / and black moss and white camas and then Saskatoon [berries]" (131).
17 Canada contains the largest number of polar bears (*Ursus maritimus*) in the world (approximately 16,000 of the estimated 25,000). British Columbia's 16,000 grizzly bears (brown bears, *Ursus actos*) constitute about a quarter of the total North American population. British Columbia has the highest number of black bears (*Ursus Americanus*) in Canada, between 120,000 and 150,000 of the 900,000 in North America and Mexico. See IUCN, "Seventy-five Per Cent," n.p.
18 Barman, "Sophie Morigeau," 181; the cookbook by the People of K'san, *Gathering What the Great Nature Provided*, gives recipes for moose nose, not to mention "Half-Smoked Bear Intestines" (109), as well as many of the creatures mentioned as game by Tate and in De Smet's account quoted by Barman of the French Canadian's feast, including porcupine and beaver.
19 See Maud, *Transmission Difficulties*.
20 Tsimshian territories are on the central coastal mainland of British Columbia just opposite Haida Gwaii (formerly Queen Charlotte Islands).
21 Boyd, "Smallpox in the Pacific Northwest," 28, 35.
22 Hyde analyzes this story in *Trickster Makes this World*, 23–7.
23 Tate, *Porcupine Hunter*, 136.
24 See also McClellan, *My Old People's Stories*, which contains these stories and many more from the Yukon; Detwiler, "Moral Foundations of Tlingit Cosmology."
25 McClellan, *The Girl Who Married the Bear*, version 3, told by Maria Johns, 28–33.
26 Tate, *Porcupine Hunter*, 40n2.
27 Tallbear, "Indigenous Reflection," 235.
28 Martin, *Stories in a New Skin*, 49–58.
29 Rockwell, *Giving Voice to Bear*, 57.
30 Gade, "South America": "The potato, manioc, and sweet potato, each belonging to

different plant families, are among the top 10 food sources in the world today. The potato (*Solanum tuberosum* and related species) clearly originated in South America, where prior to European contact it was cultivated in the Andes through a range of 50 degrees of latitude" (1254).

31 Rockwell, *Giving Voice to Bear*, 6.
32 Terralingua; see also Maffi, *On Biocultural Diversity*.
33 See Berez, "Directional Reference, Discourse, and Landscape in Ahtna."
34 Armstrong, "Land Speaking," 178.
35 Armstrong, "Community," 57.
36 Armstrong, "Constructing Indigeneity," 232.
37 Ibid.
38 Ibid., 233.
39 Ibid.
40 Atleo, *Principles of Tsawalk*, 101.
41 Ibid.
42 Although we frequently poke fun at the Canadian tendency to defer controversial action to the deliberation of commissions, such deferral does open up a space for multiple perspectives to be voiced and recorded, including Indigenous perspectives that otherwise might never reach a wide public. Further, these inquiries, trials, and commissions provide a way for Indigenous people to speak to powerful members of the dominant mainstream, many of whom, of course, are not listening or, if listening, not understanding. Nonetheless, these events also focus diverse Indigenous nations and communities on common goals, which allows for the revitalizing of their worldviews for new contexts. Recent Canadian examples of such events include the Mackenzie Pipeline Inquiry (also called the Berger Inquiry, 1974–77), Delgaamukw v. British Columbia (1984–97), the Royal Commission on Aboriginal Peoples (1991–96), and the Truth and Reconciliation Commission (2008–15). The extent to which these discussions are fiddling while Rome burns is for another paper to consider.
43 Tsing, *Frictions*, 247.
44 Brennan and Lo, "Environmental Ethics," n.p.
45 Ibid.
46 Castricano, Introduction, *Animal Subjects*, 17.
47 Nixon, "Slow Violence"; see also Huggan and Tiffin, *Postcolonial Ecocriticism*.
48 Attributed to Guha, Nixon, "Slow Violence."
49 See Brennan and Lo, "Environmental Ethics."
50 See Latour with Miranda, "A Dialog about a New Meaning of Symmetric Anthropology."

51 Ibid., 7.
52 See Latour, *Politics of Nature*.
53 Tallbear, "Shepard Krech's *The Ecological Indian*," 2.
54 Spivak, "Love: A Conversation," 61.

Bibliography

Armstrong, Jeannette. "Community: 'Sharing One Skin.'" In *Paradigm Wars: Indigenous Peoples' Resistance to Globalization*, edited by Jerry Mander and Victoria Tauli-Corpuz, 35–9. San Francisco: Sierra Book Club, 2006.

– "Constructing Indigeneity: Syilx Okanagan Oraliture and tmix^w-centrism." PhD dissertation, University of Greifswald, 2009. Accessed 7 February 2016. https://d-nb.info/1027188737/34.

– "Land Speaking." In *Speaking for the Generations: Native Writers on Writing*, edited by Simon Ortiz, 175–94. Tucson: University of Arizona, 1999.

Armstrong, Jeannette, Greg Younging, and Delphine Derickson, eds. *We Get Our Living Like Milk from the Land*. Penticton, BC: Theytus, 1994.

Atleo, E. Richard. (Umeek). *Principles of Tsawalk: An Indigenous Approach to Global Crisis*. Vancouver: University of British Columbia Press, 2011.

– *Tsawalk: A Nuu-chah-nulth Worldview*. Vancouver: University of British Columbia Press, 2004.

Barman, Jean. "Sophie Morigeau: Free Trader, Free Woman." In *Recollecting: Lives of Aboriginal Women of the Canadian Northwest and Borderlands*, edited by Sarah Carter and Patricia McCormack, 175–95. Edmonton: Athabasca University Press, 2011.

Battiste, Marie, and James (Sa'ke'j) Youngblood Henderson. *Protecting Indigenous Knowledge and Heritage: A Global Challenge*. Saskatoon: Purich, 2000.

Bennett, John, and Susan Rowley, eds. *Uqalurait: An Oral History of Nunavut*. Montreal and Kingston: McGill-Queen's University Press, 2004.

Berez, Andrea. "Directional Reference, Discourse, and Landscape in Ahtna." PhD dissertation, University of California at Santa Barbara, 2011.

Beynon, William. *Potlatch at Gitsegukla: William Beynon's 1945 Field Notebooks*. Edited by Margaret Anderson and Marjorie Halpin. Vancouver: University of British Columbia Press, 2000.

Boas, Franz. *The Central Eskimo*. Introduction by Henry B. Collins. Lincoln: University of Nebraska Press, 1964.

Boyd, Robert. "Smallpox in the Pacific Northwest: The Early Epidemics." *BC Studies* 101 (1994): 5–40.

Brennan, Andrew, and Yeuk-Sze Lo. "Environmental Ethics," *The Stanford Encyclopedia of Philosophy* (Winter 2015 Edition), edited by Edward N. Zalta. Accessed 31 August 2016. http://plato.stanford.edu/archives/win2015/entries/ethics-environmental/.

Canada. Panel on Research Ethics. "Tricouncil policy statement 2 (2014)." Accessed 31 August 2016. www.pre.ethics.gc.ca/eng/policy-politique/initiatives/tcps2-eptc2/chapter9-chapitre9/.

Castricano, Jodey. Introduction. In *Animal Subjects: An Ethical Reader in a Posthuman World*, edited by Castricano, 1–32. Waterloo: Wilfrid Laurier University Press, 2008.

Detwiler, Fritz. "Moral Foundations of Tlingit Cosmology." In *The Handbook of Contemporary Animism* by Graham Harvey, 167–80. Durham, UK: Acumen, 2013.

Gade, David W. "South America." In *Cambridge World History of Food*, edited by Kenneth F. Kiple and Coneè Ornelas Kriemhild, 1254–60. Cambridge: Cambridge University Press, 2000.

Gombay, Nicole. *Making a Living: Place, Food, and Economy in an Inuit Community*. Saskatoon: Purich, 2010.

Harvey, Graham. *The Handbook of Contemporary Animism*. Durham, UK: Acumen, 2013.

Holden, Madronna. "Restorying the World, Reviving the Language of Life." *Australian Humanities Review: Ecological Humanities* 47 [2009]. www.australianhumanitiesreview.org/archive/Issue-November-2009/holden.html.

Huggan, Graham, and Helen Tiffin. *Postcolonial Ecocriticism: Literature, Animals, Environment*. 2010. London: Routledge, 2015.

Hyde, Lewis. *Trickster Makes this World*. New York: Farrar, Straus, and Giroux, 1998.

IUCN. "Seventy-five Per Cent of Bear Species Threatened with Extinction." 12 November 2007. www.iucn.org/content/seventy-five-percent-bear-species-threatened-extinction. See also linked fact sheets.

Kiple Kenneth F., and Kriemhild Coneè Ornelas, eds. *Cambridge World History of Food*. Cambridge: Cambridge University Press, 2000.

Krech, Shepard III. *The Ecological Indian: Myth and History*. New York: Norton, 1999.

K'san, People of. *Gathering What the Great Nature Provided: Food Traditions of the Gitksan*. Vancouver: Douglas and McIntyre, 1980.

Latour, Bruno. Interview with Carolina Miranda. "A Dialog about a New Meaning of Symmetric Anthropology." 2016. Chapter for a book edited by Pierre Charbonnier, Gildas Salmon, and Peter Skafish (in preparation). Accessed 30 August 2016. www.bruno-latour.fr/article.

– *Politics of Nature: How to Bring the Sciences into Democracy*. Cambridge, MA: Harvard University Press, 2004.

Laugrand, Frédéric, and Jarich Oosten. *Hunters, Predators and Prey: Inuit Perceptions of Animals*. New York: Berghan, 2015.

Maffi, Luisa, ed. *On Biocultural Diversity: Linking Language, Knowledge, and the Environment*. Washington, DC: Smithsonian Institution Press, 2001.

Martin, Keavy. *Stories in a New Skin: Approaches to Inuit Literature*. Winnipeg: University of Manitoba Press, 2012.

Maud, Ralph. *Transmission Difficulties: Franz Boas and Tsimshian Mythography*. Vancouver: Talonbooks, 2000.

McClellan, Catharine. *My Old People's Stories: A Legacy for Yukon First Nations*. 3 Vols. Edited with additions by Julie Cruikshank. Illustrated by Catherine Kernan. Occasional Papers in Yukon History 5 (1–3). Whitehorse: Government of Yukon, Cultural Services Branch, 2007.

McClellan, Catherine [sic]. *The Girl Who Married the Bear*. Publications in Ethnology 2. Ottawa: National Museums of Canada, 1970. Canadian Museum of History. www.historymuseum.ca/cmc/exhibitions/tresors/ethno/etp1202e.shtml.

Nabhan, Gary Paul. *The Desert Smells Like Rain: A Naturalist in O'odham Country*. Tucson: University of Arizona Press, 1982.

Nixon, Rob. "Slow Violence: Literary and Postcolonial Studies Have Ignored the Environmentalism that Often Only the Poor Can See." *Chronicle of Higher Education*, 26 June 2011. www.chronicle.com/article/Slow-Violence/127968.

– *Slow Violence and the Environmentalism of the Poor*. Cambridge, MA: Harvard University Press, 2011.

"Order of Mass." Excerpts of the English translation of *The Roman Missal*, 2010. www.catholicbishops.ie/wp-content/uploads/2011/02/Order-of-Mass.pdf.

Robinson, Harry. "Saved by a Grizzly Bear." In *Write It on Your Heart: The Epic World of an Okanagan Storyteller*, edited by Wendy Wickwire, 125–37. Vancouver: Talonbooks/Theytus, 1989.

Rockwell, David. *Giving Voice to Bear: North American Indian Myths, Rituals, and Images of the Bear*. Revised ed. Lanham: Roberts Rinehart, 1991.

Squier, Susan. *Liminal Lives: Imagining the Human at the Frontiers of Biomedicine*. Durham, NC: Duke University Press, 2004.

Spivak, Gayatri Chakravorty. "Love: A Conversation." With Serene Jones, Catherine Keller, Kwok Pui-Lan, and Stephen D. Moore. In *Planetary Loves: Spivak, Postcoloniality and Theology*, edited by Stephen D. Moore, 55–78. New York: Fordham University Press, 2010.

Sterling, Shirley. "The Grandmother Stories: Oral Stories and the Transmission of Culture." PhD dissertation, University of British Columbia, 1997.

Tallbear, Kim. "An Indigenous Reflection on Working Beyond the Human/Not Human." *GLQ: A Journal of Lesbian and Gay Studies* 21, nos. 2–3 (June 2015): 230–5. Special issue edited by Mel Y. Chen and Dana Luciano.

– "Shepard Krech's *The Ecological Indian*: One Indian's Perspective." International Institute for Indigenous Resource Management. IIIRM Publications. September 2000. www.iiirm.org/publications/Book%20Reviews/Reviews/Krech001.pdf.

Tate, Henry Wellington. *The Porcupine Hunter and Other Stories: The Original Tsimshian Texts of Henry Tate*, edited by Ralph Maud. Vancouver: Talonbooks, 1993.

Terralingua: Unity in Biocultural Diversity. Accessed 30 August 2016. http://terralingua.org/.

Tsing, Anna Lowenhaupt. *Frictions: An Ethnography of Global Connection*. Princeton: Princeton University Press, 2005.

Turner, Nancy J. *The Earth's Blanket: Traditional Teachings for Sustainable Living*. Vancouver: Douglas and McIntyre, 2005.

3

Changing Tides

Indigenous Chefs at the Culinary Olympics and the Gastronomic Professionalization of Aboriginal Cooking

Sebastian Schellhaas

> "The king then seated me by him and ordered his women to bring him something to eat. They sat before him some dried clams and train oil ... of which he ate very heartily and encouraged me to follow his example, telling me to eat much and take a great deal of oil which would make me strong and fat. Notwithstanding his praise of this new kind of food, I felt no disposition to indulge in it, both smell and taste being loathsome to me."[1]

John R. Jewitt published these disparaging lines in 1815 to describe his first encounter with Aboriginal foods during his forced stay in Yaqout. The king in this passage was Mukʷina, chief of the Mowachaht-Muchalaht First Nation of what is now the western coast of Vancouver Island.[2] The unenthusiastic Jewitt, a nineteenth-century British blacksmith and armorer from Boston, England, was not a visitor but a captive of Mukʷina and lived for two years (1803–05) among the Mowachaht-Muchalaht people.[3] Jewitt reflected the collective imagination and sentiments of many newcomers to the Pacific Northwest Coast (as well as to the rest of the area that we associate with present-day Canada), notably the unpalatability of Aboriginal foods and cooking.[4] Tellingly, historian Coll Thrush also points to the reverse perspective with respect to settler foods: "Clearly, indigenous noses were turned up just as often as those of the newcomers."[5]

Two centuries later these attitudes are changing. Today, ingredients and dishes once introduced by European settlers have become an integral part of Indigenous food cultures across the country. At the same time, Indigenous cookbooks are winning international prizes, and Indigenous chefs are invited to world-class culinary think tanks like Cook It Raw, "an annual gathering of culinary luminaries who explore possibilities of cuisine."[6] They also contribute to collective cookbook projects like *Great Canadian Masters. Vol. I + II*, participate in gastro-events like Terroir Symposium or Canada 150 celebrations, give professional talks and cooking demonstrations, appear on television shows like *Top Chef* and *Chopped Canada*, and open up restaurants that attract foodies and chefs from all over North America and the rest of the world. However, these ongoing changes must not be misunderstood as a new state of symmetry between Indigenous peoples and the non-Indigenous public during the 150th anniversary of Canadian confederation. In fact, the prevailing racism on social, political, and cultural levels, and the often-precarious nutritional situation – in terms of both food security and food sovereignty with all the disastrous effects on health and cultural well-being[7] – are integral parts of the settler-colonial reality still faced by Indigenous peoples today. Nevertheless, there is change and, more importantly, change that has not happened by chance. The growing awareness of and appreciation for Aboriginal foods and cooking are intertwined with the rising presence of Indigenous gastronomy in Canadian public space. One part of this ongoing success story can be attributed to a team of Indigenous chefs who in 1992 competed at one of the world's most renowned professional cook-offs: the Culinary Olympics in Germany. As the first competitors ever to represent Indigenous people – both in Canada and the rest of the world – at the Culinary Olympics, the team's participation stands as a remarkable episode in the cultural history of Indigenous food cultures in Canada – that is, the gastronomic professionalization of Aboriginal cooking.

When the first Indigenous team made their appearance on the culinary world stage in the early 1990s, there were a limited number of Indigenous chefs and only a few Indigenous restaurants had been in operation in Canada since the 1970s. It was only after the team returned home and became actively involved in educational programs that gastronomic professionalization gained momentum among Indigenous communities. Today, the legacy of this team's competitive success and broader commitment finds expression not only in the growing number of Indigenous people working in culinary professions but also in the emergence of Indigenous-owned catering companies, food trucks, bistros, cafés, and restaurants that serve a great diversity of Aboriginal foods or offer Indigenous-inspired menus.

The Culinary Olympics

To appreciate the team's achievements, one first needs to understand the Culinary Olympics. Among the countless chef competitions around the globe, the International Exhibition of Culinary Art (Internationale Kochkunst-Ausstellung, IKA) – widely known as the "Culinary Olympics"[8] – occupies a special place. Out of the four most prestigious (the other three are the Bocuse d'Or in France, Food and Hotel Asia Culinary Challenge in Singapore, and the Culinary World Cup in Luxembourg), only the Culinary Olympics can look back on a history that extends to the end of the nineteenth century. When the first Olympics took place in Frankfurt/Main in 1900, there had been comparable events in France, England, and Germany since the 1870s.[9] These other shows, hosted by respective national organizations like the Société des Cuisiniers Française or the Verband Deutscher Köche, had a strong national focus, whereas the Olympics followed a decidedly international credo.[10] Organized by the Internationaler Verband der Köche (since 1948 Verband der Köche Deutschlands, VKD), the Olympics carried its "international" orientation in its original title. In their journal *Kochkunst* from 1900, the organizers stated: "For an exhibition of culinary art to truly deserve its name, it has to show the visitor the range of culinary art in its entirety. Not only the present state of a region's or a country's culinary art should be exhibited, but also the cuisine of the neighbouring countries has to be taken into consideration."[11] As in the case of other culinary and world exhibitions hosted at the turn of the nineteenth and twentieth centuries, culinary nationalism has played – and today still plays – an important part in the Culinary Olympics.[12] Yet, more importantly, the Olympics have been committed to the modernization of French haute cuisine as most prominently associated with the name Auguste Escoffier and his revolutionary *Le Guide Culinaire*. The "Guidelines for Exhibitors/Competitors and Jury" highlight this commitment and point to the competition's central aim: "Correct basic preparation in accordance with modern cooking principles."[13] Simply put, these "modern cooking principles" refer to the evolution of standards regarding the style of service; the organization of the physical and social structure of professional kitchens; and the canonization of basic recipes, cooking techniques, meal structures, and patterns of plating that characterize the craft of culinary arts as it is taught in culinary schools and performed in commercial kitchens of the international food and hotel industry. Without going into further detail, it is enough to recognize that the expression "modern cooking principles" conveys these standards, which are the Olympic jury's frame of reference.[14]

Figure 3.1
Canadian Native Haute Cuisine team at the 1992 World Culinary Olympics (from left): Andrew George Jr, Arnold Olson, team manager George Chauvet, Bertha Skye, and David Wolfman.

The international mix of competitors and their execution of the aforementioned standards have proven the Olympics to be timely and progressive, if not pioneering from the very beginning. Hence, since the first Olympics in 1900, chefs from all over the world have gathered every four years[15] to take part in what has become one of the most important events in the world of culinary professionals. For example, in 2016, the Olympics was a four-day event of superlatives with 28,000 visitors watching approximately 2,000 chefs from fifty-nine nations showcase their skill and passion for their profession. Even though it is difficult to measure the full importance from an outside perspective, for chefs to win medals at the Culinary Olympics is an honour that lasts a lifetime.

At the Culinary Olympics, each country can enter only one senior and one junior national team, which compete in the Hot Show.[16] The Hot Show judges the chefs' craft as a whole: from processing and plating in glassed and standardized show kitchens, to the taste of their ephemeral pieces. The Canadian Culinary Federation traditionally forms Canada's national team. Regional teams and individual exhibitors are restricted to the Cold Show, in which competitors prepare the food off-site and are judged by means of visual tasting alone. Because the Canadian Culinary Federation competed at the national level, the Indigenous team of the 1992 Olympics was restricted to the regional or individual level and, hence, the Cold Show. One of the original team's members, Andrew George Jr (Wet'suwet'en), emphasizes the Cold Show's unique challenges in his first cookbook *Feast! Canadian Native Cuisine for All Seasons*: "Our participation in the competitions was not judged on taste. It didn't have anything to do with whose pastry was flakier or whose sauce was zestier ... In this competitive pressure cooker on the world stage, it's all about the other kind of taste – presentation, imagination and artistic impression."[17]

Canadian Native Haute Cuisine at the 1992 Culinary Olympics

For George, the journey to the Culinary Olympics began in the summer of 1991 when he picked up the phone during a busy service at his restaurant, Toody-Ni Grill and Catering Company, in East Vancouver. As George described it, "from out of nowhere," the person on the other end of the phone asked if he wanted to be part of a team of Indigenous chefs that would bring Indigenous food cultures onto the world stage.[18] The caller explained they would pull together the very first Canadian Native Haute Cuisine (CNHC) team to travel to Frankfurt and compete at the Culinary Olympics in October 1992. "They" were a joint venture of Indigenous and non-Indigenous people from both the private sector and government agencies. In *Delicious Resistance, Sweet Persistence: First Nations Culinary Arts in Canada*, Annie Turner names the key figures behind the initial idea as well as the actual planning and organization of the CNHC team. She explains that, in light of the early 1990s' taut relations between Indigenous and non-Indigenous people following the Oka Crisis, the Canadian Tourism Commission (CTC) hired Métis Robert Gairns to develop "a number of Aboriginal initiatives" – and the CNHC team appears to be one of them.[19] Gairns and the CTC worked with experienced entrepreneur Albert Diamond (Cree, Oudeheemin Foods) and F&B (food and beverage) consultant Danielle Medina (Medina Foods) to organize a team of Indigenous chefs to compete at the Culinary Olympics.

Technically speaking, there were no preliminaries to qualify for the Culinary Olympics when George took that call. Today, the competition remains open to anyone who is a member of a national chef association or the World Association of Chefs Society (WACS) and who has sufficient financial support. While the CNHC team's organizers were well resourced,[20] finding enough professionally trained Indigenous cooks was a more complicated matter. Through the "moccasin telegraph," they eventually searched out ten candidates for the five-person team.[21] As with most aspects related to the CNHC team's participation at the Culinary Olympics in 1992, there is no record of the initial selection process as well as any information

Figure 3.2
Canadian Native Haute Cuisine entry from 1992 World Culinary Olympics: Impression of table display (probably "Western Canada") with Arnold Olsen (centre) and Bertha Skye (right).

about the identities of the other five (or more) candidates, or why and how they dropped out. However, the final team consisted of captain David Wolfman (Xaxli'p), Bertha Skye (Ahtahkakoop First Nation, Cree), Arnold Olson (Cree), Andrew George Jr, and Bryan Sappier (Wolastoqiyik).

Although all the team members were experienced cooks, none had ever competed in a forum like the Culinary Olympics. Being restricted to the Cold Show did not make things easier. Hence, the organizers convinced award-winning Olympic veteran and past president of the Canadian Culinary Federation George Chauvet to be the team manager. Chauvet, in collaboration with another former Olympian Niels Kjeldsen, developed a fast-track training program that took place at Toronto's Sutton Place Hotel between the fall of 1991 and the summer of 1992.[22] From the beginning, George and the other team members were asked to bring along recipes related to their traditional territories and cultural backgrounds. With Chauvet and Kjeldsen's expertise and assistance, the team developed their recipes into an Indigenous Olympic menu in accordance with the "modern cooking principles" promoted by the event. The training sessions were intense. Chauvet and Kjeldsen had them "hitting the books pretty hard," as George put it.[23] Their hands-on train-

Arnold Olson, Medina Inc. Toronto
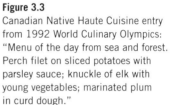

Figure 3.3
Canadian Native Haute Cuisine entry from 1992 World Culinary Olympics: "Menu of the day from sea and forest. Perch filet on sliced potatoes with parsley sauce; knuckle of elk with young vegetables; marinated plum in curd dough."

ing aligned with the unfamiliar peculiarities of the Cold Show – most importantly, the elaborate glazing techniques that would make their pieces look like food replicas coated with thin glass.

When George's CNHC team finally started their journey to Frankfurt in October 1992, they brought many materials: cooking tools, unique chef whites with the official CNHC team's crest, and distinctive ingredients like beaver, muskox, caribou, fiddleheads, and various wild berries. They also brought cultural artifacts, drums, traditional dress, and a teepee, which they set up in the exhibition hall next to the table where their creations were displayed. Upon arrival, there was no time to rest. With the first day of competition beginning the very next day, the chefs had to prepare their food during a night shift in a rented hotel kitchen. In the morning, they donned their traditional dress for the presentation, set up their display, and dove into the judging part of the event. Since they were all registered as individual exhibitors, this challenging schedule – cooking at night and (re)presenting by day – characterized their whole stay.[24] Splitting the team so that each member was scheduled for one of the five days of competition (11–15 October 1992) ensured their continuous visibility within the well-attended exhibition hall and enabled them to pay homage to the diversity of Indigenous food cultures across Canada. George explained: "Our entries – each a seven-course meal – were structured around the regions of the country, and each of us took a turn being the principal chef, while the rest acted as sous-chefs. Day one featured Native foods from the Atlantic provinces, day two the foods of the North, day three the foods of Quebec, day four the foods of Ontario, and finally day five … the foods of Western Canada."[25]

As one of the Western Canadians in the group, George was responsible for day five. Born in Smithers in the northwestern central interior of British Columbia, he grew up in the neighbouring town of Telkwa. His menu, reflecting the fact that hunting and fishing had always been a central feature of George's life, included "entree creations of Campbell River salmon," a terrine of smoked fish, an arrangement of Pacific prawns, a smoked Arctic char, a venison tenderloin, a scallop plate, and a poached pear among others.[26] A beaver tail soup, prepared according to family traditions, was a particular highlight. The soup resembled "a deep brown, but clear" consommé refined with some finely cut mushrooms, onions, and greens.[27] For most Europeans, however, the dish featured a quite unfamiliar main ingredient.[28] In the end, the positive tension between appearance and content seems to have made a lasting impression on both the flabbergasted public and the convinced judges. Finally, there was the chocolate centrepiece of George's presentation, which he described as "a bear lying on its back with a salmon clutched in its front paws, and above it an eagle swooping down to steal the salmon. It's a scene I had often seen before back home in British Columbia – but not in glazed chocolate."[29]

For each day of the Olympics, the team prepared different Indigenous-themed statues for display. One depicted a buffalo hunt in a most dynamic fashion with two horsemen spearing a buffalo.[30] Another statue, named "Indian Grandfather,"[31] was of an almost one-metre-tall man wearing buckskin and a feather headdress.[32] Unfortunately, there is almost no photographic documentation or any detailed description and contextualization of these statues and the other dishes and platters. Even the few pictures that can be found in the official 1992 Olympics catalogue, *Kochkunst in Bildern 4*, are of little help. The images by German food photographer Wolfgang Usbeck are published in low quality and with little information, but to give an idea of what their award-winning pieces looked like, I have included one of them here.

Besides Usbeck's two pictures of chef Bertha Skye's creations, Skye has also provided a written account of some of her dishes and their background in her chapter published in Jo Marie Powers and Anita Stewart's *Northern Bounty: A Celebration of Canadian Cuisine*. Skye explains that she grew up in northern Saskatchewan and learned to prepare foods in the manner of her people, the Ahtahkakoop First Nation (Cree). When she moved with her husband onto Six Nations Reserve in south-

Figure 3.4
Bertha Skye (right) with Danielle Medina (left) at the award ceremony.

ern Ontario, her mother-in-law taught her how to cook according to her husband's family's Cayuga tradition. Astounded by the differences, she conducted research on Cayuga foods and cooking, and understood that "because they were an agricultural people, they had corn, beans, and squash to sustain them."[33] Therefore, when she decided on her "Ontario" menu, she focused on "Iroquois foods" and included a Three Sisters Soup prepared according to her mother-in-law's recipe.[34] But again, no detailed information is given, as Skye only mentions, "in addition to Three Sisters Soup, some of the other Iroquois foods we made were corn soup, bannock, and corn bread."[35] On a general note, she adds: "Bannock hors d'oeuvres were one of the special foods we prepared for the Culinary Olympics ... we used salmon, Arctic char, muskox, caviar, even dandelions, on bannock."[36] Despite the lack of documentation, important details begin to emerge, pointing to the team's story as one of success. The intense training, supportive expertise, funding, and team effort paid off. Their unique combination of professional culinary skills, Aboriginal ingredients, recipes, and creativity convinced the judges, and the team returned home with eleven medals – two bronze, two silver, and seven gold.[37]

SEBASTIAN SCHELLHAAS

"More Than a Competition"

After the CNHC team's debut at the Culinary Olympics, the Indigenous news media in Canada brought specific focus to the win: "Native heritage came in for a good deal of attention in Europe recently though on unusual medium: Food."[38] As George remembered, the Germans were eager to meet the Indigenous chefs who, dressed in buckskins and wearing feather headdresses, explained their foods and cultures to the inquisitive audience. In fact, Germans have long held a fascination for Indigenous peoples in North America.[39] In line with this, the same news media reported: "German television and print media gave them wide coverage, and the native kiosk was a favorite with the thousands of paying spectators who visited the site during the five days of competition."[40] This frenetic tone was not, however, the only resonance heard. At about the same time, Canadian food writer Judy Schultz commented on the team: "The hastily assembled team worked under the direction of the Canadian Federation of Chefs de Cuisine in order to make traditional native dishes and ingredients conform to the stringent rules of the haute cuisine community. Those who know genuine First Peoples cooking might wonder why anyone could contrive to send such a natural, historic cuisine down that particular road, but the five members of the team were enthusiastic."[41]

George touched on Schultz's skepticism in conversation with me in 2016, pointing out that "Aboriginal foods and Aboriginal cuisines are two different things."[42] "Aboriginal foods" are traditional products prepared in a way that "you might find at a feast in a long house." In contrast, "Aboriginal cuisine is what we produce at a professional level." What I understood from our discussion is that professionalization does not necessarily amount to the modernization of Aboriginal foods and cooking. It is more about taking modern techniques and traditional products and "fusing" them while paying respect to both. In regard to the Culinary Olympics, George described this fusing as an effort to "bridge these two worlds, which is kind of hard, because even in the modern world there are hardly people that understand the Culinary Olympics and why we do it … Overall it is the promotion of the concept of professional cooking, and introducing that to the Aboriginal culture so that Aboriginal communities can benefit from that."

Thus, besides "going for the gold," the team and organizers chose to "bridge these two worlds" of traditional foods and professional cooking for two reasons. One of them was to foster awareness and make Indigenous foods and cultures visible to the exhibition visitors and the general European public as well as to the transnational community of culinary professionals. The other more important goal was to create role models to attract Indigenous youth to the trade of cooking and, by this, bolster positive, long-term effects in terms of education and economic growth within Indigenous communities back home. George put it clearly: "What we actually did was we fought for our right for education. It was more than a competition. It was a statement ... 'Cause right up to about 1960, Aboriginal people weren't even allowed in a lot of restaurants. So, even me going to school in 1983–84 at the Vancouver Vocational Institute, I was one of maybe half a dozen Aboriginal cooks in that whole school. But now when I go to that school there are Aboriginal cooks everywhere. So I think overall that process is working."

By talking about a "process working," George points to the fact that this change did not happen by chance. After the initial Olympic achievements, Medina and Oudeheemin initiated a program to introduce Indigenous youth into the cooking trade. With George's mentorship, the eight-week program took place at the Institut de tourisme et d'hôtellerie du Québec in Montreal twice a year from the mid- to late 1990s.[43] Its curriculum was inspired by the initial team's training program though it did not directly resemble it. The students, mostly teenagers and young adults aged fifteen to twenty-five, were brought in from all over Canada. When they returned to their communities after completing the program, they spread the seeds of gastronomic professionalization. Other CNHC team members contributed to the overall process as well. Skye ran a program at Woodland Cultural Centre on Six Nations Reserve,[44] and in 1994, Wolfman became an instructor at George Brown College in Toronto,[45] where he contributed to the general curriculum and apparently taught Indigenous culinary arts classes.[46]

Ever since the program in Montreal, there have been similar courses initiated across the country. George explained that these initiatives were entry points for Indigenous students to obtain "their prerequisites to go into real culinary school."[47] As most of these courses were community-based with no direct connection to culinary schools, there is often no detailed information available on the total number of programs, the curricula, or the number of students. There is, nevertheless, one momentous example that makes the flourishing of Indigenous gastronomic professionalization over the last quarter-century clearly evident: the Aboriginal Culinary Arts Class. This twelve-month course, which started in 2008 and ran until 2011 at Vancouver Community College (VCC), included a thorough introduction to classic French techniques followed by a deep involvement with the histories and cultural backgrounds of Aboriginal foods and cooking. The course was further complemented by learning from elders through storytelling and guided, hands-on training by cultural experts during field trips to different communities across British Columbia.[48] Furthermore, for the last four months of the program, the students ran the Wild Salmon restaurant on the VCC campus. Most importantly, chef instructor Ben Genaille (Métis of Cree Nation and French descent) realized an idea that he had been working on for years. From his students, he recruited Faith Vickers (Coast Salish, Tsimshian), Samantha Nyce (Nisga), and Paul Roy Natrall (Squamish Nation) to assemble the Aboriginal Culinary Team Canada (ACTC), which competed in 2012 as a regional team at the Culinary Olympics (this time in Erfurt, Germany).

Through a conversation with Genaille and Natrall (as well as information in Canadian newspapers and the VKD archive), I learned that their Northwest Coast–themed Cold Show table consisted of four different tapas prepared by Vickers; a platter for eight featuring the five kinds of Pacific salmon prepared in five different ways – i.e., salmon chops, confit salmon, salmon belly terrine, as well as barbequed and smoked salmon – served with rose hip beurre blanc and sage-infused oolichan grease, created by Natrall; and finally a five-course gala dinner prepared by Nyce.[49] In the end, the chefs returned home with a diploma for participation, but no medals. Still, the goal of this second team, as with the first, was not to go down in history as one-hit wonders. Instead, Genaille pointed out that it was part of an ongoing journey with the mission to create role models, foster awareness, and share pride in their cultures through the celebration of Aboriginal foods and cooking abroad.[50]

Taking into account that Genaille's team of young chefs competed in the Culinary Olympics on their own – with no support team, no organizing companies, and no big sponsorship – one can reasonably state that the twenty years separating the two teams' appearances at the event should not be perceived as a symptom of stagnation or even regression of the gastronomic professionalization process. Instead, the second team's stand-alone participation represents a clear change in tides. First, it shows that the dedication of Indigenous people to professional cooking has reached a critical mass. Alongside these rising numbers, Indigenous chefs and their food cultures have acquired their own standing among the global community of culinary professionals. Second, even though the Culinary Olympics are primarily known within an international and professional community, the ACTC's participation in 2012 is an indication that Indigenous food cultures and gastronomy have become a distinct, self-determined part of the broader Canadian foodscape.

Indigenous Gastronomy in British Columbia, 1974–2018

In light of George's statement about Indigenous people not being allowed in many restaurants before the 1960s, it is reasonable to assume that during that time, there were probably few, if any, Indigenous chefs or restaurants. This situation has changed significantly with the rise of professional Indigenous gastronomy in British Columbia, the region in which George established his own career. The very first Indigenous-themed restaurant in the province appears to have been the Muckamuck (meaning "food" or "to eat" in Chinook Wawa[51]), which opened its doors in downtown Vancouver in 1974. After closing in 1981, following a dispute between the non-Indigenous management and the Indigenous employees over labour conditions and the latter's unsuccessful attempt "to go union," as George described it,[52] the next Indigenous restaurant, Quilicum, opened in 1986. This time, the operation was all-Indigenous with some of the former Muckamuck employees among the owners. Tellingly, they used the same facilities but changed the name to Quilicum (meaning "return of the people" in Chinook Wawa[53]). In fact, it was at Quilicum where George had his first full-time job before running his Toody-Ni restaurant from 1991–93. One year after George closed Toody-Ni, the Quilicum closed too, though the facilities in downtown Vancouver did not stay vacant for long. In 1995, the restaurant reopened as the Liliget Feast House. The new Gitxsan owners ran a successful establishment until 2007 when the whole building was sold to make way for a new condominium development. Finally, with the 2010 Olympic Winter Games, the Salmon n' Bannock opened its doors on West Broadway, where it resides to this day. From the mid-1970s onward, then, there has always been at least one restaurant in Vancouver that serves Aboriginal foods and cooking. Albeit, it seems that these restaurants were the only ones that did so in the whole of British Columbia at that time.

Today, the Salmon n' Bannock remains the only year-round Indigenous restaurant in Vancouver, though not in the province. Gastronomic professionalization is flourishing with establishments in Alert Bay, Duncan, Kelowna, Langley, Merritt, Port Hardy, Victoria, Westbank, Whistler, and elsewhere, all of which serve Aboriginal foods or Indigenous-inspired menus on a (mostly) regular basis. The spectrum of contemporary Indigenous gastronomy encompasses many variations, from fine dining places that serve elk osso buco with wild asparagus and wild rice risotto alongside a glass of red wine from an Indigenous winery[54] to casual food trucks that specialize in popular dishes like Indian tacos, bannock-dogs, and burgers served in takeout boxes with a soda pop or a Saskatoon berry smoothie.

Taking into account these different approaches to Aboriginal foods and cooking, one can readily conclude that Indigenous gastronomy has grown not only in terms of the places and people involved but also in terms of culinary diversity. And there is no indication of this process slowing down. Although Indigenous apprentices, chefs, and restaurateurs still have to negotiate all kinds of social, cultural, financial, and legal obstacles, Indigenous gastronomy has already created salient landmarks in the field of gastronomy within British Columbia as well as the rest of Canada. Indigenous chefs are invited to participate in local and global events and other collaborations; they have also been awarded prizes for their cookbooks, proving Indigenous gastronomy's growing national and international reputation. Of course, the CNHC team is not the sole cause for this development. Indigenous restaurants existed prior to the 1992 Culinary Olympics, and George was not the only chef who received a call to participate. However, the first team's international acclaim and subsequent engagement in promoting professional cooking to Indigenous people and their communities undeniably accelerated the process of gastronomic professionalization – and in one way or another, still does.

The Ends

When the organizers of the CNHC team began working to send Indigenous chefs to the Culinary Olympics, they thought of professional cooking, or gastronomy, as an effective means for various ends, some planned and others unanticipated. First of all, the organizers knew that professionally trained cooks would always find employment. Gastronomy is an ever-growing market, and in an official press release, the organizers defined the team's mission as to "help establish a profitable and professional industry for Canada's Native People. The Oudeheemin-Medina connection has for [its] mission to create and commercialize a native cuisine."[55] An important part of this commercialization, the authors go on to explain, would be to "include food products from different Reserves in Canada."[56] Clearly, the process of gastronomic professionalization does not stop in the kitchen or at the restaurant's doorstep. Aside from Indigenous restaurant staff, Indigenous gastronomy creates a growing need for suppliers of raw or processed Aboriginal ingredients, which again leads to economic opportunities for Indigenous communities. This network of restaurateurs, cooks, and producers generates an additional need for knowledge about Aboriginal ingredients, their handling, and the management of resources. Ecologist and ethnobotanist Gary P. Nabhan, in *Renewing Salmon Nation's Food Traditions*, points to the fact that the demand for cultural experts also has the potential to facilitate processes of ecological revitalization, or conservation of respective resources and ecosystems.[57] Because collaboration with such experts reproduces and even multiplies cultural knowledge, the process of gastronomic professionalization may also foster cultural resurgence within Indigenous communities.

Finally, alongside economic growth, ecological revitalization, and cultural resurgence, this process might well evoke culinary re-imaginations both inside Indigenous communities – by "sharing pride," as Genaille put it, in one's historic as well as contemporary (food) culture – and outside Indigenous communities – by experiencing Aboriginal foods and cooking that might exceed non-Indigenous expectations. Indeed, the many gastronomic concepts and approaches to cooking that characterize this field of gastronomy mirror the fundamental diversity of Indigenous (food) cultures in what is now Canada, and the complexity of these contemporary life-worlds. Consequently, far from solely providing a well-funded foodie or touristic clientele with an original experience of "a natural, historic cuisine," Indigenous gastronomy reflects the vibrant, diverse, and dynamic cultures of Indigenous peoples. The argument is plausible, therefore, that Indigenous gastronomy and the different actors involved eventually challenge categories like "natural" and "historic," or "traditional" and "authentic."[58] Ultimately, the implications of gastronomic professionalization make clear that the growing field of Indigenous gastronomy calls for further research on its historic and cultural contexts, it socio-economic dimensions, and its role with respect to the politics of Indigenous identities in Canada.

Acknowledgments

This chapter includes preliminary results of my PhD research project on the gastronomic professionalization of Indigenous food cultures in Canada. The many conversations with friends, chefs, restaurateurs, artists, activists, and scholars I had the pleasure of meeting during my research provide the basis of this chapter. My deepest gratitude to all of them for their support and for sharing their knowledge and stories with me.

Notes

1. Jewitt, *White Slaves of the Nootka*, 32.
2. I use endonyms and traditional names whenever possible. I also use the inclusive term "Indigenous" for collective expressions, such as in Indigenous chefs, or Indigenous gastronomy, to refer to actors from all three groups of people with ancient roots in the lands that now make up Canada, i.e., First Nations, Métis, and Inuit. In keeping with chef Andrew George Jr's own phrasing, I also use the term "Aboriginal" to identify ingredients, foods, and cooking.
3. See Stewart, *The Adventures and Sufferings of John R. Jewitt*.
4. On unpalatability, see Thrush, "Vancouver the Cannibal," 9, 14–17. For a vivid account of this early collective imagination, see also chapter 4, "The Image of the Indian," in Fisher, *Contact and Conflict*.
5. Thrush, "Vancouver the Cannibal," 16.
6. *Cook It Raw*.
7. See Fee, "Stories of Traditional Aboriginal Food, Territory and Health."
8. Even though "IKA" is still the official name of this quadrennial event today, the VKD also employs the alternative label "IKA – Die Olympiade der Köche." I use the more popular term in this chapter.
9. See Coydon, "Food Exhibitions as Places of National Representation and International Exchange."
10. Ibid., 70.
11. Cited in ibid., 78.
12. The phrasing "culinary nationalism" refers to "the discursive construction of national cuisines as part of a constructed national culture," ibid., 71. See related discussions hereof in Teughels and Scholliers, *A Taste of Progress*.
13. Verband der Köche Deutschlands, *Kochkunst in Bildern*, 19.
14. For detailed researches and discussions of this standard and its evolution, see, for example, Mennell, *All Manners of Food*; Poulain and Neirinck, *Histoire de la Cuisine et des Cuisiniers*; Spang, *The Invention of the Restaurant*; Sikorski, *Cooking to the Image*.
15. There were only very few irregularities in the first half of the twentieth century and total cancellations during the First and Second World Wars.
16. The official titles for this part of the competition are "Restaurant of Nations" and the "Hot Kitchen" and "Cold Kitchen." I have chosen to use the informal terms "Hot Show" and "Cold Show," which were frequently used in my conversations with chefs from both Canada and Germany during the course of my research.

17 George and Gairns, *Feast!*, 11.
18 Ibid., 9.
19 Turner, "Delicious Resistance, Sweet Persistence," 83. See also ibid., 85.
20 Among their supporters were the minister of employment and immigration, the minister of industry, science and technology Canada, the Bank of Montreal, Air Canada, and the Canadian Egg Marketing Agency. Information obtained from the CNHC team's official promotion video, *Going for the Gold*, written and produced after the 1992 Culinary Olympics by Robert Gairns and Robert St-Onge.
21 Personal conversation with Andrew George Jr, February 2015.
22 George and Gairns, *Feast!*, 9–11.
23 Ibid., 9.
24 Information obtained from the VKD's archives in Frankfurt/Main. See also George and Gairns, *Feast!*, 11.
25 George and Gairns, *Feast!*, 11.
26 Thorne, "Native Chefs Sweep Culinary Olympics," 9; George and Gairns, *Feast!*, 12.
27 Tennant, "First Course," 61. When in February 2016, Andrew George Jr and I watched Gairns and St-Onge's *Going for the Gold*, he identified one of the dishes shown in the video as the respective beaver tail soup.
28 See also Gora, "From Meat to Metaphor," chapter 5 in this volume, for her discussion of the Canadian history and cultural politics behind shifting perceptions of the beaver as food. Gora refers to George's beaver tail soup and the use of this ingredient in one of his cookbooks as core examples of how imaginings of the beaver depend on the context and respective audience. She also sheds light on the almost forgotten history of European beaver consumption.
29 George and Gairns, *Feast!*, 12.
30 Seen on photograph, private archive, Andrew George Jr.
31 Information obtained from original scoring sheet found in the VKD's archives in Frankfurt/Main.
32 Seen on photograph, private archive, Andrew George Jr. See also close-up tracking shot of the statue in Gairns and St-Onge, *Going for the Gold*.
33 Skye, "Traditional Cree and Iroquois Foods," 116.
34 Ibid.
35 Ibid.
36 Ibid., 116–17.
37 George and Gairns, *Feast!*, 12–13.

38 Thorne, "Native Chefs Sweep Culinary Olympics," 9.
39 On the nature of this fascination and "striking sense of affinity for American Indians that has permeated German cultures for two centuries" see Penny, *Kindred by Choice*, xi.
40 Thorne, "Native Chefs Sweep Culinary Olympics," 9.
41 Schultz, "Olympic Scrapbook," C2.
42 The following paragraph paraphrases parts of the conversation we had in February 2016 in Chilliwack, BC. Phrases set in quotation marks are from audio recordings.
43 Information on this program's basic conditions varies depending on different sources. Here, I refer to personal conversations with Andrew George Jr from February 2015 and 2016.
44 Skye, "Traditional Cree and Iroquois Foods," 118.
45 Wolfman and Finn, *Cooking with the Wolfman*, 2.
46 Turner, "Delicious Resistance, Sweet Persistence," 86.
47 Personal conversation with Andrew George Jr, February 2016.
48 Personal conversation with Ben Genaille, February 2016, and Paul Roy Natrall, November 2016.
49 Ibid.; Narine, "Aboriginal Team Canada Takes its Place on World Stage." Again, there is almost no visual documentation or detailed information available.
50 Personal conversation with Ben Genaille, February 2016.
51 Blanchet, *Dictionary of the Chinook Jargon*, 17.
52 Personal conversation with Andrew George Jr, February 2016. See also Nicol, "'Unions Aren't Native.'"
53 Hewitt, "Quilicum," 131; Lepine, "Tradition Served with Cuisine," 17.
54 These fine dining restaurants often also serve rare Aboriginal specialties like smoked seal, herring roe on kelp, and oolichan grease as well as fresh sea food, or variations of game charcuterie.
55 Official press release. Private archive, Andrew George Jr.
56 Ibid.
57 Nabhan, *Renewing Salmon Nation's Food Traditions*, v.
58 See also Tennant, "*Terra Nullius* on the Plate," chapter 4 in this volume, for her discussion of the identity politics behind such categories. For a more detailed account of the political ramifications of these categories, see Raibmon, *Authentic Indians*.

Bibliography

Blanchet, François N. *Dictionary of the Chinook Jargon, or, Indian Trade Language of the North Pacific Coast*. Victoria: T.N. Hibben, 1883.

Canadian Museum Association. *Great Canadian Masters Vol. 1*. Ottawa, 2016.

– *Great Canadian Masters Vol. 1*. Ottawa, 2017.

Cook It Raw. Accessed 31 August 2016. www.cookitraw.org/about/vision/.

Coydon, Eva. "Food Exhibitions as Places of National Representation and International Exchange. The International Exhibition of Culinary Art in Frankfurt/Main (1900–1911)." In *A Taste of Progress: Food at International and World Exhibitions in the Nineteenth and Twentieth Centuries*, edited by Nelleke Teughels and Peter Scholliers, 70–89. Abingdon: Routledge, 2016.

Escoffier, Auguste. *Le Guide Culinaire. Aide-mémoire de cuisine pratique: Avec la collaboration de Messieurs Philéas Gilbert et Émile Fétu*. Paris, 1903.

Fee, Margery. "Stories of Traditional Aboriginal Food, Territory and Health." In *What's to Eat? Entrées in Canadian Food History*, edited by Nathalie Cooke, 55–78. Montreal and Kingston: McGill-Queen's University Press, 2009.

Fisher, Robin. *Contact and Conflict: Indian-European Relations in British Columbia, 1774–1890*. Vancouver: University of British Columbia Press, 1992.

Gairns, Robert, and Robert St-Onge. *Going for the Gold*. (Promotion film, ca 1993)

George Jr, Andrew, and Robert Gairns. *Feast! Canadian Native Cuisine for All Seasons*. Toronto: Doubleday Canada, 1997.

Hewitt, Priscilla. "Quilicum: A West Coast Indian Restaurant." *Canadian Woman Studies* 10, nos. 2 & 3 (1989): 131–2.

Jewitt, John R. *White Slaves of the Nootka: Narrative of the Adventures and Sufferings of John R. Jewitt While a Captive of the Nootka Indians on Vancouver Island, 1803–05*. Surrey, BC: Heritage House, 1987.

Lepine, Jeanne. "Tradition Served with Cuisine." *Windspeaker*, 28 March 1986, 17.

Mennell, Stephen. *All Manners of Food: Eating and Taste in England and France from the Middle Ages to the Present*. Oxford, UK: B. Blackwell, 1985.

Nabhan, Gary P., ed. *Renewing Salmon Nation's Food Traditions*. Corvallis: Oregon State University Press, 2006.

Narine, Shari. "Aboriginal Team Canada Takes Its Place on World Stage." *Windspeaker* (AMMSA) 30, no. 9 (2012). www.ammsa.com/publications/windspeaker/aboriginal-team-canada-takes-its-place-world-stage.

Nicol, Janet Mary. "'Unions Aren't Native': The Muckamuck Restaurant Labour Dispute, Vancouver, B.C. (1978–1983)." *Labour/Le Travail* 40 (1997): 235–51.

Penny, H. Glenn. *Kindred by Choice: German and American Indians since 1800*. Chapel Hill: University of North Carolina Press, 2013.

Poulain, Jean-Pierre, and Edmond Neirinck. *Histoire de la Cuisine et des cuisiniers: Techniques culinaires et pratiques de table, en France, du moyen-âge à nos jours*. Paris: Edition LT Jacques Lanore, 2004.

Raibmon, Paige. *Authentic Indians: Episodes of Encounter from the Late-Nineteenth-Century Northwest Coast*. Durham: Duke University Press, 2005.

Schultz, Judy. "Olympic Scrapbook Part 2." *Edmonton Journal*, 4 November 1992, C1–2.

Sikorski, Elaine. *Cooking to the Image: A Plating Handbook*. Hoboken: Wiley, 2012.

Skye, Bertha. "Traditional Cree and Iroquois Foods." In *Northern Bounty: A Celebration of Canadian Cuisine*, edited by Jo Marie Powers and Anita Stewart, 113–19. Toronto: Random House of Canada, 1995.

Spang, Rebecca L. *The Invention of the Restaurant: Paris and Modern Gastronomic Culture*. Cambridge, MA: Harvard University Press, 2001.

Stewart, Hilary. *The Adventures and Sufferings of John R. Jewitt: Captive of Maquinna*. Annotated and Illustrated by Hilary Stewart. Vancouver: Douglas and McIntyre, 1987.

Tennant, Zoe. "First Course: Exploring Indigenous Cuisines in the Canadian Food Landscape." MA thesis, University of British Columbia, 2015.

Teughels, Nelleke, and Peter Scholliers, eds. *A Taste of Progress: Food at International and World Exhibitions in the Nineteenth and Twentieth Centuries*. Abingdon: Routledge, 2016.

Thorne, Susan. "Native Chefs Sweep Culinary Olympics." *Windspeaker* (AMMSA) 10, no. 16 (1992): 9. www.ammsa.com/publications/windspeaker/native-chefs-sweep-culinary-olympics-1.

Thrush, Coll. "Vancouver the Cannibal: Cuisine, Encounter, and the Dilemma of Difference on the Northwest Coast, 1774–1808." *Ethnohistory* 58, no. 1 (2011): 1–35.

Turner, Annie (Catherine Annie). "Delicious Resistance, Sweet Persistence: First Nations Culinary Arts in Canada." MA thesis, Carleton University, 2005.

Verband der Köche Deutschlands e.V. *Kochkunst in Bilder*. Vol. 4. Stuttgart: Matthaes, 1993.

Wolfman, David, and Marlene Finn. *Cooking with the Wolfman: Indigenous Fusion*. Vancouver: Douglas & McIntyre, 2017.

4

Terra Nullius on the Plate
Colonial Blindness, Restaurant Discourse, and Indigenous Cuisines

Zoe Tennant

"The field of cuisine and the field of the nation are intimately connected."[1]

"It's finally time for the Aboriginal peoples' cuisine to make its presence in the world."[2]

On any given night in a Canadian city, it is possible to eat at restaurants offering a wide variety of cuisines – from Moroccan to Vietnamese, from French to Sri Lankan. However, it is almost impossible to go to a restaurant that serves Indigenous cuisines. In Canada, there are foods that are considered "Indigenous"[3] (*taas guz*, whipped *soapalillie*, and roe-on-kelp, to name a few),[4] but one is hard pressed to find these dishes on a menu. French gastronomic writer Jean Anthelme Brillat-Savarin's oft-quoted "Tell me what you eat: I will tell you what you are"[5] – better known as "you are what you eat" – sums up the basic tenet of the social science of food: that what we eat and the way we eat reflect wider cultural, social, and political processes. What if we were to flip this? What does it mean when a cuisine is not consumed? Cultural anthropologist Carolyn Morris, writing about the absence of Maori cuisine in restaurants in New Zealand, argues that restaurants are signifiers of the public visibility of cuisines and are indicators of capital.[6] According to Morris, "the public culinascape can be read as a map of the field of race relations."[7] What do Morris's remarks suggest about the culinary field, the restaurant culture, and the state of settler colonialism in Canada?

"Food, long considered trivial," explains food sociologist Krishnendu Ray,[8] is now the subject of increasing and recent academic interest. However, despite the burgeoning scholarly studies related to cuisine, culture, and power relationships,[9] academic enquiry into contemporary Indigenous foodways is underdeveloped.[10] I explore here a glaring, but overlooked, absence in Canadian restaurant culture: Indigenous cuisines. There are more than 1.6 million people in Canada who identify as Indigenous (this includes First Nations, Inuit, and Métis people).[11] However, there are no more than a couple dozen Indigenous restaurants in Canadian cities – including Salmon n' Bannock in Vancouver; Painted Pony Café in Kamloops, British Columbia; Feast Café Bistro in Winnipeg; NishDish, Pow Wow Café, and Kūkum in Toronto. Indigenous people, who make up 4.9 per cent of the population in Canada,[12] are represented in less than 1 per cent of the country's 95,000 restaurants.[13] Compare these statistics to Japanese restaurants – a culinary mainstay in cities across Canada. The Japanese population in Canada is 0.26 per cent.[14] The invisibility of Indigenous cuisines in Canada's restaurant landscape, I argue, can be understood as a continuation of a history of erasure, appropriation, and colonial blindness. A restaurant landscape, or restaurantscape, is a kind of "foodscape," a term used by sociologists Josée Johnston and Shyon Baumann that suggests perceptions of food and the food system are mediated and seen through cultural and social lenses, and that recognizes an interconnection between taste, culture, and the physical landscape.[15] The current popularity of local and foraged foods often frames restaurant discourse (restaurant reviews in the media, restaurant menus, restaurant websites, and media interviews with chefs), resulting in one expression of the invisibility of Indigenous foods. I suggest that the contemporary erasure of Indigenous foods in the restaurant foodscape can be read as a continuation of a history of colonial blindness informed by concepts like *terra nullius* (or "empty land").

A Different Kind of "Pan" in the Kitchen: Defining Indigenous Cuisines

The term "Indigenous cuisine," in the singular, is hyper-generalized and rooted in a pan- Indigenous concept, the frame that conflates the diversity of hundreds of Indigenous nations across distinct geographies and millions of kilometres.[16] There is no clear-cut definition of Indigenous cuisine because there is no *one* Indigenous cuisine. Rather, there are regionally specific Indigenous *cuisines*, in the plural. In the same way that even the most obvious cuisines, like French, have been forged, pushed, moulded, and invented[17] – not existing as such but established, developed, and created from regional or local traditions – so, too, is there no singular Indigenous cuisine. Joseph Aaron Bear Robe, a Toronto-based chef and member of the

Sisika Nation, has said of "Aboriginal cuisine": "A large misconception is that there's some sort of 'pan Aboriginal' cuisine, that because I'm Aboriginal, I'm going to cook salmon, which for me, culturally, doesn't make any sense."[18] Bear Robe's comment points to the plurality of Indigenous cuisines that can be elaborated upon by flipping through the cookbook *A Feast for All Seasons*, by Wet'suwet'en chef and hereditary wing chief Andrew George Jr.[19] In addition to Wet'suwet'en cuisine, George highlights a diversity of recipes from the Stoney Nakoda Haudenosaunee to the Wolastoqiyik.[20]

Anishinaabe chef, artist, and scholar Lisa Myers points out that the culinary genre of Indigenous cuisines can fall into the trap of authenticity.[21] She explains: "The ingredients that distinguish Aboriginal cuisine often include so-called pre-contact fare, such as wild rice, venison, and bison. The anthropological parameters of pre-contact and post-contact culture loom as legitimating factors that 'authenticate' this food genre."[22] Myers is critical of what is commonly understood as Aboriginal cuisine and questions the need for "traditional" ingredients to categorize Indigenous foods. When it comes to Indigenous foods, "traditional" gets used like a branding iron and the pre-/post-contact markers stem from romantic imaginings of "traditional" life where traditional means stasis. Myers reminds us that cuisines, like cultures, are fluid, nuanced, and complex.

Indigenous cuisines in what is now called Canada exist today against the backdrop of settler colonialism. According to Yellowknives Dene political scientist Glen Coulthard, whose definition makes explicit the continued relationships of power, "a settler-colonial relationship is one characterized by a particular form of *domination*; that is, it is a relationship where power – in this case, interrelated discursive and non-discursive facets of economic, gendered, racial, and state power – has been structured into a relatively secure or sedimented set of hierarchical social relations that continue to facilitate the *dispossession* of Indigenous peoples of their lands and self-determining authority."[23] Settler scholars Emma Lowman and Adam Barker's description of the term "settler" builds on Coulthard's work and informs my use of the word. "Settler," write Lowman and Barker, signals a "potential complicity in systems of dispossession."[24] It is a word that "voices relationships to structures and processes in Canada today, to the histories of our peoples on this land, to Indigenous peoples, and to our own day-to-day choices and actions … Settler Canadian identity is entangled both historically and in the present with the process of settler colonization, the means through which our state and nation have wrested their land base from Indigenous peoples."[25] Importantly, "settler" signals the *continuation* of the colonial project in Canada and how this is expressed in everyday instances. The invisibility of Indigenous foods and cuisines in Canada's restaurantscape is one of these instances.

"The Original Locavore Diet"[26]

Let us turn our attention to a prevalent framework of contemporary food culture and restaurant discourse: localness. I argue that "local foods" and "Indigenous foods" occupy similar territory; however, there is often silence in the locavore discourse about Indigenous foods.[27] Outlining the local foods landscape illustrates one expression of the contemporary invisibility of Indigenous foods within Canada's restaurantscape.

Eating local foods was declared the "hottest trend in food" in 2006.[28] The *New Oxford American Dictionary* subsequently named "locavore" the word of the year in 2007, the same year that Canadian writers Alisa Smith and J.B. Mackinnon published their best-selling book, *The 100-Mile Diet: A Year of Eating Local*.[29] "An increased interest in eating locally and seasonally," write Johnston and Baumann, is a "trend" and a "standout trait" in food.[30] The fame of Noma, the Nordic-cuisine restaurant in Denmark, highlights the popularity of localness. "Otherwise known as the best restaurant in the world," writes Jane Kramer, Noma – the two-Michelin-starred creation of chef René Redzepi – has topped the global culinary rankings for years and is premised upon bringing "wild," "foraged," and "local" ingredients to the table (think beach thistles, roots, berries, and wild herbs).[31]

Indigenous cuisines cannot be separated from locale. Like any other cuisine in the world, Indigenous cuisines are tied to place and are influenced by the trade routes that have passed through those landscapes. As Myers explains, "Aboriginal cuisine includes ingredients sourced or associated with the flora and fauna of specific regions ... The key indicator of Aboriginal cuisine seems to be the use of ingredients derived from an indigenous source that have strong associations with the land, wild meat, or wild edible plants."[32] United States–based Ojibway writer Heid Erdrich explains in her recent cookbook, *Original Local: Indigenous Foods, Stories and Recipes from the Upper Midwest*: "Local foods have garnered much attention in recent years, but the concept is hardly new: Indigenous peoples have always made the most of nature's gifts. Their menus were truly the 'original local.'"[33] And, Wet'suwet'en chef Andrew George Jr refers to Indigenous cuisines as "the original locavore diet."[34] Yet, despite all the foodie-talk about wild, foraged, and local, Indigenous connections to these ingredients are often overlooked.

In Vancouver, the birthplace of the 100-mile locavore diet, wild, foraged, and local are focal points on the menus of many restaurants. In this city, there is a restaurant that serves "First Nations inspired food": Salmon n' Bannock.[35] Co-owners Inez Cook (a member of the Nuxalk Nation) and Remi Caudron (a settler) describe their business on their website: "We are Vancouver's only First Nations restaurant. We specialize in wild fish, free range game meat and of course bannock, fresh baked daily. We use traditional ingredients that we prepare and present in a modern way."[36] At the top of Salmon n' Bannock's menu, adjacent to text that asks diners to advise their server of any allergies, is an acknowledgment of Indigenous territories: "Acknowledging the Traditional Coast Salish Territories of the Musqueam, Squamish and Tsleil-Waututh First Nations."[37] This assertion calls settler colonialism to the table and gestures to the inherent ties between food, land, and Indigenous sovereignty.

Now, let us compare Salmon n' Bannock to a nearby restaurant, Forage, that describes itself as serving "locally grown, sustainable cuisine."[38] The website states that Forage "connects diners to local fishers, foragers and farmers."[39] While Salmon n' Bannock acknowledges Indigenous territories, "British Columbia" is Forage's reference for the surrounding landscape: "share some delicious food, and enjoy the best of what BC has to offer."[40] The dishes on Forage's menu are similar to those served at Salmon n' Bannock; comparable ingredients are used and served in dishes sold in the same price range. For example: an entrée of pan-roasted Pacific Spring salmon at Forage is $29, a wild Sockeye salmon dinner at Salmon n' Bannock is $27; seafood chowder at Forage costs $8, wild salmon soup at Salmon n' Bannock is $8 for a small bowl and $14 for a large bowl; Turtle Valley Bison Ranch strip loin at Forage costs $43, and braised free-range Bison back ribs with Ojibway wild rice risotto at Salmon n' Bannock cost $35.[41] The two menus are not so different, but Salmon n' Bannock serves "First Nations inspired foods" and Forage serves foods that are "locally grown."

Local foods and Indigenous foods are not always synonymous – a herd of cattle is not the same as a meadow of camas. Settlers imported the former; the Coast Salish harvested the latter long before Europeans "discovered" their territories. However, one must not get hung up on pre- and post-contact as measures for Indigenous and non-Indigenous foods. Indigenous foodways, like all foodways, are comprised of foods that have always grown there as well as those that were brought to the shores or the valleys or the plains on the footpaths and grease trails or in the bellies of ships. What one must get hung up on here is land. A discussion of food is necessarily a discussion of land – food comes from somewhere. For Forage that place is British Columbia; for Salmon n' Bannock the source is Indigenous. These two Vancouver-based restaurants are located on unceded Indigenous territories, and the way in which land is referred to is political. This erasure of Indigenous territories does not only occur within urban restaurantcapes but also within smaller communities. For example, the restaurant Shelter is located in the small oceanside town of Tofino on Vancouver Island, British Columbia – also known as the territories of the Nuu-chah-nulth nations. Shelter's website invites diners to "taste the freshest fare from local farms and waters" and describes the ingredients they serve as "fresh caught seafood from the local waters, fresh cut herbs from our backyard garden, free run poultry from Vancouver Island farms."[42] No mention is made of the Nuu-chah-nulth nations whose land and waters the discourse of local simultaneously refers to. As Coulthard and Lowman and Barker have pointed out, settler Canadian identity is enmeshed both in the past and present with the process of settler colonization, the process through which the Canadian state has taken its land base from Indigenous people.[43] The colonial project continues in Canada and is expressed in everyday occurrences. The settler blindness to, and the invisibility of, Indigenous connections to local foods, particularly in the language of restaurant menus and websites, is one of these occurrences.

The rise in popularity of eating locally or localness has opened up a space for Indigenous chefs to identify local foods as their own, explains Morris. However, Morris sees a struggle for claiming the field of local/foraged/wild foods in New Zealand – a struggle between Maori and settler chefs. Morris explains what is at stake: "the ability to codify your food as the national cuisine may also signal the ability to make yourself the national subject, and in turn make the nation yours."[44] Morris suggests that Pierre Bourdieu is useful for thinking about these relationships of power within the culinary field.[45] In Bourdieu's foundational work on taste and social status, *Distinction: A Social Critique of the Judgement of Taste*, he examines how taste works to construct and reinforce social-class hierarchies and inequalities.[46] Within the culinary field, different cuisines are positioned in accordance with the cultural capital value associated with them.[47] For example, in the field of New Zealand cuisine, Morris explains that Anglo-American cuisine has the greatest capital value, and Maori cuisine has "almost none."[48] People or groups who hold valuable capital in one field are able to use their capital in other fields.[49]

KC Adams, an Oji-Cree artist whose works explore the relationship between food and colonization, speaks to these tensions between local food and Indigenous food. Adams says that some of the foods labelled as local, wild, or foraged should really be called Indigenous.[50] "It comes down to value," says Adams. "Foods that have value. There's not much value in First Nations culture, there's still a lot of racism."[51] Adams suggests that Canada's long history of colonization and systemic racism against Indigenous peoples taints how foods are described and perceived and facilitates an ongoing process of the erasure of Indigeneity on the locavore's plate. Claiming Indigenous foods as local foods can also be understood as appropriation according to Martin Reinhardt, Anishinaabe Ojibway professor of Native American Studies, and this restaurant-related issue is one that I have referred to elsewhere as "a process with a long legacy in the colonial project."[52]

Anishinaabe chef Johl Whiteduck Ringuette engages with the tension between local food and Indigenous food that Adams and Reinhardt speak to. Of Canadian restaurant culture and the locavore discourse, Ringuette has said: "There are tons of people who are into the whole farm-to-table movement. And First Nations restaurants they're going to keep coming. I know that some people think it's a trend, but it's not. It's not a trend. This food has always been here."[53] In Ringuette's Toronto-based restaurant NishDish, he uses local ingredients, but he does not use locavore discourse to describe these foods; instead, he refers to Indigeneity. For example, NishDish's website describes the restaurant as "a business built on traditional Anishinaabe (Nish) food" and goes on to explain that "our kitchen sources as many ingredients as we can from Indigenous communities and businesses."[54] Ringuette's reference to ingredients from "Indigenous communities" and "Anishinaabe food" contrasts and destabilizes the dominant restaurant discourse regarding what is understood as local. Given the cultural capital of localness, some Indigenous restaurants may also use locavore language in order to attract customers. For example, the Mi'kmaw restaurant Kiju's in Membertou, Nova Scotia, is self-described as "Fresh. Local. Friendly." Kiju's description indicates a pervasiveness of locavore discourse and an awareness of the high cultural capital that localness holds. However, an Indigenous restaurant's use of this discourse can be read another way. Morris's analysis suggests that identifying local foods *as* Indigenous foods is a political stance with ties to sovereignty. Read this way, Indigenous restaurants and chefs are rendering visible the Indigenous ties to food and land.

Colonial Blindness, Invisible Foodways

Within the discourse of Canada's restaurantscape, separation and absence of the Indigenous roots of eating local are not dissimilar to the ways in which Indigeneity has been historically erased from the landscape. Consider maps with the names of white explorers – like Alexander Mackenzie and Sir Henry Hudson – imposed on the terrain. The invisibility of Indigenous foods in restaurants today is a continuation of this history of erasure. *Terra nullius,* or "empty land," was the idea carried around by Europeans in the eighteenth and nineteenth centuries.[55] This meant that Indigenous governance and land management structures did not register in the European worldview, so Indigenous territories were seen as available for the taking. The extensive and intensive Indigenous land and food management systems already in place in the so-called "discovered" land did not count. The rock-buttressed clam gardens, the coastal beds of springbank clover and silverweed, the fields of camas, the burning of alpine meadows and lowland prairies to promote the growth of roots and berries – none of this fit the European model.[56]

Despite the large-scale Indigenous food production and management systems Coll Thrush explains how European explorers were blind to First Nations' cultivation methods along the Northwest coast during the late eighteenth and early nineteenth centuries.[57] Explorers and early settlers unloaded cattle from their ships, tore up gardens that they could not – or did not want to – see, and expropriated Indigenous lands.[58]

The invisibility Thrush refers to was rooted in a colonial conceptual framework, the effects of which continue to be felt.[59] Thrush writes: "Most Indigenous foods are completely unknown in settler society, even as 'local food' movements have achieved great popularity. With the exception of smoked salmon, the region's indigenous ways of eating are almost invisible."[60] Today, in the restaurant landscape, even with the prominence of foods that are described in terms of their ties to the land – wild, local, and foraged – Indigenous foods are somehow not seen. But Indigenous foods are there, dished up onto plates, even if they are not described as such.

Indigenous restaurateurs and chefs are pushing back against this history of erasure through the language they use on their menus. For instance, the drink menu at Nikosi Bistro in Quebec is politicized and brings colonization to the table by listing cocktails with names such as "Colonial Blues" and "Bloody Patriot."[61] Similarly, at Kū-kūm in Toronto, the restaurant centres Indigeneity on its menu by describing the corn grits served with venison osso buco as "Algonquin corn grits."[62] Whereas at the non-Indigenous, Tofino-based restaurant Shelter, two of the dishes on the menu – "Meares Island Chowder" and "Quadra Island Manila Clams"[63] – reference the non-Indigenous names of nearby islands, named after European explorers John Meares and Juan Francisco de la Bodega y Quadra. The language used by Shelter contrasts with the menu at NishDish that lists their coffee provider as "Mohawk roasted coffee from Kanestake 1st Nation." NishDish uses its menu to clearly link Indigenous nations, territory, and food.[64] Furthermore, NishDish uses wordplay to describe the types of coffee it serves and in doing so increases the visibility of Indigeneity – "Anishnakano," "Deneccino," "Creespresso" are mash-ups of Anishinabe and americano, Dene and cappuccino, and Cree and espresso. The reference to place names, Indigenous nations, and European explorers on the menus of these restaurants signals the (in)visibility of Indigenous ties to land and food. Menus are seemingly innocuous everyday objects, yet they are laden with meaning. These Indigenous restaurants can be seen as pushing back against a history of erasure and, through their menus, challenging narratives of sovereignty.

Conclusion

There is an invisibility of Indigenous cuisines in the contemporary Canadian restaurantscape, an invisibility that is most apparent when we look to the locavore terrain. This lack of seeing must be understood within the context of settler colonialism. In particular, a discussion of the concept of *terra nullius* alongside Thrush's work on colonial blindness allows us to see the invisibility of Indigenous foods today as a continuation of these early instances of blindness. Countering this narrative, however, are Indigenous restaurateurs and chefs who bring visibility to Indigenous foods and lands through their culinary work and the language they use to talk about their work (in their menus, on their websites, and in media interviews).

While the visibility of Indigenous foods in the restaurant foodscape remains low, we are witnessing a steady increase in Indigenous cuisines in Canada that can be traced over the last quarter-century through the growing numbers of Indigenous peoples working within the culinary arts and related professions.[65]

Given this growing visibility, possible areas of study include a further exploration into the ways in which the contemporary culinary field in Canada is emblematic of wider social, cultural, political, historical, and economic structures and settler colonialism.

Acknowledgments

I gratefully acknowledge the Social Sciences and Humanities Research Council of Canada for supporting research that led to this chapter.

Notes

1 Morris, "Kai or Kiwi?"
2 Andrew George Jr, Wet'suwet'en Chef and Hereditary Wing Chief.
3 Just as Indigenous foodways are diverse, overlapping, and shifting, terminology such as "Indigenous," "Aboriginal," and "Native" fall into the same pan-traps. Whenever possible, I refer to specific nations within this chapter. A further note on terms, when referring to "colonial" and "settler-colonial," I am drawing from the work of Glen Coulthard, Yellowknives Dene political scientist, whose definition makes explicit the continued relationships of power (Coulthard, *Red Skin, White Masks*, 7).
4 Wet'suwet'en chef and hereditary wing chief Andrew George Jr describes *taas guz* as a cold huckleberry soup. Whipped *soapalillie*, George explains, is a dessert made from whipping soapalillie (a tart berry also known as the soap berry) and their juice with sugar until the mixture forms peaks. Roe-on-kelp refers to a frond of kelp (a type of seaweed) that has been spawned on by herring and covered in their eggs (George and Gairns, *Feast!*, 59–89).
5 Brillat-Savarin, *The Physiology of Taste*.
6 Morris, "The Politics of Palatability," 6.
7 Ibid.
8 Ray, *The Ethnic Restaurateur*, 2.
9 See, for examples, Beriss and Sutton, *The Restaurants Book*; Johnston and Baumann, *Foodies*; and Heldke, *Exotic Appetites*.
10 Morris, "The Politics of Palatability."
11 Statistics Canada, "Aboriginal Peoples in Canada"; Statistics Canada, "Aboriginal Identity."
12 Statistics Canada, "Aboriginal Peoples in Canada."
13 Restaurants Canada.
14 Statistics Canada, "Census Profile, 2016 Census."
15 Johnston and Baumann, *Foodies*, 3. Johnston and Baumann describe the foodscape as

"a dynamic social construction that relates food to specific places, people, and meanings" (*Foodies*, 3). The term "foodscape" shares Appadurai's perspectival understanding of "scapes": "I use the terms with the common suffix scape to indicate first of all that these are not objectively given relations which look the same from every angle of vision, but rather that they are deeply perspectival constructs, inflected very much by the historical, linguistic and political situatedness of different sorts of actors" (Appadurai, "Disjunction and Difference in the Global Cultural Economy," 296). Morris draws from Appadurai's concept of scapes through her use of the term "culinascape" ("The Politics of Palatability," 25).

16 Anderson and Robertson, *Seeing Red*.
17 See Appadurai, "How to Make a National Cuisine," and Anderson, "Cooking Up the Nation."
18 Chu, "Get to Know a Chef."
19 George and Gairns, *A Feast for All Seasons*.
20 Ibid.
21 Ibid.
22 Ibid., 178.
23 Coulthard, *Red Skin, White Masks*, 7.
24 Lowman and Barker, *Settler Identity and Colonialism*, 2.
25 Ibid.
26 Abraham, "Chef Andrew George Jr Reinterprets."
27 Tennant, "Breaking Bread." As Thrush explains in "Vancouver the Cannibal," the local foods movement has largely overlooked Indigenous ties to local foods. However, the work of Nabhan is a notable exception: in *Coming Home to Eat*, he draws important connections between local ingredients and Indigenous foods and communities.
28 Johnston and Baumann, *Foodies*, 21.
29 Ibid.; Smith and MacKinnon, *100-Mile Diet*.
30 Johnston and Baumann, *Foodies*, 20.
31 Kramer, "The Food at Our Feet;" Quinn, "Noma Regains Its Crown."
32 Myers, "Serving It Up," 177.
33 Erdrich, *Original Local*.
34 Abraham, "Chef Andrew George Jr Reinterprets."
35 Salmon n' Bannock.
36 Salmon n' Bannock. "First Nations" is a term often used in a Canadian context and refers to Indigenous peoples who are neither Inuit nor Métis (Indigenous Foundations). As Maaka and Fleras point out in "Tino Rangatiratanga in Aotearoa," "first nations" can and should also be read literally: "As discourse, indigeneity refers to indigenous peoples as 'first

nations,' whose customary rights to self-determination over jurisdictions pertaining to land, identity and political voice have never been extinguished but remain undisturbed for purposes of identity, belonging and relations" (91).

37. Salmon n' Bannock.
38. Forage.
39. Ibid.
40. Ibid.
41. Forage; Salmon n' Bannock.
42. Shelter.
43. Ibid., 2.
44. Morris, "Kai or Kiwi?," 221.
45. Ibid.
46. Bourdieu, *Distinction*.
47. Morris, "Kai or Kiwi?," 213.
48. Ibid.
49. Ibid.
50. Adams, interview by author.
51. Ibid.
52. Tennant, "Breaking Bread."
53. Tennant and Macklem, "The Restaurant."
54. NishDish.
55. Smith, *Decolonizing Methodologies*.
56. Thrush, "Vancouver the Cannibal."
57. Ibid.
58. See Turner and Tuner, "'Where Our Women Used to Get the Food.'"
59. My analysis is also informed by Margery Fee's "Stories of Traditional Aboriginal Food, Territory and Health."
60. Thrush, "Vancouver the Cannibal," 26.
61. Nikosi Bistro.
62. Kukum.
63. Shelter.
64. Aksich, "What's on the Menu at NishDish, Toronto's New Anishinabe Café."
65. See Schellhaas, "Changing Tides," chapter 3 in this volume, where he discusses the increasing profile of Indigenous culinary arts in Canada over the last quarter century.

Bibliography

Abraham, Lisa. "Chef Andrew George Jr Reinterprets Native Recipes with Modern Healthy Twist." *Times Colonist*, 25 March 2014.

Adams, KC. Interview by author, 5 December 2014.

Aksich, C. "What's on the Menu at NishDish, Toronto's New Anishinabe Café." *Toronto Life*, 17 May 2017.

Anderson, Lara. "Cooking Up the Nation in the Fin-de-Siècle Spanish Cookery Books and Culinary Treatises." *Romance Studies* 27, no. 2 (2009): 121–32.

Anderson, Mark, and Carmen Robertson. *Seeing Red: A History of Natives in Canadian Press*. Winnipeg: University of Manitoba Press, 2011.

Appadurai, Arjun. "Disjunction and Difference in the Global Cultural Economy." *Theory, Culture & Society* 7 (1990): 295–310.

– "How to Make a National Cuisine: Cookbooks in Contemporary India." *Comparative Studies in Society and History* 30, no. 1 (1988): 3–24.

Bendix, Regina. "Diverging Paths in the Scientific Search for Authenticity." *Journal of Folklore Research* 29, no. 2 (1992): 103–32.

Berris, David, and David Sutton. *The Restaurants Book: Ethnographies of Where We Eat*. New York: Berg, 2007.

Bourdieu, Pierre. *Distinction: A Social Critique of the Judgment of Taste*. London: Routledge, 1984.

Brillat-Savarin, Jean Anthelme. *The Physiology of Taste*. London: Penguin Books, 1994 [1825].

Chu, Natalie. "Get to Know a Chef: Aaron Joseph Bear Robe, Keriwa Café." *blogTO*, 17 May 2012. www.blogto.com/people/2012/05/get_to_know_a_chef_aaron_joseph_bear_robe_keriwa_cafe/.

Coulthard, Glen. *Red Skin, White Masks*. Minneapolis: University of Minnesota Press, 2014.

Erdrich, Heid. *Original Local: Indigenous Foods, Stories and Recipes from the Upper Midwest*. St Paul, MN: Minnesota Historical Press Society, 2013.

Fee, Margery. "Stories of Traditional Aboriginal Food, Territory and Health." In *What's to Eat?: Entrées in Canadian Food History*, edited by Nathalie Cooke, 55–69. Montreal and Kingston: McGill-Queen's University Press, 2009.

Forage. Accessed 13 August 2016. http://foragevancouver.com/.

George, Andrew. *Modern Native Feasts: Healthy, Innovative, Sustainable Cuisine*. Vancouver: Arsenal Pulp Press, 2013.

George, Andrew, Jr, and Robert Gairns. *Feast! Canadian Native Cuisine for All Seasons.* Toronto: Doubleday Canada, 1997.

– *A Feast for All Seasons: Traditional Native Peoples' Cuisine.* Vancouver: Arsenal Pulp Press, 2010.

Greenberg, Reesa, Bruce Ferguson, and Sandy Nairne. *Thinking about Exhibitions.* London: Routledge, Press, 1996.

Hancock, Alexander. "René Redzepi on the Explosive Dangers of Foraging, Eating Bugs, and His New Book." *Eater*, 8 October 2012. www.eater.com/2012/10/8/6537747/rene-redzepi-on-the-explosive-dangers-of-foraging-eating-bugs-and-his.

Heldke, Lisa. *Exotic Appetites: Ruminations of a Food Adventurer.* New York: Routledge, 2003.

Indigenous Foundations. Accessed 27 October 2016. http://indigenousfoundations.arts.ubc.ca/home/identity/terminology.html#firstnations.

Johnston, Josée, and Baumann, Shyon. *Foodies: Democracy and Distinction in the Gourmet Foodscape.* New York: Routledge, 2010.

Kramer, Jane. "The Food at Our Feet." *The New Yorker*, 21 November 2011. www.newyorker.com/magazine/2011/11/21/the-food-at-our-feet.

Kū-kūm. Accessed 13 May 2018. www.kukum-kitchen.com/menu/.

Levenstein, Harvey. *Paradox of Plenty: A Social History of Eating in Modern America.* New York: Oxford University Press, 1993.

Lowman, Emma, and Adam Barker. *Settler: Colonialism and Identity in 21st Century Canada.* Halifax: Fernwood Press, 2015.

Maaka, Roger, and Augie Fleras. "Tino Rangatiratanga in Aotearoa." In *Political Theory and the Rights of Indigenous Peoples*, edited by Duncan Ivison, Paul Patton, and Will Sanders, 89–112. Cambridge, UK: Cambridge University Press, 2000.

Milby, Kathleen. *HIDE: Skin as Material and Metaphor.* Smithsonian: National Museum of the American Indian, 2010.

Molz, Jennie. "Tasting an Imagined Thailand: Authenticity and Culinary Tourism." In *Culinary Tourism*, edited by Lucy Long, 53–75. Lexington, KY: University Press of Kentucky, 2004.

Morris, Carolyn. "Kai or Kiwi? Maori and 'Kiwi' Cookbooks, and the Struggle for the Field of New Zealand Cuisine." *Journal of Sociology* 49, nos. 2–3 (2013): 210–23.

– "The Politics of Palatability: On the Absence of Maori Restaurants." *Food, Culture and Society: An International Journal of Multidisciplinary Research* 13, no. 1 (2010): 5–28.

Myers, Lisa. "Serving It Up: Recipes, Art, and Indigenous Perspectives." *Senses and Society* 7, no. 2 (2012): 173–95.

– Interview by author, 16 July 2014.

Nabhan, Gary Paul. *Coming Home to Eat: The Pleasures and Politics of Local Foods*. New York: W.W. Norton, 2009.

Nikosi Bistro. Accessed 13 May 2018. www.facebook.com/NikosiBistroPub/photos/a.1861118757498998.1073741828.1858314714446069/1869187416692132/?type=3&theater.

NishDish. Accessed 13 May 2018. www.nishdish.com/.

Pojar, Jim, and MacKinnon, Andy. *Plants of Coastal British Columbia*. Vancouver: BC Ministry of Forests and Lone Pine Publishing, 1994.

Quinn, Ben. "Noma Regains Its Crown as World's Best Restaurant – But Brits Are Coming." *The Guardian*, 29 April 2014. www.theguardian.com/lifeandstyle/2014/apr/29/noma-worlds-best-restaurant-heston-blumenthal.

Ray, Krishnendu. *The Ethnic Restaurateur*. New York: Bloomsbury Publishing, 2016.

Restaurants Canada. Accessed 14 December 2017. www.restaurantscanada.org/research/.

Ryan, Allan. *The Trickster Shift: Humour and Irony in Contemporary Native Art*. Vancouver: University of British Columbia Press, 1999.

Salmon n' Bannock. Accessed 13 August 2016. www.salmonandbannock.net/about.html.

Shelter. Accessed 12 May 2018. www.shelterrestaurant.com/experience/.

Smith, Alisa, and J.B. MacKinnon. *100-Mile Diet: A Year of Local Eating*. Toronto: Vintage Canada, 2007.

Smith, Linda Tuhiwai. *Decolonizing Methodologies: Research and Indigenous Peoples*. London: Zed Books, 1999.

Statistics Canada. "Aboriginal Identity." Accessed 14 December 2017. www12.statcan.gc.ca/census-recensement/2016/ref/dict/pop001-eng.cfm.

– "Aboriginal Peoples in Canada: Key Results from the 2016 Census." Accessed 14 December 2017. www.statcan.gc.ca/daily-quotidien/171025/dq171025a-eng.pdf.

– "Census Profile, 2016 Census." Accessed 14 December 2017. www12.statcan.gc.ca/census-recensement/2016/dp-pd/prof/details/page.cfm?Lang=E&Geo1=PR&Code1=01&Geo2=PR&Code2=01&Data=Count&SearchText=Canada&SearchType=Begins&SearchPR=01&B1=Visible%20minority&TABID=1.

Tennant, Zoe. "Breaking Bread." *The Walrus*, June 2016. http://thewalrus.ca/breaking-bread/.

– "First Course: Exploring Indigenous Cuisines in the Canadian Food Landscape." MA thesis, University of British Columbia, 2015.

Tennant, Zoe, and Michelle Macklem. "The Restaurant: A Table Divided." CBC, *Ideas*, 21 May 2018. www.cbc.ca/radio/ideas/the-restaurant-a-table-divided-1.4669493.

Thrush, Coll. "Vancouver the Cannibal: Cuisine, Encounter, and the Dilemma of Difference on the Northwest Coast, 1774–1808." *Ethnohistory* 58, no. 1 (2011): 1–35.

Turner, Nancy, and Katherine Turner. "'Where Our Women Used to Get the Food': Cumulative Effects and Loss of Ethnobotanical Knowledge and Practice; Case Study from Coastal British Columbia." *Botany* 86, no. 2 (2008): 103–15.

5

From Meat to Metaphor

Beavers and Conflicting Imaginations of the Edible

L. Sasha Gora

The closest most Canadians get to eating beaver is whole wheat, yeasted dough fried in oil and slathered with butter and a sweet topping like cinnamon and sugar. Grant and Pam Hooker gave this popular pastry a very Canadian name when they opened their first BeaverTails stall in 1978.[1] BeaverTails (*Queues de Castor*) have since become a quintessentially Canadian food, both at home and abroad. But tails aside, to what extent is the beaver imagined in Canada as meat and, therefore, as food? Although the beaver looms large in Canadian history, its culinary history is less apparent. Why are beavers not readily and widely consumed? Cuisine is equally defined by what it includes and excludes. Distinct beaver species are native to Europe (*Castor fiber*) and North America (*Castor canadensis*), making this animal/meat a compelling example of different cultural perceptions.

Anthony Bourdain – the late celebrity chef, promiscuous carnivore, and television host – described beaver meat as "absolutely delicious."[2] Others agree, suggesting that the taste does not prevent it from being popular.[3] Descriptions of the flavour, ranging from fatty lamb and bacon to eel and chicken, are too diverse to define. And although most Canadians have not had a chance to try the actual meat, artist Michael Farnan invited his fellow citizens to put a beaver in their mouths via the country's ever-popular culinary ambassador, maple syrup.[4] As part of the collaborative art project *oh-oh canada* (2016) organized by Leah Decter, Farnan used maple syrup to create candies representing the less-acknowledged stories in Canada's history: the nation's dirty laundry. The maple candies were then distributed to crowds on Parliament Hill in Ottawa on Canada Day. Many of the eight candies reflected the tensions between Canadian history and Indigenous peoples. Importantly, Farnan used the beaver as a dominant Canadian symbol associated with environmental stewardship and national character traits, such as friendliness and hard work, to argue that beavers are symbolically associated with what he describes as "the negative and enduring aspects of colonization."[5] Farnan cleverly rendered the "edible" beaver a challenge to the constructed notions of Canadian nationalism. The artist transformed eating a candy into a moment of critical reflection on how colonial history and popular culture have moulded the Canadian imagination into perceiving the beaver as a cute and noble animal. This, I argue, also prevents Canadians from envisioning the beaver as their next meal.

In light of this culinary predicament, there are three main reasons the majority of Canadians do not consider the beaver as food. First, beaver meat is often described as Indigenous "country food."[6] This makes it a niche food less associated with a mainstream Canadian diet. However, this narrative neglects the European history of the beaver as meat. Second, colonial history has predominantly shaped the Canadian imagination into perceiving the beaver as a cute animal that represents national ideals and that, since 1975, has been an official emblem. Moreover, under the guise of artistic representation, there has been a concerted attempt to naturalize the beaver less as food and more as a Canadian cultural symbol. Lastly, government regulations make it difficult to access beaver meat. Many Canadians do not know that the beaver is edible, let alone how to cook it. Indeed, Canadian cookbooks tell a varied and oftentimes incomplete story. Focusing more on the presence, rather than the absence, of the beaver, I refer to three types of cookbooks: those which involve cooking beavers (this includes Indigenous cookbooks, and cookbooks aimed at settlers and hunters); those for home cooks who are vaguely aware of the beaver as meat; and cookbooks authored by contemporary restaurant chefs. My examination of Canada's national animal reveals how imaginations shift around what is edible and for whom. The beaver is thus an intriguing case study signalling tensions around notions of Canadianness and how an animal has become a symbol with conflicting understandings and representations between Indigenous peoples and Canadian settlers.

Castor canadensis: The Beaver as "Country Food"

The beaver as "country food" differentiates Indigenous food from Canadian food by categorizing the former as what people traditionally ate and the latter as what people now eat. However, this categorization along temporal and racial lines fails to account for diverse culinary practices. In "'Fit for the Table of the Most Fastidious Epicure': Culinary Colonialism in Upper Canada," Alison Norman mentions

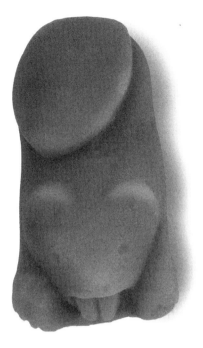

Figure 5.1
Michael Farnan, *Beaver Candy*, and Leah Decter, *oh-oh canada*, at Parliament Hill on Canada Day, 1 July 2016.

the beaver as something the Haudenosaunee ate.[7] Beaver recipes appear in a variety of twentieth- and twenty-first-century Indigenous cookbooks, such as *Nishnabe Delights*, *Gathering What the Great Nature Provided: Food Traditions of the Gitksan*, *The Rural and Native Heritage Cookbook: The Gathering*, and *PachaMama: Cuisine des Premières Nations*. All four titles represent specific regional foodways, as opposed to "pan-Indigenous" cuisine. In contrast, Health Canada's 2007 *Food Guide for First Nations, Inuit and Métis* includes a beaver illustration under the generic category of traditional meats and wild game. The beaver is not, however, included in government food guides aimed at settlers.

Although the beaver is often excluded as a food for non-Indigenous diners, this categorization changes when Canada is on an international stage and catering to different audiences. For example, during the International and Universal Exposition in 1967 (Expo 67) in Montreal, La Toundra restaurant in the Canadian pavilion served beaver. With illustrations and names of dishes referencing Indigenous peoples and places, La Toundra's menu is one interpretation of Indigenous food. Divided into three parts – *Cuisine Canadienne*, La Toundra, and International Cuisine – the menu offers "Beaver Tail Broth" as Arctic fare, a treat from up North, for seventy-five cents. La Toundra, the second section, expands its offerings, and thus claims the Arctic's culinary potential as Canadian. What significance does this have?

Sarah Wilmshurst describes Expo 67 as a "hive of activity where Canadians sought to represent their nation to the world."[8] However, Rhona Richman Kenneally argues that in presenting an "authentic" Canadian menu, the organizers served dishes foreign to many Canadians.[9] In other words, La Toundra constructs the beaver broth as an Indigenous dish but claims it as representative of the entire nation. Rather than opening a much-needed dialogue about what is edible and, therefore, included in Canadian cuisine, La Toundra's menu appears to have been more about novelty, an attempt to serve "authentic" Canadian dishes on an international stage.

As with cookbooks, restaurants, and exhibitions – spaces and places within which staging, media, and performance are enacted – television provides another medium through which to present and define Indigenous and Canadian cuisines. In *Moosemeat & Marmalade*, which premiered on the Aboriginal Peoples Television Network (APTN) in 2015, beaver meat represents Indigenous food. As in the case of La Toundra, audience is important. APTN provides a venue for Indigenous self-representation and "talking back" in the context of mainstream media accessible to Indigenous and non-Indigenous viewers. The show's premise is that "two very different chefs" – Art Napoleon from Canada, a "seasoned hunter & bush cook," and Dan Hayes from the United Kingdom, a "classically trained French chef" – together "explore culture, culinary traditions and really good food."[10] Moosemeat, food that is hunted, signals Napoleon as an Indigenous bush cook, while marmalade, food that is processed in a kitchen with imported oranges, represents Hayes as a chef. The pilot is set in Moberly Lake, British Columbia, where Napoleon takes Hayes beaver hunting. Only a couple of minutes into the episode, the culture clash begins: Napoleon is dressed in all green with an army cap, while Hayes wears a tweed jacket, tie, and knee-high socks. As Napoleon explains the importance of respecting the animal, Hayes responds that the British do not have such rituals, and then chuckles about port wine. Not only do the men dress differently but they also associate hunting with contrasting sentiments ranging from the spiritual (Indigenous) to the more hedonistic (British). With one shot, the beaver is killed, and Napoleon gives a tobacco offering to its spirit. He later explains that the beaver was once a staple, "but these days most young people haven't even tried it. Hopefully we can change this."[11] The unpopularity of the meat is not connected to the animal's history as an overhunted commodity of the fur trade. Nor is the beaver thought of as an exotic food; instead, the focus is on a lack of experience. There are many ways to cook a beaver, which Napoleon demonstrates as he turns a teepee into a smoker. He seasons the meat with soy sauce and places it in a metal net over the fire. The Indigenous bush cook prepares a dish the European chef has never tried. No reference is made to the history of beavers in the United Kingdom; however, by the twelfth century – well before the Canadian fur trade – beavers were already extinct in England and, by the sixteenth century, in the rest of the UK because of overhunting for fur, medicine, and food.[12] In 2009, beavers were reintroduced to Scotland and since 2013 have been spotted in England.[13] However, *Moosemeat & Marmalade* presents beaver as an Indigenous, Canadian meat without a European history.

Despite this televised dramatization, there are notable absences of beaver meat in other contemporary chefs' representations of Indigenous cuisines. Dolly and Annie Watts, who are from the Gitk'san Nation, ran the Vancouver restaurant Liliget Feast House from 1995 to 2007. They devote a chapter to wild game in *Where People Feast: An Indigenous People's Cookbook*, but do not mention the beaver. Because of the traditions of specific First Nations, beaver meat is not a universal Indigenous food. Rachel Poliquin writes that the tribes of the Great Plains valued beavers for managing resources and conserving water, but not as food.[14] The beaver is also absent in Surrey-based, Wet'suwet'en chef Andrew George Jr's *Modern Native Feasts: Healthy, Innovative, Sustainable Cuisine*. However, there are two beaver recipes in his first cookbook, *A Feast for All Seasons: Traditional Native Peoples' Cuisine*. Published in 1997 and then republished in 2010, the year of the Vancouver Olympic Winter Games, both editions have the same recipes: "Smoked Beaver Meat" and "Boiled Smoked Beaver." Why are these dishes included in George's first cookbook and not the more recent one? As the subtitles indicate, *A Feast for All Seasons* features "traditional" cuisine whereas the later 2013 volume focuses on cooking that is "modern" and "innovative." In contrast to placing these recipes within his traditional cookbook, "Beaver Tail Soup" was part of George's competition menu at the 1992 Culinary Olympics in Frankfurt, Germany.[15] In his work, then, George imagines the beaver as either traditional country food or contemporary cuisine depending on the context and his audience.

Castor fiber: The Beaver as Fish

Contradictions and tensions concerning the status of the beaver as food are found not just in the kinds of contemporary Indigenous references discussed in the previous section. They also animate early European culinary accounts in which the beaver's categorization changes over time. Today, the large, semi-aquatic, broad-tailed animal is classified as a rodent, but in the Middle Ages it was classified as a fish. In a study of the beaver's reintroduction to Scotland, the authors address its convenient Catholic classification: "The Catholic Church considered beavers to be primarily aquatic and therefore categorized as fish, as opposed to 'creatures which creepeth upon the land' (Leviticus 11, King James Bible). This meant that their flesh … could be consumed during fasts and holidays, when the eating of 'meat' was forbidden."[16] This contradicts the common narrative that beavers were hunted primarily for fur[17] and the belief, in Canada, that beaver meat is only an Indigenous food. Environmental historian Dolly Jørgensen states the distinction was not between mammals versus fish and birds, but land versus water.[18] The beaver was thus treated as a bifurcated creature. Both of land and sea, its belly and tail were considered fish.[19] An example emerges in John Russell's cooking manual *Boke of Nurture* from around 1460. He begins the "Carving of fish" section with a recommendation to add beaver tail to pea soup.[20] The recipe does not sound too different from French-Canadian pea soup, replacing the ham hock with a beaver tail. This beaver-as-fish debate also took place in Canada. Writing for *Scientific American*, Jason G. Goldman reports that the bishop of Quebec asked his church superiors in the seventeenth century if settlers would be allowed to eat beaver meat during Lent, implying that the animal was regularly consumed.[21] The fact that Jørgensen writes about the ambiguous classification of the beaver in the Middle Ages (with an example from the fifteenth century) and that the bishop of Quebec asked the Vatican to clarify dietary prohibitions two centuries later reveals a substantial gap in this history. Nonetheless, because the animal passed as an acceptable food in Catholic doctrine, the history of beaver hunting in Europe is also one of meat.

This European history of beaver meat is absent, however, from contemporary representations, such as the one dramatized for both educational effect and cultural contrast in the *Moosemeat & Marmalade* television show.[22] This misconception is curious. Why does so little of this history live on in contemporary culinary memory? How did the beaver lose its status and popularity as meat? Jørgensen writes about "when the past obscures the past."[23] Studying press coverage of the beaver's reintroduction to Scotland, she found that most articles explained the beaver's extinction through overhunting, with nearly a third specifying the fur trade as the main cause. Explicit references to the beaver being hunted for meat appeared in only 4 of 137 articles. She concludes that "Canadian colonial history has dominated the way we think about the historical relationship between humans and beavers."²⁴ The legacy of the Canadian fur trade has impacted how beavers are imagined both inside and outside Canada, with a history of fashionable hats obscuring a history of meat.

While popular representations curtail or "forget" the beaver's transatlantic status as food, the beaver nonetheless appears in histories of Canadian foodways. In *Canadians at Table: A Culinary History of Canada*, Dorothy Duncan mentions the beaver four times. She writes: "This fascination with beaver pelts, to the exclusion of the rest of the animal, must have surprised the First Nations. They, too, coveted the beaver, because every part of it was important to them. The meat was tasty."²⁵ In her analysis of traditional Indigenous foods in the 2009 anthology *What's to Eat? Entrées in Canadian Food History*, Margery Fee mentions a 1972 court case brought against the James Bay hydroelectric project by the Cree in order to stop the flooding of their traplines. The beaver was one of the animals they depended on for food.²⁶ These two examples once again associate beaver meat with Indigenous foodways. However, in an endnote in Elizabeth Driver's "Regional Differences in the Canadian Daily Meal? Cookbooks Answer the Question," the beaver appears in a settler context. The note reviews a menu that included "Beaver Tail" at a dinner in Ottawa in 1876 given by Sandford Fleming, engineer-in-chief of Canadian and Intercolonial Railways.²⁷ Despite modern narratives' associations of the animal with Indigenous food, Europeans and settlers in the Americas, including prominent individuals like Fleming, consumed beaver meat for centuries.

The Beaver as National Symbol and Metaphor

Clearly, the beaver's various categorizations (edible/non-edible, fish/rodent, Indigenous/Canadian/European) have shifted depending on the context, audience, and time period. Other factors that influence the (sometimes absent) stories of beaver meat are the animal's status as a national symbol and the ways in which colonial history shapes its representation as an emblem of Canadianness. The beaver appears on five-cent coins, in Molson Canadian beer advertisements, and as the official Canadian animal. The mascot of Montreal's 1976 Olympic Summer Games was the beaver, and the book *The Beaver Bites Back? American Popular Culture in Canada* casts the beaver as a metaphor for Canadians.²⁸ Contemporary artists have also used the beaver to reflect on Canada and its history. An example is Farnan's artist statement on his contribution to the *oh-oh canada* art project: "As you eat this beaver, create a link between your own personal identity and the history of colonization that shapes it."[29] As cultural historian Jody Berland argues in her research concerning the animal's appearance in today's visual and digital cultures, the beaver can be studied as a living creature, a commodity (which this chapter does in considering fragments of a dead beaver as food), and as a "material and semiotic object."[30] Turning something into a symbol is therefore a process of abstraction. Berland writes that "the hard-working beaver is both symbolic and more than symbol ... we need its animality – together with its de-animalization – to convince us that there is something certain in our shared citizenship. If we choose living entities like beavers ... for our collective symbols, according to the totemic thinking ... then the nation congregated under its sign is equally vital, natural and distinct."[31] Berland argues that by adopting a living animal and imagining it as a symbol, we give it more power than constructing a symbol from scratch.

It is through the beaver as a collective and "natural" symbol that a visual and metaphorical Canadian identity is constructed. These cultural constructions can be traced to Canada's past as an emerging nation on the global stage. In his 1941 article "The Beaver in Canadian Art," anthropologist Marius Barbeau attempted to naturalize the beaver as a Canadian cultural symbol. The article was printed in the appropriately titled *Beaver*, a publication founded by the Hudson's Bay Company, one of Canada's largest fur trading companies and today one of the country's largest retailers.[32] As Joan Sangster argues, the *Beaver* created "an ideology of Canadian 'northerness' [sic] that promoted ideals of anthropological discovery, historical pride, and liberal tolerance for other cultures, while also reinforcing colonial images of Inuit and Native peoples."[33] The journal's mandate must be considered when interpreting how Barbeau analyzed examples of beavers in his construction of "Canadian art," including his objectives for doing so, and how audiences consumed such ideas. Throughout the *Beaver*'s history, there was a concerted attempt to celebrate Canadian national identity via the beaver through its relationship to Indigenous and ancient cultures.[34] Barbeau writes: "Canada was not at first the only home of the beaver, as its present habitat and its role in our colonial history might lead one to believe ... the beaver is mentioned in the hieroglyphs of the Egyptians."[35] Writing for a Canadian audience several decades before the beaver became an official emblem, Barbeau suggests that the animal was already so much a part of the country's image that it was hard to imagine otherwise.

But Barbeau's article is not strictly about art and visual representations. He also addresses the beaver as food: "the meat was extensively consumed, and the tail was a delicacy – its 'flavour and appearance resemble those of the choicest bacon.'"[36] This description reinforces Duncan's claim that the meat was tasty. However, by comparing beaver to pork, which is not native to the Americas, Barbeau speaks of the beaver in European terms. But it is still not clear who was eating it: Indigenous peoples, settlers, or both. Did Barbeau try beaver meat? His wording suggests not, as he writes about it in the passive voice and in the past tense, the latter signalling a prejudiced attitude towards Indigenous cultures that persisted well into the twentieth century. As Fee writes in "Rewriting Anthropology and Identifications on the North Pacific Coast," "the assertion that the Indian was 'vanishing' produces the imperative to salvage Indian culture. This belief is anthropology's warrant, providing it with the mandate to work fast … 'rescue' the artefacts, languages … ceremonies and daily practices for future scientific study."[37] Fee's argument that anthropologists were trying to document something that was vanishing, as opposed to being in flux, reveals the limitations and cultural tensions surrounding Barbeau's representations of the beaver as a Canadian symbol and as a food from the past.

Beyond settler society's tactics of using the beaver to establish a national and cultural identity, Indigenous peoples also regarded the beaver with strong symbolic associations. Barbeau writes that "some … tribes made the beaver their clan name or emblem."[38] He provides examples ranging from the Haida of the North Pacific coast to the Amihonas on Lake Huron, a reminder of the beaver's vast geographical reach. The rest of the article focuses exclusively on Indigenous art, and yet by framing his argument with the title "The Beaver in Canadian Art," he claims Indigenous art as Canadian, appropriating Indigenous peoples' history of visually representing the symbolic beaver. It was therefore strategic (albeit highly problematic due to his research objectives) of Barbeau to declare the beaver "Canadian," as he placed the animal into a larger art history that generalized its importance across time and audiences. Thus, from a fur-trade commodity to an appropriated cultural symbol of Canadianness, the beaver has been re-imagined as something other than edible.[39] In the first instance, the beaver was too scarce to be eaten, and in the second, it has become too important. Indeed, beavers make countless appearances across Canada's cultural, corporate, and geographic landscapes, but rarely show up in cookbooks or on restaurant menus.[40]

Restaurants and Regulations

Even if Canadians can navigate the taboos and historical tensions surrounding the beaver as national symbol, strict government regulations around hunting and food preparation make it nearly impossible for beaver meat to reach Canadian dinner tables. Not having easy access makes it increasingly difficult to imagine the beaver as food. Wild meat regulations differ across Canadian provinces and territories, and in the majority of the country, it is illegal to buy and sell wild game. British Columbia's Wildlife Act makes it unlawful to sell game meat, which some restaurant owners might not even be aware of, according to a CBC News report.[41] In Ontario, it is only legal to sell meat that has been inspected and slaughtered in a government-licensed facility.[42] Jacob Richler writes, "if your local bistro peddles elk, duck … venison, and even 'wild' boar, that animal grew up on a farm."[43] This is the scenario I mentioned earlier that enabled Liliget Feast House restaurant to serve elk and include recipes for wild game in their cookbook. However, to label this meat as "game" is misleading and points to the tension between how some diners would like to imagine the life of the animal and the reality that government regulations require.

It is important to note, here, that hunting also connects to social hierarchies and communicates specific cultural ideals regarding which animals are fit to eat and how they should be killed. In *A Revolution in Eating: How the Quest for Food Shaped America*, James E. McWilliams describes how regional eating habits developed throughout British America. Although foodways differed from colony to colony, he describes consistent attitudes towards hunting: "As the English saw it, [hunting] may have served a purpose in rare times of need, but ultimately it was a sport, a diversion."[44] McWilliams's comment puts Hayes's reaction to bush cook Napoleon's description of the spiritual qualities of hunting into perspective. This makes "produced" food more valuable than wild game, which was considered "frontier food." Julia Roberts, however, finds the opposite true in her study of snipe in Canadian saloons and affirms a connection between hunting and nobility.[45] To be sure, the historic, cultural, and political perceptions of hunting in Canada are complex because of differences in attitudes among the British, French, and settlers from other countries. Regional differences in agriculture and foodways, and Indigenous food sovereignty further add to the complexity. Hunting implies a different relationship with the land than animal husbandry. When properly managed, hunting is understood more as managing and harvesting a landscape, rather than radically transforming it. McWilliams's argument, as well as a history of over-trapping beavers nearly to extinction,[46] provides context for understanding why Canada's commercial food industry is based on domesticated animals.

Today, if people want to eat beaver meat in Canada, they have to trap the animal themselves or know someone who will do it for them. Since it is illegal for wild meat to be sold commercially, one would have to offer something other than money in exchange. These circumstances present issues related to accessing wild foods and to food sovereignty. Who is allowed to hunt, and how is the meat distributed? This regulatory dynamic also influences cuisine in the public realm, as the opportunity to consume wild game becomes strictly a private affair. Richler is quite critical of this situation: "It is also an outrage that Canadian chefs cannot use their restaurants to showcase our own wild grouse, turkeys, deer … For game is one of our great resources, and in keeping it out of the hands of real chefs who know what to do with it, and leaving it entirely to home cooks, who do not, we have defaulted on developing what might have been the cornerstone of our national cuisine. So even today, if you really want to eat great Canadian game, as our own chefs generally lack experience with it, you do best to import for the occasion a great European-trained chef."[47] Richler assumes home cooks are less capable than trained chefs even though the former, especially if they are hunters like bush cook Napolean, are likely to be more experienced in preparing wild game. Clearly, provincial governments have tremendous influence on regulating what Canadian cuisine does and does not include. One consequence is that Indigenous peoples who grow up learning to prepare game are not able to apply their specialized knowledge to the restaurant trade. Moreover, Indigenous restaurants cannot represent their food cultures through wild meats. In the end, opportunities to consume beaver meat are severely limited, as regulatory laws indirectly enforce cultural stereotypes as well as the beaver's nationalistic associations as a symbol and metaphor.

The Beaver in Canadian Cookbooks

Because of the strict government regulations, it is primarily Indigenous peoples, hunters, and risk-taking chefs who know how to prepare beaver meat. Derek Dammann and Martin Picard are examples of the latter. Dammann – co-author of *True North: Canadian Cooking from Coast to Coast* and co-owner, with British chef Jamie

Oliver, of Maison Publique in Montreal – introduces a recipe for "Hare Ravioli" with a complaint about not being able to legally serve moose and deer in Quebec even though he can serve seal and hare. "It doesn't make any sense at all," he writes.[48] Nonetheless, *True North* includes recipes for caribou and moose, but not beaver, despite referring to it as meat. When I asked Dammann about beaver, he told me he has cooked it.[49] A recipe for beaver appears in Montreal chef Martin Picard's 2012 *Au Pied de Cochon Sugar Shack*, his second cookbook. Its controversial name, "Confederation Beaver," and six pages of intricate instructions suggest that the dish is anything but everyday fare.[50] The beaver is stripped of its sacs and stuffed with its own tail, which has been braised. The ingredients include oyster and button mushrooms, pig's blood, cream, foie gras, and maple-smoked ham. It sounds like extreme eating, food as spectacle or sport. However, as Picard suggests, his beaver recipe is about more than shock value; it is about recognizing the history of the beaver as food in Quebec and the animals he hunts on the land around his sugar shack.[51]

Still, there remains tension with including a recipe for beaver in a restaurant cookbook. After all, the public cannot actually consume beaver at Au Pied de Cochon, nor at its sugar shack. If serving wild meat were legal, "Confederation Beaver" could potentially appear on Au Pied de Cochon's menu, but is this likely? Such a complicated recipe is not any more suited for a busy restaurant chef than it is for a busy home cook. Would the price reflect the effort required? Would enough people be curious to try it, or grow to like it, to keep it on the menu? Picard is also responsible for giving Bourdain, author of the preface to Picard's first cookbook, his first taste of beaver meat in a 2013 episode of *Parts Unknown*.[52] Bourdain's show is often about extreme eating, but Picard did not serve "Confederation Beaver"; instead, he prepared a simple stew.

Beyond these examples from the exclusive realm of high-end chefs, the beaver does not have an extensive presence in Canadian cookbooks, especially cookbooks for amateurs who may only vaguely know about the beaver as food. Recipes utilizing moose, another symbol of Canada, appear to be more popular. For example, Michele Genest's *The Boreal Feast: A Culinary Journey through the North* features "*Gravad* of Moose with Pickled Radish and Morel Mayonnaise" and "Smoked, Braised, Barbecued Moose Ribs," but no beaver. An earlier cookbook focusing on a different region, Marie Nightingale's *Out of Old Nova Scotia Kitchens*, makes a passing reference. Not including a recipe can be seen as either a limited interest in eating beaver meat or a lack of knowledge in preparing it.

In all likelihood, most amateur cooks today would understand a recipe for beaver not as a meat dish but as a dessert akin to the popular treat purchased from BeaverTails vendors. In *Pemmican to Poutine: A Journey through Canada's Culinary History*, Suman Roy and Ali Brooke include a recipe for "Beaver Tails Pastries" as part of "Traditional Fare" in the Ontario chapter. "The tails of beavers were eaten during pioneer times, most often by fur traders who had killed the beavers for their fur," the authors explain, before going on to describe how the tails were cooked over a fire to remove the skin and how the meat was prepared in a bean stew.[53] Roy and Brooke mention that sometime during the nineteenth century, people started calling campfire bread "beaver tails." While the book does not include a recipe for actual tail meat, this narrative depicts the beaver as a food of the past, similar to the titles of George's cookbooks. Although Roy is a chef, *Pemmican to Poutine* differs from *True North* and *Au Pied de Cochon* because it is not associated with a restaurant and is meant to be cooked from – a clear distinction from Picard's "Confederation Beaver," which is designed to entertain and provoke. Moreover, *Pemmican to Poutine* focuses on defining Canadian cuisine whereas the cookbooks by Dammann and Picard serve to represent the authors as unique chefs with individual styles of cooking.

While many Canadian cookbooks only mention the beaver as part of a larger historical narrative, cookbooks (such as Indigenous cookbooks) that are written for hunters target those who actually cook beavers. One example is *The Wild Game Cookbook* by Jeff Morrison, the former outdoors columnist for the *Ottawa Sun*. His audience is radically different from those who cook from *Pemmican to Poutine*. Assuming that readers will be hunting their own meat, the latter includes recipes for wild game, with any additional ingredients being easy to buy. There is also an online presence of beaver recipes, such as "Beaver with Barbecue Sauce" and "Beaver Tenderloin Roast," mostly from hunting websites. Predecessors to these more recent hunting books and websites are publications targeting Canadians moving to rural settings. One example is *The Northern Cookbook*, which includes a recipe for "Sweet Pickled Beaver." First published by the Canadian Department of Indian Affairs and Northern Development in 1967, this culinary handbook encourages settlers to move to and eat well in the north. Here, the beaver is presented as a local food with gourmet potential and as part of a colonizing agenda. The recipe humorously mixes beaver meat with ingredients that travel great distances, such as pineapple juice and lemon. As in the case of "Confederation Beaver," one is left doubting the practicality of "Sweet Pickled Beaver."

Conclusion: The Beaver as Part of Canadian Cuisine

The "Confederation Beaver" recipe in Picard's cookbook demonstrates his openness to experimentation. It also creates media attention around the subject and highlights the fact that government regulations make serving beaver meat in restaurants nearly impossible. There is also the question of how many people would be willing to try it, as the public's imagination remains focused on the animal's symbolic significance. Canadians have largely forgotten beaver meat's transatlantic past. Nonetheless, there seems to be an emerging curiosity. As part of a gathering of chefs at Cook It Raw Alberta: The Shaping of a Culinary Frontier in 2015, Edmonton chef Brayden Kozak cooked beaver. Founded by Italian food entrepreneur Alessandro Porcelli, the concept of Cook It Raw is for chefs to gather and cook in the wilderness. In a promotional video, Kozak stirs a stew of beaver meat with chunks of carrot: "Beaver meat is obviously something extremely underutilized in cooking in Canada. Growing up, you learn a lot about the fur trade and how important beaver was to the pioneers. So it kind of made sense to bring something that was so important to our nation's history."[54] Interestingly, it is exactly because of the beaver's importance in Canadian history that Kozak decides to cook it. As a chef, he is presumably less sentimental about this national symbol and more concerned with the blood and bones associated with preparing and eating the animal. Describing beaver meat as "underutilized" implies that it has potential.

Although not explicitly stated in Kozak's description, there is an emphasis throughout Cook It Raw Alberta on what chef Jamie Kennedy describes as the "Indigenous influence."[55] Porcelli discusses three ingredients needed to shape a culinary identity – great people, talents, and products – and the method through which to execute it: tradition. "So what is tradition here?" Porcelli asks, and then states: "It's the Aboriginal people, it's the First Nations. All of the chefs here should be able to tap into this."[56] Cook It Raw Alberta is, therefore, more than a cooking event staged in the woods. It is a means through which to shape a new Canadian culinary identity, one that includes the beaver. When one considers that only one of the fourteen chefs is Indigenous, however, Cook It Raw Alberta also raises questions about who has the power to define that identity.

The examples I have gathered span Canada's cultural, culinary, and visual histories, revealing the beaver's shifting categorization and representations. Forgotten and misperceived culinary traditions, government regulations, and a loss of practical knowledge have all curtailed the beaver's status as food. Although the beaver has long since recovered from its endangered ranking, today one is more likely to see a piece of dough named after the beaver's tail than actual meat. Neither advocating for nor critiquing the consumption of beaver meat, I have explored the culinary and cultural life of this animal while highlighting reasons as to why it is an "underutilized" food. When identified as meat, the beaver is often framed as traditional country food, which classifies it as specialized and culturally based, not mainstream. Meanwhile, the symbolic value of Canada's national animal overshadows the fact that it is also edible. This situation is further aided by government regulations restricting most Canadians, other than hunters and Indigenous peoples, from being able to access beaver meat, and thus learn how to prepare it. The fact that the beaver is recognized more as a metaphor for Canadianness and less as a food reveals a complex story about conflicting constructions of Canada and the ongoing tensions between Indigenous and settler imaginations.

Notes

1. According to Casselman, there was already a dough dish with this name. He refers to Frank Russell's 1896 *Explorations in the Far North*: "If the traveler has no frying pan the bread is baked in a *beaver tail*. Such a loaf is long and narrow and is exposed to the fire upon a stick" (Casselman, "Canadian Food Words").
2. *Anthony Bourdain*.
3. For more about how others have described the taste of beaver meat, see Gora, "Beaver as Offal," 208.
4. Farnan's multidisciplinary artistic practice uses media such as sculpture, video, and performance to investigate representations of Canadian history and discourses regarding human relationships to nature, nationhood, and colonialism.
5. This is the artist's description of the artwork's objective. See "Michael Farnan" on the *oh-oh Canada* website.
6. I use "Indigenous" since the term includes all Indigenous peoples in Canada: First Nations, Métis, and Inuit.
7. Norman, "'Fit for the Table of the Most Fastidious Epicure,'" 34.
8. Wilmshurst, "How to Eat Like a Canadian."
9. Kenneally, "The Cuisine of the Tundra," 291.
10. *Moosemeat & Marmalade*, "About the Show."
11. *Moosemeat & Marmalade*, "Beaver and the Boys."
12. Poliquin, *Beaver*, 17, 164.

13 Jørgensen, "Beavers Are Back in England."

14 Poliquin, *Beaver*, 181–2.

15 George Jr and Gairns, *Feast for All Seasons*, 21.

16 Campbell-Palmer, Gow, Needham, Jones, and Rosell, *The Eurasian Beaver*, 17.

17 The authors of *The Eurasian Beaver* conclude that overhunting beavers for meat likely influenced the animal's decline because the forty days of Lent coincide with the season when beavers are suckling young or pregnant (17).

18 Jørgensen, "Beaver for Lent."

19 Poliquin, *Beaver*, 22.

20 Jørgensen, "Beaver for Lent."

21 Goldman, "Once upon a Time."

22 Aldred, "Scotland Wild Beaver Reintroduction Trial."

23 Jørgensen, "When the Past Obscures the Past."

24 Ibid.

25 Duncan, *Canadians at Table*, 45.

26 Fee, "Stories of Traditional Aboriginal Food, Territory, and Health," 64.

27 Driver, "Regional Differences in the Canadian Daily Meal?," 212.

28 If the beaver symbolizes Canada, is eating beaver meat acceptable, or is it taboo? Some answers may be found in "Eating Roo: Of Things That Become Food," where Probyn writes about the popularity of an Australian television show about a kangaroo named Skippy and how "Skippy" has become slang for Australians. Probyn argues that few Australians eat kangaroo, an aversion that has to do with a different culturally ingrained association: kangaroo meat is pet food. I have yet to encounter pet food made with beaver meat. Despite how unpopular it is in Australia, there is a kangaroo meat industry, which exports 80 per cent of the meat. There has never been a beaver meat industry in Canada. Still, the connections are worth pondering, as they suggest that despite long histories as food, once certain animals are commoditized for materials other than human food, these histories become muddled (36).

29 "Michael Farnan."

30 Berland, "The Work of the Beaver," 25.

31 Ibid., 27.

32 *The Beaver: Canada's History Magazine* changed its name in 2010 to *Canada's History*. Reasons behind the change include the word's many meanings, as well as spam filters ("The Beaver Gets a New Name," CBC).

33 Sangster, "'The Beaver' as Ideology," 191.

34 Ibid., 192.
35 Barbeau, "The Beaver in Canadian Art," 14.
36 Ibid.
37 Fee, "Rewriting Anthropology and Identifications on the North Pacific Coast," 19.
38 Ibid., 14.
39 The 1928 film *Beaver People*, made by the National Parks branch of the Department of the Interior, featured the controversial figure Grey Owl and his relationship with beavers, including his advocacy for conservation. For more, see chapter 6, "'They Taught Me Much': Imposture, Animism, Ecosystem, and Archibald Belaney/Grey Owl (1888–1938)," in Fee's *Literary Land Claims* and chapter 5, "Ecologist," in Poliquin's *Beaver*.
40 Examples include the Beaverhall Group, the Beaverbrook Gallery, the logos of Bell Media and Parks Canada, Beaver Lake in Vancouver's Stanley Park, and Le Lac aux Castor in Montreal's Parc du Mont-Royal.
41 Daybreak Kamloops, "Illegal Hunting Starting Early this Season," CBC News.
42 "Food Safety and Quality Act, 2001, S.O. 2001, c. 20."
43 Richler, "Wild about Eating Game."
44 McWilliams, *A Revolution in Eating*, 8.
45 Roberts, "'The Snipe Were Good and the Wine Not Bad,'" 62.
46 It is estimated that when the fur trade began, about six million beavers lived across what is now Canada. By the mid-1800s, the species was nearing extinction. At the trade's peak, 100,000 pelts a year were sent to Europe. Luckily for the beaver, the fashion in hats changed from fur to silk. Thriving populations of beavers live across Canada today ("Beaver," *The Canadian Encyclopedia*).
47 Richler, *My Canada Includes Foie Gras*, 113.
48 Dammann and Johns, *True North*, 49.
49 Derek Dammann, phone call with the author, 10 August 2016.
50 Humphreys, "Controversial Montreal Chef Martin Picard's New Book."
51 Panetta, "Martin Picard's Squirrel Sushi and Braised Beaver."
52 *Anthony Bourdain*.
53 Roy and Ali, *From Pemmican to Poutine*, 91.
54 Salminen, "Cook It Raw Alberta."
55 Salminen, "Hunting for the Future."
56 Salminen, "Cook It Raw Alberta."

Bibliography

Aldred, Jessica. "Scotland Wild Beaver Reintroduction Trial 'An Outstanding Success.'" *The Guardian*, 14 May 2014. www.theguardian.com/environment/2014/may/14/scotland-wild-beaver-reintroduced-knapdale.

Anthony Bourdain: Parts Unknown. Season 1, episode 4, "Canada." Aired 5 May 2013 on CNN.

Barbeau, Marius. "The Beaver in Canadian Art." *The Beaver* (September 1941): 14–18.

"Beaver." *The Canadian Encyclopedia*. Accessed 4 February 2016. www.thecanadianencyclopedia.ca/en/article/beaver/.

Berland, Jody. "The Work of the Beaver." In *Material Cultures in Canada*, edited by Thomas Allen and Jennifer Blair, 25–49. Waterloo: Wilfrid Laurier University Press, 2015.

Campbell-Palmer, Róisín, Derek Gow, Robert Needham, Simon Jones, and Frank Rosell. *The Eurasian Beaver*. Exeter, UK: Perlagic Publishing, 2015.

Casselman, Bill. "Canadian Food Words." Accessed 26 January 2016. www.billcasselman.com/canadian_food_words/cfw_five.html.

CBC. "The Beaver Gets a New Name." *CBC News*, 12 January 2010. www.cbc.ca/news/canada/manitoba/the-beaver-gets-a-new-name-1.865851.

Dammann, Derek, and Chris Johns. *True North: Canadian Cooking from Coast to Coast*. Toronto: HarperCollins, 2015.

Daybreak Kamloops. "Illegal Hunting Starting Early this Season." *CBC News*, 11 September 2015. www.cbc.ca/news/canada/british-columbia/illegal-hunting-starting-early-this-season-1.3224570.

Driver, Elizabeth. "Regional Differences in the Canadian Daily Meal? Cookbooks Answer the Question." In *What's to Eat? Entrées in Canadian Food History*, edited by Nathalie Cooke, 197–212. Montreal and Kingston: McGill-Queen's University Press, 2009.

Duncan, Dorothy. *Canadians at Table: A Culinary History of Canada: Food, Fellowship, and Folklore*. Toronto: Dundurn Press, 2006.

Fee, Margery. *Literary Land Claims: The "Indian Land Question" from Pontiac's War to Attawapiskat*. Waterloo: Wilfrid Laurier University Press, 2015.

– "Rewriting Anthropology and Identifications on the North Pacific Coast: The Work of George Hunt, William Beynon, Franz Boas, and Marius Barbeau." *Australian Literary Studies* 25, no. 4 (2010): 17–32. http://dx.doi.org/10.20314/als.1e6b7d2349.

– "Stories of Traditional Aboriginal Food, Territory, and Health." In *What's to Eat? Entrées in Canadian Food History*, edited by Nathalie Cooke, 55–78. Montreal and Kingston: McGill-Queen's University Press, 2009.

Flakerty, David H., and Frank E. Manning, eds. *The Beaver Bites Back? American Popular Culture in Canada*. Montreal and Kingston: McGill-Queen's University Press, 1993.

Fox, Mary Lou. *Nishnabe Delights*. Serpent River Indian Reserve, Cutler, ON: Woodlands Studio, 1975.

Genest, Michele. *The Boreal Feast: A Culinary Journey through the North*. Madeira Park, BC: Lost Moose, 2014.

George, Andrew, Jr. *Modern Native Feast: Healthy, Innovative, Sustainable Cuisine*. Vancouver: Arsenal Pulp Press, 2013.

George, Andrew, Jr, and Robert Gairns. *Feast! Canadian Native Cuisine for All Seasons*. Toronto: Doubleday Canada, 1997.

– *Feast for All Seasons: Traditional Native Peoples' Cuisine*. Vancouver: Arsenal Pulp Press, 2010.

Goldman, Jason G. "Once upon a Time, the Catholic Church Decided That Beavers Were Fish." *Scientific American*, 23 May 2013. https://blogs.scientificamerican.com/thoughtful-animal/once-upon-a-time-the-catholic-church-decided-that-beavers-were-fish/.

Gora, L. Sasha. "Beaver as Offal: The Presence and Absence of Beaver in Canadian Cuisine." In *Proceedings of the Oxford Symposium on Food & Cookery 2016*, edited by Mark McWilliams, 200–10. London: Prospect Books, 2017.

Government of Canada. "Official Symbols of Canada." Last updated 12 January 2016. http://canada.pch.gc.ca/eng/1444070816842.

Health Canada. *Eating Well With Canada's Food Guide: First Nations, Inuit and Métis*. Ottawa: Health Canada, 2007.

Humphreys, Adrian. "Controversial Montreal Chef Martin Picard's New Book Includes Recipes for 'Squirrel Sushi' and 'Confederation Beaver.'" *National Post*, 2 March 2012. http://news.nationalpost.com/news/canada/controversial-montreal-chef-martin-picards-new-book-includes-recipes-for-squirrel-sushi-and-confederation-beaver.

Jørgensen, Dolly. "Beavers Are Back in England." *The Return of Native Nordic Fauna*, 1 April 2015. http://dolly.jorgensenweb.net/nordicnature/?p=2153.

– "Beaver for Lent." *The Return of Native Nordic Fauna*, 19 April 2014. http://dolly.jorgensenweb.net/nordicnature/?p=1568.

– "When the Past Obscures the Past." *The Return of Native Nordic Fauna*, 24 August 2014. http://dolly.jorgensenweb.net/nordicnature/?p=1816.

Kenneally, Rhona Richman. "The Cuisine of the Tundra: Towards a Canadian Food Culture at Expo 67." *Food, Culture & Society* 11, no. 3 (2008): 287–313.

Kurtness, Manuel Kak'wa. *Pachamama: Cuisine des Premières Nations*. Quebec City: Les Editions du Boreal, 2009.

Lovesick Lake Native Women's Association. *The Rural and Native Heritage Cookbook: The Gathering*. Selwyn, ON: Lovesick Lake Native Women's Association, 1985.

McWilliams, James E. *A Revolution in Eating: How the Quest for Food Shaped America.* New York: Columbia University Press, 2005.

Menu "La Toundra," ca 1967, M2004.156.2 (C285/B1.1, Box 3), McCord Museum.

"Michael Farnan." *oh-oh canada.* Accessed 10 October 2016. http://ohohcanada.ca/michael-farnan.

Moosemeat & Marmalade. "About the Show." Accessed 10 October 2016. http://moosemeatandmarmalade.com/about-the-show/.

Moosemeat & Marmalade. Season 1, episode 1, "Beaver and the Boys." Aired 2015, on APTN.

Morrison, Jeff. *The Wild Game Cookbook.* Edmonton: Company's Coming Publishing Limited, 2014.

Nightingale, Marie. *Out of Old Nova Scotia Kitchens.* Halifax: Petheric Press, 1970.

Norman, Alison. "'Fit for the Table of the Most Fastidious Epicure': Culinary Colonialism in the Upper Canadian Contact Zone." In *Edible Histories, Cultural Politics: Towards a Canadian Food History*, edited by Franca Iacovetta, Marlene Epp, and Valerie Korinek, 31–51. Toronto: University of Toronto Press, 2009.

Ontario Regulation. "Food Safety and Quality Act, 2001, S.O. 2001, c. 20." Last updated 1 July 2014. www.ontario.ca/laws/regulation/050031.

Panetta, Alexander. "Martin Picard's Squirrel Sushi and Braised Beaver in New Cookbook." *Huffington Post*, 3 January 2012. www.huffingtonpost.ca/2012/03/01/martin-picard-squirrel-sushi_n_1313474.html.

People of 'Ksan, *Gathering What the Great Nature Provided: Food Traditions of the Gitksan.* Seattle: University of Washington Press, 1980.

Picard, Martin. *Au Pied de Cochon Sugar Shack.* Montreal: Au Pied Du Cochon, 2012.

Poliquin, Rachel. *Beaver.* London: Reaktion Books, 2015.

Probyn, Elspeth. "Eating Roo: Of Things That Become Food." *New Formations* 74 (2011): 33–45.

Richler, Jacob. *My Canada Includes Foie Gras: A Culinary Life.* Toronto: Viking, 2012.

– "Wild about Eating Game." *Maclean's*, 28 October 2012. www.macleans.ca/society/life/wild-about-game/.

Roberts, Julia. "'The Snipe Were Good and the Wine Not Bad': Enabling Public Life for Privileged Men." In *Edible Histories, Cultural Politics: Towards a Canadian Food History*, edited by Franca Iacovetta, Valerie Korinek, and Marlene Epp, 52–69. Toronto: University of Toronto Press, 2012.

Rose, Nick. "Eating Beaver in Search of Canadian Cuisine." MUNCHIES, 17 November 2015. https://munchies.vice.com/en/articles/eating-beaver-in-search-of-canadian-cuisine.

Roy, Suman, and Brooke Ali. *From Pemmican to Poutine: A Journey through Canada's Culinary History*. Toronto: The Key Publishing House Inc., 2010.

Salminen, Edith. "Cook It Raw Alberta and the Art of Slowing Down." *munchies*, 15 September 2015. https://munchies.vice.com/en/articles/cook-it-raw-alberta-and-the-art-of-slowing-down.

– "Hunting for the Future at Cook It Raw Alberta." *munchies*, 16 November 2015. https://munchies.vice.com/en/articles/hunting-for-the-future-at-cook-it-raw-alberta.

Sangster, Jane. "'The Beaver' as Ideology: Constructing Images of Inuit and Native Life in Post–World War II Canada." *Anthropologica* 49, no. 2 (2007): 191–209.

Watts, Dolly, and Annie Watts. *Where People Feast: An Indigenous People's Cookbook*. Vancouver: Arsenal Pulp Press, 2007.

Wilmshurst, Sara. "How to Eat Like a Canadian: Centennial Cookbooks and Visions of Culinary Identity." *CuiZine: The Journal of Canadian Food Cultures* 4, no. 2 (2013).

PART TWO
(Sub)Urban/Rural Imaginations
Producing and Representing Foodscapes

The five essays in Part 2 bring to light culinary imaginations' intricate involvement in the creation of urban, suburban, and rural environments. The contributors examine, produce, and represent past and contemporary foodscapes through both collective and individual sensibilities, engaging Canada's distinct and multi-faceted geography as a launching point for conversations about space, place, and food. In her case study of Montreal and culinary place-making, Nathalie Cooke touches on issues of cultural and linguistic heterogeneity, literary and popular culture, landmark cookbooks and restaurants, tourism, and the enduring sway of imagined food despite the city's changing demographics and geography. Moving from the urban to the suburban, artist Sylvia Grace Borda recreates disappearing rural spaces through digital technologies. Theorizing what she calls "Agri-art," Borda constructs food-producing landscapes through her multi-dimensional photographs and use of the Google Street View technology positing that while farming is not part of urbanites' routines, it is essential and merits attentive interaction. Continuing the discussion within a spectrum of rural-urban spaces, Wendy Roy examines Timothy Taylor's novel *Stanley Park* and protagonist-chef Jeremy Papier's commitment to locally sourced ingredients as a way of declaring allegiance to one particular place. Papier's decolonizing and ecocritical approach to food is similar to the one that informs the art practice of Surrey-based artists Cora and Don Li-Leger. In an interview relating their community activism through the creation of a food-sharing garden and medicine wheel, the Li-Legers reveal how the category "earth art" can be expanded and transformed to activate and nourish suburban neighbourhoods. Finally, Angela Ferreira considers food-as-spectacle through Calgary's Ghost River Theatre and its production *Taste*. A performance that magnifies the senses while raising awareness about sustainability, *Taste* facilitates creative exchanges among chefs, patrons, wait staff, audiences, and actors as they contemplate Albertan cuisine within an urban restaurant setting.

6

Montreal in the Culinary Imagination

Nathalie Cooke

Noah Richler argues that "Nowhere" becomes "Somewhere" through art, which is essential to a landscape's coming into consciousness. "The sum of stories that are told about or in a particular landscape," he writes, "create an impression of a place that is imaginary, but functions as any map would, for places are as real as persons, but they have no voice and so they speak to us through art."[1] In the case of Montreal, the city most famously sprang to life in pages penned by Hugh MacLennan, Brian Moore, Mordecai Richler, Gabrielle Roy, F.R. Scott, and Michel Tremblay, among others. Just as its writers mapped Montreal's peoples and streetscapes, so too they wrote about Montreal's distinctive foodways. Photographers and illustrators captured the idiosyncratic characters and animals – yes, live animals – that animated Montreal's restaurant food scene.

Consequently, this study asks, how do Montreal foodways – real, represented, and imagined – work in the construction and stabilization (or destabilization) of place. In what ways were and are Montreal's foodways represented in the culinary imagination? What can such literary maps tell us about Montreal cuisine, and what has shaped Montrealers' food choices? To answer such questions, this study adopts a definition of place that emerges in the 1970s from humanistic geography, one that conceptualizes space as "a particular location that has acquired a set of meanings and attachments."[2] As T. Cresswell explains, "while space was the favored object of the spatial scientist (and is still the favored object of social theorists), it is the way space becomes endowed with human meaning and is transformed into place that lies at the heart of humanistic geography." Cresswell adds that "this is the most important contribution of humanistic geography to the discipline – the distinction between an abstract realm of space and an experienced and felt world of place."[3] However, the particular notion of place discussed here gains nuance from later geographical commentators like Doreen Massey, who points out that places are constantly in process, dynamic sites that are part of the comings and goings of mobile societies.[4] Place, for Massey, is the function of practice and careful nurturing, its identity woven from the threads of, among other things, creative cultural productions, including a diversity of literary forms – in addition to such other literary forms as anecdote, folklore, brand literature, tourist narrative, and popular fiction.[5] Seen through this lens, and with a specific focus on the city's culinary sense of place, Montreal has become a city closely identified with distinctive food traditions, one known predominantly for the more popular and affordable foodstuffs like Montreal bagels and smoked meat, in addition to the culinary sophistication of some of Canada's best restaurants.

Using Montreal as an example, this study argues that the culinary imagination is not only mimetic in the sense of representing socio-historical and cultural context but also *constitutive* of place itself. That is, the city's cultural productions actually contribute to shaping as well as articulating a sense of place (where place is understood according to usage in the field of human geography). Examples explored here include cookbooks, restaurant histories, and interviews with chefs, in addition to Gabrielle Roy's popular novel set in Montreal, *Bonheur d'occasion* (*The Tin Flute*), a historical commentary on the Montreal fire by Afua Cooper, and an acerbic poem about Montreal's language politics seen through the lens of a food menu by F.R. Scott.

In particular, through an extended glance at the role of Jewish foods and foodways in Montreal's culinary imaginary, including a discussion of the endurance of Jewish foodways within the city via the restaurants, popular/iconic food items, and literary stories despite the city's changing demographics, this study points to the *enduring* hold of certain "culinary imaginaries." In this way, the city's culinary cultural productions are *constitutive* of place, where place is understood to be both process and practice. Further, the case study of Montreal reveals that the culinary imagination is at once, and paradoxically, *dynamic and enduring*. In the case of Montreal it seems like the culinary imagination holds sway – and carries certain imaginaries *through* time, *across* space, and *between* cultural groups – even as demographics shift, neighbourhoods evolve, and new food imaginings enter the mix.

What Is the Culinary Imagination?

Like other contributions to this collection, my study of Montreal necessarily poses the central question: what is the culinary imagination? W.W. Norton describes a recent book by Sandra Gilbert by that same title, *The Culinary Imagination*, as tracing "the social, aesthetic, and political history of food"[6] – food's connotations, in other words, as much as its denotations. Bee Wilson's review of Gilbert's book further emphasizes the second word in the phrase "culinary imagination," tracing Gilbert's scrutiny of the "allure" and pleasure of "imaginary" food.[7] For Wilson, as for Gilbert, the allure is not food itself, but rather its possibilities, and particularly as they are unleashed and realized in and through human imagination.

Perhaps the most potent illustration of the potential of cultural production to imbue foods with significance involves iconic foods. Jennifer Berg notes that "specific icon foods, when consumed or even just imagined, immediately suggest links to specific places, culturally bound groups, or communities."[8] Elsewhere I have argued that Expo 67 and Canada's centennial year prompted a "period of intense introspection (which continues to our own day) in which Canadians began to review and revise their culinary practices past and present – to reconceive food (sometimes retrospectively) as symbol of self, community and nation; to bestow upon humble food items (such as Red Fife wheat, the donut, tourtière, the butter tart, and, most recently, poutine) the burden of iconicity."[9] Pemmican should also certainly have been added to this list of iconic Canadian foods. There are certainly other iconic foods that evoke a particular region in Canada rather than the nation itself. Suman Roy and Brooke Ali organize their "journey through Canada's culinary history" around either foods that are sourced in particular regions or dishes traditionally prepared only in particular regions in Canada, and that therefore take on iconic status.[10] They include foods like scallops from Mahone Bay in Nova Scotia, potatoes from Prince Edward Island, maple syrup from Quebec, Saskatoon berries from Saskatchewan, and salmon from the West Coast. Examples of traditional and regional dishes include Newfoundland's Figgy Duff; Son-of-a-Gun-in-a-Sack from the Prairies; or Nanaimo Bars, which take their name from Nanaimo on Vancouver Island.

That these and other foods have gained iconic status is thanks to various kinds of cultural productions, including food histories and cookbooks like that of Roy and Ali, as well as oral histories, folklore, and marketing narratives to invite settlers (especially at the turn of the twentieth century) and later tourists to appreciate the country's bounty.

A Montreal Focus

Consequently, as we turn our attention to Montreal, it is useful to consider some of the narratives currently being offered to tourists interested in Montreal's culinary heritage. Most obviously, Montreal is one of the top sites of culinary tourism in Canada; restaurants Toqué!, Joe Beef, and Au Pied de Cochon have impressive reputations both nationally and internationally.[11] Gail Simmons writes in her introduction to *Montreal Cooks*, the "city has a very long history as a culinary destination for food lovers not only within Canada but from around the world. The ritual of eating good food and enjoying life is second nature to Montrealers. Trends may change, tastes may evolve, but our culinary scene will forever be incomparable."[12] In 2007, *Travelocity* editors published their top ten destinations for gourmet travellers, commonly referred to as foodies. Montreal, ranked sixth, is the only Canadian city to have made the list.[13] According to American travel guide *Frommer's*, Montreal ranked among the ten best cities for outdoor dining in 2011.[14] Fodor's lists Taste Montreal as one of the world's fifteen top food festivals.[15] In 2010, Statistics Canada showed that Montreal's tourists spent CA$548 million on restaurant dining. In 2011, in the touristic boroughs of Ville-Marie and the Plateau-Mont-Royal, there were on average 83.9 restaurants and 11.5 bars per square kilometre.[16] A similar emphasis on dining as preferential tourist activity in Montreal emerges from evidence that the average tourist spent CA$65.47 on restaurants per stay in Montreal in 2010; for the same period, the average tourist spent CA$54.81 on restaurants per stay in Canada.[17] However, this may be in part because in 2009 the average Montreal dinner (three courses, no drink, service included) cost CA$43 compared to CA$34 in Toronto.[18] Certainly, the Canadian dollar relative to its American counterpart makes Montreal all the more attractive as a tourist destination for American travellers.

Culinary tours of Montreal are popular and include such offerings as the Jewish Museum's "Beyond the Bagel" food tour of Montreal's Jewish culinary sites, and the Local Montréal Food Tour Company's tours of Old Montreal, Montreal's working class and multicultural Mile End district in the Plateau-Mont-Royal Borough, and the city's craft beer scene.[19] 'Round Table Tours provides an array of tours given on foot and on bicycles, including their "Iconic Dishes: Jewish Montreal, The Original Tour," "Circuit of Tapas: Iberian Montreal" food tour, and the "Sustaining City: Montreal's Living Table" biking tour.[20]

What these tours reveal is the way food and food venues have figured in Montreal's complex cultural and socio-ideological negotiations, and also the way they served and continue to serve as means of communication and bridge between Montreal's varied and distinct communities. To expand on the first: food provides an effective angle for approaching and understanding Montreal's history. Not only is the topic of interest to tourists, but it also serves as a concrete indicator of changing ideas and practices over time. Closer scrutiny of Montreal's food venues and their clienteles provides detailed glimpses of Montreal's evolution. To expand on the second point: intriguingly given the sometimes fractious relationship between Montreal's different cultural communities, foods that have taken on iconic status in Montreal are ones that appealed to those outside the particular community responsible for their origin. Indeed, the culinary imagination in Montreal seems remarkably "mobile," limited not so much to a particular location or specific moment in time but rather to *place* – that more fluid and subtle notion emerging from human geography.

Iconic Food Venues in Montreal

Popular tour operator Melissa Simard of 'Round Table Tours[21] offers three wonderful anecdotes about Montreal's colourful food history, which both engage listeners on her tours and serve here as useful starting points for further exploration of the relationship between the city of Montreal and its cultural imaginary.

First, she reminds tour participants of the success of the iconic Joe Beef Canteen.[22] The canteen was situated first along Montreal's waterfront on St Claude Street[23] and as of 1876 on Common Street, a bit further west.[24] Simard points out that the proprietor supported striking workers constructing the Lachine Canal, thereby becoming a local hero. During December 1877, he not only sent two wagonloads of food for the striking workers but also distributed bread to the soldiers, who ultimately in the spirit of things, shared it amongst the workers themselves.[25] Joe Beef – the proprietor Charles McKiernan's nickname – supported his working-class clientele in other ways as well. He kept a few bills tucked near the bar in his establishment in order to pay fines for his regular customers. Most of these were day labourers, and a jail sentence had dire consequences for their families.[26] His canteen housed workers needing a roof over their heads and provided for those needing a place to convalesce. Historian Peter DeLottinville argues that McKiernan, the tavern's owner, was able to leverage the tavern's role as a forum for the working-class community of Montreal.[27] "His role in alleviating problems of housing, job hunting, health care, and labour unrest indicated the possibility of a collective response to the common problems among casual labourers of Montreal's waterfront."[28] Arguably, Joe Beef's legacy in Montreal's cultural imaginary is one of social advocacy. The canteen initially took its energy from Charles McKiernan's big character. Then in 1893, after changing hands in 1889, the establishment became the base of the Salvation Army. That change signalled the entrance of middle-class reformers into discussions and initiatives to improve the lives of the working class.

Current-day restaurateurs David McMillan and Frédéric Morin adopted the name Joe Beef for their establishment to honour the nineteenth-century canteen. There is certainly an informal vibe to this contemporary restaurant, with McMillan confessing to wearing shorts and sandals and claiming "we're these hilbillies that have a garden out back."[29] However, ranking eighty-first on the 2015 list of *The World's 50 Best Restaurants* (which unintuitively provides a top 100 list annually), the contemporary iteration has proven itself focused on the quality of food, and has consequently appealed to a clientele enjoying culinary sophistication.[30] Nevertheless, both restaurateurs are careful to emphasize not so much the working-class ethic associated with Joe Beef's own legacy as an expansive, down-to-earth character, which they astutely equate with Canada's own national character. If Joe Beef in the nineteenth-century provided a venue and voice for Montreal's working class, then the owners of Joe Beef in the twenty-first century place themselves and their enterprise squarely in the national culinary imaginary. About the award, for example, McMillan explained: "I think it's very un-Canadian to pop Champagne bottles. There'll be an extra beer for everyone tonight."[31] That beer is more Canadian than Champagne, of course, owes much to Canada's long-standing tradition of brewing beer, but also to its iconic status as a national drink, cemented with Molson Canadian's hugely popular advertisement, "I am Canadian."[32] That the restaurant is the brainchild of a partnership between an anglophone (David McMillan) and a francophone (Frédéric Morin) extends the claim to reaching across the linguistic solitudes in Montreal, Canada's largest bilingual city.

One final link between the two restaurants includes a nod in the contemporary restaurant to its historical forebear. During McKiernan's time, the canteen served

MONTREAL IN THE CULINARY IMAGINATION

Figure 6.1
[Bear Pit illustration] Charles McKiernan, ca 1835–1889, *Joe Beef of Montreal, the Son of the People*, 1879 or 1880, Montreal: Charles McKiernan, Broadside, printed in three columns; includes text and thirteen wood engravings, some signed by J. Walker.

as a meeting place, where the local community could come together for food and conversation, certainly, even for aid, but also for recreation. The original canteen was home to an enormous variety of animals – monkeys, parrots, and most famously alcohol-loving bears Jenny and Tom, among others. One article from 1879 recounts the alarming time when McKiernan's six-year-old son accidentally fell into the bear pit to be rescued by his father, who suffered a very nasty gash on his leg.[33] But it was ultimately a buffalo that caused difficulty for Charles McKiernan, injuring him to the extent that he needed a stint in the hospital.[34] There are two stuffed animal heads in the contemporary restaurant. One is that of a bear, supposedly one of the bears McKiernan kept chained in the basement of the original restaurant.[35] The other is a curiosity – a large stuffed bison head in the main bathroom. This seems not to be a reference to McKiernan's buffalo, however, but rather a curiosity offered as a gift by loyal customer Joe Battat.[36]

Ironically enough, then, although the restaurant name suggests a preoccupation with a particular foodstuff – beef – the culinary imaginary surrounding Joe Beef past and present showcases the restaurateurs, and their ability to leverage their establishments to become platforms for outreach, advocacy, and community engagement. There are two other restaurants in Montreal that are all about a particular food product, indeed one of Quebec's most iconic foods: pork. Catherine Turgeon-Gouin rightly points out that the narrative of Quebec's traditional foodways serves as foundation for Martin Picard's Montreal restaurant, Au Pied de Cochon, which has become a tourist draw in its own right. Turgeon-Gouin goes on to argue that Picard's menu transforms Quebec's culinary traditions to appeal to an urban clientele, and what Turgeon-Gouin describes as "bohemian-bourgeois" or "bobo" ideals:[37] "Au Pied de Cochon, with its ingredient and menu choices, decor, and overall atmosphere, is steeped in Québec tradition. From the jovial attitude and lumberjack plaid-shirt attire of its owner to the flow of maple syrup on pork cooked from nose to tail, the Montreal restaurant relishes Québec folklore." She goes on to argue that "concerns about promoting *La belle province's* gastronomical culture permeate the entire book [*Au Pied de Cochon: L'Album*] as well as Picard's discourse. Au Pied de Cochon's project uses for its basic narrative the cuisine and folklore of Québec."

If Picard's Au Pied de Cochon has become a welcome attraction for Montreal and finds its home in the city, it is really more precisely one of a number of articulations of the provincial (rather than urban) culinary imaginary. Another would be the long-running restaurant Au Petit Poucet, with a menu steeped in pork-related offerings, in Val David, north of Montreal. By contrast, there was one iconic Montreal food venue that focused its attention not so much on pork as on the piglet. Like Joe Beef of the nineteenth century, it included live animals as part of its recreational offerings: piglets, in this case, often bedecked in ribbons, who entertained customers by feeding from the bottles they were invited to give them. More than 2,500 photographs were taken of such diners at a restaurant called Au Lutin qui Bouffe between 1938 and 1972, when the restaurant situated at the corner of St Hubert and St Grégoire burned down. In this venue it was the piglets, likely more than the food itself, that served to stimulate conversation and congenial interaction.

Figure 6.2
Feeding the piglet at Au Lutin qui Bouffe, 18 October 1947: Jessie Wilson, Neil Compton, Silvia Freddi, William Compton, Pauline (Freddi) Compton, Floss (Wilson) Freddi.

Montreal Bagels and Smoked Meat

Tour operator Melissa Simard shares two other anecdotes that revolve around Montreal's Jewish culinary scene, and both illustrate ways in which that cuisine is shared beyond the Jewish community. One is about a beloved Montreal food venue, the iconic deli Wilensky's. Simard explains that Moe Wilensky, proprietor of the diner lovingly commemorated in Mordecai Richler's Montreal fiction, never cut his "special" smoked meat sandwiches because he was a communist and believed that nobody should receive special treatment.[38] The second anecdote signals an apparent curiosity: that Jewish and Chinese communities co-populated what is now Chinatown in Montreal, an area situated south of René Lévesque Boulevard and north of Old Montreal.³⁹ This often comes as a surprise even to Montrealers largely because, as Christopher Dewolf points out, Chinatown's Jewish heritage has been erased by "time and redevelopment," as Chinese immigration increased after the easing of immigration restrictions, and as the Jewish population of Montreal gradually moved to neighbourhoods further west and north.⁴⁰

Tamara Myers sheds light on the enormous influx of Jewish immigrants to Montreal at the turn of the twentieth century, such that Montreal's Jewish population grew "from 881 in 1881 to more than 45,000 on the island in 1921."⁴¹ The *Histoire de Montréal depuis la Confédération*, source for Myers's insight, also notes that the Jewish population grew between 1921 and 1941 – from 45,792 to 63,898 – but this increase was less significant in terms of demographic shift. Drawing on the censuses of 1921, 1931, and 1941, Linteau observes that Montreal Jews tended to cluster in the city (93 per cent in 1921 and 80 per cent in 1941).⁴² It is understandable then that during the earlier period at the turn of century, Montreal's downtown would have been a thriving hub of Jewish culture. Writes Dewolf: "At its peak in the 1910s, Yiddish-language cultural life flourished in this downtown neighbourhood, with two bookstores on the Main, the newly-founded Jewish People's Library (the predecessor to the present-day Jewish Public Library) and a regular programming of socialist and Zionist lectures and Yiddish theatre at the Monument National. On Chenneville Street, about half of all residents were Jewish between 1900 and 1915."⁴³ However, the Jewish population of Montreal has dwindled over time in percentage terms since this "peak" period, such that in 2011, the National Household Survey revealed that of Montrealers reporting religious affiliation (85.1 per cent of the total population), only 2.2 per cent were identifying as Jewish, 5.9 per cent as Muslim, and 63.2 per cent as Roman Catholic.⁴⁴

Despite the small proportion of the Jewish population in Montreal, the city's multiple culinary tours of Jewish Montreal⁴⁵ suggest this particular cuisine continues to influence the "tastes of Montreal." Olivier Bauer points to the predominance of Jewish food establishments in a list provided by Pierre Bellerose, vice-president of public relations for Tourisme Montréal, on his 2011 blog. On his list of ten, the Jewish restaurateurs are: Fairmount Bagel (1919–), Schwartz's (1928–), Beauty's (1942–), Déli Lesters (1951–), St Viateur Bagel (1957–), and Moishes (1938–). That six out of ten are Jewish establishments is indeed striking.⁴⁶ Elsewhere, Bellerose writes that: "Is it possible for a journalist visiting Montreal's restaurants not to comment on the bagels, Schwartz's or La Binerie Mont-Royal, for instance? Our long Jewish and French-Canadian traditions, unique to North America, are reflected in the rustic counters of Schwartz's, La Binerie or Wilensky. They've become staples and have long since become part of our Montreal and Quebec's DNA, along with the tables of newer Quebecois chefs."[47] In other words, Montreal's culinary imaginary has embraced Jewish culinary traditions as its own.

In part, the popularity of Jewish venues can be attributed to the marketing successes of these establishments. Bertrand Cesvet offers a close study of the "Conversational Capital" that the small Hebrew delicatessen, Schwartz's, managed to develop. "Schwartz's enjoys incredible international word-of-mouth and an extremely loyal customer base. It has never employed *mass-marketing* techniques, and yet it continually draws in new customers while retaining its existing clientele. Show up any day of the year at lunchtime or dinner, and you are likely to stand in line outside on Saint-Laurent Boulevard."[48] For Cesvet, the ritual of standing in line is an integral part of the deli's success: waiting in line has become a ritual of initiation that "reinforces a feeling of *tribalism*."[49] More generally, Cesvet finds that Schwartz's checks all the boxes for producing the eight engines that drive conversational capital: Rituals and Tribalism (the queueing), Exclusive Product Offerings (the best smoked meat), Myths (did the recipe really come to Montreal from a Romanian Jew?), Relevant Sensory Oddity (aroma of grilled meat and spices), Icons (photos of the now late original owner, his family and friends, and of famous visitors), Endorsements (which include Céline Dion, Jean Chrétien, Ken Dryden, Halle Berry, Angelina Jolie, the Rolling Stones …), and Continuity (the deli's continuous presence in Montreal for decades). That's a lot of conversational capital for a single small Montreal delicatessen with a limited menu and minimal decor. In turn, Schwartz's success has become Montreal's success, as Montreal smoked meat has become an icon of Montreal foodways.

Olivier Bauer asks himself: "Bagels and smoked meat – some of the foods most closely identified with Montreal – are Ashkenazi Jewish in origin, yet Jews make up only 2 percent of Montreal's population. How did this happen?"[50] Such quick adoption of an ethnic foodway would indicate a fast track to what Susan Drucker describes as the fifth stage of immigrant cuisine's incorporation into the larger North American restaurant scene.[51] Bauer's answer is a practical one: Ashkenazi Jews settled on the border between French and English Montreal, offering affordable and hearty fare.[52] Bauer's explanation both points to the pertinence of geographer Doreen Massey's argument that places are sites of heterogeneity in relation to Montreal, and to one example of what Mary Pratt has called the "contact zone" in which cultural others brush up against one another. In suggesting this, I also point to the city's maps as tools through which one can begin to trace and understand the shifting boundaries of the sense of place understood to be "home," and to further conceptualize place as practice.

Interesting in themselves, Simard's two anecdotes about Montreal's Jewish heritage provide slightly different but consistent insights about ways that Jewish cuisine might have started to punch above its weight in Montreal's culinary imaginary: that Jewish food purveyors served a clientele that extended beyond the Jewish community, and that the Jewish community resided in close proximity to other cultural communities.

In particular, the close proximity of the Jewish and Chinese communities during the early twentieth century speaks to a larger North American urban phenomenon of alliances between Jewish and Chinese communities. This phenomenon is referenced by the American poet August Kleinzahler in his poem "Christmas in Chinatown," in which the poem's speaker muses on the experience of eating Chinese at Christmas, very much a part of contemporary life for Jewish North Americans since Chinese restaurants are some of the few establishments serving regular fare and open for business on the holiday.[53] The appeal of Chinese food for Jews, as fare that effectively functions as "safe treyf," is explored in detail by Tuchman and Levine.[54] Here "treyf" refers to food not authorized by the rules of Kashrut, whereas "safe" speaks to the possibility of the food "passing" as safe – or possibly allowing the willing suspension of disbelief – because of its unfamiliar configuration.

Although this is a larger North American phenomenon, Morton Weinfeld reminds us that Canadian Jewry is distinct from American Jewry.[55] One important distinction for Montreal Jewry in particular is the strong presence of French-speaking Jews, naturally drawn to a bilingual city in a country with French as one of its official languages. Consequently the relative proportion of Sephardic Jews to Ashkenazi Jews is much higher than in other North American cities, the Sephardim typically hailing from other French-speaking countries such as Morocco and parts of Africa.[56]

Artistic Renderings of Montreal Foodways

From Montreal's culinary reality has sprung lore and literature, even song. There is Mordecai Richler's Montreal, famously outlined in the novel *The Apprenticeship of Duddy Kravitz* and depicted in the film starring Richard Dreyfuss,[57] which has itself become the stuff of walking tours and tourist advertisements for the city. As readers of his works would know, Richler's home turf was Montreal's historic Mile End neighbourhood; a typical walking tour of Richler's favourite gastronomic haunts includes St Viateur Bagel Shop as well as Wilensky's, to name only a couple.[58] There is now also popular entertainment based on food establishments, including Bill Brownstein's popular book, *Schwartz's Hebrew Delicatessen: The Story*,[59] which inspired a recent musical also based on the iconic deli, Schwartz's, *Schwartz the Musical*.[60]

The startlingly unpoetic choice of topic for the musical based on Schwartz's deli leads to another question. What prompts playwrights, and authors more generally, to feed their characters? To gather their subjects to the kitchen and dining table? And what is the particular appeal of textual fare, the particular "allure" of imagined food, to use Bee Wilson's phrasing?[61]

Commentary on food in literature provides answers that fall into two broad categories: that authors use imaginary food in the service of precision and of artistic effect. First and most obviously, representations within the text of food served up in its transformed state serve as a vehicle for precision in characterization.[62] Detailed representations of food further add to a sense of the accurate rendering of socio-historical setting.[63] Second, at the level of the text, representations of food and metaphors involving food can serve either to support or challenge the text's formal and thematic frameworks.[64]

The case study of Montreal's iconic foods and food venues suggests that the culinary imagination is not only mimetic and constitutive of *notions* of socio-historical and cultural context but can also be understood as *constitutive* of place itself. In other words, our focus here on Montreal's foodways and cultural productions related to them enables us to extend existing commentary on the allure and function of imagined food.

How then can one prove that Montrealers' sense of their city has been shaped by its cultural productions? Let me begin to answer this question in relation to Gabrielle Roy's 1945 novel *Bonheur d'occasion* (translated as *The Tin Flute*), arguably Canada's first urban novel, for which Roy won the Prix Femina. *Bonheur d'occasion* is a novel in the realist tradition, offering a detailed glimpse into Montreal just prior to and during the start of the Second World War. In this novel, Montreal is described as being a part of the larger consumer society and its central characters find themselves on the lowest rungs of the consumer ladder. The consumer society is figured literally in this novel; food service and consumption set the stage in working-class Saint Henri. The young Florentine works as a waitress at the Five and Dime, surrounded by food. But her mother is unable, on the family's meagre earnings, to provide adequate nutrition to keep her children healthy. When war looms, those men who are nourished enough to pass the medical test are able to secure a wage for themselves, and to support their families. This novel's consistent emphasis on scenes of food scarcity and on instances that reveal unequal access to food build up a symbolic resonance for this novel about the perils of consumer society for those at the lower end of the food chain.[65] In this way, the novel's food scenes serve to both paint a strikingly accurate and haunting portrait of prewar Montreal, and also support and further the novel's symbolic structure.

How has Roy's novel served to shape notions of the city itself? When one walks around Saint Henri today, one seems to find references to that novel – a street and park bearing the name "Lacasse" – the surname of the family that figures in the novel, and one chosen for its relevance to a story about poverty centred on a family that is for much of the time, as the surname suggests, "broke."[66] But the street was actually named in 1907 to honour the parish priest, also named Lacasse, and not in reference to Roy's award-winning novel. Evidence of the novel's influence can be found elsewhere, however. Most obviously, there are walking tours of Gabrielle Roy's Montreal,[67] which signal the book's enduring popularity, and Montrealers' recognition that Roy's writerly imagination offers valuable glimpses of the city. As well, the novel's characters and places reverberate in the city's literary imagination. The protagonist in *My October* by Montrealer Claire Rothman, for example, returns to inhabit the real house that served as model for the home of Jean Lévesque in Roy's novel.[68]

One of the disturbing insights of Roy's novel is that the poorer classes were driven to war not out of conviction but out of necessity; they were figuratively fodder for the war machine. In another book about Montreal's history, the writer – this time a scholar writing a work of non-fiction – makes the link between humans and objects of consumption explicit. It goes without saying perhaps, but when fiction and non-fiction authors describe characters *as* food, rather than invite them to the dinner table, it is for marked effect. Here is Afua Cooper depicting what might have prompted black slave Angélique to set fire to her master's home, and eventually to much of Montreal, in the spring of 1734. Her act is a conscious one, intended to treat her slave masters to a literal dose of their own figurative medicine: "She would roast, burn, and grill them, and so do to them what they had been doing to her all her days. With determination, she blew hard on the coals on the cross beams, and they burst into flames."⁶⁹ The fire of Montreal is still widely believed to be an unsolved mystery.⁷⁰ But through this interjection of the culinary imagination in Cooper's scholarly work, Montreal's history and therefore our notion of place have been transformed in the same way that Montreal was transformed by that blaze. Through indirect narration, this passage demonstrates its affective quality – it suggests to the reader that Afua Cooper in the twenty-first century could channel the thoughts of Angélique in the eighteenth century. This too is an act of the narrative culinary imagination.

The Stories Books (and Food) Can Tell

Just as stories can be told through food, in the way that Roy and Cooper illustrate, so too can food function as a storytelling medium. This is particularly true when food is understood to be a primary vehicle for the celebration and continuance of cultural heritage. Two important Montreal cookbooks provide insights about changing attitudes towards food and cultural food practices over time. The first Canadian cookbook by a Jewish writer is *Household Recipes or Domestic Cookery* "by a Montreal Lady" (1865).⁷¹ Only one recipe hints at the author's cultural heritage and religious practice: a recipe for "ball soup," a version of the very familiar Ashkenazi matzoh ball soup, perhaps more colloquially known today as "Jewish chicken soup." By contrast, the very popular *A Treasure for My Daughter* (1950), in its fourteenth printing in 2013, is much more explicit about its cultural context. This text offers readers staple Jewish recipes such as Cold Beet Borscht and Noodle Kugel, and in doing so, asserts an important connection between the food we eat and cultural heritage.⁷² *A Treasure for My Daughter* is staged as a conversation between a mother and a daughter, where the mother passes on the legacy of food recipes and traditions to ensure their continuance. Eileen Solomon identifies this book as constituent of the process of cultural negotiation of Jewish communities in North America through the language of food.⁷³

For foods to tell their stories, of course, those "stories" and the "language" in which they are told have to be understood. The apprenticeship at the heart of *A Treasure for My Daughter* ensures that both the book's readers and "My Daughter" are recipients of culinary and cultural knowledge. But there are a number of moments when writers describe the inevitable misunderstandings in a city like Montreal, with its increasing cultural plurality, and where the stories food tells are not fully understood. In these moments, food scenes serve as sites of cultural negotiation. Poet F.R. Scott provides one wonderful example, where he includes food in his wry depiction of miscommunication between the two official languages and the people who represented them when he wrote this poem in 1954. Notice how he introduces the poem as one about two "cultures" rather than just two "languages," signalling already that the poem will touch on the intersections between a primarily Roman Catholic francophone population and an anglophone community that was primarily Protestant Christian, as well as between religious and secular rituals:

BONNE ENTENTE
The advantages of living with two cultures
Strike one at every turn,
Especially when one finds a notice in an office building:
"This elevator will not run on Ascension Day";
Or reads in the *Montreal Star*:
"Tomorrow being the Feast of the Immaculate Conception,
There will be no collection of garbage in the city";
Or sees on the restaurant menu the bilingual dish:
DEEP APPLE PIE
TARTE AUX POMMES PROFONDES[74]

Like the "profound" apples in Scott's pie, food is good to think as much as it is good to eat. Montreal, Canada's most bilingual city, is the site of significant and ongoing cultural negotiation – one that often takes place over food, just as much as it is described in the languages of food itself, and in cultural productions of the culinary imagination. The culinary imagination that Montreal conjures for itself, however, is one of inclusion. By writing this, and by signalling the strategic and self-conscious way a city (through its advocates) constructs a sense of its own place, I begin to align this study's notion of place more closely to that of critical cultural geography than humanistic geography because the former scrutinizes the way power is involved in the "construction, reproduction, and contestation of places and their meanings," to use Cresswell's phrasing of the particular subsection of the discipline's concerns.[75] So far in this study I have pointed to examples that signal food's role as catalyst for encounter between different cultural communities, and even between species (in the case of the original Joe Beef canteen). Additionally, the book written by current co-owners of Joe Beef in Montreal constructs a culinary tradition for Montreal that is inclusive of a variety of different culinary registers. Ian Mosby points out: "*The Art of Living According to Joe Beef* tries to overcome Montreal's fractured linguistic, ethnic, and class divisions through an appeal to a common history and a common love for delicious foods that extends beyond – but also necessarily includes – the usual gravy-covered and cheese-curded suspects. (You know who you are.)"[76] Mosby is particularly struck by the way McMillan and Morin gather together low with high culinary food traditions in their book, such that the blending itself becomes peculiar to Montreal's food scene: "Chip shacks and delis, for instance, are placed on as high a pedestal as groundbreaking Montreal restaurants like Toque! [*sic*] or Citrus. Recipes simultaneously look traditional and modern, high-end and low-class, French and English (and Jewish and Irish and Haitian and many of the other groups that make up contemporary Montreal) and therefore range from the fanciful tongue-in-cheek high/low hybrids like Pork Fish Sticks or a Fois Gras Breakfast Sandwich to the more traditional and straightforward Pate en Croute, Schnitzel of Pork, or Chicken Jalfrezi."[77] When asked about pivotal moments in Montreal's food scene, journalist Julian Armstrong, whose career has been devoted to chronicling Quebec's foodways, identifies 1967 as such a time.[78] Not only did Montreal's Expo bring the world and its varied cuisines to Montreal's door but it also brought the world's chefs to Montreal. She points to Peter Mueller in particular who, as she describes it, was one of a number of chefs who came from abroad, ran the restaurants of their countries at Expo, and then restaurants in Montreal, thereby launching Montreal as a more international food city. "Prior to that," Armstrong explains, "French and maybe a smattering of Chinatown restaurants would have been about it internationally."[79] Scrutiny of census data alongside Yellow Pages listings confirms Armstrong's sense of the times. Alan Nash found that between 1951 and 1971 in Montreal, there was a 244 per cent increase in the total number of ethnic restaurants in the city, with those serving Italian, Greek, and Chinese cuisine showing a marked rise in percentage share and those serving European or Jewish cuisine experiencing a decline.[80]

Mueller himself describes the restaurant scene in Montreal of the 1960s as being about "huge portions ... big plates full of steak and potatoes ... sixteen or twenty ounce portions without finesse. Cuisine chez grand mère."[81] Slowly, he explains, it became more "gourmand." Certainly he, along with the other European expat chefs in Montreal, played a lead hand in this development. Armstrong describes Peter Mueller as "a huge bon vivant, a natural leader, I think, and much liked."[82] Mueller had actually come from Switzerland to Montreal in 1962, and ran the restaurant in the Queen Elizabeth Hotel before being transferred to Vancouver. But he came back to Montreal to manage the restaurant in the Swiss Pavilion at Expo 67, where he recalls that the 140-person staff served an astonishing number of clients, usually between 2,100 and 2,200 per day. After Expo, Mueller joined the William Tell Restaurant, which had been floundering. Under his direction, and later with another Swiss-born chef, Anton Koch, as his chef de cuisine, the restaurant flourished and became central to Montreal's culinary scene. After lunch service, top chefs from the city's key restaurant venues would gather at the William Tell for conversation over "coffee cake, kirsch, and beer," as Mueller recalls. These included Albert Schnell (of the Queen Elizabeth Hotel), Christian Hitz (of the Château Champlain), Hans Burry (of the Mount Royal Hotel), Raymond Ferri (of the Mount Royal Club), and Carlo dell Olio (of the Windsor Hotel). Says Koch, "it was an amazing era for the chefs, who found each other here, and built a circle."[83] Peter Mueller explains that whereas today important restaurants are stand-alone establishments, during the 1960s and 1970s, they were largely affiliated with hotels.[84] In Montreal of 2020 there are signs that this may be changing, however, with such excellent restaurants as Rosélys in Fairmont The Queen Elizabeth Hotel and Maison Boulud in the Ritz-Carlton. Anton Koch also recalls that European chefs, with the exception of Quebec executive chef Pierre Demers (of the Ritz), ran most of the important restaurants.[85] This would slowly change with the opening of ITHQ, the Institut de tourisme et d'hôtellerie du Québec.

David McMillan – chef, history buff, and co-owner of the current-day restaurant Joe Beef – argues that, more specifically, the French expat chefs in particular contributed significantly. "These are the pillars of Montreal cuisine," to his mind.[86] But McMillan also points to one other shining light in the Montreal restaurant scene: Normand Laprise, who opened Citrus in 1989 and then the legendary Toqué!. "Toqué! was a meeting place for chefs young and old," remembers McMillan. "It was like the Bohemian movement in Paris, a powerhouse of great talent. Today it sits proudly on the edge of the old port, watching over us, keeping us sage."[87] Mueller also gives Normand Laprise top honours, saying "today Normand Laprise carries the flambeau."[88]

In conclusion, the enormous reservoir of cultural production – material gathered by tour guides, restaurateurs, writers, scholars of religion and history, chefs, and food journalists to describe Montreal's culinary imaginary – always emphasizes food's inclusive potential. The history of Montreal foodways – at least as Montrealers tell it – is punctuated by moments when different communities shared their food traditions, and when chefs brought innovative ideas to the table. Foodways in Montreal today are described as a blending together of different culinary registers, and the product of an evolution that has welcomed new culinary traditions and innovations. Food is good to think as well as to eat; and in Montreal's culinary imaginary, food lore seems to be a way to depict the good in Montreal and Montrealers.

Acknowledgments

A version of this study was presented on 20 February 2016 at the panel on "You Are Where You Eat: Stories of Urban Foodways," as part of the conference "Culinary Imaginations" held at Kwantlen Polytechnic University. My thanks to Erin Yanota, Étienne Gratton, Nora Shaalan, and Chelsea Woodhouse for their research assistance, to Quebec food authority Julian Armstrong for facilitating consultation with some of Montreal's most esteemed culinary professionals, and to McGill University librarians Martin Chandler, Eamon Duffy, and Lonnie Weatherby for their wise counsel.

Notes

1. Richler, *This Is My Country, What's Yours?*, 6.
2. Cresswell, "Place," 169.
3. Ibid., 172.
4. Massey, "Power-geometry," 60–70.
5. In adopting the term "diversity," I am cognizant of the perils of articulating the range of literary forms in terms of the false binary "high" and "low" art, as articulated by Fisher in "High Art versus Low Art."
6. See Gilbert, *The Culinary Imagination from Myth to Modernity*.
7. See Wilson, "The Allure of Imagined Meals."
8. Berg, "Icon Foods," 243.
9. Cooke, "Introduction," 6.
10. See Roy and Ali, *From Pemmican to Poutine*, 229.
11. See Meehan, "These Chefs Believe in Sticking Close to Home."
12. Simmons, "Introduction."

13 Travelocity, "Travelocity Highlights 10 Delicious." *Hotel News Resource*, 15 March 2007, cited in Tourisme Montréal, "Tourisme culinaire à Montréal." In *Tourisme culinaire à Montréal*, 64.
14 Cited in Tourisme Montréal, "Tourisme culinaire à Montréal," 64.
15 See Friesen, "North America's 15 Best Food Festivals."
16 Tourisme Montréal, "La restauration en chiffre," 54.
17 Ibid., 59–60.
18 Ibid., 55.
19 See, for example, "The Mile End Montreal Food Tour."
20 See, for example, www.roundtablefoodtours.com/. In a personal communication of 19 January 2020, owner Melissa Simard adds that she now also offers a Chinatown Tour, and tours themed around "Third Wave" Coffee, Chocolate, Afternoon Tea, Micro-Distilleries and Cocktail Bars.
21 See her blog 4cornersofthetable.com and tour website: roundtablefoodtours.com.
22 Named after the original Joe Beef canteen.
23 My thanks to Etienne Gratton who points out that St Claude is a small street running only from St Paul to Notre-Dame. It was said to be right behind the Bonsecours Market, which would place it probably between today's St Paul and Le Royer streets, perhaps even at the angle of St Paul and St Claude. In terms of the Common Street location, one advertisement listed Joe Beef as being at 4, 5, and 6 Common Street and 2 Callières (Collard, "Joe Beef's Canteen," 278; now 201–207 de la Commune, a Gallicized version of "Common Street"). The present-day restaurant Joe Beef is located at 2491 Rue Notre-Dame West in the Little Burgundy area of Montreal, a historically working-class neighbourhood, but in the process of rapid gentrification. See Walker, *Cantine de Joe Beef*. See also Collard, "Joe Beef's Canteen": "'A good many present,' Harris told his audience that night ... 'can't remember that strange place of refuge of all the tramps and "down-on-their-lucks" in town'" (271).
24 He wouldn't refuse anyone service based on their ethnicity nor refuse the poor a meal. He also had sofas set up for people to sleep on. He was very controversial. Curiously, he used wild animals, among other things, to entertain his customers. See DeLottinville, "Joe Beef of Montreal," 9–40.
25 DeLottinville, "Joe Beef of Montreal," 21. See also an article in the *Star*, 19 December 1877.
26 DeLottinville, "Joe Beef of Montreal," 16.
27 Ibid., 11.
28 Ibid., 18.
29 Tucker, "There's a Mistake!"

30 "Joe Beef Sits at #81 on World's 50 Best Restaurants List," 26 May 2015, https://montreal.eater.com/2015/5/26/8659571/joe-beef-montreal-worlds-50-best-restaurants-list.

31 Ibid.

32 For an interesting analysis, see Bodroghkozy, "'I … Am … Canadian!'"

33 "An Encounter with a Bear," *The Globe*, 17 June 1879.

34 DeLottinville, "Joe Beef of Montreal," 15. See also *The Montreal Daily Witness*, "The Second Visit," 8; and *The Montreal Daily Witness*, "McKiernan and His Dog," 8.

35 Personal communication from Max Campbell (bar manager, Joe Beef), 7 August 2016.

36 Morin, McMillan, and Erickson, *The Art of Living according to Joe Beef*, 13.

37 Turgeon-Gouin, "The Myth of Québec Traditional Cuisine at Au Pied de Cochon."

38 Simard writes in a personal communication to the author dated 3 February 2016: "Harry Wilensky (Moe Wilensky's father and Sharon Wilensky's grandfather) came from Russia and was a Communist so a secular Jew. He had a barbershop that started selling comic books and cigars and became a kind of variety store and hangout for lone Jewish male immigrants. In 1932, his son Moe Wilensky, known to be creative and charismatic, was working with his father when someone said, 'Moe, make me something special.' Moe whipped up what is now known as the 'Wilensky Special'– an all-beef grilled bologna and salami sandwich heated in an iron and always served with mustard. The sandwich was never cut, simplicity and fairness being the guiding principles. Schwartz's is the same in that 'no matter who you are, you can't cut the line.'"

39 There are further connections between these communities: for example, Wong Wings, the Chinese food establishment, was partially funded by Steinbergs – the iconic supermarket group that sold to IGA. See www.wongwing.ca/en-ca/Pages/OurStory.aspx. Here, Wong Wing tells the company story. Wing Noodles claims to have partially financed them along with Steinberg. Their page says "Mr Wing," but Wing Noodles was owned by Arthur Lee (Mr Lee) back then.

40 Dewolf, "When Chinatown Was a Jewish Neighbourhood."

41 Myers, "On Probation," 180.

42 Linteau, *Histoire de Montréal*, 325–6.

43 Dewolf, "When Chinatown was a Jewish Neighbourhood."

44 "Statistics Canada," www12.statcan.gc.ca/nhs-enm/2011/as-sa/fogs-spg/Pages/FOG.cfm?lang=E&level=3&GeoCode=462.

45 See, for example, tours by 'Round Table Tours and the "Beyond the Bagel" tour, www.roundtablefoodtours.com/tours/ and http://montrealgazette.com/life/beyond-the-bagel-a-jewish-food-walking-tour.

46 Bauer, "Bagel, Bagelry, Smoked Meat and Deli."

47 Bellerose, "Le tourisme gourmand à Montréal." "Nos longues traditions juives et canadiennes-françaises uniques en Amérique du Nord se reflètent dans ces comptoirs à l'ancienne que sont Schwartz's, la Binerie ou encore Wilensky. Ils sont devenus avec les décennies des incontournables qui font partie depuis longtemps de notre ADN montréalais et québécois, autant que les nouvelles bonnes tables de nos grands chefs québécois." Accessed 30 January 2019

48 Cesvet, *Conversational Capital*, 30.

49 Ibid.

50 "Bagels and Smoked Meat."

51 Drucker, "Ethnic Food and Ethnic Enclaves," 173–83.

52 See Bauer, "Bagel, Bagelry, Smoked Meat and Deli."

53 Kleinzahler, "Christmas in Chinatown." My thanks to Olivia Maccioni for bringing this poem to my attention.

54 Tuchman and Levine, "New York Jews and Chinese Food," 382–407.

55 For a brief summary of the history of Jewish Canadians, see Schoenfeld, "Jewish Canadians." For a history of the Jewish community in Montreal, see this document provided "by the Jewish Public Library: www.jewishpubliclibrary.org/blog/wp-content/uploads/2010/06/Immigration-Timeline.pdf.

56 According to the 2011 National Household Survey, there were 22,225 Sephardim residing in the Montreal CMA. Consequently, the Sephardim comprises 24.5 per cent of the 90,780 members of the Jewish community in Montreal. Charles Shahar, "National Household Survey 2011 Analysis, Part 7, The Sephardic Community." Courtesy of Charles Shahar, Canadian Jewish Federation, iii. In this analysis, if one's mother tongue is French, Arabic, Greek, Bulgarian, or Yugoslavian, then one is considered to be a member of the Sephardim. Whereas if one's mother tongue is Yiddish, English, Russian, Austrian (Germanic Languages, n.i.e), Czech, Danish, German, Hungarian, Irish (Celtic Languages), Dutch, Polish, Romanian, Swedish, or Finnish, then one is considered to be a member of the Ashkenazim (Shahar, 49).

57 Richler, *The Apprenticeship of Duddy Kravitz*, directed by Ted Kotcheff, DVD.

58 See Griffiths, "Mordecai Richler's Montreal."

59 Brownstein, *Schwartz's Hebrew Delicatessen*.

60 The musical was first staged at Centaur Theatre in Montreal, scripted by Rick Blue and George Bowser. See www.bowserandblue.com/centaur.html

61 Wilson, "Imagined Meals."

62 Although she does not specifically address characterization in literature, in *Fasting Girls*, Joan Jacobs Brumberg reveals how during the Victorian age, a woman's rejection of food

was an expression of her moral propriety and ideal femininity. Avoidance of meat consumption pointed to the delicate nature of a young woman, as "how one ate spoke to issues of basic character" (174). In a Canadian literary context, Elspeth Cameron provides an example of characterization-via-food through her analysis of Margaret Atwood's *The Edible Women* in which the protagonist, Marianne, stops eating as a means of personal protest against, and acquiescence to, consumer society. Characterization of course is not limited to whether or not a character eats, but also includes *what* a character eats. Alice Munro's "Half a Grapefruit" and "Royal Beatings" in her short story collection *Who Do You Think You Are?* reveal how what a character eats or claims to eat points to his or her social-economic position.

63 Critics Mary Drake McFeely and Margaret Visser suggest that food is imbued with social-cultural codes, which are both context specific and dynamic. McFeely, for instance, argues that "cookbooks have acted as agents of society, delivering expectations of women that may conflict with or support women's own goals" (3). Historical changes in domestic science, technology, and women's roles make the kitchen "a place to study women's lives" as the foods women serve point to specific social values and norms (4).

64 Traci Marie Kelly in "If I Were A Voodoo Priestess" notes that culinary autobiographies – texts that include recipes, personal stories, and public history – are an appropriate genre for the telling of women's life narratives: "For many women, sitting around a table or standing around a kitchen counter becomes the space where their stories are told. For generations, oral storytelling has brewed while dinners have simmered ... There is a power that we get from telling our stories through our recipes" (252). For Kelly, food's presence through the recipe form lends credibility to the content and telling of a woman-centred narrative. For writer Carol Shields the obvious advantages of food for a novelist is the way it affords socio-historical accuracy and precision in character portrayal. Acknowledging her use of real menus, as gleaned from newspaper clippings for example, she notes in "Parties Real and Otherwise" how "shifting menus – familiar to all of us – make for fascinating social history and allow a novelist to set a scene in a precise period in history" (211). As well, parties give the novelist a chance to bring "characters together on stage" and "show a book's characters from as many angles as possible" (211).

65 Roy and Josephson, *The Tin Flute*.

66 The street was actually named after the parish priest, also named Lacasse, in 1907; see Ville de Montréal, *Les Rues de Montréal*.

67 Montreal-based tour company Kaleidoscope offers a "Tin Flute" tour in Roy's home neighbourhood of St Henri: www.tourskaleidoscope.com/accueil/nos-visites-de-a-a-z/bonheur-doccasion-dans-saint-henri.html. Other companies offer tours of the neighbour-

hood with mention of Gabrielle Roy. Both accessed 16 August 2016. See http://lessalonsdesylvieroy.com/2014/09/visite-du-quartier-saint-henri-suivie-dun-souper-au-resto-bitoque/. See also this Quartier St-Henri walking tour: http://randopleinair.com/decouverte.

68 The protagonist of Claire Holden Rothman's novel, *My October* (Toronto: Penguin Canada, 2014), also lives in a fictional version of the distinctive little blue boat-shaped house near the train tracks that was used by Gabrielle Roy as model for the home of Jean Levesque.

69 Cooper, *The Hanging of Angélique*, 292.

70 For more on the connection between Angelique and the fire of Montreal, see "Truth and Torture: Angélique and the Burning of Montréal," accessed 10 August 2016, www.canadianmysteries.ca.

71 For full text see: Hart, *Household Recipes*, accessed 10 July 2016. https://openlibrary.org/books/OL17430229M/Household_recipes_or_Domestic_cookery.

72 For a longer selection of recipes from "A Treasure for My Daughter," see Warshaw, Davids, and Ein, "Cooking the Classics."

73 Solomon, "More than Recipes," 24–37.

74 Scott, "Bonne Entente," 56.

75 Cresswell, "Place," 172.

76 Mosby, "Joe Beef."

77 Ibid.

78 See also Kenneally, "'There *Is* a Canadian Cuisine, and It Is Unique in All the World.'" Interestingly, Michael Symon makes the case that foodways across the Western world were dramatically transformed in the mid-1960s. See Symons, "Grandmas to Gourmets."

79 Armstrong, personal communication with author, 12 August 2016.

80 Nash, "From Spaghetti to Sushi," 15.

81 Mueller, conversation with the author, 30 August 2016.

82 Armstrong, personal communication with the author, 12 August 2016.

83 Koch, conversation with the author, 26 August 2016.

84 Mueller, conversation with the author, 30 August 2016.

85 Koch, conversation with the author, 26 August 2016.

86 McMillan, "The Builders, the Brewers," 52.

87 Ibid., 52–3.

88 Mueller, conversation with the author, 30 August 2016.

Bibliography

Armstrong, Julian. Personal communication with author, 12 August 2016.

"Bagels and Smoked Meat: How Jewish Foods Came to Define Montreal's Cuisine." *Haaretz*, 12 January 2016. www.haaretz.com/jewish/food/1.696951.

Bauer, Oliver. "Bagel, Bagelry, Smoked Meat and Deli as the Jewish Part of Montreal's Culinary Heritage." Paper presented at *Food Heritage, Hybridity & Locality: An International Conference*. Providence, RI: Brown University, 23–25 October 2014.

Bellerose, Pierre. "Le tourisme gourmand à Montréal: Un attrait incontournable." *Huffington Post*, 5 April 2016. https://quebec.huffingtonpost.ca/pierre-bellerose/meilleurs-restaurants-montreal-tourisme-gourmand-foodies_b_9618738.html.

Berg, Jennifer. "Icon Foods." In *Encyclopedia of Food and Culture*, edited by Solomon H. Kats, 243–4. Vol. 2. New York: Oxford University Press, 2003.

Bodroghkozy, Aniko. "'I … Am … Canadian!' Examining Popular Culture in Canada: Recent Books." *TOPIA* (2001): 109–18.

Brownstein, Bill. *Schwartz's Hebrew Delicatessen: The Story*. Montreal: Véhicule Press, 2006.

Brumberg, Joan Jacobs. *Fasting Girls: The History of Anorexia Nervosa*. New York: Vintage Books, 2000.

Cameron, Elspeth. "Faminity, or Parody of Autonomy: Anorexia Nervosa and the *Edible Woman*." *Journal of Canadian Studies/Revue d'Études Canadiennes* 20, no. 2 (Summer 1985): 45–69.

Campbell, Max. Personal communication with author, 7 August 2016.

Canadian Heritage. "Truth and Torture: Angélique and the Burning of Montréal." *canadianmysteries.ca*. Accessed 25 August 2016. www.canadianmysteries.ca/sites/angelique/accueil/indexen.html.

Cesvet, Bertrand. *Conversational Capital: How to Create Stuff People Will Love to Talk About*. Harlow: Financial Times Prentice Hall, 2008.

Collard, Edgard Andrew. "Joe Beef's Canteen." In *Montréal Yesterdays*, 269–81. Toronto: Longmans Canada, 1963.

Cooke, Nathalie. "Introduction." In *What's to Eat? Entrées in Canadian Food History*, edited by Cooke, 3–17. Montreal and Kingston: McGill-Queen's University Press, 2009.

Cooper, Afua. *The Hanging of Angélique*. Toronto: HarperCollins, 2006.

Cresswell, T. "Place." In *International Encyclopedia of Human Geography*, edited by N. Thrift and R. Kitchin, 169–77. Oxford: Elsevier, 2009.

DeLottinville, Peter. "Joe Beef of Montreal: Working-Class Culture and the Tavern, 1869–1889." *Labour/Le Travail* 8/9 (1981/82): 9–40.

Dewolf, Christopher. "When Chinatown Was a Jewish Neighbourhood." 28 January 2008. http://spacing.ca/montreal/2008/01/28/when-chinatown-was-a-jewish-neighbourhood/.

Drucker, Susan. "Ethnic Food and Ethnic Enclaves." In *People, Places and Sustainability*, edited by G. Moser, E. Pol, Y. Bernard, and M. Giuiana, 173–83. Toronto: Hogrefe and Huber Publishers, 2003.

"An Encounter with a Bear: Joe Beef, of Montreal, Rescues His Child. A Struggle for Life in a Bear Pit." *The Globe*, 17 June 1879, ProQuest Historical Newspapers.

Fisher, John A. "High Art versus Low Art." In *The Routledge Companion to Aesthetics*, edited by Berys Nigel Gaut and Dominic Lopes, 473–74. London: Routledge, 2013.

Friesen, Trish. "North America's 15 Best Food Festivals." *Fodor's Travels*, 22 October 2013. www.fodors.com/news/photos/north-americas-15-best-food-festivals#!1-intro.

Frommer's. "World's 10 Best Cities for Outdoor Dining." January 2012.

Gilbert, Sandra M. *The Culinary Imagination: From Myth to Modernity*. New York: W.W. Norton & Company, 2014.

Griffiths, Sian. "Mordecai Richler's Montreal." *The Guardian*, 11 January 2011. www.theguardian.com/travel/2011/jan/11/montreal-mordecai-richler-literary-guide.

Harrison, Ian. "Joe Beef Sits at #81 on World's 50 Best Restaurants List." *Eater Montreal*, 26 May 2015. www.montreal.eater.com/2015/5/26/8659571/joe-beef-montreal-worlds-50-best-restaurants-list.

Hatton Hart, Constance. *Household Recipes or Domestic Cookery by a Montreal Lady*. Montreal: A.A. Stevenson, 1865. https://openlibrary.org/books/OL17430229M/Household_recipes_or_Domestic_cookery.

Holden Rothman, Claire. *My October*. Toronto: Penguin Canada, 2014.

Jewish Public Library. "Immigration Timeline." June 2010. www.jewishpubliclibrary.org/blog/wp-content/uploads/2010/06/Immigration-Timeline.pdf.

Kaléidoscope. "Circuit Littéraire 'Bonheur d'occasion dans Saint-Henri.'" *Tours Kaléidoscope*. 2007. www.tourskaleidoscope.com/accueil/nos-visites-de-a-z/bonheur-doccasion-dans-saint-henri.html.

Kelly, Traci Marie. "'If I Were A Voodoo Priestess': Women's Culinary Autobiographies." In *Kitchen Culture in America: Popular Representations of Food, Gender, and Race*, edited by Sherrie A. Inness, 251–69. Philadelphia: University of Pennsylvania Press, 2001.

Kenneally, Rhona Richman. "'There *Is* a Canadian Cuisine, and It Is Unique in All the World': Crafting National Food Culture during the Long 1960s." In *What's to Eat? Entrées in Canadian Food History*, edited by Nathalie Cooke, 167–96. Montreal and Kingston: McGill-Queen's University Press, 2009.

Kleinzahler, August. "Christmas in Chinatown." *The Griffin Poetry Prize*, 29 November 2015. www.griffinpoetryprize.com/christmas-in-chinatown/.

Koch, Anton. Conversation with author, 26 August 2016.

Linteau, Paul-André. *Histoire de Montréal depuis la Confédération*. Montreal: Boréal, 1992.

Massey, D. "Power-geometry and a Progressive Sense of Place." In *Mapping the Futures: Local Cultures, Global Change*, edited by Bird, Curtis, Putnam, Robertson, and Thickner, 60–70. London: Routledge, 1993.

McFeely, Mary Drake. *Can She Bake a Cherry Pie?* Amherst: University of Massachusetts Press, 2000.

McMillan, David. "The Builders, the Brewers, the Bankers and the Gangsters." In *The Art of Living according to Joe Beef, A Cookbook of Sorts*, edited by Frédéric Morin, David McMillan, and Meredith Erickson, 45–80. Berkeley: Ten Speed Press, 2011.

Meehan, Peter. "These Chefs Believe in Sticking Close to Home." *The New York Times*, 6 April 2008. www.nytimes.com/2008/04/06/travel/06choice.html.

The Mile End Montreal Food Tour. n.d. "The Mile End Montreal Food Tour." *Local Montréal Food Tours*. Accessed 25 August 2016. http://localmontrealtours.com/food-tours/mile-end-montreal-food-tour/.

The Montreal Daily Witness. "McKiernan and His Dog," 22 March 1881: 8.

– "The Second Visit. The Magistrates Visiting the Saloons," 17 March 1881: 8.

Morin, Frédéric, David McMillan, and Meredith Erickson. *The Art of Living according to Joe Beef, A Cookbook of Sorts*. Berkeley: Ten Speed Press, 2011.

Mosby, Ian. "Joe Beef and the Invention of Culinary Tradition." *ActiveHistory.ca*, 14 June 2012. http://activehistory.ca/2012/06/joe-beef-and-the-invention-of-a-culinary-tradition/.

Munro, Alice. "Half a Grapefruit." In *Who Do You Think You Are*, 38–54. Toronto: Macmillan of Canada, 1978.

– "Royal Beatings." In *Who Do You Think You Are*, 1–22. Toronto: Macmillan of Canada, 1978.

Mueller, Peter. Conversation with the author, 30 August 2016.

Myers, Tamara. "On Probation: The Rise and Fall of Jewish Women's Antidelinquency Work in Interwar Montreal." In *Negotiating Identities in 19th- and 20th-Century Montreal: A Collection of Essays*, edited by Bettina Bradbury and Tamara Myers, 175–201. Vancouver: University of British Columbia Press, 2005.

Nash, Alan. "From Spaghetti to Sushi, An Investigation of the Growth of Ethnic Restaurants in Montreal, 1951–2001." *Food, Culture and Society* 12, no. 1 (2009): 5–24.

Pratt, Mary Louise. "Arts of the Contact Zone." *Profession* (Modern Language Association) (1991): 33–40.

Randonnées Plein Air. "Marches Citadines." *randopleinair*. n.d. Accessed 22 August 2016. http://randopleinair.com/decouverte.

Richler, Mordecai. *The Apprenticeship of Duddy Kravitz*. Directed by Ted Kotcheff. Produced by Alliance Atlantis. Performed by Richard Dreyfuss, Micheline Lanctôt, Randy Quaid, and Mordecai Richler. 2001.

Richler, Noah. *This Is My Country, What's Yours? A Literary Atlas of Canada*. Toronto: McClelland & Stewart, 2006.

'Round Table Tours. "Select a Montreal Food Adventure." 'Round Table Tours. Accessed 20 August 2016. www.roundtablefoodtours.com/tour/.

Roy, Gabrielle, and Hannah Josephson (Geffen). *The Tin Flute*. New York: Reynal & Hitchcock, 1945.

Roy, Suman, and Brooke Ali. *From Pemmican to Poutine, A Journey through Canada's Culinary History*. Toronto: Key Publishing House, 2010.

Roy, Sylvie. "Visite du quartier Saint-Henri suivie d'un souper au resto Bitoque." *Les Salons de Sylvie Roy*. 29 September 2014. http://lessalonsdesylvieroy.com/2014/09/visite-du-quartier-saint-henri-suivie-dun-souper-au-resto-bitoque/.

Schoenfeld, Stuart. "Jewish Canadians." *The Canadian Encyclopedia*. 3 December 2012. www.thecanadianencyclopedia.ca/en/article/jewish-canadians/.

Schwartz, Susan. "Beyond the Bagel: A Jewish Food Walking Tour." *The Montreal Gazette*, 26 August 2015. http://montrealgazette.com/life/beyond-the-bagel-a-jewish-food-walking-tour.

Scott, F.R. "Bonne Entente." In *Events and Signals*, 56. Toronto: Ryerson Press, 1954.

Shahar, Charles. "2011 National Household Survey The Jewish Community of Montreal, part 7 The Sephardic Community." April 2015. www.federationcja.org/media/media Content/2011%20Montreal_Part7_Sephardic%20Community_Final-E.pdf.

Shields, Carol. "Parties Real and Otherwise." In *Sharing the Journey: Women Reflecting on Life's Passages*, edited by Katherine Ball Ross, 209–15. Seattle: Sterling Editing, 1997. First published in *Victoria*, June 1995, 44–6.

Simard, Melissa. Personal communication with author, 3 February 2016 and January 2020.

Simmons, Gail. "Introduction." In *Montreal Cooks*, edited by Jonathan Cheung and Tays Spencer, xi. Vancouver: Figure 1 Publishing, 2015.

Solomon, Eileen. "More than Recipes: Kosher Cookbooks as Historical Texts." *Jewish Quarterly Review* 104, no. 1 (2014): 24–37.

"Statistics Canada." *NHS Focus on Geography Series (Montréal)*. Statistics Canada. 13 March 2017. www12.statcan.gc.ca/nhs-enm/2011/as-sa/fogs-spg/Pages/FOG.cfm?lang=E&level=3&GeoCode=462.

Symons, Michael. "Grandmas to Gourmets: The Revolution of 1963." *Food, Culture and Society* 9, no. 2 (2006): 179–200.

Tourisme Montréal. "Tourisme culinaire à Montréal." In *Tourisme culinaire à Montréal*. 3rd ed. Montreal: Tourisme Montréal, 2012.

Travelocity. "Travelocity Highlights 10 Delicious Destinations for Foodies in 2007." *Hotel News Resource*, 15 March 2007. In *Tourisme culinaire à Montréal*. 3rd ed. Montreal: Tourisme Montréal, 2012.

Tuchman, Gaye, and Harry G. Levine. "New York Jews and Chinese Food: The Social Construction of an Ethnic Pattern." *Contemporary Ethnography* 22, no. 3 (1993): 382–407.

Tucker, Rebecca. "'There's a Mistake!' Joe Beef's David McMillan on Being Named One of the World's Best Restaurants." *The National Post*, 26 May 2015. http://news.nationalpost.com/life/food-drink/theres-a-mistake-joe-beefs-david-mcmillan-on-being-named-one-of-the-worlds-best-restaurants.

Turgeon-Gouin, Catherine. "The Myth of Québec Traditional Cuisine at Au Pied de Cochon." *CuiZine* 3, no. 2 (2012). www.erudit.org/en/journals/cuizine/2012-v3-n2-cuizine0288/1012454ar/.

Ville de Montréal. *Les Rues de Montréal: répertoire historique*. Montreal: Éditions du Méridien, 1995.

Walker, John Henry. *Cantine de Joe Beef, rue de la Commune, Montréal*. McCord Museum, Montreal, ca 1860–85.

Warshaw, Anne, Mary Davids, and Sarah Ein. "Cooking the Classics from 'A Treasure for My Daughter.'" *Forward*, 16 August 2015. http://forward.com/food/319026/recipes-from-a-treasure-for-my-daughter/.

Weinfeld, Morton. *Like Everyone Else – but Different: The Paradoxical Success of Canadian Jews*. Toronto: McClelland & Stewart, 2001.

Wilson, Bee. "The Allure of Imagined Meals." *The New Yorker*, 26 August 2014. www.newyorker.com/books/page-turner/the-allure-of-imagined-meals.

7

Creating Contemporary Canadian Agri-Art

Learning from Practice, Responding to Place,
Working with Immateriality

Sylvia Grace Borda

Setting the Scene

When you go to grab a head of lettuce in the supermarket, how often do you ask which is locally produced and which is imported? Sadly, local farms often remain far from public view and consciousness in everyday life. This mindset is especially true when it comes to farming as a subject in art. As farmlands continue to diminish with urbanization, this topic is overdue for attention.[1] For me personally, there are challenges in working with agriculture and art, or what I term "Agri-art," because few Canadian artists choose to deliberate on the role of farming in their own practice. Agri-art is not a recognized term or genre within the visual arts in Canada, and this gap has led me to create a broad definition informed by my artworks and my passion to foster dialogue about sustainable food and farming: "Agri-art represents an examination of how the contemporary arts can be relevant not only by extending the platform of artistic interpretation but also through the ability to comment on past, current, and future agricultural narratives for public dialogue." This working definition will inevitably change over time, but for now, it has been shaped by the creation of my artwork series *Farm Tableaux*, a set of panoramic, interactive photographic portraits profiling local food producers. I wanted to make the series tangible to a wide audience so that the public would get a sense of an operational farm by experiencing the space more intimately than through a standard snapshot. I wanted to show the real world of owners attentively working their fields, hand-picking beans, or weeding. To do this, I developed the series as navigable 360-degree images with an unbroken view of the farms surrounding the observer within an accessible, online, immersive environment, namely Google Street View. I chose this open contemporary medium because of its capability to provide panoramic views from positions along streets and roads, and I liked the idea of going "off-

Figure 7.1
Sylvia Grace Borda, *Viskaalin Farm, Muhos, Oulu* from *Mise en Scene: Farm Tableaux*. Finland Google Street View Project, 2015, Google Street View Dimensional Tableaux rendered as a C-41 Digital Panorama Photograph.

road" with the technology. The process of drilling down from Google Maps or Google Earth to a farm site was also a powerful way of exploring the scale of a geospatial image from a macro to micro view. In this way, *Farm Tableaux* enables audiences to consider the position of agriculture today and the role of the artist in challenging urban residents' notions of farming through digital media.

Farm Tableaux: Foundations

The *Farm Tableaux* series was initially produced as part of a larger body of work, *This One's for the Farmer*, commissioned by the Surrey Art Gallery in British Columbia.[2] This opus of work profiled farmers who collaborated on the art production and shared their stories of the region – that is, the city of Surrey and the surrounding area of the Fraser Valley (Abbotsford, Chilliwack, and Langley). Within this framework, I started *Farm Tableaux* as a series of works where viewers could enter multiple image frames to better understand the expansiveness of farm sites and their placement within changing urban environments. I opted to experiment with multi-dimensional photography based on older techniques, such as rotoscope imagery, in order to stage tableaux portraits within Google Street View.[3] My partnership with Northern Ireland–based Google Street View trusted photographer

John M. Lynch was pivotal to this process.[4] Prior to the development of the *Farm Tableaux* series, Google Street View was largely used to record road systems. Through the Google Trekker program that began in 2013, a wearable backpack imaging system gave Google photographers the ability to venture to locations accessible only by foot. This program was already working in tandem with heritage organizations and park boards to open up iconic global park regions and landmarks to online viewers. While Google Trekker allows specialized groups and communities to record everything from Arctic weigh stations to Grand Canyon trails, I noted that more intimate views of agricultural land had been neglected. Working with John provided an unrivalled opportunity to create off-road trails in Google Street View that could showcase regional farms. The result was the creation of what have since been internationally recognized as the "first" artworks to be directly embedded in the Google Street View engine.[5]

The initial iteration of *Farm Tableaux* depicted city farmers undertaking routine activities, from tending crops to managing livestock. All of the scenes were staged and then captured by John using a high-definition (HD) camera to create Google panosphere images.[6] Although initially reluctant to be part of the Google Street View photo shoot, the farmers were not averse to profiling their methods of farm management or to putting themselves in the photographs. Their main concern was that if their farms could be mapped with detailed coordinates through Google Street View, they could be easy targets for burglars and trespassers looking for valuable tools and equipment. Farmers managing livestock had further worries. One had experienced activists coming onto his farm to release animals and, on several occasions, had found his machinery vandalized. After consultation, the consensus was to capture a limited frame of view. Certain buildings, for instance, were not included in the shoot and/or machinery was removed from the background. Some farmers chose isolated locations, and understandably, a few decided not to participate.

The *Farm Tableaux* process of finding a location, developing a scene, and capturing it took several visits. The photo shoots themselves were all-day affairs that involved planning where the camera would be situated and which path it would follow in real time so that the images could be readily translated to a dimensional and navigable space in Google Street View. To create the tableaux, each participant farmer stood motionless for up to forty minutes in order to be recorded in the HD format specific to Google Street View. During this capture time frame, the camera would move to a number of positions around the portrait sitters to create what would appear to be a seamless image in time for the online viewer. However, the required length of the capture created some unforeseen challenges.

Fieldwork, for example, proved difficult to capture in a steady state, but the farmers found their routine activities of tending crops could be isolated into discrete and plausible poses if their bodies could be anchored against a prop or tool to support their weight. The youngest farmers, Doug Zaklan and Gemma McNeil of Zaklan Heritage Farm, were the first to be recorded, and Gemma decided on a crouching position, as though she were collecting organic beans in the field. What John and I did not realize, as we staged the scene, was that the farmers had great dexterity and could endure back-breaking tasks. The long exposure time is not, however, amenable to an active pose, and like the forerunners of early photography, we learned that any movement could offset how the HD camera would record the scene. In this instance, Gemma's dynamic pose of leaning downward and forward became a problem, as her muscles tensed up and began to shake wildly. After this experience, John and I worked with our participants to find postures that each could maintain for longer periods of time so as to emulate a "steady state" of naturalness.

Figure 7.2
Sylvia Grace Borda in collaboration with John M. Lynch, *Farm Tableaux*, 2013, Google Street View Dimensional Tableaux rendered as a C-41 Digital Panorama Photograph profiling Kevin Bose changing the water feeder in the turkey barn at Medomist Farm, Surrey, BC.

Figure 7.3
Sylvia Grace Borda in collaboration with John M. Lynch, *Farm Tableaux*, 2013, Google Street View Dimensional Tableaux rendered as a C-41 Digital Panorama Photograph profiling Pam Tamis reviewing accounts at the farm shop, Rondriso Farms, Surrey, BC.

A greater challenge was capturing a tableau among livestock. For example, while Kevin Bose of Medomist Farms appears in focus, a number of the turkeys do not. Longer camera exposures were needed for the tableau to be recorded in high-definition resolution, resulting in birds moving across the scene as blurred subjects. Subjects with the smallest movements often appear as "ghosts" in a photographic plane. The capture of the flocks could have translated into a ghostly scene because the birds quickly reacted to the presence of camera equipment; however, John ingeniously used sock puppet actions to keep the birds' attention. The few flighty birds appear as a sort of stop-motion effect in relation to the stillness of the other livestock, creating a dynamic scene rather than a static portrait. In my artworks, this ghosting recalls past photographic processes and evolutions, but it also occurs for other reasons with respect to the farmers themselves. Unlike a family album in which the subjects are clearly recognizable, the human subjects portrayed in *Farm Tableaux* have their faces blurred in accordance with Google Street View's privacy terms. While this loss of identity might seem unsettling, the farmers actually felt that the depictions of their farmland and their activities defined even more strongly who they are and what they do.

These scenes of actual farm labour were what I most wanted to address and validate in the field. It became my personal quest to use Google Street View as a way to insert the farmer back into a geographical frame of our digital culture, while at the same time giving an artist's nod to the past. For instance, throughout the sixteenth and seventeenth centuries in Western art, the farmer appeared as a pastoral or idyllic figure. With the advent of photography by the mid-nineteenth century, British photographer Henry Peach Robinson created a set of montaged images in which farmers and labourers were placed in fields to illustrate the passage of the seasons. Since that time, the use of photography within a fine art context has rarely returned the farmer to the foreground.[7]

By using multi-dimensional photography, I purposely move beyond Google's GPS coordinate system to portray the human endeavour of agricultural labour, enabling users to have instant access to immersive experiences of place and production. The ability for online audiences to navigate through Google Street View from a city and/or road perspective and then to a farmscape provides an immediate contrast in land use. The *Farm Tableaux* scenes illustrate how urban agriculture is functioning today and where its margins of success and failure may lie. Many of the Surrey *Farm Tableaux* sites were once part of larger swaths of agricultural lands. Through redevelopment and urbanization, the farms have become discrete packages of terrain operating adjacent to residential districts.

The *Farm Tableaux* series offers, therefore, perspectives on how regional farms thrive in metropolitan areas; their perseverance creates food self-reliance and food security for the region.[8] These farmers yield substantial vegetables, fruits, and dairy products beyond what many residents might assume. With its escalating population, Surrey is a prime example of a city that could maintain a balance of active, viable farms supported through the direct marketing of locally produced food to its residents.[9] The portrayed farms (such as Zaklan Heritage Farm, Rondriso Farms, and Medomist Farms) are small to mid-scale and urban-situated. They are potentially part of a wider flourishing of local food producers providing better livability through the promotion of improved air quality, among other benefits.[10] However, there are looming concerns for family farms. Many suburban, regional farms are often in conflict with their adjacent neighbours of large-scale housing and industrial developments. Not long after my collaboration with Clover Valley Organic Farm and

Finley's Rhododendrons, both closed due in part to the older age bracket and lower income levels of the owners/operators. Property developers offered more secure ways to retain positive retirement and financial prospects. Thus, the challenge with *Farm Tableaux* was not only to make the public aware of local agricultural production but also to bring attention to the crisis of farmers in regard to real-world issues and the placement of food production within Surrey's diverse neighbourhoods.

To illustrate the dynamics of farmland in the face of ongoing urbanization and challenging economies, I chose Google Street View in large part to engage audiences through visual scenarios and to promote dialogue on how municipalities can become proactive guardians through the establishment of farm land trusts and community farms to facilitate food security (i.e., supply) and food sovereignty (i.e., control). My aim was to extract food production and farming from their usual commodity status in order to create new representations about an age-old subject. By contrasting elements of space, time, labour, and farming in *Farm Tableaux*, I made a conscious effort to elicit public engagement with farming, its practice, and its possible misalignment within an individualistic society.[11] After all, where does food come from, if not from farming?

Farm Tableaux: Photographic Influences

If I could profile how urban agriculture is changing while remaining intrinsic to a city's well-being, could I also challenge how contemporary art produces new inroads in photographic practice? The use of "tableaux" in the series' title draws from *tableaux vivants*, French for "living pictures." Historically, tableaux were comprised of costumed actors posed in dioramas illustrating particular events for public viewing. My series consists of independent artworks framing farming subjects, their labour, and their experiences in accessible ways for audiences to engage with in a similar vein to a diorama.[12] While actors have been used by past and present artists in staging such visual representations, I believe the staging of *real farmers* in my tableaux, as partners in the creation of the work, imbues the photographs with critical perspectives and nuances that reach audiences far beyond the arts. The *Farm Tableaux* series is an expression of its in-the-field production and its embedded imagery within Google Street View, enabling multi-dimensional viewpoints. Co-authoring in the Google Street View with John allowed me to validate how this genre could become part of a distinctly Canadian narrative.[13] The *Tableaux* scenes push bound-

Figure 7.4
Sylvia Grace Borda in collaboration with John M. Lynch, *Farm Tableaux*, 2013, Google Street View Dimensional Tableaux rendered as a C-41 Digital Panorama Photograph profiling the Zaklan Heritage Farms, Surrey, BC. Young farmers Doug Zaklan and Gemma McNeill are posed harvesting beans while in the distance new residential homes illustrate the encroaching urbanization.

aries by questioning the evolving role of contemporary art creation while commenting on current socio-economic conditions considered on the margins of public interest (i.e., suburban farms).

While my pioneering efforts to create a multi-dimensional photograph are based on older techniques – the diorama and *tableaux vivant* – these were successfully migrated into a contemporary medium, the Google Street View platform. I undertook a similar direction based on historic art references by including myself within the portraitures, positioned on the periphery. This visual sign is my way of enacting a real and virtual role as witness to the events being documented. By placing myself as a photographer at work, I also embody my own "signature" within the *Tableaux* scenes.[14] In these self-assisted portraits, I am caught behind the apparatus of an

Figure 7.5
Sylvia Grace Borda in collaboration with John M. Lynch, *Farm Tableaux*, 2013, Google Street View Dimensional self-assisted portrait rendered as a C-41 Digital Panorama Photograph, taken at Medomist Farm, Surrey, BC.

actual camera that is in the act of capturing the scene before me. Who and what I record acquire layers of interpretation through my visible gesture as the photographer embedded in the scene. In standing behind the camera, I further avoid becoming a blurred identity within the Google Street View engine – which critically distinguishes me (my artist signature) from the portraits of the farmers (the subjects).

A larger philosophical evocation surrounds both the staged portraits and self-portraits. In any portraiture, there is often melancholy or a sense of death, according to semiotician Roland Barthes, who suggests that every image offers an instance of stillness, or the end of one's own existence, through the act of being captured. "Whether or not the subject is already dead, every photograph is this catastrophe," writes Barthes.[15] So we might ask ourselves: Do these farms still exist? Do farmers and their work have a future?

Visual Narratives: *e*-xperiences

In developing my series, I was always motivated to collaborate with farm communities. This initiative was about more than creating a series of artworks – it was meant to foster dialogue about the complex role of civic food production, conservation, and stakeholders in its management. As an artist, I pushed the boundaries of what constitutes contemporary art while also defining a new "commons" to replace the visible loss of greenbelts and public lands. This newly translated commons, in turn, becomes a digital commons that is a media representation of farming and an open opportunity for the online viewer, regardless of location, to experience first-hand the small-scale practices of farming and food production.

I relish the fact that through any web-enabled device viewers can explore the *Farm Tableaux* artwork from the privacy of their own homes.[16] And as these artworks "age" in Google Street View, their subject matter of agricultural landscapes and farmers' routines can impact understandings of local physical geography and urban farms in Metro Vancouver. Moreover, the introduction of artworks in Google Street View has the potential to expand cultural-identity expression online. The agreement of individual farmers from one urban locale to participate in staged tableaux has offered viewers an opportunity to experience a counter-cultural diaspora not readily visible in social media or in our city centres. My project depends on online users exploring the artworks, but this "virtual," immersive viewing also offers critical opportunities for audiences to appreciate external geographies that are marked and searchable beyond the physical computer. In other words, *Farm Tableaux* is an invitation for online participants to rediscover real places – that is, the working farms in one part of Canada.

Intangible Heritage: Tangible Legacy

The context for expression in the *Farm Tableaux* series is complex, taking its definition from its digitized platform (space) and within a physical geography (place).[17] While online games, such as FarmVille in Facebook, mimic farming, they do not ground viewers in day-to-day operations. The *Tableaux* artworks are silent purveyors; there are no audio tracks or descriptions. Viewers explore these spaces and gain a sense of what is being achieved artistically through an interpretive process that enables them to understand a working farm. Some viewers may see my artworks as incidental; others may explore them without finding a particular narrative. This dilemma parallels the reception of historical avant-gardes whose innovative concepts were misunderstood in their originating context and time.[18] Since the avant-gardes challenged existing ideas and traditional processes and forms, their works were considered controversial and even deviant. I see my own response to technology, art, and farming as similarly unexpected.

Combining Google technology with the subject of farming is not a process for artistic creation in and of itself. Through a response to the times in which we live, however, an artist can shift cultural values to challenge current conventions. Past avant-garde artworks were best understood through cultural responses, debate, and time. I aspire for *Farm Tableaux* to mature and remain accessible to audiences in a similar manner. However, I am also conscious that the artworks are embedded in Google Street View and are under eminent threat whenever the application might be re-engineered or overtaken by another technology, or when the content is deemed obsolete. Launched originally in September 2013, the series continues to reach audiences beyond farm and local geographies, inviting viewers to engage with contemporary art values as well as food production. These embedded artworks have much to tell us about contemporary experiences, about new possibilities for art in a digital society, and about our perceptions of agricultural industries. Therefore *Farm Tableaux* acts simultaneously as staged scenes of the present (or recent past) for viewers to bear witness to into the future. Simply put, the project represents specific moments of time that have been "stilled." Each artwork creates a moment, but also moves forward in time to become an archive of farm practice. Without this continuing acknowledgement of Canadian farming as having a role in our shared identity, we will be left disconnected from the land.[19]

Perhaps a better term will attract artist practitioners and even art schools to respond to what I call Agri-art. Let this be a call to artists! We need more artists to be active participants continuously creating artworks that address farms and food production. What else can we do to ensure this movement remains relevant? The im/materiality of agriculture and food in both actual form and visual representation are key strengths to enduring legacies. Agriculture and food production present us with critical and challenging situations from which to comment. Art, after all, offers new perspectives on how we see and define ourselves today and into the future. What we see, feel, touch, and react to in public artworks such as *Farm Tableaux* serve as aesthetic and cultural environments, creating reflective spaces on farming, food, and artistic intervention. Agri-art has the potential to define not only new directions in contemporary Canadian image making but also the future of farming and our relationship to increasing urbanization.

Acknowledgments

In the writing of this paper and in the realization of the artworks described herein, I would like to acknowledge the tremendous support of the following: Surrey Art Gallery (BC) and particularly Jordan Strom, Liane Davison, Alison Rajah, and Brian Foreman; Surrey, BC Farms: Historic Collishaw Farm, Zaklan Heritage Farm, Medomist Farms Ltd, Rondriso Farms and General Store, Clover Valley Organic Farm, Finley's Rhododendrons; BC Young Farmers Association and its director, Ravi Bathe; John M. Lynch, Google Street View Trusted Photographer; Malcolm Dickson, Street Level Photoworks; J. Keith Donnelly, artist; Dorothy Barenscott and Shelley Boyd (Kwantlen Polytechnic University), Culinary Imaginations; and my immediate family for their unwavering support and belief in the development of the *Farm Tableaux* project.

Notes

1 Redwood, ed., *Agriculture in Urban Planning.*
2 Surrey Art Gallery, *Sylvia Grace Borda: This One's for the Farmer.*
3 Rotoscoping is a technique that goes back to the early days of cinema when animators would trace live-action footage projected frame-by-frame onto paper, either to use as an action or motion reference or to create an image to superimpose on it.
4 Google Street View, "What It Takes to Be Trusted."
5 The Lumen Prize, "Farm Tableaux: Sylvia Grace Borda and John M. Lynch."
6 The *Farm Tableaux* series was expanded in 2014–15 in collaboration with John with the use of Google panosphere cameras to encompass regional farms and farm operators in Finland. I subsequently developed multi-dimensional photographic artworks using the open Google Street View API. These later works examine the built environment and interaction of people and perspectives, such as in the *Kissing Project* launched in Nelson, BC (2017).
7 Prior to the advent of photography, depictions of farmers, their land, and/or labour by artists such as Vincent van Gogh and Jean-Francois Millet offered new visual and social interpretations of agricultural subjects while challenging academic painting conventions. They innovated stylistic approaches to their subjects, placing them into what is now understood as the avant-garde. In the 1860s, English photographer Henry Peach Robinson produced a composite set of photographic images of farmers who were staged in the

studio, again challenging prevailing conventions about subject matter and what could be placed in front of the lens. At this time in the development of photography, farmers and farming were rarely considered suitable subjects. With the rise of industrialization and urbanization, painters and photographers (with the notable exception of social realists) ignored farms, farmers, and agricultural activities. In 1932, the Soviet state proclaimed that all artists must embrace the socialist realism philosophy and style. Works of art had to reveal the spirit of socialism with the purpose of furthering the goals of communism and glorifying the working classes, such as factory workers and farm labourers. Consequently, farm workers became a popular subject. This overt idealism would later be shunned by the art world, and farming would remain a neglected subject not only by artists but also by the general public. In my artistic practice, I was keen, therefore, to reinstate the farmer as a relevant subject long overdue for re-examination.

8 The Food and Agriculture Organisation (FAO) recognizes there is a strong potential for urban agriculture to strengthen food security, as it is not impacted as much by large market shifts associated with fuel prices, inflation, or other transport costs. See Food and Agriculture Organization of the United Nations, "Urban and Peri-Urban Agriculture, Household Food Security and Nutrition."

9 A large percentage of the province's farm revenue is generated in Metro Vancouver, of which the Surrey region is one of the larger producers with 490 registered farms. Agriculture in Metro Vancouver contributed over $789 million in gross annual farm receipts in 2010 (27 per cent of the BC farm total) on only 1.5 per cent of the province's agricultural land. See Metro Vancouver, *Farming in Metro Vancouver*.

10 The Environmental Performance Index developed at Yale University indicates a good amount of green space can assist in the preservation of local civic air quality. See Environmental Performance Index.

11 Farm Art, *Sylvia Grace Borda: Farm Art*.

12 It can be argued that contemporary Canadian photographer Jeff Wall has also utilized staged tableaux for the camera, though the term is now more often associated with theatrical and stage performances.

13 My working processes are strongly informed by the photo-conceptual traditions associated with the so-called Vancouver School of art. Key artists loosely grouped under this association have embodied in their works responses to thought-provoking questions about what constitutes contemporary photographic art and what it can become. I am particularly drawn to Vancouver School associated artist and luminary Jeff Wall and to his staged tableaux and ideologies: "The only way to continue in the spirit of the avant-garde is to experiment with your relation to tradition" (Wall, "Lightbox, Camera, Action!," 222).

14 Similar to Hipplotye Bayard's *Self-Portrait of a Drowned Man* (1840), these choreographed scenes suggest a broader enquiry into both a conceptual and personal relationship with image making. Also see Sapir, "The Impossible Photograph," 1994.

15 Barthes, *Camera Lucida*, 96.

16 Much like the work of contemporary visual artist Felix Gonzales Torres, the *Farm Tableaux* artworks are open multiples supported, in this case, by being strategically placed on a web platform for all to access.

17 While *Farm Tableaux* resides as documents of people and farms, it is also a series of artworks. There is a duality here that resonates with past photographic practices in which political and social agency came visibly to the foreground. The experiences of creating the *Farm Tableaux* series in Surrey may have had an indirect impact in a similar way. I argue that the City of Surrey's latest endeavour to promote economic development negates its past. The City's current strapline is "the future lives here." However, through the ongoing debates, exhibitions, and the recent Lumen Award acknowledging *Farm Tableaux* as a pioneering artistic intervention, the City of Surrey is gaining an increasing awareness of the role of urban farms in its catchment. In 2016, Surrey's Department for Agricultural Development gained a more prominent position on the city's website, and there is a direct contact for the public to learn more about its agribusinesses and "How to start a farm." See City of Surrey, "Agriculture and Farming."

19 Peter Bürger is one of the most quoted theorists in this context. Bürger considered the "institution of art" as autonomous from society and it was the avant-garde's attempt to break down that autonomy and return art to its place in society. See Bürger, *Theory of the Avant-Garde*.

19 Comparable to UNESCO's statement on intangible cultural histories – "Intangible culture plays a major role in giving the community its sense of identity and continuity, it supports social cohesion" – there is a necessity to realize that Canadian agricultural histories are intrinsically part of our food system and are aesthetically worthy subjects (UNESCO, "What Is Intangible Cultural Heritage?").

Bibliography

Adams, A. Jensen. "Competing in the Great Bog of Europe: Identity and Seventeenth-Century Dutch Landscape Painting." In *Landscape and Power*, edited by W.J.T. Mitchell, 35–76. Chicago: University of Chicago Press, 1994.

Barthes, R. *Camera Lucida*. London: Vintage, 1980.

Bower, S. "Get Information, Give Information: Facilitating the Production and Teaching of Environmental Art." *Art Journal* 65 (2006): 78–80.

Bürger, P. *Theory of the Avant-Garde*. Translation by Michael Shaw. *Theory and History of Literature*, Vol. 4. Minneapolis: University of Minnesota Press, 1984.

Carruthers, B. "Mapping the Terrain of Contemporary Ecoart Practice and Collaboration." *Art in Ecology – A Think Tank on Arts and Sustainability*, commissioned by the Canada Council for the Arts, the Canadian Commission for UNESCO, the Vancouver Foundation, and the Royal Society for the Encouragement of the Arts, 27 April 2006. London, UK, and Vancouver: Royal Society for the Encouragement of the Arts and Vancouver Foundation, 2006.

City of Surrey. "Agriculture and Farming." Accessed 29 October 2016. www.surrey.ca/business-economic-development/1422.aspx.

Coles, L.L., and P. Pasquier. "Digital Eco-Art: Transformative Possibilities." *Digital Creativity* 26 (2015): 3–15. https://doi.org/10.1080/14626268.2015.998683.

Condon, P., K. Mullinix, A. Fallick, and M. Harcourt. "Agriculture on the Edge: Strategies to Abate Urban Encroachment onto Agricultural Lands by Promoting Viable Human-Scale Agriculture as an Integral Element of Urbanization." *International Journal of Agricultural Sustainability* 8, nos. 1 & 2 (2010): 104–15. https://doi.org/10.3763/ijas.2009.0465.

Environmental Performance Index. "Home page." Accessed 29 October 2016. http://epi.yale.edu/.

Farm Art. *Sylvia Grace Borda: Farm Art*. Accessed 29 October 2016. www.farm-art.ca/?tag=this-ones-for-the-farmer.

Food and Agriculture Organization of the United Nations. "Urban and Peri-Urban Agriculture, Household Food Security and Nutrition." Accessed 29 October 2016. www.fao.org/fcit/upa/en/.

Frey, H., and P. Yaneske. *Visions of Sustainability: Cities and Regions*. London: Taylor & Francis, 2007.

Google Street View. "What It Takes to Be Trusted." Accessed 29 October 2016. www.google.com/streetview/earn/.

Huebner, J. "Art on the Farm." *Public Art Review* 23, no. 2 (2012): 38–9.

Kagan, S. *Art and Sustainability: Connecting Patterns for a Culture of Complexity*. 2nd ed. Bielefeld: Transcript Verlag, 2012.

Levi Strauss, D. "Essay: Troublesomely Bound up with Reality." In *Words Not Spent Today, Buy Smaller Images Tomorrow: Essays on the Past and Future of Photography*, 134. New York: Aperture Press, 2014.

The Lumen Prize. "Farm Tableaux: Sylvia Grace Borda and John M. Lynch." Accessed 29 October 2016. http://lumenprize.com/artwork/farm-tableaux.

Marks, M., L. Chandler, and C. Baldwin. "Environmental Art as an Innovative Medium for Environmental Education in Biosphere Reserves." *Environmental Education Research* (2016): 1–15. https://doi.org/10.1080/13504622.2016.121486.

Matilsky, B.C. *Fragile Ecologies: Contemporary Artists' Interpretations and Solutions.* New York: Rizzoli Publications, 1992.

Metro Vancouver. *Farming in Metro Vancouver: Metro Facts in Focus.* Burnaby, BC: Metro Vancouver, 2014.

Polli, A. "Eco-Media: Art Informed by Developments in Ecology, Media Technology and Environmental Science." *Technoetic Arts: A Journal of Speculative Research* 5, no. 3 (2007): 187–98. https://doi.org/10.1386/tear.5.3.187_1.

Redwood, M., ed. *Agriculture in Urban Planning: Generating Livelihoods and Food Security.* London: Routledge Earthscan, 2009.

Rhodes, R. "Newsmakers: The Vancouver School." *Canadian Art* 21, no. 3 (2004): 49.

Rosenthal, A. "Bridging the Binaries: Assessing Eco-Art Practices within the Context of Environmental Activism." *Paradoxa* 9 (2002): 27–9.

Sapir, M. "The Impossible Photograph: Hippolyte Bayard's Self-Portrait as a Drowned Man." *Modern Fiction Studies* 40, no. 3 (1994): 619–29. https://doi.org/10.1353/mfs.1994.0007.

Scott, Colin. *Street Photography: From Atget to Cartier-Bresson.* London: I.B. Tauris, 2013.

Surrey Art Gallery. *Sylvia Grace Borda: This One's for the Farmer*, 21 September–15 December 2013. www.surrey.ca/culture-recreation/17363.aspx.

UNESCO. "What Is Intangible Cultural Heritage?" Intangible Cultural Heritage. Accessed 29 October 2016. www.unesco.org/culture/ich/en/what-is-intangible-heritage-00003.

Wall, J. "Lightbox, Camera, Action!" *Artnews* 94, no. 9 (1995): 220–3.

Weintraub, L. "Final Thoughts: Eco-Art in Practice." *Art Journal* 65 (2006): 81.

– "Introduction: Eco Art Is, Eco Art Is Not." In *To Life! Eco Art in Pursuit of a Sustainable Planet*, 3–16. Oakland: University of California Press, 2012.

8

Food, Place, and Power in Timothy Taylor's *Stanley Park*

Wendy Roy

In a discussion of some of the ills of contemporary Canadian literature, literary critic Lawrence Mathews criticized a passage in the 1987 novel *Swann* by Carol Shields.[1] While his negative judgment was about the quality of the prose, I could not help but wonder if he was also implicitly criticizing the subject matter of the passage: food, prepared and eaten by a woman. Literary representations of food, and readers' responses to those representations, tell us a great deal about ourselves as individuals and as a society. As historians Franca Iacovetta, Valerie Korinek, and Marlene Epp argue in their introduction to *Edible Histories, Cultural Politics: Towards a Canadian Food History*, "the study of food – its production and consumption, its exchange and evolution, its abundance or scarcity – can illuminate social relations between individuals and groups, the exertion of power (political and otherwise), how cultural norms and aberrations are created, and how personal and group identity is constructed."[2] As I considered Mathews's comments, I wondered about the power relations and cultural norms evident in both Shields's literary depictions of food and Mathews's response to those depictions. Is the preparation and eating of food a fundamental and fascinating part of human life that deserves to be explored fully in literature, or is it a boring or trivial matter that is best ignored?

I considered this question again when I reread Timothy Taylor's 2001 novel *Stanley Park*. The novel's central character is a young chef, and thus much of the book is taken up with representations of food: recipes; accounts of the purchase, sourcing, and preparation of food ingredients; descriptions of meals; and depictions of the act of eating. However, because the chef is a man, food takes on a different resonance and meaning than it does in Shields's novel, in effect highlighting its gendered nature. In *Stanley Park*, rather than just being a private human necessity, food planning and preparation becomes a public, mostly masculine-associated form of artistry. This artistry is emphasized as *Stanley Park* presents explicit arguments about food as craft and art, and incorporates ekphrastic descriptions of food in real and imagined works of visual art.³

As the novel's title suggests, another compelling aspect of *Stanley Park* is the way that it links food to the politics of place. *Stanley Park*, as those of us who have lived in or visited or read about the city of Vancouver, British Columbia, know, is a thousand-acre park just west of the city's downtown. On a forested peninsula, with the ocean and bays on three sides and Lost Lagoon on the fourth, the park is a threatened near-island of nature encroached on by city skyscrapers, harbours, bridges, and humans. Like all of Vancouver, it sits on unceded Indigenous land, specifically Coast Salish land. However, its name is a masculine, British, colonial one, acquired at the park's opening in 1888 in honour of Lord Stanley, the British politician newly appointed governor general of Canada. In the collection of Canadian ecocritical writings *Greening the Maple*, editors Ella Soper and Nicolas Bradley note that "the names of places illustrate the important difference that language makes in relation to physical space,"⁴ and indeed because of its name, Stanley Park is discursively distanced from its Indigenous roots and its actual location in a Canadian city. Founded during the late nineteenth century when world exhibitions and nation-building led to the creation of designed spaces of shared leisure, the park was not only a colonial endeavour but also part of a worldwide trend in park development and urban planning that attempted to tame and control both nature and human populations.

Taylor's novel explores that control, as well as interrogating what is indigenous in terms of both food – plants and animals – and the humans who consume that food. In *Stanley Park*, Taylor asks readers to consider an ecocritical and a decolonizing approach to food, place, and social power. Post-colonial theorist Graham Huggan argues that despite the apparent contradictions of these theoretical perspectives, they have some convergences and similar goals, including "the inseparability of current crises of ecological mismanagement from historical legacies of imperialistic exploitation and abuse."⁵ In their introduction to a special issue of *Ariel* on post-colonial ecocriticism, Travis Mason, Lisa Szabo-Jones, and Elzette Steenkamp argue that "ecocriticism challenges many of the assumptions the humanist tradition supports and perpetuates, particularly entrenched anthropocentric views that alienate nature from human culture."⁶ While Taylor's novel is anthropocentric, focusing almost exclusively on human experience, nature in *Stanley Park* is shown to be not alienated from human culture but instead, literally as well as figuratively, part of that culture through its acknowledged role as a source of human food. Most significantly, Taylor interrogates local versus global approaches to food through a sustained reflection on how the protagonist, chef Jeremy Papier, is economically coerced into betraying his commitment to locally sourced foodstuffs.[7] Jeremy ultimately resists that coercion in an artistic and political expression of his connection to the food that can be harvested from one particular place: Stanley Park. In the climactic scene and what leads up to it, food is figured as a way of declaring connections and "allegiance"[8] to place and to what lives in that place: the plants, animals, and humans. The novel complicates these connections by highlighting what feminist writer Adrienne Rich calls the "politics of location" that empowers or disempowers people in terms of gender, race, and social class, as well as geography.[9]

Taylor's novel begins with an exploration of geographical location and its social and political implications. Jeremy meets his semi-estranged father, known throughout the book only by the authoritative title "the Professor," at Lost Lagoon, described in the second line as "an in-between place, the city on one side, Stanley Park on the other" (Taylor 3). The park is thus figured as a marginal location, one that is both of the city and outside it. While Jeremy is trying to keep his portentously named The Monkey's Paw bistro in Vancouver's Crosstown district afloat,[10] the Professor is a participatory anthropologist, living with and studying the purportedly homeless people who in fact make their homes in Stanley Park. The two men immediately begin talking about the non-human inhabitants of the park in terms of food – apparently starlings are delicious – and the Professor uses a net to catch a canvasback duck complacently swimming in the lagoon. At the Professor's makeshift camp near Prospect Point, father and son roast and then eat the duck, "tough to cook directly over such a low flame" but not "badly done" (22). As they eat, the two men talk about Jeremy's approach to food: in his restaurant, he uses mostly local ingredients because he is "trying to remind people of something. Of what the soil under their feet has to offer. Of a time when they would have known only the food that their own soil could offer" (23). In other words, Jeremy is trying to maintain a connection between the place where people live and the food that they eat.

This connection of food to place, readers learn, has been ingrained in Jeremy during his studies in Dijon and his apprenticeship at a restaurant in rural France. Borrowing the names of two rival Los Angeles street gangs, a fellow culinary student has identified the kind of cook one might become.[11] One might be a "Crip," a cook whose food is not linked to any particular place but who, using the formula "Classic Ingredient A plus Exotic Technique B plus Totally Unexpected Strange Ingredient C" (50, 298), "stack[s] things like mahi mahi and grilled eggplant in wobbly towers glued together with wasabi mayonnaise" (32). Or, one might be a "Blood," a cook who is "respectful of tradition ... interested in the veracity of things culinary, linked to 'local' by the inheritance or adoption of a culture." While a Crip cook may be vegetarian, a Blood is attracted to dishes such as sweetbreads – animal organs – and "pot-au-feu" – beef stew (32). After working at the rural Burgundy restaurant where the food comes from traditional recipes and most of the ingredients are produced in the community, Jeremy recognizes himself as a Blood cook.

While the references to street gangs are an intriguing way of categorizing food preferences, they also implicitly evoke relations of power, especially racialized and gendered conflict and violence. The Crips and Bloods gangs are made up primarily of young African American men, struggling for dominance over one another in their activities of drug dealing and prostitution rings as a way of compensating for their lack of power in the society at large. Their activities are gendered, since they are mostly men and some of them are engaged in controlling and profiting from the sexual work of women. One gang name evokes the power of violence: Blood refers to the colour of clothing they wear but also to the visible evidence of human conflict. The other name evokes the social relations of ability-disability: Crips is short for "cripples" and is an example of the adoption by a social group of what was originally the dismissive epithet of outsiders.[12] Taylor's metaphoric use of these terms forces readers to recognize locations of social and economic power, and in particular the gendered and human-centric nature of professional cooking: the top chefs will be men, with the women chefs for the most part *sous* or under them, and the literal blood spilled will be that of the animals being killed, cooked, and eaten.

Social and cultural power is also explored in *Stanley Park* through references to visual art. On his way back to Canada after his studies and work in France, Jeremy stops in Amsterdam and visits the Rijksmuseum to look at sixteenth- and seventeenth-century paintings of food, and of people or animals presented as food: *The Well-Stocked Kitchen* by Joachim Bueckelaer (1566), *The Beheading of John the Baptist* attributed to Carel Fabritius (c. 1640–45), and *The Threatened Swan* by Jan Asselijn (c. 1650). Literary scholar Travis Mason has analyzed these textual representations of visual art in Taylor's novel and has concluded that because ekphrasis highlights the main character's relationship to each work of art under scrutiny, it emphasizes "the uncertainty and partial knowing of interpretation" and highlights "shifting notions of place." He argues, further, that ekphrasis "provides strategies for negotiating Jeremy's developing, at times contradictory relations to other characters,

Figure 8.1
Joachim Bueckelaer, *The Well-Stocked Kitchen*, 1566, oil on canvas.

to political ideologies, and to a sense of place."[13] Inclusion of descriptions of the paintings by the Dutch masters asks readers to think about Jeremy's location in multiple senses: not only geographical but also in terms of culture, gender, and species. The artworks enforce a consideration of animals (and humans) as food, although as Mason notes, the interpretations of the paintings by Jeremy that the narrative presents are not always accurate; instead, they indicate his own position in the world, or what the paintings evoke for him subjectively. For example, while the narrative positions Asselijn's *Swan* as potential food, to be killed, plucked, and prepared for the table by a junior chef like Jeremy (Taylor 45), Mason argues that he eventually identifies with the swan, since he, too, feels himself threatened by outside forces that seem bent on consuming him.[14] He is thus in some ways not only animalized but also feminized, aligned with the animals and women who are the more common objects of consumption in literature and visual art.[15]

These paintings become significant later in the novel when it is evident that food itself can be a transient form of performance art, ephemeral but no less powerful than more permanent works of art. In the meantime, though, the novel traces the

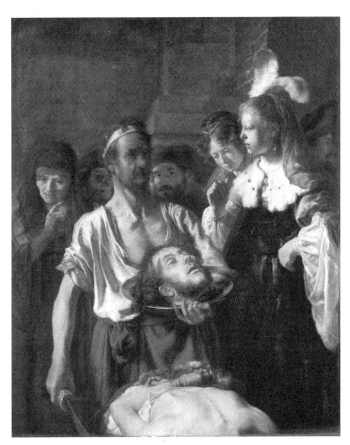

Figure 8.2
Carel Fabritius, *The Beheading of John the Baptist*, ca 1640–45, oil on canvas.

Figure 8.3 *Below*
Jan Asselijn, *The Threatened Swan*, ca 1650, oil on canvas.

development of Jeremy's Vancouver restaurant, including an erotic market scene in which Jeremy sees a young woman, Jules Capelli, inhaling the scent of a celery root, and instead of asking her to be his lover, sublimates that interest into food as he invites her to be his sous chef (45–8). What follows are pages describing shopping, menus, cooking, and eating, and even the extended use of metaphors of cooking: Jeremy's thoughts are described as "simmering, reducing and strengthening," as though they are soup stock (61). The food of the place is also introduced, in varied forms that emphasize how food locates people in terms of social class: Jeremy buys and eats not only chanterelles from the local public market but also the hamburgers available at Save On Meats on East Hastings Street (45, 47).

The implicit gendering of food is highlighted both by the references to works of art, and by the role women play in the narrative. While the paintings that Jeremy views in Amsterdam are by male artists, women are significant figures in two of them. In *The Well-Stocked Kitchen*, women are pictured prominently in the left foreground preparing fowl for roasting, while the background, but central, section of the painting illustrates the biblical story in which Martha is chastised by Jesus for continuing to cook for their guests while her sister, Mary, receives praise for sitting at Jesus's feet to listen to him (Figure 8.1).[16] While the painting foregrounds food, the background scene implicitly criticizes women (and perhaps others) for placing too much importance on comfort and consumption. Taylor's narrative emphasizes this critique of Jeremy's occupation by describing mainly the relatively insignificant background scene, as well as the food but not the people of the foreground scene (44). However, the ekphrastic description of the painting also implicitly allies Jeremy with the female cooks through a reference to the way in which he imagines working with "the large clay oven in the background" (45).[17] Meanwhile, in *The Beheading of John the Baptist*, the young Salome is prominent in the right foreground as instigator of the butcher who is serving up John's head on a platter (Figure 8.2).[18] Looking over Salome's shoulder, however, is the mastermind of this violence: her mother Herodias, who is angry that John has reproved her for marrying her husband's divorced brother. In this painting, a human rather than an animal is depicted as something to be killed, served, and consumed, and as with *The Threatened Swan*, the painting seems to foreshadow the way in which Jeremy is eventually served on a platter to the powerful international food financier Dante Beale, with help from one of the women in his life.[19]

The role that women characters play in the novel is paradoxically insignificant. While in most cultures, including in Canada, food is most often prepared domestically by women, *Stanley Park* revolves around the experiences of a classically trained male chef working in a restaurant.[20] The novel thus raises the question of whether food can be called art, rather than simply craft, only if it is prepared by a professional man who works in the public sphere rather than by an amateur woman who works privately and domestically. In addition, women characters in Taylor's novel are less fully developed than male characters and are presented only in supporting roles: as mother, friend and former lover, current lover, and cooking partner and future lover.[21] Given the novel's culinary emphasis, it is not surprising that the female characters' associations with the protagonist are almost all through food. Jeremy remembers his deceased European-born mother, Hélène, who is presented only in flashbacks, through the traditional Roma recipes she prepares (38, 149, 204). Jeremy's friend and former lover, Margaret, is a "steady customer" at his restaurant (68) who is nevertheless introduced to the reader as she cooks him a meal in her home rather than the other way around (143–4). He meets his current lover, Benny, when she enters The Monkey's Paw as a customer. She later becomes design assistant for Dante Beale's new restaurant, in the process abandoning Jeremy and his aspirations; however, like Jeremy, she is used and rejected by Dante. Although a small part of the novel is focalized through Benny's perspective (79–80), she is described in terms that objectify her, as "a Barbie from the toy section of the 1978 Sears catalogue" (76). The only female character who is reasonably well developed is Jules, the fellow chef with whom Jeremy should be in a romantic relationship. It is she who comes up with the formula for Crip cooking (50); she is described as a formidable, creative, and professionally trained chef who also has "strong green eyes" and a "magnificent nose and eyebrows" (206); and the novel is also briefly focalized through her perspective (210). However, throughout much of the narrative Jeremy keeps Jules at arm's length, never making her a full partner and not revealing to her the extent of the financial kite he is flying until he has signed away his rights to the restaurant. It is only at the end of the novel that Jeremy takes Jules into his confidence, and she becomes more than just a minor supporting character (423).

Jeremy's father figures are much more fully developed: both the Professor and the ruthless financier Dante Beale, who lives next door to the Professor and who has initially presented himself as like family to Jeremy (190, 282). These two masculine figures help Jeremy to interrogate ideas of the local and global in relation to food. Through their support and their betrayal, they in turn empower and emasculate him. For example, in a second conversation Jeremy has with his father about his approach to food, Jeremy briefly but tellingly mishears the words "cultural homelessness," a term the Professor uses to describe the condition of people in our contemporary global society, as "*culinarily homeless*" (136). People are not just displaced from their culture in general, Jeremy concludes; they are displaced from an essential part of that culture, the food that they eat. This term is reiterated when Jeremy is thinking about what he identifies as "culinarily homeless" seafood risotto made with farmed Chilean salmon. He thinks that "a fish pen up the coast from Santiago might as well be up the coast from Osaka or Vladivostok or Campbell River. The fish in such a pen lived independent of geography, food chain or ecosystem … There was no *where* that these fish were *from*" (171). Jeremy's father thus helps him to develop and name the important association between food, place, and ecology. As such, the Professor is a benevolent and helpful figure, but as his title implies, he is also a figure of masculine intellectual power who aims to name and control the world around him.

Jeremy comes to a clearer conception of the relationship between food and location in the midst of the painful, drawn-out financial demise of his own metaphorical offspring, his restaurant, provoked by his other more menacing father figure.[22] As in the story "The Monkey's Paw" by W.W. Jacobs, Jeremy wishes for his debt to be paid but gets something much more sinister than he has bargained for. Jacobs's story is especially significant because of the parallels that can be drawn with the often-destructive father-son relationships in Taylor's novel, as well as the focus in both texts on the relationship between paternalism and money. Under the guise of helping Jeremy get his finances in order, Dante takes over and closes The Monkey's Paw. He then starts remodelling the building, which he has owned all along, into the pretentiously decorated and named Gerriamo's, described as not "even a room, really; it had moved beyond that to become what designers called a *space*" (309). As Dante says to an appalled Jeremy of the young "*fooderati*" he wants to attract, "they want something wired, post-national, with vibrant flavours. They want unlimited new ingredients, they want grooviness and sophistication, and both purple and gold score very well" (256). Jeremy's connections to local space have been both literally and figuratively severed. In the new restaurant, he will be forced to cook and serve the latest Crip concoctions of unmoored, global, and unnaturally coloured food, evident in the menu that takes up the whole of pages 336–7. Thus this 2001 novel exemplifies the 2013 statement by Soper and Bradley affirming the global "interconnectedness of environments and economies."[23] What Jeremy will be able to accomplish in this environment is almost entirely controlled by Dante's international financial interests.

During the section of the novel in which Dante's betrayal becomes evident, Jeremy's relationship with his actual father begins to mend, in part through a reconnection to local food through the bounty of Stanley Park. In a series of passages set in the park, father and son are described as killing or gathering, and then cooking and eating, red and grey squirrels, starlings, rabbits, Canada geese, huckleberries, and dandelion greens (249, 293, 301). Eventually the people of the place join them, bringing their own offerings of trapped, netted, and found food, ranging from "items salvaged from dumpsters" to "items harvested from the forest around them" (301). As Jeremy becomes increasingly alienated from the stark, shiny placelessness of the restaurant under construction, he finds the cold and wet outdoors of Stanley Park over Christmas a much more welcoming place. As he cooks for the growing collection of so-called homeless people, who are constructing a group identity through the sharing of food, he smiles and feels "wonderful" (292).[24] When he walks to his father's camp in Stanley Park, it is "like coming home" (346). He finally tells the Professor after cooking Christmas dinner for two dozen people that while the new restaurant is not a bad place, "I'd rather cook here" (303).

Jeremy's feelings are remarkable in part because Stanley Park has not always felt like home to him. Even though it is part of the city, and a visitor can walk from one end to the other in a few hours, it has earlier struck Jeremy as a kind of wilderness. In his first meeting with his father in the park, he muses that "if he were abandoned here, he would be lost until morning" (20), and later, when he drunkenly tries to find his father's camp spot at night, he becomes utterly "lost" (106). While the park clearly shows the mark of human involvement – after all, it is bisected by a major road connecting downtown to the Lions Gate Bridge, parts of it have been cleared of trees, and as Jeremy notes, it has "thousands of visitors a day" (20) – it is what Canadian poet Don McKay identifies as wilderness: "not just a set of endangered spaces, but the capacity of all things to elude the mind's appropriations."[25] As Taylor suggests in these passages, nature in Stanley Park is endangered and at the same time eludes appropriation by humans.

Jeremy's growing connection to Stanley Park leads to his decision to turn the opening of Gerriamo's into a kind of participatory "performance art" (416) that is at the same time guerrilla warfare (318). In her discussion of food as a performance medium, Barbara Kirshenblatt-Gimblett argues that food is "already highly charged with meaning and affect" and "already performative and theatrical."[26] While Kirshenblatt-Gimblett then analyzes primarily food that is part of artistic works but is not eaten, or food prepared and served in a way that is profoundly unsettling for its recipients, *Stanley Park* initially presents the food people commonly eat as both art and craft. As Jeremy prepares fish fritters for Benny, he labels "how the fritter was conceived" as "art" and "how it was tossed together back there, out of sight, in just a few minutes" as "craft" (78). The production, circulation, and display of art is again emphasized when Jeremy goes to the new restaurant to see the works of visual art that Benny and the other designers have chosen for the walls. The paintings are fictive, part of the world of the novel rather than the real world, but they echo and at the same time subvert the real paintings by Dutch masters. One hyperrealist painting shows maggoty meat and rotting fruit, but "each silky patch of mould, each broken pit, each rejected mouthful was rendered in achingly precise strokes."[27] In a second set of decorative paintings, "healthy fruit and plump vines" are presented on separate panels that are "arbitrarily segmented." Another surrealist painting presents traditional arrangements of "fruit, vegetables, meat and cheese on tables, slaughtered game birds on chopping blocks," but elements such as light are "intentionally wrong" and the perspective is "skewed" (311–12). Through these paintings, like the ones in the Rijksmuseum, Jeremy's position in the world is both delineated and undermined. In this new restaurant, he will unwillingly serve unnatural, rotten food, arbitrarily separated from its origins in a way that is both "wrong" and "skewed."

A final painting described in this scene is the only one by a contemporary artist who exists in the world outside the novel, Canadian Attila Richard Lukacs. Unlike the other paintings, this one is a portrait rather than a still life, and it is described to evoke any one of Lukacs's many paintings that depict skinhead men. The canvas, referred to as "phallic National Socialist imagery" (312), is placed by Dante at the entrance to the kitchen, suggesting that it is his fascist style, rather than Jeremy's more collegial approach, that will predominate in the restaurant's kitchen, but also implying that there may be homoerotic as well as fatherly overtones in his attempted control of Jeremy.[28] The narrative then moves into an exploration of Dante's approach to gender relations, as he explicitly shows Benny her place in his social world by forcing her to put his "browning half-eaten apple" in the garbage and then demanding that she strip to show off the underwear that will be part of the servers' uniforms (313–14).[29] Instead of valuing her role as assistant designer of the new space, Dante emphasizes her role as caretaker of discarded food and as human edible to be sexually consumed.[30]

Readers are initially kept in the dark about the details of the artistic performance that Jeremy plans as a way of reasserting his power, although his father evokes the artistry of music to call it "A Blood overture to Dante's Crip opera." Jeremy replies, however, that it is "more ... a tribute" (347), to his father and to others who live and die in Stanley Park. Inspired by a local food truck operator who runs an illegal "Guerrilla Grill" (318), Jeremy hires, trains, and swears to silence an entire crew of cooks just out of culinary school, initially practising with them the set Crip menu (343–5, 349–51). Just before opening night, with the help of one of the so-called homeless men, Jeremy stocks the restaurant kitchen with animals and plants from Stanley Park: Canada Geese, rock doves, canvasbacks, rabbits, grey squirrels, raccoons, goldfish, and periwinkles, as well as dandelion greens, fiddleheads, mushrooms, salal berries, salmonberries, and huckleberries (355–6). Chladek also brings a swan, which Jeremy has not requested and which he violently rejects, saying, "It's not even indigenous" (356). As noted above, this exchange can be linked to Jeremy's identification with Asselijn's *The Threatened Swan*, especially because in the meantime Jeremy has prevented a park-dwelling friend of his father's, Caruso, from killing a swan. The narrator notes during this incident that had Jeremy "lived in Asselijn's day, he would have ... killed it without remorse," "roasted it in a stone oven and served it in fatty pieces," but now he tells Caruso to "stop!" (285). As well as this personal association, Jeremy's reaction to Chladek's swan raises questions of indigeneity. Chladek points out that the grey squirrels are also not indigenous to this part of Canada (356), and readers know that neither are the rock doves, rabbits, nor dandelions, all of which have been at some time in the past released into the park by humans.[31] Like the people who live in Stanley Park, however, these animals and plants are now *of* this place: they have become indigenous, which Jeremy acknowledges by accepting them as part of his menu.

In an extended passage, Jeremy is described as turning animals into food: plucking the birds, setting aside the geese livers for the faux foie gras, skinning and boning the squirrels and simmering the meat to make consommé, jointing the rabbits and cooking rabbit meat and mushrooms to make stock, gutting the raccoons to remove the tenderloin and grinding the rest of the meat for a terrine (356–7). As this passage suggests, Taylor's novel is anthropocentric in that it does not privilege or focus on animals except in their role as human food, unlike other Canadian novels such as Yann Martel's *Life of Pi* and Barbara Gowdy's *The White Bone* in which animals are central and their consciousness is explored and imagined.[32] The novel makes it clear that as a Blood cook, Jeremy will exercise his human power over other species by killing them and turning them into food. However, in Taylor's book animals are respected as part of the wilderness that is Stanley Park and as an integral part of human culture. As noted above, Jeremy is also at times figured as an animal, and this figuration is emphasized when, just as he is completing his preparation of the plants and animals from Stanley Park, he cuts himself with his sharp knife and a few drops of his own blood fall into the pan he is using to make blood sausage. According to health regulations, he should throw out what he has made; instead, he sets the pan aside to cool (359). Just as he is intimately connected to Stanley Park, Jeremy is now part of the food that he plans to serve. However, his role as fodder is now empowering, in contrast to previous scenes in which he appeared edible because others such as Dante were arranging and controlling him.

Jeremy has earlier described the upcoming opening night as "like theatre, like a culinary monologue" (353), suggesting that it is an artistic performance to which all the important people of the city have been invited. Further connecting what he is doing to a work of art, the kitchen with all the supplies from Stanley Park is said to look "not unlike how Bueckelaer would have painted it" (355). Just before the opening night food service starts, British food journalist Kiwi Frederique interviews Jeremy about the restaurant. His responses reflect only Dante's vision, contradicting and concealing his own opinions about the connection of food to place and the people who live there. The food they will serve, he *says*, is "beyond international. Beyond globalized. We aren't the restaurant of *all* places – Europe and Africa, Asia and the Americas ... We are the restaurant of *no* place. We belong to no soil, to no cuisine, to no people, to no culinary morality" (364). Meanwhile, however, he is *thinking*, "Eat and be unconsciously connected to this place" (365). This place is, of course, Vancouver, especially the small semi-island in the city where it may still be possible to live off the land. Jeremy's guerilla warfare/performance art is to serve the opening-night glitterati animals and plants gleaned from Stanley Park disguised as other foods: the "pork" wontons contain squirrel meat, the "squab" are really rock doves, and the "El Chaco Angus beef tenderloin" is actually highly seasoned raccoon. Jeremy's performative attack will involve breaking conventional social practices and customs surrounding food, including health regulations. As Jeremy acknowledges to a friend, his father will not be there physically but will be there in spirit, through the foodstuffs harvested from Stanley Park (368).[33]

By concealing from the recipients of the meal the reality of what they are eating, Jeremy takes away one of the standard aspects of performance – a knowing and responsive audience.[34] The climax of the novel comes when some of the guests become aware that the dinner is a performance. Kiwi Frederique, hidden behind a counter in the kitchen, has heard one of the young cooks refer to a dish as "raccoon" and another as "squirrel," and while Jeremy denies that this is really what he is serving, he tells her that his cooking is "always part performance" (389) and admits that his "post-national" cuisine contains "reminders about what ... had been lost," perhaps "even something of the family itself" (389) – hinting, of course, both to food from the soil of Vancouver and to his own blood in the sausage. Kiwi returns to her table, where she excitedly tells her dinner companions that this "wasn't just a meal, it was a performance" in which "Jeremy had fed them ... a range of delicious, forbidden things": "He performed for us. He showed us some things and kept some things secret ... We should all be *thrilled* to have been part of it" (391).

Kiwi understands the symbolic significances of and potential exhilaration in being unknowingly fed food that Euro-North Americans have labelled *vermin* and thus have a culturally conditioned revulsion towards, what Carolyn Korsmeyer calls the attraction of "that which disgusts, endangers, or repels."[35] However, others, such as Dante, are far from thrilled. In the face of a rapidly expanding and ironically inaccurate urban legend – picketers surrounding his company's head office over the next few weeks are convinced that for Gerriamo's opening night, "exotic and rare animals from around the world" were served (405) – Dante fires Jeremy.[36] Despite, or perhaps because of, the protest, the restaurant becomes wildly successful, although its new chef serves unrooted, unchallenging, and ultimately uninteresting food. Jeremy thinks of what he has done in almost religious terms, believing that those who ate his food are now "satisfied and strengthened and full of unknowable joy. Sanctified by his efforts" (402). The blood of the animals of Stanley Park, and of himself, has been transformed into the wine of a communion, in this case with the natural world and other humans. With this understanding of connectedness, Jeremy is able to open his own small, illegal underground Blood restaurant at the southern edge of Chinatown, where Jules comes to help him and where, as when he was cooking in Stanley Park, he finds himself "smiling uncontrollably" (423).

In *Stanley Park*, Jeremy Papier has declared allegiance to a particular place and to the people who live in that place, including his father, by turning its plants and animals into food. The book complicates notions of the ownership of place, however, by briefly and thus somewhat problematically highlighting Stanley Park as contested space through a further questioning of who or what is indigenous to the park. Taylor's novel refers to Indigenous peoples several times, the first time explicitly when the Professor tells Jeremy that there have always been people in the park, beginning with "a First Nation" (14). Many of the other references are implicit, such as when Siwash Rock, a large rock outcropping on the northwestern sea edge of Stanley Park, is mentioned and its legend is described (20). "Siwash" is a pejorative Chinook jargon term for Pacific Coast Indigenous peoples.[37] In *Stanley Park*, Siwash is the name not only of the rock, which is known in Squamish as Slhx̱í7lsh, or "standing man," but also of an inhabitant of the park who lives near the rock and spends his time counting people who pass that specific spot (24). References to this character emphasize the importance of place; he calculates the position of others using a high-tech GPS, while he himself remains almost motionless (334–5).

Jeremy's musings about the indigenous in food ingredients and in food preparation techniques take a critical turn when he becomes lost in the park at night and stumbles upon a small group of Indigenous people: a woman, two men, and a baby. Their cultural group is not specified, but they are described as speaking "an ancient-sounding tongue that mirrored the sound of cedar branches hitting one another in the wind overhead, or the sound of wave slaps on algae-ed [*sic*] stone" (107). Presumably, they come from a nation such as the Squamish or Musqueam who traditionally lived in or used the park until they were forcibly removed in 1888, and who have never ceded that land to European settler-invaders. When the Professor hears of Jeremy's encounter with them, he describes them as "cultural holdouts," "taking a last stand. Homing in on a place that cannot be taken from them" (135). The professor interprets their inhabitation of this place as a protest against its occupation by colonizing forces – an ironic interpretation since he himself is a kind of colonizer of the park, using his social and cultural power to turn its current inhabitants into objects of study. Certainly, the food these doubly Indigenous peoples bring with them carries particular significance for questions of indigeneity. Transported in a black plastic garbage bag, their victuals include a box of pastries, some apples, and a "furry row" of squirrels (106). This encounter indicates that Stanley Park is indigenous land in more senses than one, since the Indigenous people who still live there claim it through the food it offers both as it once was, and as it has now become.

Concerns about indigeneity have long been left out of discussions of both localism and ecocriticism as they relate to food. Soper and Bradley acknowledge this gap in their anthology, noting that "Canadian literary studies have traditionally ignored or marginalized indigenous cultures, and Canadian ecocriticism to date has not focussed sufficiently on indigenous texts and contexts."[38] Similarly, in her article on the post-colonial politics of locally produced food, Susie O'Brien argues that "while localism does not in theory preclude respect for indigenous culture or politics, these elements receive little to no attention in most discussions," often being simply "refracted into thematic concerns with place, economics, representation, and morality."[39] In her essay in this volume, Zoe Tennant provides a provocative discussion of the politics of identifying food as either *local* or *Indigenous*. She argues that what is important is not "pre- and post-contact as measures for Indigenous and non-Indigenous foods," since these consist of "foods that have always grown there as well as those that were brought to the shores or the valleys or the plains on the footpaths and grease trails or in the bellies of ships." What is important, she argues, is an acknowledgement of land, since "food comes from somewhere."[40]

Taylor's discussion of indigeneity is primarily connected to thematic questions about place. The brevity and the limited context of these references point to an ideological and cultural distancing and marginalization of Indigenous peoples and questions of colonialism in *Stanley Park*, and critics of the novel often reinforce this marginalization. Sarah Banting's discussion of the role of Siwash Rock, for example, avoids mention of the Indigenous origins of both the name and the legend that surrounds it, noting only that "Siwash Rock is named before it is described in more abstract terms," at first alienating non-local readers and then giving them "enough guidance to begin constructing the landmark's significance."[41]

Despite this shortcoming, Taylor's *Stanley Park* explores food and place as imbricated in and reflective of relations of social and cultural power, in many complicated and interrelated ways. The novel celebrates the natural world as an integral part of even urban human culture, through its material existence both as a home for humans and as a source of human food. In doing so, *Stanley Park* combines ecocritical, gendered, and decolonizing approaches to food and place. As Iacovetta, Korinek, and Epp argue, food provides a "vantage point" on questions of "cultural politics and power, gender relations, ethnic and racialized histories of inclusion and exclusion, [and] imperial designs and nation building," among other questions.[42] Through its focus on food, *Stanley Park* offers many such significant vantage points. It demonstrates the power of local and global economies through the ideologies and actions of chef Jeremy Papier and food financier Dante Beale. It explores gender relations through its representations of female and male characters and their connections to the artistry of food and its preparation. It alludes to the power imbalance between human beings and the animals that become their food. And it evokes the colonizing practices of displacement through its discussions of what it means to be indigenous in terms of plants, animals, and humans.

Acknowledgments

I would like to thank the editors of this collection, Shelley Boyd and Dorothy Barenscott, for the astute suggestions that helped me to expand and hone my arguments during revision of this essay.

Notes

1 The passage, which Mathews calls "bland" and "plodding" ("Not Where Here Is," 80–1), includes this sentence about small-town librarian Rose Hindmarch: "She takes a packed lunch to work, a sandwich of tuna fish or egg salad, which she eats at the library desk, and afterwards she makes herself a pot of tea, boiling the water on the little hotplate in the storeroom at the back" (Shields, *Swann*, 151).
2 Iacovetta, Korinek, and Epps, eds., "Introduction," 10.
3 In its simplest form, ekphrasis is a textual or dramatic description of a work of visual art, either existing (i.e., a painting or sculpture that can be seen in the real world) or imagined by the author of the text. The word comes from ancient Greek and thus has associations with the long histories of visual and literary art.
4 Soper and Bradley, Introduction, xxvi.
5 Huggan, "Postcolonialism," 164.
6 Mason, Szabo-Jones, and Steenkamp, Introduction, 4.
7 Sarah Banting's essay about cities in Canadian fiction, "Reading from a Distance," discusses the way in which novels such as *Stanley Park* appeal to particular audiences, both "distant" and "local," through their descriptions of place. Banting argues that *Stanley Park* and a novel by Dionne Brand "address several audiences, positioned at a variety of distances from the cities in which they are set" (115). Indeed, *Stanley Park* often describes Vancouver and its park in a way that is most intelligible to readers who are familiar with the city, despite the opportunity for wider audiences to know Vancouver through the Internet and social media. However, while Banting uses food puns to discuss the notion of location in *Stanley Park* (136, 139), she does not talk in detail about how the novel explores and theorizes the relationship between food and place.
8 Taylor, *Stanley Park*, 51. All subsequent references to the novel are in parentheses after the quoted passage.
9 Rich, "Notes," 215. For the purposes of this study, I would add species to this list of political locations.
10 In the 1902 story "The Monkey's Paw" by W.W. Jacobs, the White family is given the paw of a monkey that can purportedly grant wishes. Mr White wishes for money to pay off the

mortgage on their house, which is granted when his son is killed in a factory accident and the owner pays the family the exact amount of the mortgage. See my discussion of the relationship of this story line to Jeremy Papier's experiences with his restaurant later in this essay.

11 Crips are an African-American street gang founded in Los Angeles in the late 1960s whose genesis was in part social ills such as racial segregation, poverty, and unemployment among African-American male youth. Bloods are a rival gang that originated in the early 1970s; they are identified by their red clothing as opposed to the blue clothing of the Crips (Harris, *Gangland*, 51–2).

12 According to one of its founders, the gang name was originally Cribs, to signify the extreme youth of the first members, but evolved into Crips (short for "cripples") when gang members began to carry canes and walk in a particularly stilted way (McRuer, *Crip Theory*, 65–6).

13 Mason, "Placing Ekphrasis," 13, 29. Mason examines not only these three paintings by sixteenth- and seventeenth-century Dutch masters but also several fictional paintings by real and fictive contemporary North American artists, as well as three sculptures by a fictional Vancouver artist and reproductions of paintings by real French Cubist artist Georges Braque.

14 Ibid., 19.

15 See Patnaik, "The Succulent Gender," for a detailed discussion of women as literary food.

16 *The Holy Bible*, Luke 10:38–42.

17 In fact, the painting appears to show a fireplace in the left middle ground, indicating Jeremy's faulty interpretation of works of art in relation to his own life.

18 *The Holy Bible*, Matthew 14:1–12 and Mark 6:14–29.

19 The inaccurate narrative description of the painting, referring to "the proffered head … held high in the hand of the workmanlike executioner" (Taylor, *Stanley Park*, 44), emphasizes the male cook or butcher figure rather than the two female instigators. It also fails to note that pictured between Herodias and the butcher, in the centre of the painting, is a male figure gazing directly at the audience and thus activating viewers as witnesses to the scene.

20 Significantly, the practice of training cooks in Europe originated in the medieval guild systems out of which art traditions and schools also emerged (Jovinelly and Netelkos, *Crafts and Culture*, 6–9).

21 When I taught the novel in a university class on Canadian fiction, several students were disturbed by what they saw as its brief and dismissive representations of women. Mason

notes the novel's troubling gender relations in a footnote, in which he connects "the marginalization of the women" in the narrative description of Bueckelaer's painting to women characters' "minor" and "undervalued" roles ("Placing Ekphrasis," 30n6).

22 Jeremy is also a father figure to Margaret's son, to whom he is godfather. His godson carries the evocative name Trout and thus also figures as a person who has the potential to be consumed, especially in a chilling scene in which Jeremy finds Dante standing menacingly over the sleeping child (Taylor, *Stanley Park*, 273).

23 Soper and Bradley, "Introduction," xxiii.

24 Significantly, while a few women are part of the group in the park, those who are emphasized and named – the Professor, Caruzo, Chladek, and Siwash – are all men.

25 McKay, "Baler Twine," 131.

26 Kirshenblatt-Gimblett, "Playing to the Senses," 1.

27 Korsmeyer notes that historically such paintings have been employed "to foreground rot and decay, transience and loss, and ultimate mortality" ("Delightful, Delicious, Disgusting," 221).

28 Mason argues that "the shaven-headed image signifies Dante's characteristics" ("Placing Ekphrasis," 26). The placement of this painting at the entrance to Jeremy's kitchen has additional significances, however, since as Piet Defraeye points out, while almost every review of Lukacs's paintings from the 1980s and 1990s acknowledges their expression of homoerotic desire, the paintings also clearly reflect "structures of exploitation and repression" ("Above Mere Men," 82).

29 Dante has earlier connected gender to sexuality as a way of denigrating both women and lesbians. Because Jules is an assertive woman who dislikes him, he has referred to her as a "dyke" (Taylor, *Stanley Park*, 66).

30 This passage demonstrates, as Kirshenblatt-Gimblett argues in another context, "the materiality of food, its dynamic and unstable character, its precarious position between sustenance and garbage, its relationship to the mouth and the rest of the body, particularly the female body" ("Playing to the Senses," 11).

31 Meanwhile, some indigenous animals such as beavers have been driven out of areas of the park because they were considered too disruptive (Kheraj, "125 Years of Stanley Park").

32 See Huggan, "Postcolonialism," 161–80, for his exploration of the ecocritical posthumanist in these two novels.

33 See Gora, "From Meat to Metaphor," chapter 5 in this volume, about consumption of beavers in Canada, in which she points out that in British Columbia, as in many provinces, it is illegal to serve wild game in restaurants.

34 Kirshenblatt-Gimblett, "Playing to the Senses," 2.

35 Korsmeyer, "Delightful, Delicious, Disgusting," 218, 219.
36 The rumour may have started as a result of an overheard telephone conversation in which Trout's father jokingly describes the opening-night food as including "Walrus" and "Elephant" (Taylor, *Stanley Park*, 381). The incident with the picketers raises an intriguing question about what the reaction would have been to animals from Vancouver being trapped, killed, and fed to unknowing people. Would the connection to the local have appeased the protesters, or would it have incensed them even further? Or is their protest simply over the unequal power humans have over animals?
37 The name is under review by the Vancouver Park Board and may be changed (Schmunk, "Siwash Rock").
38 Soper and Bradley, "Introduction," xli.
39 O'Brien, "'No Debt Outstanding,'" 232.
40 See Tennant, "*Terra Nullius* on the Plate," chapter 4 in this volume.
41 Banting, "Reading from a Distance," 137.
42 Iacovetta, Korinek, and Epps, eds., "Introduction," 22. O'Brien argues that even "alternative food practices occupy sites of race and class privilege" ("'No Debt Outstanding,'" 232).

Bibliography

Banting, Sarah. "Reading from a Distance in/and Canadian Cities: Negotiating the Stylistics of Locality." *English Studies in Canada* 39, no. 4 (2013): 113–44.

Defraeye, Piet. "'Above Mere Men': The Heterogenous Male in Attila Richard Lukacs." In *Making It Like a Man: Canadian Masculinities in Practice*, edited by Christine Ramsay, 79–100. Waterloo: Wilfrid Laurier University Press, 2011.

Harris, Donnie. *Gangland*. Oak Ridge: Holy Fire, 2004.

Huggan, Graham. "Postcolonialism, Ecocriticism and the Animal in Recent Canadian Fiction." In *Culture, Creativity and Environment: New Environmentalist Criticism*, edited by Fiona Becket and Terry Gifford, 161–80. New York: Rodopi, 2007.

The Holy Bible. Authorized King James Version. New York: Consolidated Book Publishers, 1982.

Iacovetta, Franca, Valerie Korinek, and Marlene Epp, eds. "Introduction." In *Edible Histories, Cultural Politics: Towards a Canadian Food History*, 3–28. Toronto: University of Toronto Press, 2012.

Jacobs, W.W. "The Monkey's Paw." In *The Monkey's Paw and Other Tales of Mystery and the Macabre*, compiled by Gary Hoppenstand, 17–30. Chicago: Academy Chicago Publishers, 1997.

Jovinelly, Joann, and Jason Netelkos. *The Crafts and Culture of a Medieval Guild*. New York: Rosen, 2007.

Kheraj, Sean. "125 Years of Stanley Park: Before and After." *ActiveHistory.ca: History Matters*. Accessed 15 July 2016. http://activehistory.ca/2013/09/125-years-of-stanley-park-before-and-after/.

Kirshenblatt-Gimblett, Barbara. "Playing to the Senses: Food as a Performance Medium." *Performance Research* 4, no. 1 (1999): 1–30.

Korsmeyer, Carolyn. "Delightful, Delicious, Disgusting." *The Journal of Aesthetics and Art Criticism* 60, no. 3 (2002): 217–25.

Mason, Travis. "Placing Ekphrasis: Paintings and Place in Stanley Park." *Canadian Literature* 194 (2007): 12–32.

Mason, Travis, Lisa Szabo-Jones, and Elzette Steenkamp. "Introduction to *Postcolonial Ecocriticism Among Settler-Colonial Nations*," special issue of *Ariel* 44, no. 4 (2013): 1–11.

Mathews, Lawrence. "Not Where Here Is, but Where Here Might Be." *Essays on Canadian Writing* 71 (2000): 79–87.

McKay, Don. "Baler Twine: Thoughts on Ravens, Home, and Nature Poetry." *Studies in Canadian Literature* 18, no. 1 (1993): 128–38.

McRuer, Robert. *Crip Theory: Cultural Signs of Queerness and Disability*. New York: New York University Press, 2006.

O'Brien, Susie. "'No Debt Outstanding': The Postcolonial Politics of Local Food." In *Environmental Criticism for the Twenty-First Century*, edited by Stephanie LeMenager, Teresa Shewry, and Ken Hiltner, 231–46. New York: Routledge, 2011.

Patnaik, Eira. "The Succulent Gender: Eat Her Softly." In *Literary Gastronomy*, edited by David Bevan, 59–75. Amsterdam: Rodopi, 1988.

Rich, Adrienne. "Notes toward a Politics of Location." In *Blood, Bread, and Poetry*, 210–31. New York: Norton, 1986.

Schmunk, Rhianna. "Siwash Rock Needs Its 'Derogatory' Name Changed, Park Board Commissioner Says." CBC News Online, 29 September 2017. www.cbc.ca/news/canada/british-columbia/siwash-rock-renaming-1.4312151.

Shields, Carol. *Swann*. 1987. Toronto: Vintage, 1996.

Soper, Ella, and Nicholas Bradley. "Introduction." In *Greening the Maple: Canadian Ecocriticism in Context*, xiii–liv. Calgary: University of Calgary Press, 2013.

Taylor, Timothy. *Stanley Park*. Toronto: Vintage, 2001.

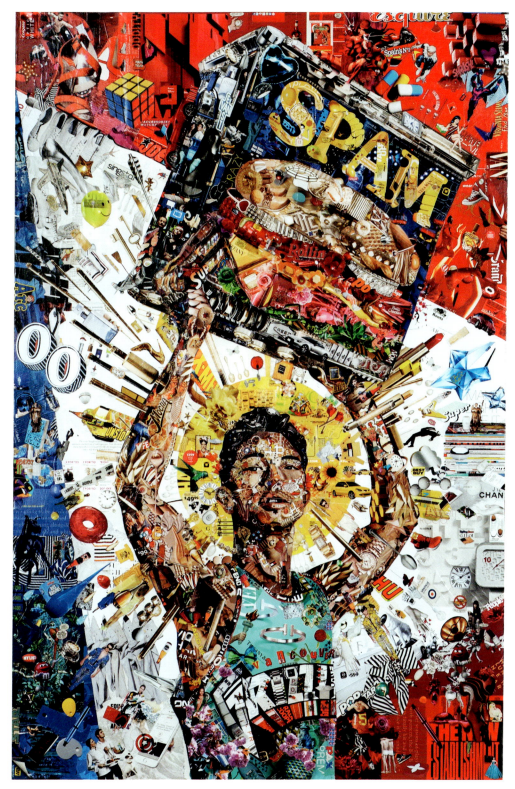

Figure 0.3
Jay Cabalu, *De Los Reyes*, 2018.

Figure 0.5
Lawrence Paul Yuxweluptun, *Haida Hot Dog*, 1984, acrylic on canvas.

Figure 1.1
Barry Pottle, *Starting the Feast*, 2012.

Figure 7.1
Sylvia Grace Borda, *Viskaalin Farm, Muhos, Oulu* from *Mise en Scene: Farm Tableaux*. Finland Google Street View Project, 2015, Google Street View Dimensional Tableaux rendered as a C-41 Digital Panorama Photograph.

Figure 7.2
Sylvia Grace Borda in collaboration with John M. Lynch, *Farm Tableaux*, 2013, Google Street View Dimensional Tableaux rendered as a C-41 Digital Panorama Photograph profiling Kevin Bose changing the water feeder in the turkey barn at Medomist Farm, Surrey, BC.

Figure 8.3
Jan Asselijn, *The Threatened Swan*, ca 1650, oil on canvas.

Figure 9.4
PLOT aerial view, June 2016.

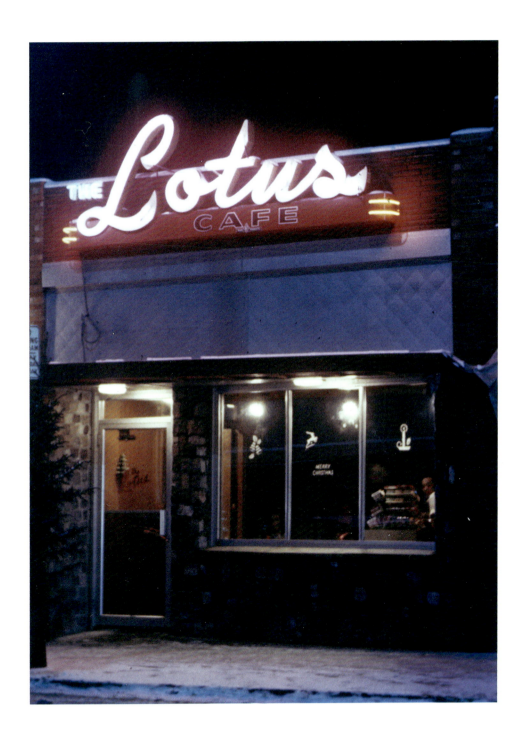

Figure 12.4
The Lotus Café neon sign.

Figure 13.5
Elyse Bouvier, *Coffee at Chin's*, 2016, digital photograph.

Figure 13.6
Elyse Bouvier, *Lan in the Dragon Room*, 2015, digital photograph.

Figure 15.4 *Opposite*
Jason Wright, *Tragedy of Open-Faced St Sebastians or The Sacrifice of Artisanal Sandwiches for the Redemption of the Ethical Glutton* (detail), 2013, framed c-prints on paper.

Figure 17.3
Sandee Moore, *In Sick & Hunger*, 2011; materials: gingerbread sculpture; performance.

Figure 17.6
Sandee Moore, *The Taste of Someone Else's Mouth*, 2003 [Version 1]; materials: cast gum, video, cast rubber sculpture.

Figure 19.1
Traversée des Sentiments, for *The Tableaux Blog*, Canadian Literary Fare.

Figure 20.1
Children playing at MacIntosh Brook Campground, 2017.

Figure 20.5
Ursula Johnson's *(re)al-location* design pattern, 2017.

PLOT

An Interview with Cora and Don Li-Leger (The People's Food Security Bureau)

Cora and Don Li-Leger (interviewed by Dorothy Barenscott)

This is the story of an art project, a social experiment, and the food that connects a community – a story that involves some very diverse players: artists, gardeners, families, new immigrants, long-time multi-generational residents, seniors from a nearby activity centre, women from a nearby shelter, the homeless, those struggling with addictions, security guards, and police. PLOT (a.k.a. Peas Lettuce Onions Tomatoes) was conceived as art in the form of a participatory food garden in Newton, a community of need in Surrey, British Columbia. Large in geographic area and among the fastest growing cities in Canada, Surrey's population is projected to surpass Vancouver's in the next decade. Located in the Lower Mainland, Surrey comprises six town centres, of which Newton is the most populated and the one that in recent years has borne the unfortunate distinction of being an area troubled by crime, violence, substance abuse, poverty, and homelessness. Once known for its early settlements of foresters and farmers, and today for its large, ethnically diverse immigrant populations, Newton is presently deemed one of the two most vulnerable communities in Surrey: a place of social isolation where a great number of fundamental needs are not being met.[1]

In an effort to rejuvenate the area, the City of Surrey invited artists to beleaguered Newton in 2015. Several pop-up exhibitions and installations resulted that sought to establish a contemporary art presence in an attempt to effect positive change. It was through this initiative that we became involved and the People's Food Security Bureau was born. The question we posed: Could sharing and connection, in place of fear and mistrust, be collectively experienced by such a diverse community? Inspired by a history of social practice art projects, we turned our attention to using imagination and energy towards a direct response through action. We also looked to guerilla gardening projects and social practice art that involved food and food production. What follows is our account and reflections on PLOT, as both art project and local community engagement, captured at the end of the growing season (in fall 2016) when we sat down with art historian Dorothy Barenscott for an interview.

PLOT as Art Project

DOROTHY: *Tell us about how* PLOT *first came about as something more than an idea, as a work of art to create.*

DON: Just prior to beginning PLOT, we had produced *The Encyclopedia House* (2015) in the Newton Grove, a unique urban space with tall trees about a block from the King George Boulevard. Old encyclopedias headed for the dump were used to construct a small house that could be an artist residence and a place for discussions about poverty, homelessness, and micro-housing while being surrounded by books of knowledge from the Western perspective. Newton was known to be an area in Surrey that was experiencing a lot of problems with drug addiction and homelessness, so we thought it would be a good opportunity to have *The Encyclopedia House* as a focus for discussion. We had challenges with the City at that time, with many bureaucratic concerns raised about feasibility and safety. But the project was very well received, even though the City was initially quite reluctant to have it. Out of that project came the idea of doing other interventions in Newton that might have a more lasting impact and yet could be artistic and transformative in their nature. A discussion started about doing something agricultural, something that could perhaps spin off into public markets or farmers' markets. There was this large vacant lot, and so the discussion moved towards converting that space into something that would be meaningful and artistic, yet produce a social environment and food for that neighbourhood. Through *The Encyclopedia House* we had earned the trust of the City, so PLOT was a much "easier sell" to the powers that be.

DOROTHY: *Why is it important for you to conceive of* PLOT *as an art project? Could it not exist more simply as a sharing garden without the added weight and expectation of associations to "art"?*

CORA: I've always really respected the use of art to challenge dominant thought. I think we had already identified so many issues – social disconnectedness, poverty,

Figure 9.1
People's Food Security Bureau (Don and Cora Li-Leger), *Encyclopedia House*, 2015.

disengagement of people in the community – that seem to be fed by the dominant culture, because we live in this culture where everybody owns something. Land is owned, everything is commodified, and it felt like an intervention to be able to do something that could really turn that upside down. That to me is where the power of art really lies, to transform an experience. And I know it might be hard to articulate to people around the community – even to other artists – who said, "well, you're just going to garden." But to us, it was always more than gardening, and really, it turned out to be much, much more.

DON: Our first artistic ideals went way beyond what PLOT is right now, considering the restrictions that were placed on us to follow the rules of the City, which owns the land. Originally we came up with ideas for a garden, a teahouse, a meeting place, communal connections, animal husbandry, that sort of thing. People already loved the idea of the garden, but if you added even a few more things, it could be much more than that. And so our ideals were very high to do things in an artistic manner, but also to think of PLOT in terms of an immersive experience. This was its potential.

DOROTHY: *What special considerations did you make planning the design and layout of PLOT that aligned with your goal of creating an art project?*

DON: We had a very limited budget, $5,000, and people were amazed that we could do it for that small amount – developing a piece of raw land with soil and all of the other needs of a garden, including a basic irrigation system. We really wanted it to be a very welcoming place for everyone, which included the homeless people, the drug addicts, the neighbours, and the people who drive by in their Lexuses and BMWs. We wanted something for everyone and a place where people could connect. We allowed it to slowly evolve along the way. We welcomed people to come in, plant, and work the soil; and then they themselves made social connections, so it gradually developed in that way. And then we brought in picnic tables, a barbecue, a sink, and different amenities. As we brought these in, we were always very aware that the City had placed limitations on things added to the site, so we knew we couldn't go too far. We couldn't get City water, build a shelter, or have a toilet. So we borrowed water from the neighbours, renovated another neighbour's shed for our tools, and solicited a donation of a portable toilet. By improvising, PLOT grew in a kind of natural way.

Initially there was a rough plan. It was to look something like a palm leaf with garden beds radiating so it could look good from the air. Then we were introduced to a local Cree elder, who was joined by some other women interested in aspects of universal Indigenous and First Nations spirituality. They spontaneously formed a committee, and it was decided that we would put a medicine wheel as a focal point on the east side of the site. And when that was installed, it quickly evolved that the wheel would be the hub from where the garden beds would radiate. Until this time, I had not dreamed of such a connection to the First Nations and how much people would respond to this.

CORA: There was an intent to always make something that would not necessarily be visual from the ground, but from a higher perspective – something that would tie PLOT together as a whole statement. But the other intent was to avoid being top-down about it. We don't live in Newton, and we were dealing with a pop-

Figure 9.2
PLOT planning, 2016.

ulation demographic that is very different from where we live. So to be respectful of that, we decided early on that we would be social observers, and would work with people at a grassroots level. We really felt that we wanted to get to know the neighbourhood in this way. We couldn't go in with the intention, "We've got this garden design. Come and help us execute it." What happened instead was that initially people who might be interested in doing a project like this were invited. We had artists, gardeners, students, people who were active in the Newton community, and people who were interested in food security. There were about twelve people in the beginning, and it was very spontaneous! It was in a way just what we wanted, what we were hoping for. I shouldn't even say *wanted*, because we didn't know exactly what we wanted. Reflecting our interest in swarm theory, we were hoping to see how people would self-organize to get this to happen. Otherwise, it might not have had the same power as a communal project. I think there is this tricky line to tread when you are doing a social practice in that you have to obviously provide some kind of guidance – I hate to even use the word "leadership" because I feel, especially after having been affected by this experience ourselves, that the real leaders were all around us.

DOROTHY: *Do you think your audience changed its interactions with* PLOT *when they understood your intentions, and does this matter to you?*

CORA: I don't think that everybody even to this day understood that it was an art project. And I've really thought and wondered about how much this really mattered, because it still provided very meaningful engagement for those people involved. I think for those who did begin to get into PLOT as an art project – and I'm even talking about fellow artists that wondered what I was doing with my summer, like "Shouldn't you be in the studio?" – I think for them it could provide a chance to think a little more deeply about the role of art. It certainly did that for me. I gained a deeper appreciation of how an artistic intervention could really make a difference – to feel the transformation in myself, but also to see it in the participants. It made me feel good about PLOT as an intervention because I think it offered up another point of conversation about "what is art." It also lives as an example of how art can have a transformative dynamic.

DON: Initially, we had talked up this project as a community garden, growing vegetables. Volunteers came in with the concept of raised beds, squared off, everything lined up and gridded, and clearly that wasn't going to happen. We showed them the plan, and they reacted in odd ways to it. But when we explained the concept of aerial photography, and that this whole thing would be growing in a unique and different pattern radiating out from the medicine wheel, they responded to that. When we put in the radiating lines – even though it wasn't all that practical or efficient, but more a creative thing – they actually started to really get into it and wanted to see it growing and evolving. And then along the way, the idea of creating mystery became important. Like initially it was thought that there would be beds of broccoli, beds of lettuce, beds of tomatoes, etc., but instead of that, we encouraged people to mix it up and create a sort of exploratory garden. So if you wanted a tomato for your salad, you had to walk through the whole garden. You couldn't just go to one bed and harvest everything that was there. People seemed to get into that, they seemed to respect that, and they liked the idea of the mystery aspect. We didn't push the idea that this was necessarily art. For the most part, people just re-

Figure 9.3
A family explores the garden, 2016.

acted to it as this special unique environment with vegetables and flowers, and it was just a very pleasant space.

DOROTHY: *What connections do you make between* PLOT *and other land art, or approaches to making art that touch on social practice and relational aesthetics? Are you inspired by any local or international artists?*

DON: Yes, Bryan Mulvihill and the World Tea Party. I first encountered this artist many years ago through Centre A in Vancouver, and I've been to a number of his tea parties since then.[2] Tea is a way of bringing people together: civilizing, calming, and also enlightening. It was during the PLOT project that those thoughts came to mind, having people come together over something so simple as food, as growing food, and then, later on, sharing food at PLOT when we had Sunday potluck lunches. Food and drink bring people together who don't agree politically, who

Figure 9.4
PLOT aerial view, June 2016.

have economic and ethnic differences, whose home countries are at war – an incredibly wide selection of people. They can come together, and they are civil, congenial, and communicative. It is a beautiful thing.

CORA: Absolutely. It's interesting because our first intention was, as Don said earlier, to make something like a palm leaf design. But the way that PLOT evolved, because of our desire to allow it to come along on its own, I think it actually became more profound than our original idea. I am really drawn to the earth art of Andy Goldsworthy, because as an artist, perhaps at my age and stage in life, I look at some things that people do, and I think who is going to need a closet full of stuff to deal with.[3] PLOT was also a very attractive project to us in that every summer Don and I are very intense gardeners. In fact, we call what we do small-scale agriculture! I feel like I have to put my art aside each year so that I can do my growing and canning and all the food preservation, and I started thinking why couldn't those things be integrated? But getting back to what I love about Andy Goldsworthy – he's using things on the land. It just goes back into the land, and you don't end up with a closet full of stuff, of things your children will have to deal with after you go. When we look at the medicine wheel, it is a beautiful thing. Medicine wheels, unlike other monuments like a Stonehenge or cathedrals, are right on the land. They don't grow up from the land, they are of the land itself. At PLOT, the medicine wheel then radiates these cultivated beds, indicating people using the land, and then beyond that there is this formal square of wildness reminding us again of what

PLOT: AN INTERVIEW

that space all around us was and where we all came from. So in a way, that triad of shapes actually stands as a piece of land art, more profound than I think we had initially conceptualized.

DON: Drone photography is important here in terms of documentation. We had put the word out that it would be nice to have this kind of photography of PLOT, and it just happened that there was somebody connected to someone else who was doing drone photography for real-estate sales. I told him that I wanted to put together a video that showed the garden in a sped-up time frame growing and morphing into what it is now. So this individual started coming weekly and doing overhead shots, sending me copious files of stills and video. And again, PLOT changed along the way as we were doing it. Ultimately it became this pattern of shapes with the medicine wheel, the radiating lines out into the squash circles, into what we called the "Great Square," the wild bee habitat with this serpentine pathway. So PLOT has some great symbolic meanings when you look at it from the air.

DOROTHY: *How are you planning for the afterlife of PLOT as an artwork? What are your modes of documentation, and do you see PLOT as forming part of a future art exhibition?*

DON: Since PLOT was actually conceived of as a one-year project and it was going to be dismantled at the end of the season, we have always thought of it that way and taken lots of photo and video documentation. And now there is some potential for PLOT continuing year to year being run by volunteers who have helped put it together, so that could also be its legacy going into the future. But as for putting it into the category with the Robert Smithsons of the world, no I don't think of it that way.[4] Although I much admire his work, I don't think of us in that sort of elevated "museums of the world" stature.

In terms of an archive or an exhibition based around PLOT, I can see that as video stills, documentation, an installation, and a form of social art – it could be all of these. For an installation, we might take the concept of freedom, the concept of growing things, food-sharing, sharing open to anyone, a tea room, a warm place to sit, a comfortable place to make those connections, and create a sort of atmosphere that has beauty, yet has the power to connect. Food would be a big part of that connective tissue.

PLOT as Local Community Engagement

DOROTHY: *You have spoken about the sharing economy represented in* PLOT. *How is this different from the economy of the typical community garden we see around other parts of Vancouver and the Lower Mainland?*

CORA: Regular community gardens are pretty widespread in the Lower Mainland. There are waiting lists, there are registrations, there are fees involved, and then each person is given an allotted piece to look after, and all that grows on it becomes theirs. It's also known that occasionally produce gets stolen from these gardens when people walk through and spot a beautiful squash over the fence – it might get pinched or something. At PLOT, you can't possibly steal anything because everything is free. There are no wait-lists, registrations, or fees, and anyone can come into the space. Anybody can take stuff whether they have worked there or not, and people that work there have to be pretty comfortable with letting stuff go. This was something that we conceptualized at the beginning of the project, and interestingly, it was one of the most difficult things for people to accept.

Initially we experienced people were reluctant to harvest vegetables. And we also experienced people who had worked with us, having emotionally invested their physical labour and time, feeling like somebody came and took too much broccoli, and they'd ask what they were using it for. It became a real experience for people to get their minds around this kind of sharing space. We've been informed so much by the medicine wheel, and we've had various Indigenous people come and share in our circle when we've had solstice and equinox celebrations. They've not only participated but they've also facilitated; they've even led and taught at the medicine wheel. It seemed that this population most easily got what we were doing. And when we reflected upon it, it seemed like wow, of course, the potlatch, which was actually banned by the dominant culture. So we are still dealing with the resistance of the dominant culture around sharing. But as soon as people at PLOT became comfortable with that, it was like a feeding frenzy. Not only was PLOT's produce freely given and taken, but neighbours began spontaneously bringing excess from their home gardens to give away too.

DON: It was our original concept to have PLOT completely open and shared. We knew there were a lot of homeless people in the area, and a lot of issues, a lot of drug problems, but we just welcomed everyone. At first we had an overabundance

Figure 9.5
The free fruit stand, 2016.

of produce we could not give away and had to take to the food banks. And then we soon had the opposite problem of people harvesting too much and harvesting some stuff before it was ripe, just because it was there. But it was not just about the sharing of produce, but also about the sharing of the space. With more "rules," we likely could have had a more orderly and productive garden, but we also felt that might have made PLOT less welcoming by excluding some groups of people we really wanted to reach out to.

DOROTHY: *What do you believe was the uniting feature of PLOT that attracted the community?*

CORA: I think food was the true uniting feature of PLOT. That was what first drew people in. It is interesting – having a psychology background, I look at Maslow's hierarchy of needs. Basic needs like food are the foundation of the pyramid and spirituality is at the top. So we knew from the beginning that we were dealing with fundamental needs. That's what *The Encyclopedia House* was originally about too, and really that was the entry point of PLOT. So it wasn't about gardening as much as it was about food. I think that when you see it in action across cultures, how people come to harvest food for themselves and bring food to share with others, you see how food is that fundamental need. And while the medicine wheel physically and visually anchored the garden, it also spiritually anchored the garden in that it kept us – those who participated – on track, keeping our priorities right, our philosophy in place, and our culture of sharing going forth for all the people who entered the site. At PLOT we did not have the social barrier of private ownership; it was a level playing field for everybody. Many people also came to PLOT and talked about how healing it is to be out-of-doors, to see plants growing, to have a hand in touching dirt and watching things grow. So nature could be another uniting feature that attracted people.

DOROTHY: *What unites the reactions of the people who get involved with PLOT? Could you provide examples of the public reaction and interaction with PLOT?*

DON: It was food, it was community, it was sharing and being free and open. It was not a confining or restrictive environment. There is a community centre right there next to PLOT with some multi-purpose rooms with tables and chairs, and you can go in there and have tea and coffee anytime and meet with people. But there is something different about having a very open and free place, and so you are not just going to meet your fellow seniors there, you are going to meet a seven-year-old and their dog, or talk to people from a country you have never met someone from before. PLOT potluck lunches are a good example. Initially this was not at all organized. Cora just started bringing a snack to share with the volunteers who gathered on Sundays to work. Soon, others began bringing food as well. At one point, a suggestion was made for an ethnic potluck feast. And it suddenly transformed the lunch: people brought things they were proud of, they shared recipes and stories, and it has since continued to evolve.

Then there is a story of a mother and her two children. The boy was ten when he first came; the girl was seven. They came and wanted to be involved, very cautiously at first, but we welcomed them to come and plant a garden. We gave them instructions, and the boy planted a wide variety of vegetables with his mother's help. Everything was very neat and organized; he put signs on everything and made

Figure 9.6 *Top*
PLOT garden beds, spring 2016.

Figure 9.7 *Bottom*
Sunday potluck lunch, 2016.

a unique little patch. And then he would come, almost daily for the first while, with his measuring stick and his notepad, and he measured every little shoot coming up and the height it was growing. He had a chart with this growth, and everything named. It was pretty amazing. He said he wanted to be a scientist. The family got very involved in the project, and then the boy started giving PLOT garden tours to people who came by. He even made a video in French to show his class what he did all summer.

DOROTHY: *We have spoken about the notion of a Canadian imagination around food, food choices, and food sovereignty and security. How do you think PLOT functions to bring about individual and community imaginaries? How are these imaginations particularly Canadian?*

CORA: I think that culinary imaginations are everywhere. They are in all the diverse cultures, and to me, as someone who loves to go in the garden and figure out what to do with what we have, how to eat what is local and seasonal, it feels just great to be able to play with that. And I think it was empowering for people at PLOT, when they looked around and discovered what they could do with food that they grew and harvested themselves. One of our core volunteers suggested, for example, that we should have a kale challenge. People love to eat, and when they can taste how good and how different something tastes, that they have grown in the ground and picked when it's ripe, it brings eating to another level. That sadly doesn't happen enough in our culture. I also want to say something around Canadianness as I am from the United States, and we always talk about the melting pot. In Canada, we talk about the salad bowl. PLOT was *literally* that salad bowl, because you could go around PLOT and make salad whenever you wanted, alongside people from many very diverse walks of life. This is also related to the medicine wheel and its four quadrants. The wheel can be looked upon as representing the four races, and how after creation, the four races dispersed around the earth, only to one day, return to be reunited again.[5] And isn't that an incredible metaphor for Newton? A place that is now possibly getting some of the most intense immigration influx of almost anywhere in British Columbia.

DON: At PLOT we had that influence of universal Indigenous philosophy and tradition, which I think was very important. The Canadian multi-ethnicity we've experienced is also profound. One of our members wanted to count the number of languages of people that were in PLOT at that given moment, and she went around and asked everyone. There were about thirty! Some of them were very new immigrants; some had only been here for a month from Syria. We also had an ESL [English-as-a-second-language] group come one day with people from all over the world, and countries from which Cora and I had never met people before – from Africa, the Middle East, and Eastern Europe, from all over the place. There were many different levels of English, but all asked questions about the garden, and tried to get their heads around the idea that it was for sharing. When they understood it *really* was for sharing, even though they were on a field trip, they started gathering food and asking for bags.

I think that Canada is about sharing our land, sharing our resources, and we welcome people who will come to participate and contribute. The people who came to the garden were also contributors and a lot of them have asked, "What can we do to help?" Communities are important. Traditionally we had our small communities, our churches, we had people coming together in community halls and places for sharing meals where they had communal kitchens and that sort of thing. We still use those, but not always in the same way, and we don't seem to have anything as inclusive in the neighbourhood. We no longer have our fall fairs or public market in Newton. That's gone. So PLOT has brought out some of those older, time-honoured ideas of people coming together in one space, sharing food, and welcoming all in the community. I think this is a very Canadian thing.

Acknowledgments

Before the publication of this book, artist Don Li-Leger passed away in 2019 following a courageous battle with cancer. This interview is a tribute to the boundless energy and creativity that Don shared with the Newton community through the collaborative art project PLOT.

Notes

1 City of Surrey, "Vulnerability Score." In the words of one recent *Vancouver Sun* report by Tara Carman entitled "Riding Profile Surrey-Newton," "Newton is a community that is desperate to be known for something, anything, else."

2 According to the World Tea Party's webpage "About WTP," Bryan Mulvihill is a Canadian artist and artistic director of the World Tea Party: An Interactive Transcultural Tea Salon (1993–present), incorporating "exhibitions, concerts, conferences, poetry readings and

multicultural events involving dozens of organizations, hundreds of artists, thousands of works of art and infinite cups of tea." During and immediately following the 2010 Vancouver Olympic Winter Games, Mulvihill organized the World Tea Party Exhibition at the Centre A Vancouver International Centre for Contemporary Asian Art (21–28 February; 12–21 March).

3 Andy Goldsworthy is a British sculptor, photographer, and environmentalist associated with the land art and environmental art movements. See Friedman and Goldsworthy, eds., *Hand to Earth*.

4 American artist and land art pioneer Robert Smithson became internationally famous for his earthwork sculpture *Spiral Jetty* (1970), a project built from mud, salt crystals, and rocks that forms a 1,500-foot-long and 15-foot-wide counterclockwise coil that juts from the shores of the Great Salt Lake near Rozel Point, Utah. The sculpture gained attention from the art world through Smithson's documentation process via film and photography, and the work today is best known through the aerial photographs that have been widely disseminated in high-profile art exhibitions and reproduced in art history survey textbooks as a seminal example of land art. See Cooke, et al., *Robert Smithson*.

5 The traditional medicine wheel is often associated with Indigenous peoples of the North American plains but has been widely adopted as a symbol by a number of aboriginal groups whose ancestors did not traditionally use the wheel. Researcher Ann Dapice in "The Medicine Wheel" describes the medicine wheel as a healing and therapeutic tool providing "a conceptual framework that is culturally grounded and also supported by solid scientific research" and a universal symbol of wholeness where each of the represented races of the four quadrants of the wheel are considered equal, an idea that is captured in the Lakota prayer "All my relations," often evoked at Indigenous ceremonies (251).

Bibliography

Carman, Tara. "Riding Profile Surrey-Newton: Crime Remains Top of Mind for Voters," *Vancouver Sun*, 4 October 2015. www.vancouversun.com/news/riding+profile+surrey+newton+crime+remains+mind+voters/11413331/story.html.

City of Surrey. "Vulnerability Score." Accessed 6 August 2016. www.surrey.ca/files/vulnerability_map.jpg.

Cooke, Lynne, et al. *Robert Smithson, Spiral Jetty: True Fictions, False Realities*. Berkeley: University of California Press, 2005.

Dapice, Ann. "The Medicine Wheel." *Journal of Transcultural Nursing* 17, no. 3 (2006): 251–60.

Friedman, Terry, and Andy Goldsworthy, eds. *Hand to Earth: Andy Goldsworthy Sculpture, 1976–1990*. London: Thames and Hudson, 2004.

World Tea Party. "About WTP." Accessed 6 August 2018. www.worldteaparty.com/about.

A Case Study on Ghost River Theatre's Food Performance

Angela Ferreira

Taste: An Event for the Senses

Taste is a complex sensorial and physiological process, comprised of olfaction and gustation, that facilitates nourishment. The tongue differentiates taste through "one or a combination of sweet, sour, bitter, salty, and umami,"[1] which are, as theatre historian and theorist Stephen Di Benedetto argues in *The Provocation of the Senses in Contemporary Theatre*, primal features to signal danger or other "vital information about anything we put in our mouths."[2] But eating is not a purely biological process. Shared eating experiences create community, memory, and a place for new narratives. As such, can controlling sensorial elements through isolation magnify the power of each human sense to achieve new flavours or heighten a theatrical experience? This experiential perception is explored in the Ghost River Theatre performative event *Taste* at Beakerhead, a festival that blends art and science. Based in Calgary, Alberta, Ghost River focuses on "performance creation," and *Taste* is part of the "Six Senses" performance series.[3] Eric Rose, artistic director of Ghost River Theatre Company, and Bruce Barton, director of the School of Creative and Performing Arts at the University of Calgary and artistic director of Vertical City Performance, co-created the concept for *Taste*. Ghost River is the only Canadian theatre company that has created a series of performances based on the senses that not only expands the field of performance but also highlights the importance of food sustainability. As the artistic creators and restaurant staff work together to introduce local ingredients, aromas, and flavours, *Taste* enables discussions of depletive and finite food sources by linking food sustainability to regional origins.

Performance: Purpose and Structure

Taste allows one to understand the experiential potential of food in performance. Arguably, Ghost River Theatre's approach stimulates a mind-body consciousness to create action and change in each participant's daily life, such as reducing food waste and appreciating the act of consumption. *Taste* was first presented in 2015 by the University of Calgary's Faculty of Arts and took place at Calgary's River Café. It is designed for a group of ten participants, five performers who act as guests, three wait staff, and the chef, with two forty-five-minute sittings per evening over three nights. The restaurant is open to regular patrons, but five tables are reserved for Ghost River Theatre: two tables sit one performer to one participant, two tables have one performer to three participants, and one table has one performer to two participants. River Café's proprietor, Sal Howell, collaborated with the company, while chef Andrew Winfield initiated the chef concept; he was part of the "generative process" until Matthias Fong took over midway as chef to pursue the original plan and to actualize ideas in a "smooth transition that was not disruptive."[4]

Meal as Nostalgia

Rather than a traditional three courses, the meal is structured around several canapés and is comprised of locally sourced, fresh ingredients, such as corn from Molnar's Taber Corn & Pumpkin Farm. The smells and tastes permit participants to recall past memories that conjure nostalgia. Sharing these memories at the table acts as a moment of "presencing," defined by theorist Otto Scharmer as a process in which individuals or groups suspend past patterns by "seeing with fresh eyes," redirecting their attention by "sensing from the field," and finally "letting go" by "connecting to source."[5] The experience incorporates Albertan cuisine, defined as what is local within a reasonable distance from Calgary, for the purpose of conjuring Albertans' memories.

The café sources sustainable ingredients from local producers as well as herbs grown in the restaurant's garden. Every canapé is paired with a wine or non-alcoholic drink, and the selection, along with dessert, comprises a participant's tasting menu, which is considered a "movement,"[6] or a culinary étude that serves a narrative purpose within the larger structure of the event. The flow of the experience is significant

Figure 10.1
Ghost River Theatre tasting, 2015.

to Rose since participants are blindfolded while tasting. The goal is to lead participants into mindfulness and consciousness. Rose maintains, "to think about taste, to place your consciousness and your very being inside of your mouth, inside a flavour, you need to be led, you need to be triggered; it's not something that happens naturally."[7] This process is a crafted experience that can be viewed as mimesis of relationship foreplay and the sensuality involved with intimacy.

Building Trust

Sight is used to make judgments and acts as a "survival" tool, according to Di Benedetto, which makes it a source of protection on a primal level.[8] *Taste* increases participant vulnerability by removing vision from the process of eating. At the same time, this experience builds trust. By the time the blindfolded participants are seated, the gradual process of making their way to their tables has removed their fear of the environment and attuned their senses. The participant transforms into active participant. Blindfolding has no negative impact on the tasting experience, as taste is "actually a combination of taste and smell sensory information, more properly defined as flavor. Researchers explain that about 80% of the tastes we describe are actually aromas."[9] To initiate the experience, Rose sends an e-mail to participants a week in advance. This information explains the process and requirements, which serves as the contract between performer and participant. The agreement to accept the blindfold parameter and to eat from a menu without knowledge of the ingredients fortifies the trust needed for the performance.

Transitioning from Outdoor to Indoor

On the day of the performance, the participants gather at a bridge to Prince's Island Park, located in downtown Calgary and accessible only on foot or by bicycle. The walk to the restaurant is "symbolic of crossing over into the experience"[10] and allows the participants to experience an outside/inside moment, preparing them to be blindfolded. Laurel Green, in her role as "Audience Experience Manager and Dramaturg," organizes the group to focus their presencing by walking slowly across the bridge to the riverside restaurant, which looks out toward the sunset. This dramaturgical choice to lead the group through a natural setting parallels Catalan chef

Ferran Adrià's conceit of starting a feast outdoors to highlight the Spanish coastline before heading indoors, as he deems "the meal as event" and the transition between the natural and man-made space as a "theatrical 'interval.'"[11]

Politicizing the Body

By positioning the participants' bodies at the centre of the performance, *Taste* opens up a discourse on body politics and thus the politics of food; a visceral connection is created between performer, participant, and the medium of food. The participant's body not only serves as the vessel through which food is consumed but also acts as a source responding to local ingredients through the senses (except for sight as that would externalize experience). The performance, as Di Benedetto argues, mediates the sensorial relationship, as "the human body as a receiver of outside stimuli can assist the artist in using sensorial stimuli to compose a live theatrical event and create an in-between state of experience and awareness."[12] This changes the participant relationship within the performance, repositioning participants from passive consumers of narrative to receivers of sensory stimuli. The composition of this piece is one of creating textural stimuli, which allows the participants to encounter the foods presented and consumed through their tactile quality and, in turn, through the theatrical experience.

Food as Performance Art

The physical and mental connection begins when the participants are blindfolded before the River Café doors open; they are then individually led to their tables. Rose affirms that "nobody in fact knew each other in the group; generally speaking, it was a way of allowing the community of people … to come together, and to not be inhibited by somebody that you are familiar with."[13] The participants are seated and, unbeknownst to them, there is one non-blindfolded performer at each table, which enables the blending of predetermined and spontaneous behaviour. The table formations allow the recounting of personal stories by participants as reactionary counterpoints to the fictional stories told by the performers. The restaurant staff and non-participatory patrons act as a naturalistic yet also designed soundscape, which creates a hybrid of scripted, improvised, and natural sound. Wait staff are trained to time their seamless serving of tables so that participant consciousness is not distracted. They recite specific memorized text and communicate with the performer to ensure dishes are presented and cleared so as to create flow in the transitions. This orchestration reveals, as Di Benedetto theorizes, that "the usefulness of vision, hearing, touch, taste, and smell lies in how they each aid cognition, and for our purposes, it is how they aid the creation, reception, and interpretation of mimetic representation."[14] *Taste* is a theatrical experience that is naturalistic while layering realism in a restaurant with mimetic performance.

Narrative as Conduit to Consumption

In *Taste*, the primary function of food as nourishment interweaves with participant responses and pre-existing text created by the theatre company. The participants thus become activated into the performance through their physical and verbal integration within the piece. For Rose, "the most successful dish and narrative pairing" is when the story leads the participants to dig in a garden.[15] With the telling of that particular scripted story, a dish is simultaneously served and eaten by hand: it consists of a carrot and its edible top, followed by a radish, which is "buried in a mixture of hummus with textured crisp onions to make it feel like dirt; the participants dug down ... visceral, playful and childlike," which served as a "climactic act."[16] This moment is a culmination of the senses, taste, and shared food memories, which acts as a hybrid. The participants engage in the physical act of eating in a way that extends their normal dining behaviour, as exemplified by digging deep to reach the hummus on their plates. The performer reveals to the participants that they have no sense of taste, which is another climactic act important in augmenting the participants' engagement with the senses. This revelation heightens the performance by forcing the participants to immerse fully in their experience so that when they describe memories that the food elicits, their articulation is clear, which allows them to serve as taste surrogates. The dessert is ice cream and goat feta, which serves as a parallel climax for the performed text. The "denouement" occurs with the completion of the tasting when the performer leaves the table without the participants seeing, and the menu is finally revealed post-consumption and after performances at all the tables have finished.[17]

The Brain and Memory

Food historian Massimo Montanari maintains that "the organ of taste is not the tongue, but the brain, a culturally (and therefore historically) determined organ through which are transmitted and learned the criteria for evaluations."[18] If the brain is the real organ of taste, it necessarily draws on the senses to categorize specific flavours. By removing a sense or by linking it to the performance, *Taste* changes the relationship of the food to the brain. Traditionally, the brain expects to *see* a performance; here, the brain is rewired to *taste* performance. This relationship of food and narrative is further reinforced with the participants responding to how the meal evokes memories of similar tastes or textures. Each meal can be viewed as a series of compositions that are, in live performance, a hybrid of the performers' rehearsed stories and the participants' shared memories, provoked by what they are eating and what stories are told during each specific meal portion. By shifting the context of taste experiences, Rose sets up a performance for the participants to sense in new and different ways, as "everything that we did was designed [for] the amplification of taste … I was always evaluating how it was enhancing the taste experience."[19] *The Calgary Herald*'s Stephen Hunt deems the event an "equally brilliant meeting of drama and tasting,"[20] which solidifies Ghost River's performance as both theatre and performance art.

Embodied Awareness and Sustainability

The audience is shocked as its primary sense is removed; however, *Taste* differs from Antonin Artaud's Theatre of Cruelty in that the goal is not to assault the audience with the senses, but to heighten the remaining ones, creating an open experience. Ghost River Theatre is not the only company that integrates food in performance, but with the rising cost of food and increasing food waste, these performances may run the risk of being unsustainable. The potential to raise awareness of sustainability must therefore be integrated into this genre to fully realize its capacity for addressing systemic world issues. Performances that use food to create an experience can seem superfluous or wasteful, which exacerbates a perilous narrative. In this sense, Rose is also challenged by the elitist nature of *Taste* due to the expensive ticket price, which influences the audience type.[21] Humans need food to survive, and *Taste* could perhaps be interpreted from a broader perspective as approaching

Figure 10.2
Ghost River Theatre tasting with actor Joe Perry, 2015.

an Aristotelian tragedy in that it "is the imitation of an action that is serious."[22] When the spectators consume food, they embody the magnitude of nourishment that privileges the spectators above those individuals who cannot afford the ticket to *Taste*, which elicits an interpolated form of pity. This embodied process is about human survival and, on some level, elicits the fear that our food-producing ecosystems are being destroyed.

One of the benefits of *Taste* is that the performance brings consciousness to the participants' food consumption in order for them to carry away a deepened appreciation of ingredients while being educated in an embodied format. This embodiment of awareness brings to light the importance of paying attention to what we eat, and how we eat it, through the frame of sustainability driven by the restaurant's philosophy, which is "taste of place [focusing on] locally sourced food and vegetables that are sustainably grown and made."[23] In turn, this philosophy affects the performance implicitly. Rose clarifies the performance objective in that it is a "sensory experience involving taste … my idea is that the ultimate goal is that the audience walks away understanding [the senses and the] incredible resource that one has within their tasting palate and capacity. Those tastes are obviously affected by how that food is made and where it is grown."[24]

Economics of Food

Sustainability is a critical topic in a world where the human population is growing exponentially and there is an unbalanced food system. What is the value of having food integrated into performance with food prices on the rise? In order to justify the exploitation of food in the name of art, it must be rooted in the name of a performative experience that transforms food beyond the material. The *Taste* ticket price of $80 is valued at half the actual cost of the food used in creating the dishes. With approximately 4.9 million Canadians living in poverty, public discussions typically focus on housing, education, and food costs.[25] Rose understands the complexity of a larger problem in that modernism and globalization are issues that a single performance cannot resolve. However, Rose's agenda is to use food and the senses to awaken consciousness, inviting reflections on capitalism in an embodied experience that ultimately is set up to reject globalism and embrace local practices. Do performances within this genre have to be elitist? Once food combines with entertainment it tends to become disconnected from nourishment, and the socio-economic background of the participant inevitably contextualizes the performance. However, the several gourmet canapés, which frame each performance, balance portion size with storytelling; this equal pairing reconnects, in each bite, the functionality of nourishment.

The Future

Rose is open to *Taste* being performed in other Canadian cities and globally, with future performances designed in collaboration with the people and food of those communities. The aim is not to create an exact replica of the Calgary experience, but to model the "best practices of that, to a new location, to a new city."[26] Municipal and federal practices, such as Vancouver's aim to be the Greenest City with zero waste by 2020 and France's banning of food waste from supermarkets, aim to create a food-conscious world. Indeed, the food performance genre may be at peril of vanishing due to the soaring cost of food and criticisms of its misuse. Meanwhile, the price of tickets heightens the popularity of such events for those who can afford it, potentially making food performance an elitist experience. Despite these factors, it is imperative that performances such as *Taste* survive in one iteration or another. They create new social experiences and facilitate the conscious tasting of food so that eating returns to a social form of presencing while focusing on the senses to enrich the participants' experience.

Acknowledgments

Ghost River Theatre (GRT) in collaboration with Vertical City Performance and River Café presented *Taste* at River Café as part of Beakerhead 2015. *Taste* is the second instalment of GRT's "Six Senses" performance series, designed to explore the theatrical potential of our senses. Show credits: Concept/Co-Creator/Director – Eric Rose; Playwright/Co-Creator – Bruce Barton; River Café Proprietor/Artistic Collaborator – Sal Howell; River Café Chef/Artistic Collaborator – Matthias Fong; Audience Experience Manager/Dramaturg – Laurel Green; Dramaturg – Pil Hanson; Assistant Director – Nicola Elson. Featuring: Kris Demeanor; Joe Perry; Bobbi Goddard; Emily Promise Allison; and Edward Ogum. River Café Servers & Staff: Andrew Winfield; Jenn Lamb; Courtney Robinson; Ethan Trillana; and Kelly Beames.

Notes

1 "Umami" is a savoury taste picked up by taste receptors that identify glutamate in the food being consumed (Di Benedetto, *The Provocation of the Senses*, 93).
2 Di Benedetto, *The Provocation of the Senses*, 93.
3 Ghost River Theatre, "Company."
4 Rose, interview by author, 19 January 2016.
5 Scharmer, *Theory U*, 42.
6 Rose, interview by author, 19 January 2016.
7 Ibid.
8 Di Benedetto, *The Provocation of the Senses*, 7.
9 Ibid., 111.
10 Rose, interview by author, 11 November 2016.
11 Abrams, "Mise En Plate," 9, 10.
12 Di Benedetto, *The Provocation of the Senses*, 1.
13 Rose, interview by author, 19 January 2016.
14 Di Benedetto, *The Provocation of the Senses*, 2.

15 Rose, interview by author, 19 January 2016.
16 Ibid.
17 Ibid.
18 Montanari, *Food Is Culture*, 61.
19 Rose, interview by author, 19 January 2016.
20 Ghost River Theatre, "Taste."
21 Rose, interview by author, 19 January 2016.
22 Gerould, *Theatre, Theory, Theatre*, 49.
23 Rose, interview by author, 11 November 2016.
24 Ibid.
25 "Just the Facts."
26 Rose, interview by author, 19 January 2016.

Bibliography

Abrams, Joshua. "Mise En Plate: The Scenographic Imagination and the Contemporary Restaurant." *Performance Research* 18, no. 3 (2013): 7–14. https://doi.org/10.1080/13528165.2013.816464.

Di Benedetto, Stephen. *The Provocation of the Senses in Contemporary Theatre*. London: Routledge, 2010.

Gerould, Daniel Charles, ed. *Theatre, Theory, Theatre: The Major Critical Texts From Aristotle and Zeami to Soyinka and Havel*. New York: Applause, 2000.

Ghost River Theatre. "Company." *Ghost River Theatre*. Accessed 7 November 2016. www.ghostrivertheatre.com/taste.

– "Taste." *Ghost River Theatre*. Accessed 11 November 2016. www.ghostrivertheatre.com/#grt.

"Just the Facts," *Canada without Poverty*. Accessed 8 November 2016. www.cwpcsp.ca/poverty/just-the-facts.

Montanari, Massimo. *Food Is Culture*. New York: Columbia University Press, 2006.

Rose, Eric. Interview by author, 19 January 2016.

– Interview by author, 11 November 2016.

Scharmer, Claus Otto. *Theory U: Leading from the Future as It Emerges: The Social Technology of Presencing*. 2nd ed. San Francisco: Berrett-Koehler Publishers, 2016.

White, Ann Folino, and Dorothy Chansky. *Food and Theatre on the World Stage*. New York: Routledge, 2016. PDF e-book.

PART THREE

Culinary Lineages
Collective and Personal Reflections

The five essays in Part 3 explore how culinary imaginations play a crucial role across time, creating both continuity and disruption through shared memories. The culinary past is remembered in a range of contexts, with creative interventions and one's chosen media shifting perceptions and consciousness. Themes of identity formation, cultural authenticity, and loss serve to construct, question, or resist the complicated legacies of colonialism, nationalism, multiculturalism, and diasporas. Shelley Boyd opens the conversation with an examination of totem foods, mythologies, and counter-cuisines as expressed by writer and artist Douglas Coupland in his *Souvenir of Canada* coffee-table books. Highlighting Coupland's interrelated modes of expression with respect to popular culture, consumerism, and globalization, Boyd raises questions about how Canadian tastes are defined through "edible" texts. Glenn Deer analyzes taste of another kind in photographer Janice Wong's award-winning culinary memoir *Chow*, based on her parents' Chinese restaurant on the prairies. Deer contends that as a genre, culinary memoir has not been closely scrutinized for its rhetorical and multimodal strategies, and his close reading of Wong's text, images, and book design provides a new interpretive framework. Closely connected to the photo-textual analysis offered by Deer, the artworks produced and discussed by artist Elyse Bouvier trace her self-reflexive tour of Chinese cafés across rural Alberta. For Bouvier, these restaurants are present in many time periods and cultural identities all at once. If personal experiences through food are significant means of re-imagining home-places and identities, then Asma Sayed's examination of South Asian diaspora writing and the notion of "currybooks" reveals immigrants' nuanced negotiations of the positive and challenging aspects of Canada's multicultural foodscape. Culinary scenes are also the focus of artist Jason Wright, who creates environments and situations through which to consider religion, gender roles, and consumer culture. Grotesque and comedic food rituals tied to place have shaped Wright's personal memories, work experience within the restaurant industry, and art practice as he continually "plays with his food."

11

Chewed a Book Lately?
Douglas Coupland's *Souvenir of Canada* Coffee-Table Books

Shelley Boyd

> "You take the book, and you remove the pages and soak them in a Tupperware container and then you chew the pages one at a time. I always did it when I was watching T.V."
> – Douglas Coupland[1]

Transforming his own words into a kind of food, writer and artist Douglas Coupland once chewed the pages of his novels, including *Generation X: Tales for an Accelerated Culture*, into malleable pulp, which he used to replicate hornet and wasp nests. Reflecting on his "edible" book sculptures, Coupland writes that his aim was to call on educators and institutions "to broaden their thinking about what books are or can be."[2] Provoking reconsiderations of the book's materiality and mutability, Coupland's physical consumption of his books is a complement to his books *about* consumption within historical contexts. In particular, his coffee-table books *Souvenir of Canada* and *Souvenir of Canada 2* are compendia that examine national (food) mythologies in light of the socio-economic forces of colonialism and globalization. When the first volume was published in 2002, Coupland introduced it as a coffee-table book by comparing it to 1976's *Between Friends/Entre Amis*, an exploration of Canada-United States relations that was given to the American president on the occasion of that country's bicentennial and that "joined *The Best of Life* and the family's thrashed atlas as a coffee table classic."[3] With the publication of *Souvenir of Canada* some thirty years after *Between Friends/Entre Amis*, Coupland noted how much had changed along the border in the post-9/11 world, with heightened surveillance, explosives detection, and racial profiling. Published two years apart, both of the *Souvenir* books were launched on Canada Day – opportunistic timing to be sure, but also a way to invite conversations about the nation, its celebrations, and its rituals and objects of consumption (particularly books, media, and food) that accompany such occasions and form a central part of citizens' daily lives.

At the time of its launch, Coupland saw *Souvenir of Canada* as alerting Canadians to their "myth-starved nation," marking an historical moment just as other celebrities and authors have done more recently by publishing books to commemorate Canada's 150th anniversary of Confederation.[4] The discourses and images that circulate in such popular texts magnify Canadian consumerism and the tensions that surface when it comes to discussions of national "taste." Coupland's *Souvenir* series is arguably a confluence of the physical book shaped by a popular genre, the material culture and marketplace that inspired it, the written text (replete with food-related metaphors and word play), and numerous visual representations of food. Together these components invite readers to reflect on their Canadian consumer world and their own predilections and actions within it.

Despite the *Souvenir* books having been best-sellers, critics have been dismissive largely because of the genre. One way of appreciating the more critical aspects of Coupland's coffee-table books is to examine them in relation to his edible book art, his earliest market-driven food writing, and his most acclaimed novel *Generation X*, with its avant-garde exploration of American consumerism. In this context, one discovers Coupland's creative manipulation of the coffee-table book genre through his use of food visuals, food-related behaviours, and creative textual arrangements – all of which highlight class-based, enculturated modes of consumption and the mutability of "Canadian" tastes.

Coffee-Table Books: A Feast for the Eyes

Whenever Coupland's reviewers use the term "coffee-table book," it is not a promising sign: "sounds suspiciously like one of those coffee-table books to me"; "more a coffee-table flipbook than an earnest collection of essays"; "a coffee-table guide" of "no intellectual weight."[5] In many ways, these comments signal sociologist Pierre Bourdieu's theory of "tastes" with respect to clothes, food, works of literature, and art "as markers of 'class.'"[6] According to Bourdieu, peoples' differing levels of education and socio-economic backgrounds shape a cultural hegemony of taste, which in turn, "classifies the classifier."[7] Not surprisingly then, most glossaries of literary terms contain no entry for coffee-table book, and scholars who do touch on the genre's conventions and market-focused genesis often note its dearth of educational and critical value.[8] The coffee-table book signals popular or low-brow literature; *Wikipedia* even indicates that the term has derogatory connotations.[9] In contrast, popular news media revel in the genre's sensual appeal as affordable entertainment since these books "provide a lot of magic ... for the sticker price."[10] Coffee-table books are large-scale "digests" designed for quick, random consumption when lounging or entertaining guests in one's home, waiting at the dentist's office, or browsing bookstore displays with a coffee in hand. Their size, weight, and full-colour illustrations indelibly tie these books to privilege and leisure, signalling what comparative literature scholar Koel Mitra sees as the "haute couture" world of fashion and material goods to which many middle-class readers aspire.[11] To this, I would add that the tremendous growth in the publication of oversized, fully illustrated cookbooks, not necessarily as practical guides but as reading material for armchair cooks, suggests that with the rise of foodie culture the cookbook and coffee-table book have merged – or, at very least, the former has borrowed conventions from the latter. And while one newspaper reviewer observes that coffee-table books function as "status symbols for those who would ostentatiously leave them out for public inspection,"[12] it is important to note that the food visuals in Coupland's *Souvenir* series (spilled corn syrup, Windsor Table Salt, and raw bacon dangling from a snow shovel) do not necessarily signal an aspirational or even appetizing aesthetic.

Coupland's aim in using the conventions of this popular genre is two-fold: to lay bare how market forces, governments, education, and other nations shape Canadians' collective and even individual tastes; and to suggest that citizens possess agency in how they consume and thereby transform their worlds. Such a critical approach to the genre challenges scholars who argue that what distinguishes a coffee-table book is that it "does not define the reading market; it is the other way [a]round where the market gives shape to a specific genre."[13] But this generalized claim does not necessarily hold true for either coffee-table books or literary genres. After all, the supposedly banal coffee-table book has served as political propaganda, and Coupland himself was clearly thinking about Canada's history of boosterism when outlining the content for *Souvenir of Canada*.[14] His manuscript notes include his initial thoughts on the topic and its intersection with the publishing industry: "who were those books about Canada being written for? These endless odes to endless resources ... they were written under the guise of being for outsiders, when they were actually meant to be read only by Canadians."[15] At the turn of the twenty-first century, the Canada book genre "'needed some defibrillating paddles,'" as Coupland puts it, so he gives his *Souvenir* series a mixture of the familiar and the odd (glossy visuals, sparse text, landscape photographs, and still lifes of grocery store goods split open, skewered by nails, and spilling over).[16] With respect to the familiar, reviewers often fault Coupland for including a coffee-table-book standard: poignant panoramas of the Canadian wilderness. But Coupland also charts the nation in a variety of private and political ways: through the rec room, his mother's pantry, his father's (hunting and fishing) den, the bedside table and kitchen counter of a crack house, and the road shoulder outside of Saskatoon where police officers abandoned a Cree man in the middle of winter.[17] These juxtaposed spaces and "uncomfortable symmetries" in life circumstances, as Ryan Melsom describes them, are key to Coupland's unconventional approach.[18] Indeed, in *Souvenir of Canada 2*, Coupland parodies the generic pan-Canadian landscapes of prairie grain elevators and arctic igloos through the inclusion of artist Colwyn Griffith's *Eye Candy 3*, photographs of three-dimensional models of iconic tourism sites composed entirely of junk food, and sculptor James Carl's *Spring Collection* (1991), an interactive igloo constructed out of antifreeze bottles at which Carl served the public glasses of dyed-blue water.[19]

While these artists' consumer-related artworks are key to the unusual yet familiar presentation of his coffee-table books, Coupland and Ken Mayer's still lifes (arranged by Coupland, lit and photographed by Mayer) in *Souvenir of Canada* particularly create a pan-Canadian landscape of citizens' "tastes" for technologies, popular entertainment, art, music, literature, and food. Peter Goddard observes that the *Souvenir* still lifes are "a contemporary reference to the images of prosperity found in 17th-century Dutch and Flemish paintings ... where semi-luxurious bourgeois objects could be found flowing in the centre."[20] Goddard adds that one photograph even alludes to the work of the American still-life painter William Michael Harnett, an artist whose work hung in print form on the walls of the Coupland family home. While Goddard accentuates the celestial reverence afforded to Canadian "comfort food," one should also note that the still-life photographs are composed in the vanitas genre, challenging viewers to contemplate death and the superficiality of life's pleasures.[21] If this is comfort food, it is unsettling. In *Canada Picture No. 6*, a skull rests near a dead fish as a toy polar bear stands atop a bag of garbage, and in *Canada Picture No. 9*, a sliced bag of Robin Hood flour spills out its now-unsanitary contents, a veritable avalanche threatening a nearby model train track and partially covering the *Saskatoon StarPhoenix* headline "Parasite Invasion."[22] These un/familiar edible landscapes, home-spaces, and still lifes (an art genre that, like the coffee-table book, venerates the commonplace) enable Coupland's readers to move beyond what Bourdieu calls the purely "functional" roles of food so that they may become conscious of their everyday consumer environments, behaviours, and predilections.[23]

Through the highly palatable coffee-table book genre, then, the *Souvenir of Canada* series presents a disconcertingly edible Canadian landscape. But given the genre's low-brow culture of reception, the sparse scholarly attention paid to Coupland's work is not surprising.[24] Reviewers even suggest that Coupland may be "cashing in on pedestrianism."[25] *Souvenir of Canada* has been described as "a nostalgic glossary" of "sucky sentimental feelings," "a melange of tossed-off banalities," and "tired cliches of pioneers."[26] *Souvenir of Canada 2* has been compared to "the immortal Vachon cake," which "isn't particularly nutritious."[27] The series may have its shortcomings, but one must question if the stigma of its mass-market genre is largely to blame for these dismissive comments. Positive reviews are the exception, such as Sarah Milroy who praises Coupland for countering the "numbing sameness" of the "predominantly horizontal (like the country) coffee-table books."[28] Coupland presents Canada as a world of "prepackaged plenty," but his *Souvenir* books are not without their satirical edge even though, or rather *because*, they assume the highly consumable coffee-table book form.[29]

Restaurant Reviews and Edible Books as Media of Exchange

To gain a new perspective on the *Souvenir* series, I would first like to situate it alongside some of Coupland's other consumer-conscious texts in order to understand his critical and playful explorations of popular, national tastes. Appreciating the intersection of food, writing, and the marketplace came early in Coupland's career when in 1987 he worked as a freelance restaurant reviewer for *The Vancouver Sun*. Under the byline "Budget Gourmet," Coupland evaluated affordable restaurants, reporting on the flavours and textures of his meals. Food writers strive to avoid clichéd descriptions, and the young Coupland certainly infused his reviews with the unexpected. Overcooked calamari had the "consistency of an Adidas insole,"[30] and the German dish Hasenpfeffer (rabbit stew) was "what Elmer Fudd was always threatening to make out of Bugs Bunny."[31] His signature use of pop culture makes evident that even as a young writer, Coupland had imaginatively absorbed his media environment, using it to interpret what travelled from his plate to his mouth and then from his mind to the page. His unusual restaurant reviews intimate that popular media and consumer brands are powerful forces in shaping notions of taste, even if the editor at the time was not amenable to some of Coupland's distinctions.[32] Now that Coupland, the novelist and artist, has long since become his own kind of celebrity brand with cultural capital, it is hardly surprising that a copy of his 1987 review of the Sitar Restaurant is today proudly posted outside this establishment's entrance to attract patrons.[33] In the 1980s, food was primarily the target, not the source, of Coupland's figurative language. But if as a food journalist he initially explained taste and texture to the Canadian public, Coupland would eventually go on, as a creative writer and artist, to interpret his readers and their consumer culture *through* food, communicating larger narratives about the nation's socio-economic identity in a global context by turning to other popular text-based forms (such as the coffee-table book) and prompting readers into thinking about how they can be transformative in the ways they consume their worlds.

Coupland's clear fascination with everything edible, acts of consumption, and text-based expressions of popular culture makes him a writer-artist inspired by what literary critic Terry Eagleton refers to as "media of exchange."[34] Eating and writing about food, as Eagleton theorizes in "Edible Écriture," are two activities that accentuate the mouth's role as conduit: "Words issue from the lips as food enters them," making language and food embodied forms of experience, meaning, and knowledge.[35] For Eagleton, "food is what makes up our bodies, just as words are what constitute our minds; and if the body and mind are hard to distinguish, it is no wonder that eating and speaking should continually cross over in metaphorical exchange."[36] In other words, eating and speaking (or writing) are interrelated ways of interacting and communicating with the physical and cultural world and, at the same time, delineating our subjectivities.

Eagleton emphasizes the constitutive roles of food and language, and individuals are not passive in these processes of exchange. Consumption can be creative and transformative, a delineation that Barbara Kirshenblatt-Gimblett makes in her study of food as a performance medium. Just as some performance artists "externalize" ingestion and digestion, a similar argument can be made that Coupland makes visible the concrete, edible realities of Canadian society and their conceptual significance, fully appreciating the mouth as a site of physical and imaginative exploration (the metaphorical crossover that Eagleton describes).[37] Indeed, when Coupland masticated his books to create insect nests, his process/artwork was not unlike conceptual artist John Latham's *Art and Culture* (1966–69). In the 1960s,

Latham invited guests to a party entitled *Still and Chew* at which they chewed pages from Clement Greenberg's edited collection *Art and Culture*. Latham then distilled the substance into a bottle and later returned it to the library at St Martin's School of Art in London.[38] Kristine Stiles refers to the liquefied book and related materials as "action-objects," relics of an artistic act that serve to reconnect art-as-object to art-as-behaviour, in turn prompting viewers to reflect on their own behaviours both in terms of the "*now*," and the "*after now*."[39] In chewing and thereby altering the use and meaning of his novels, Coupland writes that he wanted to consider how books transmit culture through time and are "vital to the survival" of our species just as insect nests are about "defending against intruders."[40] His comments activate ideas about boundaries: the nature of international borders, cultural exchange over time, the bodily conduits of eyes and mouths, and the media that allow the imagined and the concrete to shape one other – all aspects that inform his Canadian coffee-table books. Reflecting on his book-nests, Coupland concludes with the insight that chewing a novel "really trashes your saliva ducts" and advises his reader-consumers to "drink lots of water and spit regularly or your teeth will turn grey."[41] His playful instruction foregrounds the physical act of consuming a text, but also suggests that words matter – stories shape tangible experiences of the world and mark collective and individual consciousness. Moreover, his question "Have you ever chewed a book?" invites readers to consider their own behaviours and perceptions and, perhaps, to experiment.[42]

Digesting America: *Generation X*

"The world made edible makes for unusual meals," according to Kirshenblatt-Gimblett, and Coupland's creative acts of consumption and pairings of popular book genres, food, and food-related behaviours certainly merit careful consideration since these artistic strategies defamiliarize readers' sense of their consumer worlds and tastes.[43] In this regard, Coupland approaches the critical role that Marshall McLuhan envisioned for artists in their mediated societies: "the preparing of an environment for human attention."[44] These "antienvironments" or "counterenvironments," as McLuhan refers to them, "open the door of perception to people otherwise numbed in a nonperceivable situation."[45] With respect to food and books as media of exchange, Coupland formulates unique counter-environments, or what I would like to call "counter-cuisines," with respect to his many critical uses of food.

Figure 11.1
Douglas Coupland, File 177-17: Chewed Paper Samples.

His representations of the mass-market, edible world enable his reader-consumers to become conscious of their mediated tastes, appetites, and identities, and their own ability to shape these ever-changing environments. Furthermore, Coupland's transnational counter-cuisine vision is in keeping with McLuhan's claim that Canada itself plays a "corporate, artistic role" by acting as a counter-environment to America.[46] McLuhan's ideal artist is a "frontier boundary-hopper," a role that Coupland assumed when writing his first novel, *Generation X*, with its critique of American consumerism, and when formulating his Canadian coffee-table books in a post-9/11 world.[47] Between Coupland's most acclaimed literary novel and his dismissed coffee-table books, there are several points of contact with respect to his counter-cuisine vision. Indeed, a consideration of the former – which was first commissioned as a non-fiction guidebook, another market-driven genre, before Coupland transformed it into his avant-garde novel – helps to strengthen the argument for a critical appreciation of the latter.[48] Thus, before returning to the *Souvenir of Canada* series, I would like to consider how the notion of popular genres as edible books, food imagery, and creative acts of consumption inform *Generation X*.

Predominant lines of inquiry on *Generation X* pertain to its dystopian presentation of late capitalist consumer culture: its wastefulness, pervasive commoditization, and advertising language.[49] Food, however, has not figured prominently within this criticism, even though it makes visible the excesses of consumer culture as a consciousness-shaping force. Nevertheless, for the book-phenomenon and narrative of *Generation X*, the mouth has played and plays a critical role. When the novel was first published, Christopher Doody notes that its sales were largely "attributed to word-of-mouth publicity," leading to its cult following on university campuses and eventual best-seller status.[50] Its slogans, graphics, and symbols – all of which invite the public's awareness of how they consume and communicate their (textual) worlds – and the book's physical size make the novel conspicuous. Indeed, the dimensions of *Generation X* are similar to that of the *Souvenir* coffee-table books, and not surprisingly, one *Gen-X* reviewer disliked the novel's shape and feel, even using a food metaphor to describe its tactility.[51] Weighing these factors, Andrew Tate contends that the novel "displays a heightened sense of textuality and an awareness of its status as a material object."[52] One implication of this approach *within* the narrative, as Terri Zurbrigg notes, is that Andy, Dag, and Claire (a generation raised in a postmodern, late-capitalist environment) "appear to be deprived of a language not previously co-opted by advertising."[53] For this reason, the novel's glossary is particularly compelling when one considers that a "gloss" is both "a brief explanation ... of a difficult or obscure word" and a "tongue," suggesting that the mouth is the primary means of exploring and relating the world. Many of the annotations are food-related, and Coupland has been credited with popularizing terms such as "McJob" by naming into existence the effects of America's late twentieth-century capitalist society. Coupland is even cited in the *Oxford English Dictionary*'s definition of "McJob," suggesting that he has given form and expression to certain socio-economic, cultural experiences, or to what semiotician Roland Barthes would call the modern mythologies of mass culture.[54] As Barthes contends, neologism is a "constituting element of myth" by enabling one to "name concepts" that develop out of historical forces and "contingencies."[55] The fact that Coupland's terms have been added to the dictionary is evidence that they have shifted away from the particularities of history and into the realm of myth, the so-called "natural" order of a consumer world, albeit with Coupland's satirical twist.[56]

In addition to *Generation X*'s guidebook origins, word-of-mouth marketing, materiality, and heightened use of language, other kinds of consumer-focused mediations occur *within* the novel between the characters and their environment that involve defamiliarized representations of food and eating. In many ways, Coupland's *Generation X* is a late-capitalist reimagining of the mythical land of Cockaigne, a plentiful utopia found in both literature and the visual arts.[57] In Cockaigne's many variations, people reside in an entirely edible world: roasted geese fly through the air on spits, stewed larks alight in people's open mouths, rivers flow with wine, pigs run around with knives in their backs ready for carving, and nuns are reduced to sexualized flesh. In *Generation X*, equally voracious appetites are signalled through Claire's account of her retail experience where wealthy shoppers "gobbl[e] up the jewels and perfumes" like "children who are so spoiled ... they can't even wait for the food to be prepared. They have to reach for live animals placed on the table and suck the food right out of them" (9). Extending Cockaigne's bodily objectifications, *Generation X* also presents literal and figurative cannibalism, with Coupland's counter-cuisine vision capturing individuals' transformations by their late-capitalist environment. Like industrially prepared food, humans circulate in the novel as commodities, such as in the opening scene when Andy wipes yellow gunk from the snouts of his dogs, unsure if the substance is cheese from his microwave pizza or "yuppie liposuction fat" from the dumpsters behind the nearby cosmetic surgery centre (4). Or when Dag, who once survived on Kraft Dinner sandwiches when working for a meagre salary in Toronto, describes his former office cubicle as a "veal-fattening pen" (19–20). These grotesque presentations of humans-as-food expose

DOUGLAS COUPLAND'S *SOUVENIR OF CANADA* COFFEE-TABLE BOOKS

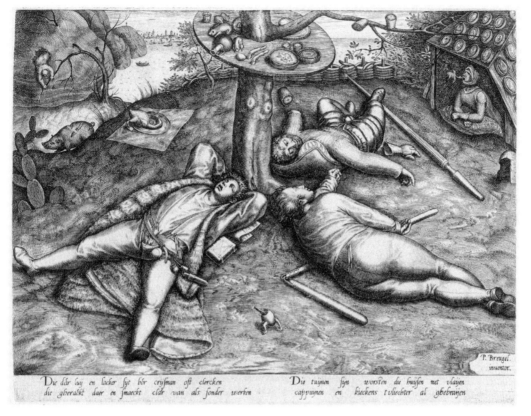

Figure 11.2
Pieter van der Heyden, after Pieter Bruegel the Elder, *The Land of Cockaigne*, after 1570, engraving.

the fact that individuals, caught up in routines of mindless consumption, are themselves utterly absorbed by the gluttonous world they inhabit.

Ultimately, what enables Andy, Claire, and Dag to perceive and critique their consumer world is a counter-cuisine food ritual focused on the exchange of both the imagined and the material. Critics agree that the friends' decision to live in the California desert is symbolic, providing a strategic distance from American culture as they search for meaningful narratives that challenge the status quo.[58] But it is the refuge of the desert *picnic*, in particular, that takes the main characters outside their usual modes of interaction, generating an alternative "nutritional consciousness," to use Barthes's term, that creates a situational framework of food-related behaviours and an imaginative "inoculation" against a ubiquitous consumer myth.[59] Driving to a failed housing development in West Palm Springs Village, parking the car with the tailgate lowered, and dining on mesquite chicken breasts and iced tea (16), the friends induce a "carbohydrate coma," which puts them in a "listening mood" (39). As they digest their lunch and shared stories, an altered consumer consciousness and sense of community take hold, not the feelings of grotesque greed that alienate consumers while also homogenizing society. A similar event occurs at the conclusion of the novel when Andy stops his car alongside the highway, eats oranges (first pilfered from and then given by a forgiving farmer), and watches what appears to be a thermonuclear cloud on the horizon. California's Imperial County is fecund – "*Everything* secretes food here" – and although the image suggests another Cockaigne-like landscape, Andy's experience represents the possibility of differently shared "commons" with new ways of perceiving and relating (175). This "restful unifying experience" includes other drivers, such as travelling salesmen who munch on microwaved 7-Eleven hamburgers as they exit their cars and take in the sky (177).[60] For Coupland, portable convenience foods become counter-cuisine when they paradoxically allow the comforts of home and daily life to facilitate moments of critical distance from the habituated consumer world.[61]

Souvenir of Canada: The *ABC*s of Canadian Taste

As with the dystopian *Generation X*, the *Souvenir of Canada* coffee-table books adapt a heightened, critical use of media of exchange (food, words, and a market-driven genre). The *Souvenir* series operates in ways that McLuhan would endorse: "Art makes the corporate and communal accessible to the individual, whose task it is to assimilate the tradition, to modify it in relation to new situations that are continuously forming."[62] Attentive to the twenty-first century and globalization, Coupland creates what McLuhan would call "mirrors of the present" in much the same way that "Emily Carr's paintings made accessible … the British Columbia experience," or "The Group of Seven made Canada visible."[63] Of course, these painters have often been the subjects of coffee-table books themselves, and the regional and national mythologies in which they circulate have also been questioned.[64] In a similar vein, Coupland critiques the nation's socio-economic character through counter-cuisine narratives that render stereotypical fare and its cultural and class-related associations unfamiliar, foregrounding so-called Canadian tastes and consumer mythologies.

In keeping with *Generation X*'s physical presentation and guidebook origins, the *Souvenir of Canada* series pushes readers to reconsider how they consume their textual, edible worlds, but this time through an alphabetical arrangement. Reviewers typically make brief references to the alphabet or set it aside altogether.[65] But careful reflection on the conventions of the alphabetical form and Coupland's challenging of them illuminates his counter-cuisine vision of Canadian consumerism. Jacquelyn Ardam observes that "alphabetic texts from all genres ... routinely raise questions of cultural and institutional understanding, learning, mastery, and genius. Even the phrase 'the ABCs' is shorthand for foundational knowledge," and texts that use this structure make "an implicit promise ... that they will re-create, organize, and make legible their worlds from A to Z."[66] It is important to note, here, that food's recurrence across the alphabets of Coupland's *Souvenir* series suggests it plays a foundational role in Canada's material culture and knowledge, what Barthes views as the mythology of a nation's everyday fare. Analyzing food's associations with letters (and their entries) across the books uncovers Coupland's experimentation with the alphabet form – that is, his attention to its meta-discursive framework and potential failures as such. Ardam observes that the alphabet appeals to artists and writers of the avant-garde because they are interested in "institutional and cultural critique" and enjoy the "sequence's intrinsic tension between sense and nonsense, meaning and arbitrariness, order and chaos."[67] The *A*-to-*Z* form also makes it, according to literary scholar Hilary A. Clark, an "encyclopedic enterprise" that "necessarily comes up against the inability to totalize or include all that can be known" since "knowledge is not fixed and eternal" but changes "with the material conditions of life."[68] "Incompletion," "obsolescence," and "ideological blind spots" always shape "the categories of a particular culture at a particular time."[69] In keeping with this convention, Coupland's *Souvenir* books – with their revised alphabets, gaps in sequence, new entries, and repeated nods to the disappearance of the country's material culture through globalization and other contingencies – apprise readers of the incoherence and mediated aspects of their so-called national cuisine and tastes. Moreover, his manipulation of the alphabet highlights the fact that the project is conscious of its incompleteness, its randomness in its selection – and that it, to use Coupland's words, "creates its own logic."[70] Tellingly, when an interviewer asked Coupland why he wrote the sequel *Souvenir of Canada 2*, Coupland replied, "a better question is more like, 'When is number 3 coming out?' I think Canadian identity isn't as finite as one book."[71]

In the same spirit as a school primer that connects *A* with "apple" (an act of enculturation that teaches children which tastes are foundational within their culture), the *Souvenir* series names iconic Canadian foods such as maple syrup, Kraft Dinner, and beer. These "totem" foods, as Barthes theorizes them, are ubiquitous, nationalized, and capable of supporting "a varied mythology which does not trouble about contradictions."[72] Yet Coupland brings contradiction and arbitrariness to the fore in much the same way that Melsom argues the film adaptation of Coupland's *Souvenir* project "refuses ... cliché while employing its structure" in order to challenge gendered stereotypes and the traditional family home.[73] Thus, food unites Canadians in the *Souvenir* coffee-table books, but not in the ways one would expect, since what is being signified appears both ambiguous and ephemeral. In other words, Coupland creates dissonance by suggesting that citizens have been unreflective, passive consumers who are superficially united and unaware of the gaps in their understanding when it comes to past exploitations and ongoing social inequalities and exclusion.

Setting out to define Canadian taste through suggestive and loaded signifiers, Coupland reveals a relational, class-based cuisine. In the entry "Cheeseheads" in *Souvenir of Canada*, Coupland distinguishes the nation's cuisine by its portability: "The foods of France may be legendary, and American cuisine may be a joyous hash of Pop Art and military science, but Canadian food? A French newspaper once asked me to try to define Canadian food, and the best description I could come up with was, 'It has to come from a box.'"[74] This prepackaged, processed food has high concentrations of carbohydrates, fat, and salt, and while Coupland initially suggests through his references to camping trips and the northern climate that this diet is "imperative," his alphabetical entries question if Canadian taste is synonymous with a leisured life in the great outdoors. Coupland likens these high-calorie foods to "fuel" that facilitates the work of citizens defined by a resource-sector economy. This working definition of Canadian cuisine carries over to *Souvenir of Canada 2* under the entry "Energy," which features both a list and still-life photograph of products (petroleum, lard, charcoal, baked beans, uranium, beer, etc.) necessary to run both humans and machines as though they belong within the same category.[75] Coupland intimates that Canadians are a kind of serfdom, pillaged by other countries – a suggestion he first makes under *R* for "Rapeseed, Zinc, and Cod" and later includes under the all-important *C* in *Souvenir of Canada 2* when he notes that "rapeseed" was renamed "Canola," after "Canada" (15). Relative to other nations,

Canada is primarily "a commodity economy," Coupland observes, which means as citizens, "we don't actually *do* anything with what we reap – we ship it somewhere else, and then other people ... sell it back to us."[76] Canadians' diet, therefore, is about keeping citizens fuelled for the work of harvesting and supplying raw materials to global markets, a narrative that most Canadians have internalized.

With respect to the nation-as-serfdom, Coupland ironically points to Kraft Dinner as a definitive Canadian dish since this inexpensive boxed food requires nominal cooking skills and is produced by an American company. In *Souvenir of Canada*, Coupland's Kraft Dinner musings are included under the important *C* section with the identifying terms "Canada™" and "Cheeseheads." Tongue-in-cheek, Coupland acknowledges the latter term is a "slur" that Americans use to refer to Canadians (11). This relational term, like "beefeaters" for the British and referencing their French adversaries as "frogs," accomplishes what food metaphors often do, according to Michiel Korthals: "organize humans into different groups, [and] distribute in an unequal way status ... by incorporating different appeals to the body and senses."[77] Cheese and Kraft Dinner constitute part of the "totemic" mythology of Coupland's Canadian counter-cuisine in that, as Barthes observes, these national myths "are ... not innocent" but are very much tied to capitalism and histories of expropriation.[78] Elsewhere, food scholars have examined Kraft Dinner through the critical lenses of class differences and poverty *within* Canada, but Coupland's aim is to scale outward.[79] Americans are predominant shapers of Canadian food culture, and Coupland also acknowledges that other countries have left their mark. For example, maple sugar, the "symbolic blood" that unites the country, grew in popularity because it was an inexpensive, geographically accessible sweetener for the British.[80] And the once ubiquitous stubby beer bottles, Coupland writes, were "an industry standard" tied to British nepotism.[81] This last claim is incorrect, as any beer historian will testify.[82] In other words, Coupland purposely thwarts the nonfiction genre of coffee-table books in order to construct his own counter-cuisine mythology. On the topic of beer, Coupland's manuscript includes the handwritten note "Fake history," suggesting this totemic beverage and its associated commercial fictions are Coupland's means of critiquing a national consciousness founded upon trade relations in much the same way that Barthes theorizes myth as a form that distorts historical details so as to naturalize bourgeoisie norms.[83] Coupland's aim is not to uphold popular tastes, but rather to promote an anti-capitalist, anti-corporate view that awakens Canadians from their "Cheesehead" mentality. Just as the characters from *Generation X* retreat to their desert picnic in order to reflect on American consumerism, Coupland creates distance through his Canadian counter-cuisine to render visible the nation's compliant economic role and identity. To this end, in *Souvenir of Canada 2*, he describes his picnic lunches as a young man seated next to the Eaton family's crypt in Toronto's Mount Pleasant Cemetery. Coupland recontextualizes this popular food ritual of the nineteenth century, when public green spaces were sparse, to acknowledge the now-defunct Canadian department store as a kind of lost "consumer commons." In the *Souvenir* books, the domestic marketplace and other homegrown initiatives (such as Quebec's poutine) continually appear destined for rebranding and absorption within the global economy.[84]

With Canadians functioning as passive consumers of a relational cuisine – in other words, food that is produced elsewhere and that signals an enduring colonial-economic mentality – Coupland occasionally turns to local fare and distinct tastes tied to the land. Significantly, his representations of locally harvested foods differ from the still-life photographs and captions detailing the shifting parameters of his mother's kitchen cupboards – a pantry replete with boxed and canned items that Coupland claims "could easily win a Most Canadian Shelves award."[85] Yet again, the alphabet structure brings to light contradictions and omissions, but especially those tied to "ideological blindspots," historical injustices, and systemic inequalities.[86] With respect to indigenous animal species, for instance, gaps in knowledge and destroyed ecosystems become apparent. The "Moose" entry in *Souvenir of Canada 2* recounts a dinner party at which a young Coupland consumed three portions of spaghetti until the host announced that the sauce was made from "ground moose meat" – a realization that made him want to vomit, even though it "*was* really delicious" (78). Coupland writes that moose occupy "the quiet nooks of the national imagination," and his visceral reaction suggests that many Canadians are, for the most part, disconnected from, and ignorant of, Indigenous foodways (78).[87] In her review of *Souvenir of Canada*, Sugars takes Coupland to task for his "myopically Anglo-European" vision of the country and for his exclusionary referencing of Inuit and First Nations as "alien others."[88] Sugars reads the book as a tedious "Coupland-centric version of Canada (and the world)."[89] Yet according to Clark, the "self-figuring turn" that typically appears within an encyclopedic text is not about a "'narcissistic'" vision, but about a "self-representation [that] generates an excess, opening outward onto the freedom of infinite *speculation* on knowledge."[90] The fact that Coupland includes an entry for "Doug" that acknowledges the popularity of his name – there being more men named "Doug" in Canada than any other name – suggests that he is trying, within this personalized alphabet, to undermine and relativize his own book's authority.[91]

If Coupland has in the past suffered from his own ideological blindness, then the revised alphabet of his second book *Souvenir of Canada 2* addresses some of the earlier gaps with respect to Indigenous foodways. For example, when it comes to Pacific and Atlantic salmon, and Atlantic cod (popular meals at Canadian dinner tables), Coupland highlights the species' near-destruction. In his manuscript notes under the heading "Cod," Coupland writes one word: "Extinct."[92] This entry never made it into *Souvenir of Canada*, but under "Fish" in *Souvenir of Canada 2*, Coupland recounts the imperiled fish stocks, the chemically modified flesh colour of farmed Atlantic salmon, and the pollution and invasive organisms that are destroying fresh-water fish. In Coupland's view, "fish … give us a potent, undeniable health report on our land and our culture," and if Canadians do not become environmental stewards and "start adding brains to our resources, it'll probably be the end of us."[93] Tellingly, the sterile white kitchen and bare cupboards of the *Canada House* installation featured in *Souvenir of Canada 2* includes *The Spawning Ladder* painted in flesh tones selected from the colour-wheel assigned to synthetic astaxanthin, the chemical fed to farmed Atlantic salmon to modify their appearance.[94] Displaced from the river, *The Spawning Ladder*, which ushers no fish to nowhere, stands as an indictment of Canada's environmental exploitation and a warning against present and future scarcity.

The *ABC*s of Canada's Future Tastes

The counter-cuisine of the *Souvenir of Canada* books includes popular Canadian tastes intricately tied to colonialism, American cultural and economic imperialism, globalization, and the expropriation of Indigenous peoples' traditional territories and resources. The series invites readers to consider the objects and myths of Canadian consumerism via the still-life photographs and alphabetical word play; the coffee-table book itself as a digestible good and national genre; citizens' actions with respect to sustainability and social inequalities; and popular and relational tastes within the nation's changeable, edible landscapes. Rather than "skip past the Canola chapter and photos of Ma Coupland's cupboards," as one reviewer suggests,

I urge readers to slow down and reassess un/familiar ways of ordering and consuming the world.[95] Coupland states: "Some books are heavier than others. Some are deliberately bonbons"; his coffee-table books hold both critical and consumer appeal as glossy counter-cuisine.[96] Because the *Souvenir* series alphabetizes a more than tenuous and fraught edible Canada in a globalized reality, then one must question what the future holds for the nation. In his alphabets, Coupland repeatedly gestures to the space-age qualities of Canadian fare: the bilingual packaging of "Capitaine Crounche" cereal evokes "a parallel-universe country" like in *Star Trek*,[97] and the nation's multicultural society resembles not the American melting pot but "the outer-space cocktail-lounge … from *Star Wars*."[98] Relative to the United States, Canada will always be young in Coupland's mind and therefore free from being "permanently locked into … myths and identities."[99] His space-age allusions, while paradoxically backwards-glancing in their pop-culture references, imply that Canada will have a highly changeable future, unbound by any singular sense of nation, and this potential for new mythologies subtly distinguishes Coupland's treatment of Canadian consumer culture from that of the United States.[100] Or does it?

While critics read the coffee-table books as brimming with nostalgia, Coupland rejects such interpretations as wrong about his intentions.[101] He is steadfastly suspect of wistful longings for the past, especially in terms of the edible world. A case in point is his 2014 article "Douglas Coupland: Worcestershistershire" (a Bugs Bunny allusion reminiscent of his restaurant reviews) in which Coupland surveys the "found food" in his Vancouver studio and home fridge. There is no maple syrup or beer but instead "Pre-9/11 Worcestershire sauce," "Catalina salad dressing from Michael Jackson's wake," "Mustard from the Bush years," and "Ketchup from the first Obama election night."[102] The non-perishable condiments form a kind of museum of American cultural history and contrast with the vanitas-inspired, edible terrain of the *Souvenir* series (published a decade earlier) and with Coupland's more recent memory of a Chilean dinner party where the food was so fresh it was "decomposing … on the plate."[103] For Coupland, this permanence is disconcerting and ultimately refuted when his body has a conversation with a three-week-old egg salad sandwich. Thinking about "science-enhanced" food, Coupland asks, "If food doesn't rot outside the body, then what's supposed to be happening inside the body? Am I technically starving?"[104] For Coupland, the edible world is, or rather should be, forever in flux as thoughtfully eating one's way in and through time is one of the most physically and politically transformative actions one can take.

When contemplating Canadian tastes as defined by the *Souvenir of Canada* coffee-table books, therefore, one must keep in mind that this series is a critical reaping of a *past* consumer world. They are popular book-form mementos of a place and time once experienced, tasted, and now imaginatively remembered. As such, Coupland's coffee-table books serve as warnings to Canadians to be open to change and not to take for granted the edible world they presently enjoy (salmon, fresh water). This world will inevitably disappear if they do not change their modes and perceptions of consumption and address ideological bias and its consequences. To date, there has been no *Souvenir of Canada 3*, and such a volume is doubtful. In the twenty-first century, Coupland's space of critical commensality has become digital. For his Twitter followers, the counter-cuisine has transformed from the "light" fare of his best-selling coffee-table books to the even shorter, quicker, and electronically dispersed bytes of the Internet. In a world of online sharing, Instagram-worthy restaurant meals circulate in abundance, but alongside these, Coupland's tweeted Kraft Dinner helpings and instructions gesture to other acts of consumption, those counter-versions of taste and their evolving (Canadian) distinctions.

Notes

1 Milroy, "Coupland's Literary Lunch," R2.
2 Coupland, "Insects."
3 Coupland, "Strong and Free."
4 Coupland, "The Encyclopedia of Us." *Souvenir of Canada* was published in 2002 to coincide with Canada's 135th anniversary of Confederation.
5 Sugars, "Souvenir of Coupland"; Faulkner, "A Perfect Fit"; Good, "Coupland's Canada."
6 Bourdieu, *Distinction*, xxv.
7 Ibid., xxix.
8 In his "Review of *The Maple Leaf Forever*" in *The Canadian Historical Review*, Ryan Edwardson notes that he was "certainly surprised when asked to write a review" of a coffee-table book for the academic journal, adding "academic snobbery should not ... get in the way" of analyzing "a cultural artefact" through which "non-academics glean and reify their own sense of Canadianness" (257). See also Jeremy M. Black's criticism of historical atlases and their use of colour for marketing purposes.
9 *Wikipedia* suggests that the term "can be used pejoratively to indicate a superficial approach to the subject."

10 Wigod, "Coffee-table Books of Note," G2.
11 Mitra, "Culture and the Market."
12 Covert, "The Best Coffee Table Books."
13 Mitra, "Culture and the Market."
14 See the *Wikipedia* entry for mention of this in relation to the lives of political leaders.
15 Coupland, manuscript notes for *Souvenir of Canada*.
16 McGregor, "Been There, Done That."
17 The still lifes of the crack den are from *Leon's Palaces* series by photographer Karin Bubaš. (Coupland, *Souvenir of Canada*, 64–5). The photograph of the site where the Cree man was abandoned, titled *Road Shoulder and High Voltage Tower Beside the Queen Elizabeth Power Station, Saskatoon, Sasktachewan* (2000), is by photographer Chris Gergley (Coupland, *Souvenir of Canada*, 97–8).
18 Melsom, "A (Queer) Souvenir of Canada."
19 Griffith's *Northern Lights* appears on the inside cover, and *Inglis Manitoba* appears on page 9 of *Souvenir of Canada 2*. On his website, Griffith describes the process of making *Eye Candy 3*: "I developed my impressions using virtual postcards and tourist brochures as a visual and experiential compass. Some of the "foods" used in the images include coloured sugars, Cheez Wizz, fruit roll-ups, hickory-sticks (French-fries), wafer cookies, tic-tacs and canned gravy" (Accessed 1 May 2018, www.colwyngriffith.com/eyecandy3.html). Appearing on page 13 of *Souvenir of Canada 2*, James Carl's *The Spring Collection* (1991) was both a public sculpture and performance at which Carl "serv[ed] drinking water tinted bright blue that looked more like Prestone windshield wiper fluid than 'naturally pure' drinking water" (Grande, "James Carl").
20 Goddard, "Still Life with Table Hockey."
21 Ibid.
22 Coupland, *Souvenir of Canada*, 72–3, 89.
23 In *Distinction*, Bourdieu writes: "And nothing is more distinctive ... than the capacity to confer aesthetic status on objects that are banal or even 'common' (because the 'common' people make them their own, especially for aesthetic purposes)" (xxviii–xxix).
24 The one exception is Ryan Melsom's "A (Queer) Souvenir of Canada." Melsom challenges critics who argue that Coupland offers "a reductive view of the nation" by analyzing the books and the film as an entire *Souvenir of Canada* project (but without considering the implications of the coffee-table book genre) and by focusing on a flexible definition of "queerness" and its expression within family relationships.
25 Faulkner, "A Perfect Fit."
26 Goddard, "Still Life with Table Hockey"; Sugars, "Souvenir of Coupland."

27 Dymond, "Grade School References." The Vachon Bakery Inc. began operating in Quebec in the 1920s and sells boxed pastries, such as the Jos Louis snacking cakes.
28 Milroy, "A Gen-Xer's Love Letter," R2.
29 Ibid.
30 Coupland, "When in the Roma," F6.
31 Coupland, "Nostalgic Treat," D8.
32 In a 2010 interview, Coupland recalls "the moment in my life when I learned the clear fork in the road between irony and no-irony. I was writing a restaurant review for *The Sun* and I described a serving portion as resembling the bronto ribs that tip over the Flintstones' car in the show's opening credits. The [section] editor crossed it out and wrote in, 'caveman like,' and my mind blanked out and I said to myself I can't do this any more" (McRanor, "From Bronto Ribs," D7).
33 On the topic of celebrity endorsements of restaurants, see Cooke, "Montreal in the Culinary Imagination," chapter 6 in this volume.
34 Eagleton, "Edible Écriture," 448.
35 Ibid., 446.
36 Ibid., 448.
37 Kirshenblatt-Gimblett, "Playing to the Senses," 8.
38 Stiles, "Uncorrupted Joy," 227.
39 Ibid., 230–1. Housed in the Museum of Modern Art's collection in New York, Latham's *Art and Culture* includes a briefcase, the stilled book, a party invitation, Latham's dismissal letter, and other items (Stiles, "Uncorrupted Joy," 227).
40 Coupland, "Insects."
41 Ibid. A related work of art that presents words as consumables is Coupland's *Viktor & Rolf* (2003), which positions text atop TV test patterns: "The artist considers the works still lifes, with the words arranged and presented as if on a platter" (Iyer, "When Words Become Art," 171).
42 Coupland, "Insects."
43 Kirshenblatt-Gimblett, "Playing to the Senses," 22.
44 McLuhan, *Essential McLuhan*, 339.
45 Ibid., 342.
46 McLuhan, "Canada," 106.
47 Ibid., 120.
48 On the genesis of *Generation X*, see Doody, "X-plained," 10–13.
49 For examples, see Tate, *Douglas Coupland*, for his discussion of consumerism, identity, and waste; Zurbrigg, *X = What?*, for her focus on the search for authentic narratives in a

postmodern world; Katerberg, "Western Myth," for his discussion of Coupland's frontier narratives of white middle-class America; and Lainsbury, "Generation X and the End of History," for his examination of the novel as a postmodern, avant-garde reflection on the late capitalism of North American.

50 Doody, "X-plained," 16.
51 See Doody's detailed examination of the novel's reception where he quotes a Montreal review: "'it droops in your hands like wet Wonderbread'" (qtd. in Doody, "X-plained," 19).
52 Tate, *Douglas Coupland*, 11.
53 Zurbrigg, *X = What?*, 9.
54 In *Mythologies*, Barthes describes myth as having two semiological systems: language (the signifier and signified); and *metalanguage*, "a second language, in which one speaks about the first," as the "details of the linguistic schema" fall away for the "total term, or global sign" – constituting the pervasive values and norms of a nation (115).
55 Barthes, *Mythologies*, 120–1.
56 In *Mythologies*, Barthes explicates myth's "naturalizing" effects within the context of daily life. Regarding France, Barthes argues that bourgeoisie norms, representations, and consumer tastes merge with the concept of *nation*, forming a kind of "natural order" through the semiological system of myth (129, 140–1).
57 "Cockaygne" is described in a satirical Middle English poem of the fourteenth century. Pieter Bruegel the Elder's painting *The Land of Cockaigne* (1567) is the most famous visual representation of this utopian landscape. On Coupland's satirical use of other western myths, see Katerberg, "Western Myth," for his examination of Coupland's parody of the (modern) West as a promised land, a place of beginnings and endings.
58 Katerberg examines the mythologized West as both a literal and figurative desert. Citing John Ulrich, who describes Coupland's desert as a negation of the consumer world, Tate notes in *Douglas Coupland* that the "infertile landscape … resists commerce … but promotes imaginative endeavour" (125). In *X=What?*, Zurbrigg similarly suggests this "desert detox" is where "irony has dried up, where capitalism and consumerism do not flow freely," and where the friends are able to share authentic narratives (11, 21).
59 Barthes, "Toward a Psychosociology," 25, and Barthes, *Mythologies*, 150–1. According to Barthes, food operates as "a system of communication," as societal norms and ideals associated with particular foods generate a shared "nutritional consciousness" for France's population ("Toward a Psychosociology," 21, 25).
60 This scene occurs when Andy is leaving the United States to join Dag and Claire in Mexico, a nation "whose role in the development of late capitalism," Zurbrigg suggests in *X=What?*, "is much less conspicuous" (34).

61 I agree with Katerberg's argument that in Coupland's re-imaginings of the mythical West, individuals "search for communities and connections to something larger than themselves"; however, I diverge from his suggestion that "the wilderness strips people of the familiar comforts and habits that allow them to repress the alienating reality of late modern life" ("Western Myth," 286–7, 286).

62 McLuhan, "Canada," 119.

63 Ibid.

64 See Darias-Beautell who points in "The Production of Vancouver" to Jin-me Yoon's famous installation *Group of Sixty-Seven* (1996), which featured photographs of Korean Canadians looking out from a Lawren Harris painting and looking at an Emily Carr painting: "*Group of Sixty-Seven* asks a fundamental question about how different people relate to ideas of the national/regional and the kinds of mythologies they often need to confront or subvert" (133).

65 One reviewer observes that the alphabet is imperfect with no entries for *A* but two for *Z*, yet does not provide interpretations as to why (Faulkner, "A Perfect Fit"). An interviewer from *Border Crossings* briefly notes the playful associations in "the drift from 'piss' to 'vinegar' to 'poutine'" but then asks how the book is organized "other than alphabetically" ("Je me souvenir").

66 Ardam, "The ABCs," 140.

67 Ibid., 133.

68 Clark, "Encyclopedic Discourse," 97.

69 Ibid.

70 "Je me souvenir."

71 Cooperman, "The Most Canadian Thing."

72 Barthes, *Mythologies*, 58.

73 Melsom, "A (Queer) Souvenir of Canada."

74 Coupland, *Souvenir of Canada*, 10. All subsequent references to this book are in parentheses after the quoted passage.

75 Coupland, *Souvenir of Canada 2*, 22–3. All subsequent references to this book are in parentheses after the quoted passage.

76 Coupland, *Souvenir of Canada*, 103, 102. In an interview, Coupland states, "our economic mentality is entirely colonial. Still" (Cooperman, "The Most Canadian Thing").

77 Korthals, "Food as a Source," 79.

78 Barthes, *Mythologies*, 61.

79 For an analysis of Kraft Dinner and charitable Canadians' misperceptions about poverty, see Rock, McIntyre, and Rondeau, "Discomforting Comfort Foods."

80 Coupland, *Souvenir of Canada*, 70.
81 Ibid., 104.
82 The stubby was a "homegrown industrial design" rolled out Canada-wide in the spring of 1962 (Coutts, *Brew North*, 88).
83 Coupland, manuscript notes for *Souvenir of Canada*.
84 The entry for "Poutine" features a photograph of a menu from the American franchise Burger King advertising the option of "switch your fries to poutine" (Coupland, *Souvenir of Canada*, 87).
85 Coupland, *Souvenir of Canada 2*, 71.
86 Clark, "Encyclopedic Discourse," 97.
87 For further analysis of these issues in this volume, see Tennant, "*Terra Nullius* on the Plate," chapter 4 in this volume, for discussion of "colonial blindness" within Canada's restaurant landscape and Gora, "From Meat to Metaphor," chapter 5 in this volume, for discussion of the beaver.
88 Sugars, "Souvenir of Coupland."
89 Ibid.
90 Clark, "Encyclopedic Discourse," 98.
91 In his review "A Nation of Dougs," Semley praises the "Doug" entry for foregrounding the "free play of signifiers and souvenirs, to laugh through the lack," and for underscoring the fact that Canada's is a manufactured identity.
92 Coupland, manuscript notes for *Souvenir of Canada*.
93 Coupland, *Souvenir of Canada 2*, 24.
94 Ibid., 65, 68–9.
95 Faulkner, "A Perfect Fit."
96 Gray, "A Conversation," 264.
97 Coupland, *Souvenir of Canada*, 10.
98 Ibid.; Coupland, *Souvenir of Canada 2*, 81.
99 Coupland, "The Encyclopedia of Us."
100 In "Western Myth," Katerberg suggests that in Coupland's dystopian fiction, America and Canada "suffer the same problems" in his re-mythologizing of the West at the end of history (287). He states that Coupland's novels, unlike science fiction, do not "repla[y] the classic Western or the mythic frontier process in outer space (*Star Wars*, for example)" (296). References to *Star Trek* and *Star Wars* within the *Souvenir* series imply, however, that Coupland imagines Canada somewhat differently than the United States.
101 An interviewer from *Border Crossings* magazine makes the comment, "The word souvenir … carries with it a sense of nostalgia," to which Coupland replies, "Really? Not for me"

("Je me souvenir"). See also Gray's interview "A Conversation with Douglas Coupland" in which Coupland rejects nostalgia in relation to Canada's past (259).

102 Coupland, "Worcestershistershire."
103 Ibid.
104 Ibid.

Bibliography

Ardam, Jacquelyn. "The ABCs of Conceptual Writing." *Comparative Literature Studies* 51, no. 1 (2014): 132–58. Project Muse.

Barthes, Roland. *Mythologies*. 1957. Translated by Annette Lavers. New York: Noonday Press, 1993.

– "Toward a Psychosociology of Contemporary Food Consumption." In *Food and Culture: A Reader*, edited by Carole Counihan and Penny Van Esterik, 20–7. New York: Routledge, 1997.

Black, Jeremy M. "The Historical Atlas: Teaching Tool or Coffee-Table Book?" *The History Teacher* 25, no. 4 (1992): 489–512. doi:10.2307/494356.

Bourdieu, Pierre. *Distinction*. 1984. Translated by Richard Nice. Introduction by Tony Bennett. London: Routledge, 2010.

Clark, Hilary A. "Encyclopedic Discourse." *SubStance* 21.1, no. 67 (1992): 95–110. JSTOR. www.jstor.org/stable/3685349.

Cooperman, Liza. "The Most Canadian Thing He Can Think Of: Questions & Answers." *National Post*, 19 June 2004. Canadian Newsstream.

Coupland, Douglas. "Douglas Coupland: Worcestershistershire." *Financial Times*, 19 December 2014. www.ft.com.

– "The Encyclopedia of Us: For Doug Coupland, 'Canada-osity' Is in the Details: Capitaine Crounche, Daytime Headlights, and Peeing in the Snow. An Irreverent Tribute to a Myth-Starved Nation." *National Post*, 29 June 2002, SP1. Canadian Newsstand Major Dailies.

– *Generation X: Tales for an Accelerated Culture*. New York: St Martin's Press, 1991.

– "Insects." *The New York Times*, 31 August 2006. http://coupland.blogs.nytimes.com/2006/08/31/insects.

– "Nostalgic Treat for a Lover of German Food." *The Vancouver Sun*, 22 May 1987, D8. Canadian Newsstand Pacific.

– Notes for Souvenir of Canada. RBSC-ARC-1643-Douglas Coupland fonds. Literary Projects. File 40-12. University of British Columbia Rare Books and Special Collections, Vancouver.

– *Souvenir of Canada*. Vancouver: Douglas & McIntyre, 2002.

– *Souvenir of Canada 2*. Vancouver: Douglas & McIntyre, 2004.

– "Strong and Free." *Maclean's*, 25 November 2002, 22. Canadian Periodicals Index Quarterly.

– "When in the Roma, You'll Eat Well." *The Vancouver Sun*, 1 May 1987, F6. Canadian Newsstand Pacific.

Coutts, Ian. *Brew North: How Canadians Made Beer and Beer Made Canada*. Vancouver: Greystone Books, 2010.

Covert, Kim. "The Best Coffee Table Books Are a Treat for the Senses." *Canadian Press NewsWire*, 2 December 2003. Canadian Newsstream.

Darias-Beautell, Eva. "The Production of Vancouver: Termination Views in the City of Glass." In *Unruly Penelopes and the Ghosts: Narratives of English Canada*, edited by Eva Darias-Beautell, 131–56. Waterloo: Wilfrid Laurier University Press, 2012.

Doody, Christopher. "X-plained: The Production and Reception History of Douglas Coupland's *Generation X*." *Papers of the Bibliographical Society of Canada* 49, no. 1 (2011): 5–34. Canadian Periodical Index.

Dymond, Greig. "Grade School References Make Us Canadian." *National Post*, 3 July 2004. Canadian Newsstream.

Eagleton, Terry. "Edible Écriture." In *Eating Words: A Norton Anthology of Food Writing*, edited by Sandra M. Gilbert and Roger J. Porter, 445–9. New York: W.W. Norton, 2015.

Edwardson, Ryan. "Review of *The Maple Leave Forever: A Celebration of Canadian Symbols* by Donna Farron Hutchins and Nigel Hutchins." *The Canadian Historical Review* 89, no. 2 (June 2008): 257–8. doi: 10.3138/chr.89.2.257.

Faulkner, Rob. "A Perfect Fit for Canada's Birthday; Douglas Coupland Returns to Reinventing Canada as *Souvenir 2* Picks Up Where Its 2001 Predecessor Left Off." *The Spectator*, 26 June 2004. Canadian Newsstream.

Goddard, Peter. "Still Life with Table Hockey: With a New Book and Photo Exhibit, Douglas Coupland Maps Canada from the Rec Room Out." *Toronto Star*, 29 June 2002. CBCA Complete.

Good, Alex. "Coupland's Canada; Souvenir's Sequel's Nostalgia Is Marred by Author's Obsession with Garbage as Art." *The Guelph Mercury*, 3 July 2004. Canadian Newsstream.

Grande, John K. "James Carl." *Sculpture Magazine* 18, no. 3 (April 1999). Accessed 1 May 2018. www.sculpture.org/documents/scmag99/april99/carl/carl.shtml.

Gray, Brenna Clarke. "A Conversation with Douglas Coupland: The Hideous, the Cynical, and the Beautiful." *Studies in Canadian Literature* 38, no. 2 (2011): 255–78. Accessed 28 September 2016. https://journals.lib.unb.ca/index.php/SCL/article/view/18926.

Griffith, Colwyn. "Eye Candy 3." Colwyn Griffith. Accessed 1 May 2018. www.colwyngriffith.com/eyecandy3.html.

Iyer, Pico. "When Words Become Art." In *Douglas Coupland: Everywhere Is Anywhere Is Anything Is Everything*, edited by Daina Augaitis, 161–75. London, UK: Black Dog, 2014.

"Je me souvenir [*Souvenir of Canada*]," *Border Crossings* 21, no. 3 (August 2008): 11–12. CBCA Complete.

Katerberg, William H. "Western Myth and the End of History in the Novels of Douglas Coupland." *Western American Literature* 40, no. 3 (Fall 2005): 272–99. JSTOR. www.jstor.org/stable/43022399.

Kirshenblatt-Gimblett, Barbara. "Playing to the Senses: Food as Performance Medium." *Performance Research* 4, no. 1 (1999): 1–30. doi: 10.1080/13528165.1999.10871639.

Korthals, Michiel. "Food as a Source and Target of Metaphors: Inclusion and Exclusion of Foodstuffs and Persons through Metaphors." *Configurations* 16, no. 1 (Winter 2008): 77–92. doi: 10.1353/con.0.0044.

Lainsbury, G.P. "Generation X and the End of History." *Essays on Canadian Writing* 58 (1996): 229–40. MLA International Bibliography.

McGregor, Glen. "Been There, Done That: Douglas Coupland Once Defined a Generation. In His Latest Book, *Souvenir of Canada*, He Takes on a Nation." *The Ottawa Citizen*, 30 June 2002. Canadian Newsstream.

McLuhan, Marshall. "Canada, the Borderline Case." In *Understanding Me: Lectures and Interviews*, edited by Stephanie McLuhan and David Staines, 105–23. Toronto: McClelland & Stewart, 2003.

– *Essential McLuhan*, edited by Eric McLuhan and Frank Zingrone. Concord: Anansi, 1995.

McRanor, Graeme. "From Bronto Ribs to the Apocalypse; Douglas Coupland Gives a Lecture the Best Way He Knows How – By Writing." *The Vancouver Sun*, 12 October 2010, D7. Canadian Newsstand Pacific.

Melsom, Ryan. "A (Queer) Souvenir of Canada: Douglas Coupland's Transformative National Symbols." *Canadian Literature*, no. 216 (Spring 2013): 35–49. Academic Search Premier.

Milroy, Sarah. "Coupland's Literary Lunch." *The Globe and Mail*, 6 September 2005, R1–R2. ProQuest Historical Newspapers.

– "A Gen-Xer's Love Letter to Canada." *The Globe and Mail*, 29 June 2002, R2. ProQuest Historical Newspapers.

Mitra, Koel. "Culture and the Market: The Emergence of Coffee-Table Books." *Aainanagar*, 26 July 2014. https://aainanagar.com/2014/07/26/culture-and-the-market-the-emergence-of-coffee-table-books/.

Rock, Melanie, Lynn McIntyre, and Krista Rondeau. "Discomforting Comfort Foods: Stirring the Pot on Kraft Dinner and Social Inequality in Canada." *Agriculture and Human Values* 26, no. 3 (2009): 167–76. doi: 10.1007/s10460-008-9153-x.

Semley, John. "A Nation of Dougs." *The Globe and Mail*, 6 September 2014. Canadian Newsstream.

Stiles, Kristine. "Uncorrupted Joy: International Art Actions." In *Out of Actions: Between Performance and the Object, 1949–1979*, edited by Russell Ferguson, 227–329. Los Angeles: Museum of Contemporary Art and Thames and Hudson, 1998.

Sugars, Cynthia. "Souvenir of Coupland." *Books in Canada* 31, no. 9 (December 2002): 15–16. CBCA Complete.

Tate, Andrew. *Douglas Coupland*. Contemporary American and Canadian Writers Series. Manchester: Manchester University Press, 2007.

Wigod, Rebecca. "Coffee-table Books of Note." *Leader Post*, 16 December 2006, G2. Canadian Newsstream.

Wikipedia. S.v. "Coffee Table Book." Last modified 26 March 2018. https://en.wikipedia.org/wiki/Coffee_table_book.

Zurbrigg, Terri Susan. *X = What? Douglas Coupland, Generation X, and the Politics of Postmodern Irony*. Saarbrücken, Germany: VDM Verlag, 2008.

12

Phototextual Remembering in Janice Wong's *Chow: From China to Canada: Memories of Food + Family*

Glenn Deer

Introduction

In 2005, Vancouver artist Janice Wong published an elegant mixture of stories and recipes titled *Chow: From China to Canada: Memories of Food + Family*. The enticing front cover features a close-up photograph of a gleaming white rice bowl with the word "chow" in black lower-case sans serif typeface overlain across its reflective surface. "Fill me with food," the empty bowl seems to assert. Indeed, "Chow," as the author reminds us, signifies both the Cantonese term for "stir fry" and the Western colloquialism for "food" and "eating."[1] Below this bowl, six wooden chopsticks – an auspicious or lucky number in Chinese numerology and ancestral rituals – in oiled hues of teak and dark mahogany are casually piled on a sand-coloured woven mat, and create a strong horizontal pull across the bottom foreground. The arrangement compels us to imagine how we might pick them up and prepare for eating.

The empty bowl and clean chopsticks signify both literal and metaphoric meanings: a bowl and chopsticks are literally implements for handling food or chow. But the empty bowl and the clean chopsticks metaphorically suggest a longing for food, even fulfillment, and the social sharing of food. They equally connote a liminal state and a deferred futurity: such metaphoric connotations of suspended temporality emphasize the "absent food" that has yet to be cooked. Within the same visual frame, a second series of images enacts not longing for the future, but memories of the past. A prominent column of six black-and-white images on the right side of the cover competes for our attention and pulls our line of sight vertically like the stills from a vintage filmstrip: two vernacular family snapshots, one studio photograph, an immigration document, a Chinese stamp, and the neon sign of The Lotus Café represent the historical journey in the subtitle, "From China to Canada." The photographic filmstrip serves as an appetizer for the family stories and recipes to follow,

Figure 12.1
Front cover of Janice Wong's *Chow*.

and the cover visually enacts how this culinary memoir is a hybrid form. As the author proclaims in the subtitle of her preface, "*Chow* is a cookbook + a story." It conjures the past through memory and simultaneously gestures to future readers and cooks who might take up the empty bowl and clean chopsticks to create their own versions of *Chow*.

While I will return to a closer analysis of the front cover, these images serve as the prelude to this multimodal study: this essay situates Wong's *Chow* within studies of Canadian foodways by analyzing how the book employs textual and visual elements to construct the communicative orality of culinary experience. First, I am especially interested in how this culinary memoir employs textually represented orality through reported speech and dialogue, and print artifacts like handwritten and typed recipes. Second, I will consider how the textual motifs of orality are supplemented with visual representations in the form of photographs. Finally, I contend that when these textual and visual expressions are employed together, they become a complex, multi-sensory substitute for meals that cannot be eaten again. In other words, the recipes in culinary memoirs like *Chow* imaginatively resurrect idealized meals and a social orality from the past through written and visual substitutions.

Asian Canadian Culinary Memoirs

Asian Canadian writers have especially emphasized motifs of food in community experiences of diasporic displacement and transcultural encounters, whether through the narrative of First Nations' sharing of food with the starving Chinese bone-searcher, Wong Gwei Chang, at the beginning of SKY Lee's *Disappearing Moon Café* (1990); through the difficulties of blending cultural recipes evoked in the image of the "stone bread" in Joy Kogawa's *Obasan* (1981); in the sensuous conjunction of words and food in Hiromi Goto's *Chorus of Mushrooms* (1994); through the violent punishment of children who reject parental cooking in Madeleine Thien's *Simple Recipes* (2001); or in the dystopic future where characters smell of pungent durian and have relationships with bioengineered clones in Larissa Lai's speculative fiction *Salt Fish Girl* (2002). While these important Asian Canadian works of fiction employ food, cooking, and eating in different ways to explore and critique the Canadian politics of cultural consumption, another genre of literature presents an even more personal investment in these foodways: the culinary memoir.

In Canada, the Asian Canadian culinary memoir[2] is represented by Fred Wah's biotext *Diamond Grill* (1996), Janice Wong's *Chow: From China to Canada: Memories of Food + Family* (2005), and the anthology *Eating Stories: A Chinese Canadian and Aboriginal Potluck*, edited by Brandy Liên Worrall (2007). As a blend of family stories, recollected anecdotes, cultural and social history, shared recipes, and, often, photographs, the Asian Canadian culinary memoir is usually not produced by the professional cook, nor is it presented as a series of books, such as the cookbooks of the famous Indo-Canadian restaurateurs, Vikram Vij and Meeru Dhalwala (for example, see *Vij's Elegant and Inspired Indian Cuisine*, 2006). The Asian Canadian culinary memoir is often driven by special exigencies, such as the need to write in a prose form because of a personal writing challenge[3] (Fred Wah), the desire to preserve cultural history for the use of future generations of the family (Janice Wong), or the desire to participate in the community-building experience of creating an anthology of food stories (Brandy Liên Worrall).

While the personal urgency to tell the story of one's family experiences is central to the Asian Canadian culinary memoir, we must respect the creative varieties of food memoirs that can feature many other motives. Outside the special category of Asian Canadian, there is considerable variation in the food memoir sub-genre. Sandra Gilbert in *The Culinary Imagination* helpfully surveys this diverse range:

> There is the food memoir as coming-of-age story, even Künstlerroman – generally a portrait of the artist and sometimes a portrait of a troubled soul; the food memoir as the story of a marriage or cook's tale; the food memoir as history of origins; the food memoir as cultural record; the food memoir as polemic; and on and on: all modes of culinary writing that fit into customary literary genres, but now oddly transformed by a newly intense focus on stove and table, market and fridge. Many of the most famous food memoirs draw, of course, on all these genres. Fisher's *The Gastronomical Me*, for instance, arguably the paradigmatic twentieth-century work of this sort, is primarily a coming-of-age story, but it is also a cultural history, a culinary polemic, a first-person tale of love and death – and thus a grief memoir – and even an informal cookbook.[4]

Gilbert's comprehensive survey includes "The Many Courses of the Culinary Memoir"[5] and convincingly ranges across history and cultures, with close engagements with Jean Anthelme Brillat-Savarin, M.F.K. Fisher, Julia Child, and even Anthony Bourdain. However, there is a tendency in many studies of the food memoir to focus on the personality of the writer or the details of the food rather than the language and visual modes that mediate the writer's persona and the tastes of the meals. For example, while Gilbert's *The Culinary Imagination* surveys many different genres, and while she touches on visual motifs of eating and food in paintings by Goya, Rubens, Cézanne, and even Wayne Thiebaud,[6] food photography is largely absent. Food photography is also absent in Wenying Xu's *Eating Identities: Reading Food in Asian American Literature* and Anita Mannur's *Culinary Fictions: Food in South Asian Diasporic Culture*, though the latter does address South Asian films in which food "orients the narrative toward a critique of race, class, and gender."[7] Lily Cho's introduction to *Eating Chinese: Culture on the Menu in Small Town Canada* begins to address the photographic construction of Chinese Canadian restaurants by considering a melancholic photograph of the abandoned "N.D. Café" in southern Alberta.[8] However, she does not address the role of photographs in the culinary memoir even though she insightfully explores the problematics of Chineseness and memory in Fred Wah's *Diamond Girl*. Hence, there has been a tendency by some literary critics to sideline the relationship between language and visual elements in culinary discourse. This essay begins to address this apparent gap in the existing research, or at least point the way for future analyses that will pay more attention to language and visual images in foodways genres like the culinary memoir.[9]

Multi-sensual Effects and Phototextualities

It is important to note that this proposed focus on the culinary memoir by Janice Wong is not narrowly confined to the illustrative function of photographs as adjuncts to the writing, nor is writing regarded simply as an extended caption for the photographs. The combinations of text and photographs in a culinary memoir like *Chow* are more than simply the illustrations of a life narrative with family photographs; more significantly, they constitute a hybrid form that places text and photographs in dialogue to evoke stories and multiple senses, including sight, sound, taste, smell, touch, and proprioception. This powerful combination of different dimensions of orality with photography (the oral pleasures of taste in images, the oral conversational exchanges in the text, and the indexicality of original eating latent in the photograph) convert the eating experiences in this culinary memoir into what Barbara Kirshenblatt-Gimblett in *Culinary Tourism* identifies as "edible chronotopes" or "sensory space-time convergences."[10] Such sensory space-time convergences are also a principal feature of what Alex Hughes and Andrea Noble identify as "phototextual" constructs. In *Phototextualities*, Hughes and Noble examine how "photo-centered textual constructs – autobiographies, photograph albums, documentary films, travelogues, mixed media montages – that deal in memory work" evoke multiple senses, not just the visual. Hughes and Noble emphasize that "phototexts make their appeal to the viewer-reader not simply on an intellectual or even purely visual level but rather on a multisensual basis ... phototexts can work against the culturally consecrated primary of intellect over emotion, of mind over body. The implication is that as we engage with the realm of the photographic, we are given access to alternative ways of knowing: ones that offer the possibility of understanding, differently, matters of self, Other, history, and culture."[11]

This emphasis on the "multisensual" mode is directly connected to food and photography in Susan Bright's introduction, "Eye Candy," in *Feast for the Eyes: The*

Story of Food in Photography. She points out that food is already socially constructed as an expression of more than just physical nourishment: "photographs of food are rarely just about food. They hold our lives up to the light ... It can be a carrier for all kinds of fantasies and realities, and photographs of food can be complicated and deceptive, touching on many aspects of our lives."[12] Bright highlights how cookbooks serve many interests and functions, and she reminds us that since the Internet is now a primary source of recipes, cookbooks have consequently become "coffee-table book[s]" or "collectible, as fetishized objects ... like photobooks" that are "aligned with still life and art practices." No longer stained by actual cooking, the cookbook now provides, according to Bright, "an aspirational experience that situates the reader in a very particular time and sensibility. [Cookbooks] are [now] for show, for seductive visual pleasure and for longing – all very far away from the labours of shopping, cooking, and washing up, but not so far away from the very first cookbooks."[13]

While I would modify Bright's broad claim by noting that *some* uses of cookbooks can be "aspirational," and veer to fantasy, cookbooks can be used for any number of purposes, whether for "seductive visual pleasure," or for actual guidance in cooking, or even multi-sensory nostalgic recollection of previous meals. Bright persistently emphasizes that the powers of food photography, currently extended through social media, are centred in its ability to arouse feelings and thoughts that are beyond the simply visual. While referencing Marcel Proust's famous memory of sweet madeleines dipped in tea in *À la recherche du temps perdu*, Bright states: "Food can arouse repeated and constant links between perception and memory, and when photographed, it is likewise transformed into a network of comparable connections and associated symbolic orders. Much like literature, photography is a medium closely woven with desire and longing – a vehicle for memory and a generator of *metaphor* and symbol. It also describes in the minutest detail [emphasis added]."[14]

It is this generative and even *metaphoric* power that I aim to describe in closer readings of Janice Wong's *Chow* by posing questions that engage closely with language and visual elements. The critical term "metaphor" here is crucial because it is often regarded as the foundational rhetorical figure that underlies the basis of language: as the figure that represents the comparative substitution of one term with another, metaphor embodies the conceptual compression and transference that is central to the thinking of rhetoricians, from the classical precepts of Aristotle to the motivational analyses of Kenneth Burke, and even cognitive linguists such as

George Lakoff and Mark Turner.[15] For example, the analysis demonstrated in the introduction to this essay, of how the empty bowl and chopsticks conceptually compress the longing for food and social contact, unpacks these images as metaphors. The bowl and chopsticks stand for something beyond their material utility as eating utensils.

Rhetorical Mapping

Along with the metaphoric power of the language and visual elements in Wong's culinary memoir, there are other key questions that I think should be posed to engage more closely with these same elements in all culinary memoirs generally: How are memories of culinary traditions preserved and transmitted? What happens to experiences of cooking and eating when these are remediated through different discourses and media, such as visual, oral, and textual forms? What are the implied motives for the remediation of culinary traditions? What is the role of temporality in the memorializing discourses of the culinary memoir?

My method of reading the language and visual elements of the culinary memoir is a form of rhetorical mapping. The map I am proposing draws upon a well-known Aristotelian rhetorical model of the dynamic exchange between authors, texts, and readers.[16] This has been a surprisingly underdeveloped area in foodways theory despite the influence of structuralist and semiotic approaches to cooking and the conventions of eating in classic studies of foodways by Claude Lévi-Strauss, Roland Barthes, and Mary Douglas.[17] I want to go beyond the culinary triangle of Lévi-Strauss, and beyond the social status semiotics of Barthes and Douglas, in order to map the communicative dynamics in the *reading* of culinary memoirs. While this discursive anatomy could apply to cookbooks and even menus, I will limit this practical application to Janice Wong's culinary memoir, *Chow: From China to Canada: Memories of Food + Family*.

The culinary memoir is a distinctive and blended sub-genre of both life writing and cookbooks, and it displays discursive features and functions that helpfully illustrate the dynamics of food as a form of communication. Because the culinary memoir obviously emphasizes the acts of remembering and the periodization of time, it provides examples of how memories of culinary traditions are preserved, for example, through repeated use of recipes, or remembered acts of learning how to cook in the home kitchen, or in the family restaurant, along with remembered multi-sensory scenes: such remembered scenes could include seeing, smelling, and tasting prepared foods. Therefore, one aspect of my project, briefly sampled here, involves tracking the different uses of memory as an essential rhetorical and conceptual element in the culinary memoir, along with related terms that signify recovery, revival, renewal, recreation, and reproduction. The culinary memoir is here regarded as a dynamic artifact that recovers, in the first instance, the culinary practices of the past, and subsequently sets up a program of continuation from the present and into the future. The hope implied in all cookbooks, and in culinary memoirs, is that meals enjoyed in the past can be faithfully resurrected and prepared again. Certainly, this is a hope that requires material, perceptual, and imaginative investments – investments of material ingredients, of preparation time, of imaginative and intellectual engagements with the instructions for cooking. Most importantly, at the higher level of theoretical inquiry, I am interested in what happens when the material exchange of food enters the social imagination, a level of exchange that is addressed by the following additional question: when we map the material exchange of food in the culinary memoir, how are we also mapping the *imaginary* exchange of food? This important question is compelled by my critical stance on previous culinary commonplaces about eating and identity, inherited from canonical authors like Brillat-Savarin, that need to be revised. In this case, the aphorism that "we are what we eat,"[18] should be supplemented with another aphorism that emphasizes the constructed nature of what we eat: "we are what we imagine what we eat."[19]

In the dynamics of food as a form of communication, the following schematic can be applied in which cooks prepare meals for diners in different situational contexts of time and space. The meal serves as a message sent from the cook to the diner:

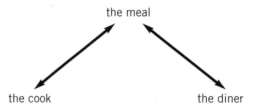

the meal

the cook   the diner

context of the situation

This pragmatic culinary triangle corresponds to the following communication triangle that is well known in rhetoric and discourse studies:

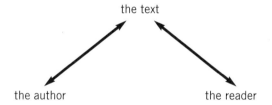

We can map a simple example of how the two previous triangles merge when cooks become writers, or memoir writers evoke meals from the past. We can also add the multimodal combination of text and images to account for cookbooks or culinary memoirs that combine the two modes of representation:

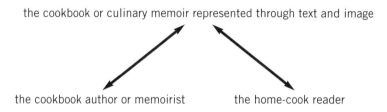

These mappings of the dynamics of communication are superseded by another central dynamic: while the preceding triangles of communication show the exchange of material texts, these can also map the imaginative recreation of absent authors and absent foods that are imaginatively conjured by the reader's act of reading, as in the following:

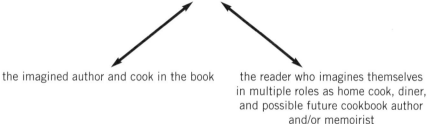

The fourth schematic map attempts to show how the material work of the cook (gathering ingredients, measuring portions, cutting, grinding, and otherwise manipulating the ingredients) is re-imagined by the implied reader, the home cook, who will attempt to imitate the instructive example of the imagined cook in the book. This home cook can imaginatively cook and consume the recipe purely by reading, but the material cooking and consuming could also take place. There is no guarantee that the reader will follow through by actually cooking the imagined food, and certainly the language of the cookbook will play a crucial role in shaping the experience of the reader. When we apply this triangle of imagined author, food, and the roles of the reader to the culinary memoir, we can ask how imagined cooks and foods from the past are conjured by the language and images of the family memoirist. The language of the memoir carries the burden of mediating the material experience in an effective manner that will revivify the culinary experiences of the past. Culinary memoirs, obviously, are about more than just the food, and the memoirist conjures absent people, places, and events that can supersede the food itself. Still, this mapping is meant to be suggestive rather than fully explanatory, and its heuristic purpose is to highlight how the relationship between authors of culinary memoirs, like Janice Wong, and readers are involved in a highly mediated relationship that relies on the rhetorical resources of language.

Mediating *Chow*

I now turn to some specific examples of the mediating textual and visual elements in *Chow*. I am especially interested in how Janice Wong's particular culinary memoir resurrects sights, sounds, and tastes of family dining experiences that have ultimately been lost, and how the author attempts to recreate these lost moments through the nostalgic uses of the photographic album genre and remembered conversations, reproductions of handwritten letters, and recipes for Chinese "comfort foods."

The extensive uses of textual and visual elements set this book apart from other well-known North American culinary memoirs, yet Wong's work shares the poignancy of unfulfilled longing, and evokes the felt absence of the original food, a culinary nostalgia that is often reflected in these memoirs. Many culinary memoirs, and even works of culinary fiction, refer to the inadequacy or limits of expression in capturing remembered experiences of eating, and emphasize that the text is merely a suggestive substitute. The lack of food, and even memories of inadequate or inedible food, haunt culinary histories like Sally Tisdale's *The Best Thing I Ever Tasted* (2000) in which the constricted life of her unhappy mother shadows her efficient yet uninspired cookery. Tisdale notes that thousands of recipes were collected by her mother but were never attempted, and that Tisdale, herself, also continues the collecting. She suggests that the reading of the recipes themselves becomes a substitute for oral gratification, especially for working parents, like her mother, who would often return home from work and face the preparation of yet another family meal with grim surrender to a cooking routine that had lost its gusto. In the poignancy of the daily grind for her mother, the reading of recipes provided an escape into imagined meals that would never be cooked but also would tantalize rather than satisfy, and thus impel further bouts of recipe collecting and reading.[20]

Janice Wong comments on a similar gap between readerly experience of her father's recipes and the gustatory reality at the end of her introduction to *Chow*: "As I transcribe the recipes from his handwritten notes, I marvel at how simple they seem. But I feel certain that even if I follow carefully, I won't be able to duplicate his flavourful wizardry" (17). Even though Wong feels that she will fall short of recreating her father's authentic meals of the past, the process of transcription and textual substitution is one way of evoking the past and keeping the memories vital. This connection to the past is reiterated in the author's essay "Making Chow": here she describes how a project that began as a "gift" to her family grew into a published memoir that "was also a gift to [herself]" because it "created a connection" and gave her "a sense of community. She writes: "What I didn't know about my dad I was to learn – through the book, through the generosity of shared stories and memories."[21]

The distinctive commemorative power of Wong's *Chow* is apparent in its artful design that blends stories, recipes, and photographs. The central goal of her work was to bring the family stories and the recipes together. Indeed, she has described how she changed the design of her book in the following note: "The final format of *Chow*, with the stories interspersed throughout and the titles that I gave to each small story, came together after my editor asked me 'what kind of a book are we dealing with?' And, I decided that the world didn't need another Chinese cookbook, but a food book, interlaced with personal stories could be something special. In true hands-on artist fashion, I quickly took scissors to the manuscript and collaged it into its current form. I was so relieved when I did this because, prior to this, the bulk of the book, the stories, were all at the front, the recipes at the back, and nothing seemed integrated."[22]

Thus, Wong purposely *integrates* domestic narrative, family recipes, and exquisitely composed photographs of Chinese cooking utensils and foods. The photographs capture the curvaceous ceramic sheen of bowls and spoons, and the gnarled textures of dried mushrooms on woven trays and wood cutting blocks. Unlike most authors of culinary memoirs, Wong is also a professional visual artist[23] and her aesthetic skills significantly shape the visual and tactile originality of her book, with its mix of colour and black-and-white photography. Students of photography might recognize echoes of the still lifes of Edward Weston or Imogen Cunningham in some of Wong's work in *Chow*:[24] her photographs focus on simple objects to reveal nuances of form, pattern, texture, and light. It is noteworthy that she does not include a single photograph of a cooked and plated dish to represent the prepared recipe: instead, the minimalist design and the recipes invite our imaginative and hands-on participation in creating the final dish. In another note, she remarks that the publisher, Whitecap Books, provided her with significant input "with design, composition, and overall look and character," and she worked closely with the book designer, Jacqui Thomas. Such a close collaboration between the book designer and the author is actually rare in the publishing industry, since the design of the book's cover is often beyond the control of the author. Janice Wong has commented that "all aspects of myself went into the final book, my aesthetics, [and] my preference for minimalism likely finds its way into writing as well, and my love of detail and historical tidbits that feed the imagination, my comprehension of balance, rhythm, counterpoint, detail, cohesiveness … all of those things that I make use of in my art practice, found their way into this book as well."[25]

As noted earlier, the movements between personal and social history, between material objects and social exchange, and between signs and food are adumbrated by the design of *Chow*'s front cover. The original cover designed for the first family version of the memoir was simpler, but still featured chopsticks and an empty bowl with a fish motif, with the addition of a fortune cookie and its furled paper "fortune": this initial version of the cover also foregrounds the name and culinary legacy of the author's father: "dennis edward wong / collected recipes." In the published version of *Chow* (Figure 12.1), the empty white bowl and dark chopsticks, overlaid vertical column, and concise black-and-white family filmstrip serve several rhetorical and multi-sensory functions. The motif of oral storytelling is much more prominent in the imagery and arrangement. The top photograph features the artist's younger brother, Joe Wong in 1959, holding a telephone. This deceptively simple image elegantly links an obvious metaphor of oral communication to *Chow*, a book that cele-

Figure 12.2
Original cover of the unpublished family version of *Chow*.

brates the oral pleasures of taste and talk. The *mouth*, as we shall see, is the site of primary experiences and the means for revisiting and recirculating those experiences as well. Wong's book is distinctive for demonstrating how such oral sensory experiences become communicable through combinations of sensations.

The second photograph in the column, a more formal group portrait of four Chinese women, taken in 1937 in Guangdong, China, includes Wong's mother, Mary Mar (Mah). She was born in Nanaimo in 1922 but spent the years between 1935 and 1938 in the company of her grandmother, leaving after "the Japanese military had begun a full-scale invasion"[26] and before she could be pressured into taking a Chinese village husband. Mary Mar returned to Victoria where she met her future husband in 1940. This photograph represents the trans-Pacific movement of her mother, influenced by family obligations and by international conflict.

The third image is a portion of a Certificate of Head Tax Exemption for the maternal side of the family. While most Chinese immigrants were forced to pay the federal head tax (which was $50 in 1885, then $100 in 1900, and $500 in 1903), there were exemptions for six classes of people: "diplomats, clergymen, merchants, students, tourists, and men of science."[27] Chan Yu Tan, the maternal grandfather of Janice Wong's father, entered Canada "registered as a man of science," but "was in fact a minister in the Chinese Methodist Church" who "worked with congregations in Victoria, New Westminster, and Nanaimo" (28–9). On the maternal side, the

Mah family of the author's mother was from the merchant class and was also spared the head tax, thus providing the family with initial economic advantages in establishing their family business. However, these fortunate circumstances are marred when the maternal grandmother dies in 1924, leaving her infant daughter Mary, at the age of one and a half, in the care of her grandmother. The head tax exemption attests to the mixed fortunes of the family, and also connects their history to the racist exclusions commonly experienced by Chinese immigrants (58).

The fourth image in the vertical album represents the paternal protagonist and emotional soul of the book, the writer's father, Dennis Wong, at the front counter of the Lotus Café in Prince Albert, Saskatchewan, in the 1960s, with his signature welcoming smile – "impish," according to his daughter (15). The photograph shows the genial public man, popular with his loyal customers, but also surrounded by modern confections that serve the oral appetites. He holds a pipe, as if pausing in mid-conversation. The pipe, of course, is an obvious metaphor for orality, and even pensiveness, but there are also the rows of candy bars at Dennis Wong's elbows, and the neat stacks of cigarettes in the display case behind him. Tobacco sales and losses figure significantly in the fortunes of the family.

We learn that Dennis had previously been forced to close a Vancouver-based coffee shop because of the theft of a large stock of cigarettes. The theft sinks the business and forces the family to relocate to Prince Albert (14). Dennis Wong's restaurant business in Prince Albert is initially met with skepticism by the extended family, who wonder "*what would he do in a restaurant? ... he doesn't know how to cook!*" (51). As the narrator states, "they knew him only as a sporty young man ... perhaps he would just charm the customers" (51). Dennis Wong's chutzpah seems akin to the mode of "faking it," the improvisatory and creative tactics employed by Fred Wah and his father in *Diamond Grill* – the agile slip of the tongue that turns into a deliberate self-racializing joke,[28] since Dennis is a joker, but a keen observer and listener who had kept a "close eye on the cooks, noting the knife handling, each distinctive method" (51). He is entirely self-taught and never works from a recipe, keeping the alchemy of cookery in his memory.

The last two images in the vertical photo album feature, respectively, a Chinese "chop," or seal-styled stamp of Dennis Wong's family name, and the neon sign of the Lotus, taken in the 1960s. The Chinese chop juxtaposed against the neon sign semiotically marks the problem of reproducing identity, authenticity, and origins, and the indexical nature of the original "signified." The Chinese ideogram is itself a stylized pictogram, a picture whose mimetic origins have long faded into conven-

Figure 12.3
Original photograph of Dennis Wong that appears in cropped form in Janice Wong's *Chow*, p. 133.

tion. The figure of the father has in effect left his mark through signs and through food, and the stamp of Dennis continues to exert its lasting effects through the process of re-stamping his name through the voice and text of his daughter, the artist Janice Wong. The Lotus neon sign is also an important means of branding or even stamping the street space with the presence of the restaurant. The neon sign is not only at the bottom of the film strip but another version also appears on the back cover of the book: a matchbook cover that depicts the distinctive signage, stone facade, doorway, and windows of the Lotus Café, complete with address (1310 Central) and phone number (ROger 3-6646). Such customized matchbook covers were common enough in the decades when smoking was accepted and even encouraged in restaurants, which often sold cigarettes. The reproduction of the Lotus sign in

Figure 12.4
The Lotus Café neon sign.

Figure 12.5
The Lotus Café matchbook cover.

matchbook form evokes multimodal sensations, not just the visual but also the olfactory and oral flavours of the cigarettes and even pipe tobacco referenced in the other cover photograph of Dennis Wong.

The dining room of the Lotus Café is a place for taste and talk. The "mouth" of the family is therefore a site not only of culinary sustenance but also communicative remembrance. Food enables talking, as much as talking supports the revival of appetites and the sharing of recipes. Within the discursive registers of *Chow*, we read about the father "musing" (10), or telling (12, 14) about how he excelled in chemistry in high school, or the mother recollecting or recalling (13), or how family dinners during the 1940s would feature guests sitting "together, chatting about food, reminiscing about certain dishes" with the family friend Ngui Suk (16). Thus, oral storytelling accompanies eating, and is also captured in the photographs.

Janice Wong's culinary memoir employs visual media to generate two key distinct levels of orality. First, photographs of food and of family dining showcase the orality of tasting and eating family food through a process of what is rhetorically known as ekphrasis, or the representation of one aesthetic form through a different aesthetic form. Since the specific material foods and meals of the past cannot obviously be preserved for future consumption, the photographs iconographically convey those instances of communal dining at kitchen tables and restaurants, and oral pleasures that cannot be physically recreated in the present. The visual representation of oral enjoyment in *Chow* is represented by several photographs of active eating by groups of family members and friends. The placement of photographs in the memoir is strategically designed to show the communal, multi-generational, and repeated patterns of oral consumption. For example, the last photograph in the book, accompanied by the subtitle, "the weekend repertoire," shows Janice Wong's sister and brother (foreground) and their two "Mar" cousins in bow ties happily tucking into a traditional Christmas turkey dinner. The accompanying narrative emphasizes that "Mom was keen to have our family fit in with everyone else in the neighbourhood" and "once she realized that her oldest daughter, Judy, then two years old, couldn't understand the postman when he said hello, she made certain the rest of us grew up speaking only English" (171). This affirmation of English oral conversational skill is followed by a tantalizing description of how the family enjoyed "Thanksgiving and Christmas turkeys ... always perfectly stuffed and roasted, with a little secret, a Chinese twist – they were basted with a bit of soy sauce and *ho yu* (oyster flavoured sauce)" (171).

Second, these photographs comprise a *photo album* that enables a dialogue, or conversational orality. As the author glosses the photographs and provides a frame narrative for the depictions of different periods of family dining, she also attributes oral comments and reactions to imagined but absent family members who assess the dining experience. For example, in the second-last narrative, with the subtitle, "from the back to the front," the author remembers how she would visit the restaurant and have conversations with her father and the customers: "While I didn't work in the restaurant, I loved my occasional, indulgent visits. I had a habit of stopping by for hot chocolate topped with a dollop of whipped cream. Invariably there were one or two regular customers seated next to me at the curvy counter. Dad would tease us and we would chat, sitting side by side, enjoying our hot chocolate or coffee. They all seemed comfortable, familiar, at ease in a favourite place" (169). This narrative of gustatory and conversation pleasure is accompanied by a photograph of three smiling women, including employees of the Lotus, seated at a café booth, at ease in the presence of the photographer.

This visual-oral conversational dynamic is an example of what Martha Langford describes in her groundbreaking work on "the afterlife of memory in photographic albums." Langford argues that the photographic album is "one way of preserving the structures of the oral tradition for new uses in the present"[29] because an album provokes conversations and performances from participants: it serves to "stir up memories and stimulate re-enactments of the informant's stories."[30] Wong's culinary memoir exemplifies these features of the oral traditions as outlined by Langford.

Finally, the *indexical* qualities of several photographs of dining and handwritten letters (69) and handwritten recipes by Dennis Wong (76) reinforce the poignant gap between the frozen past moment and the longing of the present. An indexical framing of photographic meaning emphasizes the causative linkage between past material phenomena and the enduring photograph in the present.[31] The original foods prepared in the Wong restaurant and family kitchen, though part of the irrecoverable past, are still the physical source of the images captured by the camera: this concept of indexicality reinforces the sense of contact with an authentic relic of a previous history.

Culinary memoirs like *Chow* – a hybrid of family stories, photography, and cooking instructions – emphasize what is known but not often acknowledged: that cookbooks can be read for their narrative insights and pleasures as well as their utility. The aptly named Rachel Cooke surveys her extensive cookbook library and concedes that she will never cook most of the 8,000 recipes in her collection, and confirms that "cookbooks are not just for those who cook": if you like eating, "reading about food is the next best thing to eating it."[32] As Bee Wilson has recently commented, "the vast majority of the recipes we read are hypothetical," and while we might never cook most of the recipes in a cookbook collection, even in a work like *Chow*, "the imaginary version tastes incredible."[33]

Acknowledgments

I am deeply grateful to Janice Wong for her patience and generosity in sharing her knowledge and artistry, and for her gracious consent to publish personal photographs from *Chow* in this collection. My special thanks to Janice and her mother, Mary, for their visit to my English 480 class on "Asian Diasporic Literatures: Reading Culture through Food, Cooking, and Eating" on 1 November 2016. I extend my thanks to Shelley Boyd and Dorothy Barenscott for their encouragement and many helpful suggestions.

Notes

1. Wong, *Chow*, 8. All subsequent references to Wong's book are in parentheses after the quoted passage.
2. While practical space constraints limit this study to the Asian Canadian culinary memoir, other works, such as Clarke's *Pigtails 'n Breadfruit*, are also important for shaping this sub-genre of life writing.
3. Wah, in an interview with Ashok Mathur, has referred to how the "writing" of *Diamond Grill* "was actually spurred along by bp Nichol challenging [him] to open up to other stylistic possibilities, particularly prose," and also a continuation of the prose poem *Breathin' My Name With a Sigh* (1981). It was also a means to "talk" to his late father. See "Interview with Ashok Mathur" in *Faking It*, 98.
4. Gilbert, *The Culinary Imagination*, 144.
5. Ibid., 141.
6. Gilbert considers the images of "terrible eating" and cannibalism in paintings by Francisco Goya and Peter Paul Rubens, and touches on Paul Cezanne's *Three Apples* (1878–79) and Wayne Thiebaud's *Girl with Ice Cream Cone* (1963). She also presents a concise overview of selected food films in a section titled "Lights! Camera! Eat!" However, photographs are not part of her visual analysis.
7. Mannur, *Culinary Fictions*, 119.
8. The problem of how photographs capture only the surface of the lives of small-town Asian Canadian restaurant workers is explored by Bouvier in "The Royal Cafe Experience," chapter 3 in this volume. Bouvier, who is not of Asian Canadian ancestry, deliberately sets out to connect with her nostalgic childhood memories of eating "Western" food in "Chinese-Western" restaurants in towns like Vulcan, Alberta. In contrast, Janice Wong's culinary memoir, an insider perspective on Chinese-Canadian life, is less focused on the restaurant space and its menu, and more concerned with diasporic family history and recipes.
9. Obviously, culinary memoirs that lack photographs or other visual material will not evoke the same degree of visual attention as artifacts that are conspicuously visual. By comparison, there has already been much scholarly attention paid to the staging of food in cincma. See Bower, ed., *Reel Food* and Zimmerman, "Food in Films." Bower usefully points out that "food as a cultural construct" is a relative newcomer to interdisciplinary studies in universities, though the foundational scholarship "had been part of agricultural, home economics (human ecology), and industrial studies earlier and had been a topic also in anthropology and some sociology courses. 'Food studies' as a separate (though highly interdisciplinary) field is of very recent vintage. It is thus not surprising that the

putting together of food and film as a subject of investigation has only occurred recently" (*Reel Food*, 11–12). Bower's comments could also apply to the "putting together" of culinary memoirs, food, and photographs.

10   Kirshenblatt-Gimblett, "Foreword," xiii.
11   Hughes and Noble, eds., *Phototextualities*, 5–6.
12   Bright, *Feast for the Eyes*, 6.
13   Ibid., 18.
14   Ibid., 22.
15   See Burke, *A Grammar of Motives*, 503. Also, Turner, *The Artful Mind*, 93–114; and Dancygier, ed., *The Cambridge Handbook of Cognitive Linguistics*, 93–8.
16   The rhetorical triangle that provides the basis for social discourse approaches to literature has its origins in Aristotle's rhetorical model that identifies the persuasive power of a speech in the elements of the speaker, the audience, and the speech.
17   See Lévi-Strauss, "The Culinary Triangle," Barthes, "Toward a Psychosociology," and Douglas, "Deciphering a Meal."
18   Brillat-Savarin's classic *The Physiology of Taste* is the source for this aphorism. As translated by M.F.K. Fisher, the original is aphorism "iv," "Tell me what you eat, and I shall tell you what you are" (15).
19   Dillon's *Rhetoric as Social Imagination* is a very helpful guide to understanding how the interactions between authors and readers depend on social imagination, and this in turn is guided by the "footings" established by the discourse.
20   Tisdale, *The Best Thing I Ever Tasted*, 85–6.
21   See Wong, "Making *Chow*," in Worrall, ed., *Eating Stories*, 251–4.
22   Janice Wong, e-mail correspondence, 3 May 2018.
23   Janice Wong studied fine art at the University of Saskatchewan, and received her BFA with distinction, honours painting, from the Alberta College of Art + Design. She is the recipient of numerous awards and scholarships, including Canada Council Project and Travel Grants, the Elizabeth Greenshields Foundation Grant, and Provincial Project and Travel Awards. Her work is exhibited and collected in Canada, Europe, Asia, and the United States. See www.janicewongstudio.com.
24   See "Edward Weston," 71, and "Imogen Cunningham," 107, in Bright, *Feast for the Eyes*.
25   Janice Wong, e-mail correspondence, 2 May 2018.
26   Ibid., 100.
27   See "Head Tax," *Chinese Canadian Stories*, University of British Columbia Library. Accessed 30 March 2016. http://ccs.library.ubc.ca/en/chronology/chViewItem/1/0/10.
28   See Wah, *Diamond Grill*, 65–6. Fred Wah's father's inaugural speech to the Nelson, BC,

Lion's Club features an unfortunate slip of the tongue when he mispronounces "soup" as "sloup." He turns the slip into a self-denigrating racial joke, but the poet recognizes an improvisatory "faking it" in his father's joke, a tactic that the poet also employs.

29   Langford, *Suspended Conversations*, 21.
30   Ibid.
31   See de Duve, "Time Exposure and Snapshot."
32   Cooke, "Why There's More to Cookbooks than Recipes."
33   Wilson, "The Pleasures of Reading Recipes."

Bibliography

Aristotle. *The Rhetoric and Poetics of Aristotle*. Translated by W. Rhys Roberts and Ingram Bywater. New York: Modern Library, 1954.

Barthes, Roland. "Towards a Psychosociology of Contemporary Food Consumption." In *Food and Culture: A Reader*, edited by Carole Counihan and Penny Van Esterik, 20–7. New York: Routledge, 1997.

Bower, Anne L. *Reel Food: Essays on Food and Film*. New York: Routledge, 2004.

Bright, Susan. *Feast for the Eyes: The Story of Food in Photography*. New York: Aperture, 2017.

Brillat-Savarin, Jean Anthelme. *The Physiology of Taste, or Meditations on Transcendental Gastronomy*. Translated by M.F.K. Fisher. New York: Knopf/Everyman's Library, 2009.

Burke, Kenneth. *A Grammar of Motives*. Berkeley: University of California Press, 1969.

Cho, Lily. *On Eating Chinese: Culture on the Menu in Small Town Canada*. Toronto: University of Toronto Press, 2010.

Clarke, Austin. *Pigtails 'n Breadfruit: A Culinary Memoir*. New York: The New Press, 1999.

Cooke, Rachel. "Why There's More to Cookbooks than Recipes." *The Guardian*, 15 August 2010. Web.

Dancygier, Barbara, ed. *The Cambridge Handbook to Cognitive Linguistics*. Cambridge, UK: Cambridge University Press, 2017.

de Duve, Thierry. "Time Exposure and Snapshot: The Photograph as Paradox." In *Photography Theory*, edited by James Elkins, 120–1. New York: Routledge, 2007.

Dillon, George. *Rhetoric as Social Imagination*. Bloomington: University of Indiana Press, 1986.

Douglas, Mary. "Deciphering a Meal." In *Food and Culture: A Reader*, edited by Carole Counihan and Penny Van Esterik, 36–54. New York: Routledge, 1997.

Gilbert, Sandra. *The Culinary Imagination*. New York: Norton, 2014.

Goto, Hiromi. *Chorus of Mushrooms*. Edmonton: NeWest Press, 1994.

Hughes, Alex, and Andrea Noble, eds. *Phototextualities: Intersections of Photography and Narrative*. Albuquerque: University of New Mexico Press, 2003.

Kirshenblatt-Gimblett, Barbara. "Foreword." In *Culinary Tourism*, edited by Lucy Long, xi–xiv. Lexington: University Press of Kentucky, 2004.

Kogawa, Joy. *Obasan*. Markham, ON: Penguin, 1981.

Lai, Larissa. *Salt Fish Girl*. Toronto: T. Allen, 2002.

Langford, Martha. *Suspended Conversations: The Afterlife of Memory in Photographic Albums*. Montreal and Kingston: McGill-Queen's University Press, 2001.

Lee, SKY. *Disappearing Moon Café*. Vancouver: Douglas and McIntyre, 1990.

Lévi-Strauss, Claude. "The Culinary Triangle." In *Food and Culture: A Reader*, edited by Carole Counihan and Penny Van Esterik, 28–35. New York: Routledge, 1997.

Long, Lucy, ed. *Culinary Tourism*. Lexington: The University Press of Kentucky, 2004.

Mannur, Anita. *Culinary Fictions: Food in South Asian Diasporic Culture*. Philadelphia: Temple University Press, 2010.

Marks, Laura. "Thinking Multisensory Culture." *Paragraph* 31, no. 2 (2008): 123–37.

Thien, Madeleine. *Simple Recipes*. Toronto: McClelland and Stewart, 2001.

Tisdale, Sally. *The Best Thing I Ever Tasted: The Secret of Food*. New York: Riverhead, 2000.

Turner, Mark, ed. *The Artful Mind: Cognitive Science and the Riddle of Human Creativity*. New York: Oxford University Press, 2006.

Vij, Vikram, and Meeru Dhalwala. *Vij's Elegant and Inspired Indian Cuisine*. Vancouver: Douglas and McIntyre, 2006.

Wah, Fred. *Diamond Grill*. Edmonton: NeWest Press, 1996.

– *Faking It: Poetics and Hybridity: Critical Writing 1984–1999*. Edmonton: NeWest Press, 2000.

Wilson, Bee. "The Pleasures of Reading Recipes." *The New Yorker*, 26 July 2013. Web.

Worrall, Brandy Liên, ed. *Eating Stories: A Chinese Canadian and Aboriginal Potluck*. Vancouver: Chinese Canadian Historical Society of British Columbia, 2007.

Wong, Janice. *Chow: From China to Canada: Memories of Food + Family*. North Vancouver: Whitecap Books, 2005.

Xu, Wenying. *Eating Identities: Reading Food in Asian American Literature*. Honolulu: University of Hawai'i Press, 2008.

Zimmerman, Steve. "Food in Films: A Star Is Born." *Gastronomica: The Journal of Food and Culture* 9, no. 2 (2009): 25–34.

13

The Royal Cafe Experience

Elyse Bouvier

In downtown Toronto, it is a familiar sight to come across trendy new pop-ups or mom-and-pop shops, or to see in the window of a small, converted pharmacy the words "ROYAL CAFE" in bright-red letters. This is not, in fact, a new stylish café; it is the Ryerson Artspace gallery and the location of my final thesis exhibition, *Royal Cafe: Chinese-Western in Alberta*. The installation – a collection of memorabilia, sounds, objects, and photographs (of spaces, landscapes, and food) – features documentation of Chinese restaurants in rural Alberta. The gallery acts as approximation of these Chinese-Western cafés (the unique moniker for Chinese-Canadian cafés in Alberta) that I photographed over the course of the summer in 2015, recreating my experiences of visiting them both as a child and now as an adult.

Inside the gallery, light streams in the windows forming horizontal shadows through the white, slatted blinds, highlighting a lone hanging plant. As you walk in, the wall on the right features a tattered map of Alberta (the one I used on my route and marked up with pen and other notes) and clusters of images and memorabilia: vintage postcards of prairie towns with restaurants named "Royal Cafe," the fortunes and fortune cookies from the places where I ate while driving across the province, photographs of the cafés' interiors, and pages from my journal recording the journey.[1] These pieces form mini-collections around the map that relate directly back to locations connected through red string and T-pins that I bought in Toronto's Chinatown. On a shelf beside the map is a *menaki neko*, or "Lucky Cat," which is a colourful, plastic cat with one arm that moves, often found on the front counters of Chinese restaurants. Originally Japanese, Lucky Cats have been adopted by many. On the wall opposite the map hangs a grid of fifteen photographs: plates of food printed on thin Japanese Awagami paper. Fourteen of these images feature a "Ginger Beef combo for one" from various places, while one image is of a grilled cheese sandwich, my childhood favourite and another restaurant staple. All of the

Figure 13.1
Elyse Bouvier, *Royal Cafe* installation, outside view: vinyl cut letters and window blinds, 2016.

Figure 13.2
Elyse Bouvier, *Royal Cafe* installation, inside view: grid of fifteen photographs of meals I ate over the course of one summer, digital prints on Awagami Japanese photo paper, 2016.

photographs document meals that I consumed in rural Alberta while working on the project.

In the front, near the gallery door, are pink plastic cherry blossoms. At Ben Wong Restaurant in Blairmore, Alberta, the owners had many of these blossoms in the waiting area. Mrs Wong told me how each flower represents a relationship; many cherry blossoms symbolize the potential for many friendships. I keep these cherry blossoms in my home now. The front counter hosts an orange plastic basket filled with fortune cookies. In the back corner, a strip of floral wallpaper – printed from a photograph of the wallpaper at the Wainwright Steak House, a Chinese, Western, and Thai restaurant in the oil town of Wainwright, Alberta (about two hours east of Edmonton) – highlights a small table with three stools. A speaker, suspended above, projects the recorded sounds and chatter of the rural cafés that I visited, and on the table rests a small handmade book, its cover wrapped with the same floral wallpaper. This book, a series of photographs from my trip, forms the heart of the exhibition.

Memories of the Royal Cafe

When I was a child, my family would drive to visit friends in my birthplace, Vulcan, Alberta. A farming town of fewer than 2,000 residents, it is about a two-hour drive from Calgary and is known mainly for its replica starship *Enterprise* and annual Star Trek convention. Back then, we would almost always meet our friends at the Royal Cafe, one of the town's Chinese-Western establishments that was situated comfortably in the middle of Centre Street beside Vulcan's only bakery and across from the New Club Cafe, a pizza and steak restaurant, also run by a Chinese family.[2] Years ago, before beginning this project, I found myself in Vulcan out of nostalgic curiosity. I ate at the New Club Cafe, and before I left town, I took this instant photo (analog, with a Diana camera) of the sign for the Royal Cafe. I had recently become fascinated with the ways in which the plastic Diana camera, with its instant film attachment, created a dream-like print, as if documenting something from the mid- to late twentieth century. Like a Polaroid, with its internal self-developing capabilities and on-the-spot processing of a physical object, the Diana camera creates an image that is more than just a digital snapshot: it is a material reminder of specific memories attached to a locatable place. In many ways, this print became the inspiration for this project. The Royal Cafe featured in my instant photo has since been replaced by the Town Cafe (with a similar interior and new owners), but the restaurant remains a Chinese-Western space. Despite my foggy childhood memories of the Royal Cafe, what I remember most is the food. Known for its Chinese cuisine, Royal Cafe also served a full Western menu, including hamburgers and grilled cheese sandwiches.

People from the Prairies understand what I mean when I talk about Chinese-Western restaurants. These cafés are standard fixtures in nearly every rural town. Friends who grew up in Alberta reminisce about stopping to eat Chinese on long road trips or frequenting the local café. They always rave about the delicious fries, chow mein, and ginger beef. These places are familiar, a comfort to customers, creating a sense of shared identity and community. There are many cafés spread across Western Canada, and although distinct in each town, they are instantly recognizable and have much in common.

To define Chinese-Western restaurants, from my own observations, they usually have a Chinese menu, but may also offer Vietnamese and Thai cuisine, and always have at least a few Western-Canadian menu items, like beef dip and grilled cheese.[3] In the early stages of my research, I came across scholar Lily Cho's foundational book *Eating Chinese: Culture on the Menu in Small Town Canada*. Over the course of my project, I met with Cho several times in Toronto, and our discussions not only confirmed what I had observed on my journey but also provided a deeper understanding of the importance of such spaces. In *Eating Chinese*, Cho points out that it was Chinese-Western owners that presented to Canadians not only an idea of what it was to be Chinese, and eat Chinese cuisine, but also what it was to be "Western" or "Canadian" and to eat Canadian cuisine. She writes: "Boldly ignoring any sort of existential crisis about the definition of Canadian culinary culture, Chinese restaurants have gone ahead and named Canadian food for Canadians."[4] These spaces, as Cho argues, define what Canadian food is by what is and is not featured on the Western or Canadian side of the menu.

Eating Ginger Beef and Photographing Chinese-Western

During the early stages of photographing this project, I was uncomfortable – and I mean that in the best possible sense. I *should* be uncomfortable. Although born in a small town, I no longer live in one, nor do I identify as a minority of any kind. I am a white, cis-gendered, middle-class woman from the city. I was then, and still

Figure 13.3
Elyse Bouvier, *Vulcan Royal Cafe*, 2010, instant photograph.

am, keenly aware that by taking on a project about rural Chinese restaurants, I am an outsider of some privilege and photograph from my own perspective and experience. Even when part of a collaborative effort, photography is a solo activity. Only one person pushes that shutter button.

To ease my way into the restaurants, I did the only thing I could think of: I ate. Before I took out my camera, before I recorded any audio, before I asked questions or poked my nose around, I ate. What better way to explore both difference and familiarity than to eat? This is how the grid of photographs of ginger beef was born. It also became a performative act – eating the same thing over and over, at many different places across the province. I was consuming my own perceptions of my Albertan identity and history of place.

Ginger beef holds a mythical status in the minds of many Albertans. If I bring it up in conversation, someone inevitably says, "It was invented in Calgary!" Research shows that this claim may not be entirely true, but whatever the case, it doesn't matter.[5] It's the myth of ginger beef and the ways in which people come to its defence that are evidence of something deeper. And it makes perfect sense to me that this dish with its deep-fried beef – which brings to mind images of the rolling

Figure 13.4
Elyse Bouvier, *Plate #2 – Peking Cafe*, 2015, digital photograph.

foothills, the renegade cowboys of the Old West, and the early pioneers who "settled" the land – and its rich, sweet ginger sauce takes pride of place in the province's culinary mindset. Ginger beef is, in many ways, a marriage between cultures that have permeated the idea of place in Alberta. In Chinese-Western restaurants, one senses the histories, the resilience, and the strength of the Chinese and other Asian immigrants (who remained in rural areas despite vicious discrimination) to become a permanent and important part of cultural life on the Prairies.

Chin's Cafe and Chinese-Western Spaces of Eating

When I began my project, I didn't know who I would meet, but over time I met owners and managers who were Chinese, Thai, Korean, and Vietnamese, all managing restaurants that nonetheless advertise themselves as Chinese-Western.[6] In Vegreville, I met Lan, a Vietnamese immigrant and self-described "boat person,"

Figure 13.5
Elyse Bouvier, *Coffee at Chin's*, 2016, digital photograph.

who was flown to Edmonton to start a new life with her husband. She started working at the local Chinese-Western, Chin's Cafe, and eventually became the owner. The space remains remarkably unchanged since the 1950s, and Lan is very proud of this fact. While I was there, Lan's grandson was playing computer games at a booth and customers came and went mostly to pick up takeout orders. Lan pointed out some of the original features: a wonderful mix of red and orange vinyl booths, chrome coat racks, tasselled lanterns, and wallpaper with illustrated scenes from China. Cho says that the interior of places like Chin's Cafe offers "some sense, however problematic, of entering a space that is clearly not Euro-Canadian. It is a space that is identified as Chinese by both the Chinese and non-Chinese members of the community."[7] These two sides of the restaurant – "Chinese" and "non-Chinese" for lack of better terms – are what I tried to capture in the photograph *Coffee at Chin's Cafe* (2016). The Bunn-O-Matic, two coffee pots (one with a ceramic tea pot lid balanced on top), a box of Orange Pekoe tea in the corner, and yellow patterned tiles bring together these common Prairie elements. Here, two seemingly disparate cultures intersect in a distinctly rural Chinese space.

I spent a long time in Chin's Cafe talking with Lan. She was hesitant about being photographed, so when she took me into "The Dragon Room," a party room in the back with shiny red wallpaper, I documented her reflection through the mirror. She told me about her life back in Vietnam and the journey it took for her to become the owner of this restaurant. The gold mirror, red patterned wallpaper, fake plants, and Lan turned away in contemplation are an invitation into this world that has been created, again and again, in small towns across Alberta.

Chinese-Western Restaurants as Spaces of Shifting Identities

Multiple decades are represented in Chinese-Western cafés, which may explain why I was drawn to combined patterns of floral and mismatched wallpapers, carpets, and fabrics, such as those captured in *Booth with Cups* (2015). I twice visited the E&W Family Restaurant in Three Hills, once when scouting locations and, later, when driving across the province. Both times, I was struck by the variety of the decor, the plastic cups, and the paper placemats. In this photograph, two wildly different floral patterns meet: those of the booth seats and the carpet that rises up the sides. The image tells you a great deal about what kind of place E&W Family Restaurant is without ever seeing a plate of Chinese food on the table or hearing the sounds of semi trucks rushing past on the highway. From what time period is this photograph, and in what space does this restaurant exist? As Cho has written, "there is no prescriptive and coherent list of physical elements that mark these restaurants, and yet we know one when we see it ... The ordinary spaces of diaspora are fraught with problems of definition and delineation. These are spaces remade through memory and some sense of what 'home' should and could be."[8] In other words, these spaces are familiar to both the owners and the customers who share a sense of belonging. In these restaurants, Cho notes, "a range of people will, at least for a moment, be eating Chinese. Through the consumption and production of something that will be called Chinese food, a series of interactions and negotiations unfold."[9] The Chinese-Western cafés that I visited, photographed, and ate within are spaces where many different identities, cultures, and histories collide and move towards understanding each other.

Consider the photographs *The Diana Restaurant* and *Lucky Cat Lucky Dragon* (2015). Even if you have not been to these places, both photographs present a familiar scene to many, and especially to people from Alberta and the Prairies who regularly visit rural towns. These images, arguably evoking a kind of nostalgia through form and content, are also a nod to twentieth-century photographers

Figure 13.6
Elyse Bouvier, *Lan in the Dragon Room*, 2015, digital photograph.

Figure 13.7
Elyse Bouvier, *Booth with Cups*, 2015, digital photograph.

Figure 13.8
Elyse Bouvier, *The Diana*, 2015, digital photograph.

Figure 13.9
Elyse Bouvier, *Lucky Cat Lucky Dragon*, 2015, digital photograph.

working primarily with analog film, like American artist Stephen Shore, who travelled by car in the United States and Canada, stopping in small-town diners and photographing ordinary, even banal, scenes along the way. Where Shore and I differ is in scope and intent. Whereas Shore was interested in life in the American West, I photograph the unexpected in Chinese-Western restaurants on the Prairies. Shore says that "to see something spectacular and recognise it as a photographic possibility is not making a very big leap. But to see something ordinary, something you'd see every day, and recognise it as a photographic possibility – that is what I am interested in."[10] I would like to take this idea further and say that to see something as a "photographic possibility" is also to see it as an experience and part of a larger narrative. This is especially relevant to my approach as an artist in documenting Chinese-Western spaces and recreating them as a full sensory experience.

On my journey, the Chinese-Western café was often the only restaurant in town, serving as *the place* to gather for any occasion: daily breakfast dates, after-church coffee, family birthday dinners, and after-school gatherings for teenagers. The Asian families who owned and managed these cafés were frequently only one of a handful of non-white families residing in these rural communities. So, this begs the question, how did these places of cultural difference come to be a place of familiarity and comfort for so many Albertans, regardless of their own histories? I do not pretend to be any sort of cultural theorist. I am instead an image-maker and an artist interested in experience and story. In part, this project was a way for me to understand my own role in the Canadian narrative of Chinese-Western restaurants, and to place my childhood memories of the Royal Cafe in a greater context. I began telling this story in the only way I know how, through photography. What I quickly learned, especially from a complicated history of photographic documentation, was that the images I took often revealed only a surface-level view. An image is worth more when it is part of a larger experience. In doing this project, I was not interested in merely creating a series of images on a gallery wall or in a book. I wanted instead to recreate and represent, as best I could, a multi-sensory experience of these spaces and lead viewers, myself included, to a new understanding of both the rural and the immigrant experience.

The installation of *Royal Cafe: Chinese-Western in Alberta* was so important to my project because in assembling common elements that I noticed in the cafés, the map, the collected mementos, the audio recordings, and the photographic grid of ginger beef dishes, I recreated my own experiences of these spaces. All of these details communicated the deeper understanding that I gained of Asian-Canadian histories and the many identities housed within Chinese-Western cafés. During the *Royal Cafe* exhibition, Lily Cho interviewed me about the project as I made ginger beef, filling the gallery with the sounds of cooking and the fragrant smell of ginger. After the talk, a friend's dad remarked that he was amazed at how many senses were involved during the performance. Other visitors noted the repeating patterns and photographs in the book, on the walls, and in the other elements. In this way, the photos come to life, offering not simply a window into another world, but an entry point into a more complete experience of Chinese-Western restaurants on the Canadian Prairies.

Ultimately, I can only understand the rural Chinese-Western restaurant from the point of view of a visitor, a customer who enters and eats. I cannot know what it is like to be Chinese or an Asian minority in a small Alberta town, or what it is like to work tirelessly to run a restaurant, rarely, if ever, taking a day off. What I can bring to this conversation is a sincere love of Alberta and its people in its many representations and an appreciation for the ways in which food is central to human experience. Our histories become intertwined when we sit down to eat together, when we take the time to engage in conversation and connect with individuals who are central to rural communities and to our own personal narratives of place.

Notes

1. In the course of my research for this project, I stumbled across the Peel Prairie Postcard Archive at the University of Alberta, which is a great resource for anyone interested in the rural towns of the Prairies. To my surprise and delight, I found three separate postcards depicting streets of three different towns that featured a "Royal Cafe."
2. I interviewed Esther Leung (owner of the New Club Cafe at that time) who talked about her family's time in the town of Vulcan (where they stayed after retirement) and about running a Chinese-owned restaurant in rural Alberta. Esther was especially proud to tell me that their café was the first place to serve pizza in the town and only occasionally served Chinese food.
3. The Wainwright Steak House in Wainwright, Alberta, is run by a Laotian family and features a Chinese menu, a Western menu, and a Thai menu.
4. Cho, *Eating Chinese*, 53.
5. There is an entire *Wikipedia* article devoted to ginger beef from Calgary. The main theory is that it was invented by The Silver Inn Restaurant in the 1970s (the Silver Inn's website also makes this claim). However, during my research, I interviewed Michael Ho, the father of my friend, who, along with his father, ran and owned one of the early high-end Chinese restaurants in town. He disputes the claims made online and asserts that it was, in fact, a Chinese dish that goes well with beer and that his customers loved it. He claims that this is the true reason that ginger beef became so beloved and popular in Calgary. I cannot say for sure whether it is Ho's story or one of the various *Wikipedia* claims that is the truth but only that, from my own experience, ginger beef has become a popular food to eat in Calgary and across Alberta. In fact, the favourite restaurant of my grandparents (who don't often stray far from their meat and potato dishes) is the local chain that is named after the popular dish, Ginger Beef.
6. Canadian residents of Chinese background make up less than five per cent of Alberta's population, according to a 2011 Statistics Canada profile ("NHS Profile").
7. Cho, *Eating Chinese*, 129.

8 Ibid., 127.

9 Ibid., 126.

10 Shore, "Stephen Shore's Best Shot."

Bibliography

Cho, Lily. *Eating Chinese: Culture on the Menu in Small Town Canada*. Toronto: University of Toronto Press, 2010.

Shore, Stephen, interviewed by Leo Benedictus. "Stephen Shore's Best Shot," *The Guardian*, 27 September 2007. www.theguardian.com/artanddesign/2007/sep/27/photography.art.

Statistics Canada. "NHS Profile, Alberta, 2011." Accessed 28 December 2015. www12.statcan.gc.ca/nhs-enm/2011/dp-pd/prof/details/Page.cfm%20Lang=E&Geo1=PR&Code1=48&Data=Count&SearchText=Alberta&SearchType=Begins&SearchPR=01&A1=A11&B1=A11&GeoLevel=PR&GeoCode=48.

Writing beyond "Currybooks"
Construction of Racialized and Gendered Diasporic Identities in Anita Rau Badami's *Can You Hear the Nightbird Call?*

Asma Sayed

Food is central to cultural life, especially for diaspora subjects who have moved from one place to another. It not only sustains ties to the home left behind but also helps to create a new home space in adopted lands, triggering memories of places, people, and cultures. Connection to food is reflected in South Asian diasporic writing through the ways that authors use gastronomy to signify intersectional issues of race, class, and gender, and represent matters of identity and belonging central to understanding migration. For people in diaspora, food can also be a reminder of their "otherness," especially if it is not considered part of the "mainstream" culinary trends. In fact, in multicultural countries such as Canada, diasporic culinary arts are often invoked as symbolic of cultural diversity thus leading to "celebratory multiculturalism," which further exoticizes certain outward components of culture such as food, clothing, dance, and music, while ignoring embedded social inequities.[1] Nonetheless, many diasporic authors invoke cuisine and eating places in more nuanced ways, using them to demonstrate cultural differences and fractures, and also as productive spaces for pushing socio-ethnic boundaries. Anita Rau Badami's novel *Can You Hear the Nightbird Call?* is one such work in which gastronomy plays a significant role. Badami is an Indo-Canadian author of four novels and has contributed extensively to the Canadian literary scene through her continued erudite engagement with issues affecting Canadians of South Asian origin. Her second novel, *The Hero's Walk*, was a finalist in the 2016 CBC Canada Reads competition. References to South Asian food are common in Badami's work; at times, she has been criticized for her "food politics."[2] *Can You Hear the Nightbird Call?*, her third novel, is about the lives of three women from India – two now living in Vancouver and one in Delhi – and focuses on issues of migration, displacement, religious identity, memory, violence, and trauma. In the novel, food is central to the Indo-Canadian community that comes together at The Delhi Junction Café, a restaurant, and an Indian grocery store, both of which, run by the protagonist, Bibi-ji, are at the centre of the South Asian community in Vancouver from the 1940s through to the 1980s. These two locations are also spaces where social ties are first solidified and then, over time, rupture after political upheavals in India and Canada. On the other hand, the sharing and exchange of home-cooked meals is foundational to the development of a relationship between the two main female characters, Bibi-ji and Leela, from vastly different backgrounds in India, who end up as neighbours in Canada. Thus, in *Can You Hear the Nightbird Call?*, food images become indicative of many things: a desire for migration; a means of empowerment; diaspora subjects' sense of memory, nostalgia, identity, and belonging; and community building. This chapter theorizes the ways that the novel symbolically mobilizes food as a source of comfort, as a mnemonic to evoke happy memories and resist historical injustices, and as a representation of religious and cultural divides. Understanding the role of South Asian gastronomy and culinary motifs in the novel allows for a nuanced reading of the intersections of racialized and gendered identities in diaspora, particularly in the context of South Asian immigrant experience in Canada.

Food in South Asian Diasporic Writing

Food, culture, and gastronomic references are pervasive in South Asian and South Asian diasporic literary works. Many novels and memoirs carry such references even in their titles.[3] Some South Asian diasporic literary representations of gastronomy include Yasmin Alibhai-Brown's *The Settler's Cookbook: A Memoir of Love, Migration, and Food*, Jhumpa Lahiri's *The Interpreter of Maladies*, Nisha Minhas's *Chappati or Chips?*, and Anita Desai's *Fasting, Feasting*. Cookbooks have also been one of the emerging genres. Writing about the role of cookbooks in South Asian diaspora, Arjun Appadurai, a socio-cultural theorist specializing in globalization studies, argues that they "belong to the literature of exile, of nostalgia and loss."[4] Foodways in both fiction and non-fiction have been used to explore issues of identity. In the South Asian Canadian literary context, works focusing exclusively on or including culinary arts are few, but many novelists use gastronomical references in their writing.[5] Two recent non-fiction publications include one by celebrated chef Vikram Vij and a critical analysis by Naben Ruthnum, a Canadian author and cultural critic. Vij's 2017 memoir *Vij: A Chef's One-Way Ticket to Canada with Indian Spices in His Suitcase* tells the story of his trials and tribulations as he went on to become one of the most renowned chefs globally. Vij has also published three cookbooks. Ruthnum's *Curry: Eating, Reading, and Race* is a critical study of South Asian diaspora literature and the use of curry as a metaphor. Ruthnum offers a very interesting argument about the way curry unites and serves as a symbol for South Asian culture, while also falsely perpetuating the myth of a monoculture that erases the vast and diverse cultural-scape and associated flavours, smells, and colours that are the reality.

Ruthnum writes that although there is no single "authentic" curry, it has come to assume an identity for South Asians in diaspora. By extension, curry in South Asian diasporic literature is "an abiding metaphor for connection, nostalgia, homecoming, and distance from family and country."[6] At the same time, Ruthnum worries about the metaphor's overuse and its limitations: "Thinking about and writing about a food as culturally complex as curry as though it were a marker of an authentic past that is now lost, or a signifier of a broken bond between generations due to geographical dislocation, does a major disservice to how delicious curry is, and to how particular a South Asian diasporic experience can be."[7] He calls South Asian diasporic novels "currybooks;" these books, he argues, "typically detail a wrenching sense of being in two worlds at once, torn between the traditions of the East and the liberating, if often unrewarding freedoms of the West."[8] He argues that South Asian diasporic writing focused on gastronomic metaphors has led to a certain kind of a stereotypical single story, and thus South Asian authors need to move away from the trope.

Similarly, Ruth Maxey in her study of food in transatlantic South Asian writing has argued that "the tropes of food and eating, particularly in a familial setting, undoubtedly inform much current writing by South Asian Atlantic authors" and that "food has become a tired means of depicting South Asian diasporic life."[9] Maxey discusses various roles that food has played in literature written by South Asian Atlantic authors. She writes that through the examination of "mealtimes; shopping, especially for 'authentic' ingredients; the cultural and economic importance of restaurants; the binary of South Asian versus 'American' or 'British' food; and the notion of cultural syncretism," food offers authors "the opportunity to explore a number of major themes at the same time: gender roles; family and especially matrilineal connections; regionalism; and cooking as labour, in ways which sometimes become key to socio-economic status."[10] On the other hand, South Asian writers have been criticized for "food pornography," to use a term first popularized by Frank Chin, an American author and playwright, of overusing food metaphors in their writing and using food imagery such as mangoes and chilies on book covers.[11]

Yet, Anita Mannur, in her groundbreaking study, *Culinary Fictions: Food in South Asian Diasporic Culture*, rightly notes that while food has started taking a central place in literary and visual texts and scholarship since the 1990s, "there is a relative dearth of critical analyses of film and literature about food that moves beyond critical engagement out of representational analyses and into interrogative spheres which would trouble the ways in which food is used to buttress narratives about belonging, kinship, and dissent."[12] She is critical of many narratives in which food is presented as a way of furthering "culinary citizenship," an idea that uses food as a medium of remembering and creating national identities, a kind of nostalgia rooted in memories of culinary spaces. However, Mannur asserts, scholarship "has not adequately emphasized the importance of viewing food as a discursive space able to *critically interrogate* the nostalgia and affective rendering of food in relationship to racial and ethnic identity [emphasis added]."[13] She further notes that "more often than not food is situated in narratives about racial and ethnic identity as an intractable measure of cultural authenticity."[14] Thus, it is imperative for scholars to study these intersectional elements given that South Asian literature is full of gastronomic signifiers that are presented in various forms: references to recipes, religious offertory, meals at wedding gatherings, day-to-day consumption of food with friends and family, and communal exchange of food. South Asian diasporic writers invoke poetics and politics of food in many nuanced ways, using them to demonstrate immigrant experiences of inclusiveness as well as otherness. Thus, as a diasporic author, Badami's use of such food tropes to further her female protagonists' story of migration and survival is not atypical. In *Can You Hear the Nightbird Call?* Badami represents people from various socio-economic, religious, and national backgrounds through the medium of food, which not only serves the protagonist's nostalgia but also allows her to negotiate power in her adopted homeland.

Food, Resistance, and Solidarity

Can You Hear the Nightbird Call? is about the interconnected lives of three women: Sharanjeet (also known as Bibi-ji), her niece Nimmo, and her friend Leela. Bibi-ji and Leela migrate to Vancouver and their lives are affected by various events both in India and Canada: the aftermath of the *Komagata Maru*, a Japanese liner carrying more than 300 Indian migrants, which was turned away from the shores of Vancouver in 1914 as the Canadian government refused to let those on board, mostly Sikhs, to enter Canada[15]; the Partition of India in 1947; the 1984 anti-Sikh riots in Delhi after the assassination of Prime Minister Indira Gandhi; and the 1985 Air India bombing carried out by extremists retaliating against the 1984 riots. Badami weaves all these historical details around the lives of the women through food metaphors. Bibi-ji, the protagonist, first opens a grocery store and then a restaurant in Vancouver. Shweta Khilnani, an academic, reminds us that "a sizeable portion of South Asian immigrants make their living through food either by opening Indian restaurants or grocery stores" thus rendering food as a trope that "defines them as the Other and gives them a sense of selfhood in terms of financial stability."[16] Bibi-ji achieves class status, economic empowerment, and fulfilling personal relationships, through her culinary ventures. In fact, Bibi-ji's desire to migrate to Canada emanated from love of food.

Yearning for certain sensory delights that Bibi-ji associates with luxury and success – even the basic satisfaction of enjoying a meal, or using beautifully perfumed soaps – is what drives her motivation to emigrate from her Indian village to Canada. As a child, Sharanjeet (Bibi-ji) dreamt of moving away from her village, to a place where she did not have to do her daily chore of making cow-dung cakes for fuel. The cow-dung made her hands smell and Sharanjeet, who "loved eating," could not enjoy her meals: "Her joy at the sight of food turned even the simplest combination of rice and dal into a feast, but when she raised a morsel of food to her mouth she could only smell the overpowering odour that had written itself into her skin, instead of the fragrances of turmeric, fresh rice, butter melting on hot phulkas, green chillies frying."[17] Her love of food makes her dream of a foreign land where she could enjoy a meal and the aromas of Punjabi cuisine without having to worry about cow-dung cakes: "She wished then, with all her heart, that she, like the Arabian princess in a tale the wandering storyteller had told her, might wake up and find herself in a different home altogether, carried there by the jinns in the service of a handsome prince" (6). It is interesting that young Sharanjeet's dreams of a romantic life with a prince are constituted around her desire for food. In her imagined land, she would have lavender soap to wash her hands and food would be plentiful.

In South Asian culture, as in many others, abundance of food is a sign of upward mobility and financial stability. Once Bibi-ji has fulfilled her dream of moving to a distant land by marrying Pa-ji, a Punjabi immigrant who became a Canadian citizen, she measures her status in Vancouver in proportion to her kitchen and, implicitly, her ability to nourish her family and community. She is thrilled that she now has "a kitchen with more pots and pans than she knew what to do with" (38). Here, kitchenware is symbolic of her upward mobility. At the same time, food can also trigger memories of home and a desire to be with the family left behind. Thus, while enjoying her successes in Vancouver, Bibi-ji is also nostalgic about her past. She remembers her old kitchen in Punjab as a place where her family gathered together and shared meals. As Cheryl-Ann Michael, who specializes in South African cultural studies, argues, "food and food memories offer simultaneously a means of connection to particular places and people."[18] For Bibi-ji, it is the space of the kitchen that becomes a memory of the homeland left behind: "She yearned for the return of that time when her family was entire – her mother squatting by the clay stove, the harsh angles and hollows of her exhausted face exaggerated by the glow from the fire" (6). She has now forgotten the smell of cow dung, the small kitchen, and the few pots and pans she had in Punjab. What she remembers from her new location in Canada is the communal aspect of her mother's kitchen in India. She aims to recreate the inviting kitchen atmosphere of her childhood memories in her house in Vancouver, which is open to all the newcomers from Punjab. New immigrants are welcome to eat and stay at Pa-ji and Bibi-ji's house until they get their footing in the new country. Later, when Bibi-ji runs a grocery store, East India Foods and Groceries, she again measures her success via food. The shop of which she was the "unchallenged owner – no, *proprietor*; that sounded grander" had "four rows of shelves loaded from one end to the other with sacks of rice, bags of mung, toor, chana, masoor dal, kidney beans, chick peas, navy beans and spices from India" that made Bibi-ji feel empowered, a "woman of substance," as she proudly thought, "this is all mine" (37, 39). Bibi-ji's home kitchen, her grocery store, and later her restaurant are all sites for forming relationships among the members of the South Asian immigrant community. Thus, as much as food accords some power and financial freedom to Bibi-ji, it also allows her to be a community builder.

Cooking and consuming food in Bibi-ji's kitchen, which is a space for female solidarity, are also acts of resistance to historical injustices. As Dan Ojwang, who has published widely on East African Asian writing, reminds, "the burden placed on women to reproduce the immigrant community socially through the preparation of 'traditional' food is turned into a resource by the women who take control of kitchens."[19] Bibi-ji's kitchen is a communal space always humming with activity.

Women in the house, newcomers to Canada and staying with Bibi-ji until they find their own place, "made themselves useful around the apartment, cooking and cleaning, washing dishes," and men helped in the grocery store. The house kitchen had a musical rhythm of its own: "three women were busy making stacks of parathas. Bib-ji watched absent-mindedly when two of them squatted on the floor, their knees bent, their chins resting on their knees, their hands spinning as they rolled out the dough into circles and triangles. A third woman stood at the stove slapping one paratha at a time into a hot pan and frying it rapidly. The smoky odour of cooking flour and oil filled the kitchen. Their movements were mesmerizing, their gold bracelets set up a rhythmic *chink-chink-chink* and gossip bubbled and frothed around the kitchen like a small river" (196). These women bond over cooking. Parathas, or rotis, have a special resonance for South Asian communities. Julie Mehta, an author and journalist specializing in Southeast Asia, argues that roti is "a signifier of struggle" and "a crucial cultural symbol" as it "awakens familial, community, and cultural memory."[20] Especially in the context of Sikh immigrants to Canada, Mehta argues, roti is linked to the history of the steamship *Komagata Maru*. She writes that Indo-Canadians "made rotis in their homes and supplied these to the 'prisoners' aboard the steamer" thus making wheat "the currency of life" and roti "a unifying symbol."[21] Against this historical backdrop, women making rotis in Bibi-ji's kitchen are symbolically supporting and remembering those who had not been allowed into Canada; food is the medium of their resistance. For Bibi-ji, the connection is personal. Her father was one of the passengers on board the *Komagata Maru*. He, like others on the ship, was sent back to India and spent the rest of his life depressed, eventually disappearing from his village and leaving Bibi-ji, her mother, and her sister alone fending for themselves in a highly patriarchal society. Bibi-ji then, by welcoming new immigrants in her house and making food together, is indirectly resisting Canada's history of rejecting South Asians. Ojwang, writing about African Asian literature, argues that "not only do food and drink evoke in members of immigrant Asian communities a sense of their past ... they are also a powerful index of a sense of security and belonging, or the feeling of being cast adrift in strange new worlds."[22] Bibi-ji's house, and later her restaurant, offer this sense of security and belonging to Punjabi newcomers while reminding them of the past inequities.

ASMA SAYED

The Delhi Junction Café: Invoking Memories and Building Communities

Bibi-ji and Pa-ji's restaurant, The Delhi Junction Café, is a gathering place that provides a feeling of "home" to South Asian immigrants as they invoke their memories. Communities are formed as people from wide-ranging ethno-religious backgrounds get together over a meal at the restaurant. At the same time, socio-political tensions also lead to ruptures in the community, making the restaurant a potential site of difference. Restaurants have played an important role in establishing immigrant communities in North America. Thus, ethnic restaurants feature in many South Asian immigrant literary texts, as authors use the trope to invoke multiculturalism or as a way of showing otherness. Socially, such restaurants have become trendy as people pay symbolic respect to "other" cultures by consuming "ethnic" food. Many scholars have critiqued the exoticization of ethnic restaurants and consumption of food as a mode of living superficial multiculturalism.[23] At the same time, restaurants can also serve as "gastronomic contact zones" that are typically "situated in cafes, kitchens, and homes where displaced individuals meet and reestablish identities and communities."[24] In her study of Chinese cafés in rural Canada, Lily Cho, a professor at York University, identifies restaurants as a "culturally productive space" where immigrants may build friendships and communities.[25] Bibi-ji's Vancouver restaurant is such a space where South Asian immigrants relive their memories and have discussions about their own families and development of various political scenarios in the lands they have left behind. For both Bibi-ji and Pa-ji, the restaurant serves multiple purposes: a place for gathering, a place to perform altruistic deeds, and mostly a place of joy as they watch their neighbours enjoy memories over some food. Both were "glad to see new immigrants. They felt a deep affection for these people, even when they were not from Punjab. Fuelled by frequent infusions of tea, they liked to *discuss* things" (61). The Delhi Junction Café serves South Asian food: samosas, chholey-bhaturey, curries, sweets, lassi, and chai. Partaking of the culinary delights offered at the restaurant becomes "a transformative experience – either as an assertion of community values or a zone of familiarity and identity in the midst of interracial tensions *among minorities within* Canada."[26] People from India, Pakistan, Bangladesh, with varied religious backgrounds, all gather at the restaurant. For instance, Hafeez Ali and Alibhai are Pakistani Muslims. Dr Majumdar, a Bengali; Harish Shah, a Gujarati; and Menon, a Malayali, are Hindus from India. Before tensions arose among communities because of changing circumstances in India, including the Indo-Pakistani War of 1971 and the Khalistan separatist movement, these migrants forgot the differences that divide people in the subcontinent: "In the early years of the restaurant's life, the Indians and the Pakistanis had sat hunched around the same table, fuelling their conversations with samosas and endless cups of boiling sugary chai tinged with ginger and cardamom, discussing their lives, their families, cricket matches, their work, and most of all, the politics of their country of origin" (65). These political discussions, which often happen while consuming rice and mutton curry, get heated at times until everybody realizes that they are now Canadians; they do not live in South Asia and can do very little about political changes happening there. In such instances, the only connection that characters can feel to their homeland is through food.

Food can also be a source of socio-cultural and religious tensions. Bibi-ji is careful about the implications of such pressures and uses food as a means to mediate potential cultural conflicts. She is aware that people's food habits are tied to their beliefs. As Appadurai, writing about food's connection to people's moral and cultural status, notes, "food taboos and prescriptions divide men from women, gods from humans, upper from lower castes, one sect from another. Eating together, whether as a family, a caste, or a village, is a carefully conducted exercise in the reproduction of intimacy. Exclusion of persons from events is a symbolically intense social signal of rank, of distance, of enmity."[27] Thus, a restaurateur must be careful in preparing the menu. Bibi-ji is aware that some religious traditions ban certain foods, and makes sure "that neither beef nor pork were included so as not to offend any religious group" (60–1). Typically, Muslims do not consume pork and followers of Hinduism do not eat beef. Bibi-ji ensures that she does not hurt the sentiments of these communities so that food becomes a connecting rather than dividing force. Newcomers feel comfortable at Bibi-ji's restaurant where they not only get a free bowl of sugary kheer, an Indian sweet, but also "advice on visas and immigration procedures, work permits and rents, the best places to buy vegetables and groceries" (61). The restaurant, by extension, becomes a second home and a place of comfort for new immigrants. It is "a ritual, a necessity, a habit for many of the city's growing population of desis who stopped by for a quick meal or afternoon tea" (59). As they all discuss matters over a cup of tea, new communities are formed and friendships forged. In this context, food becomes a symbol of togetherness rather than divisiveness, further adding to the intercultural framework of the restaurant and thus, by extension, lives of immigrants in Canada.

Bibi-ji's vision of the restaurant as an inclusive place is reflected both in its name and the decor. The Delhi Junction Café was meant to host "if not exactly the multitude, then at least a semblance of the crowds that streamed through New Delhi's railway station daily" (59). Delhi station sees the movement of people from all classes and religions in India. The café, by extension of its name, is meant to have a "broader appeal" and attract people from all backgrounds in Canada (59). Bibi-ji's vision furthers the idea of "culinary multiculturalism," to use Mannur's words, that as people share a meal, they share stories and in turn may forget their differences and come together. The decor of the restaurant similarly reflects Indian political and popular culture but also an interesting mingling of Eastern and Western ethos: "On one wall hung lithographic prints of the ten Sikh gurus, a highly coloured painting of the Golden Temple with a garland of flashing bulbs around it, maps of India and Canada, pictures of Nehru, Gandhi, Bhagat Singh, Marilyn Monroe, Meena Kumari, Clark Gable and Dev Anand" (60). The wall could be read as signifying cultural hybridity as it brings together cultural and political icons from India as well as North America. The other wall of the restaurant held "clocks displaying the time in India, Pakistan (East and West), Vancouver, England, New York, Melbourne and Singapore" (60). For Pa-ji these clocks are a reminder of Sikhs living across the globe. The visitors to the restaurant also have relatives in different parts of the world; thus, the clocks jog people's memories about migration patterns of their communities, but also allow them to imagine the daily lives of their family members far away. The Delhi Junction Café then is a place where "here" and "there" come together as the owners and patrons create a diasporic culture of their own.

At the same time, the restaurant represents ethnic and racial tensions between the characters and racism they face in Canada. Irrespective of Bibi-ji's attempts to keep her restaurant an impartial and inclusive place of gathering, occasionally it becomes a ground of political and divisive discussions and fears. Such contradictions are not unusual; Appadurai in his article about gastro-politics in South Asia argues that "food can serve two diametrically opposed semiotic functions. It can serve to indicate and construct social relations characterized by equality, intimacy, or solidarity; or, it can serve to sustain relations characterized by rank, distance, or segmentation."[28] For instance, in Badami's novel, during the war between India and Pakistan in 1971, two Pakistani regulars, Hafeez and Alibhai, stop visiting Bibi-ji's restaurant. Pa-ji notices their absence and feels "regret mixed with anger" (249), as he wants people to forget their differences from their homelands. The two Pakistanis refusing to eat with Indian patrons indicates their fear of verbal attacks as they are self-conscious of their minority status within the restaurant. However, as the tensions ease in the subcontinent, the two patrons return soon after as "a good meal, with familiar spices in a foreign country, meant more than the enmities generated by distant homelands" (67). Similarly, The Delhi Junction Café again becomes a place of tension after Pa-ji is killed in India during his visit to the Golden Temple, which was attacked by the Indian government to oust extremists seeking refuge inside the temple. When the usual visitors come to the restaurant to mourn Pa-ji's death, discussions about what happened in India lead to tensions between Sikhs and Hindus. Shah, one of the Hindu patrons, wonders if the Sikh owners and waiters were seeking revenge and contaminating their food by spitting into it before serving. Thus, just as food bonds different communities, it also becomes a medium of division.

Food not only creates frictions among members of the South Asian community but also leads to confrontations with the non-Asian group. For example, Colonel Samuel Hunt, who served in the British Indian army and lived in India for some twenty-five years, visits the restaurant for its mutton curry and naan, but he dislikes the presence of the South Asian community in Canada. The tension here is replete with irony; he fetishizes Indian food while disliking Indians. The orientalist and racist attitude of Hunt, "who had become known for his uncomplimentary sentiments towards immigrants who did not share his racial heritage," serves as a reminder of colonial history and of the presence of the British in India and Canada (57). Hunt wants to be served, but he will not engage with any of the brown owners or patrons. His love for Indian food is counter to his hatred for Indo-Canadian people. While eating in The Delhi Junction, he asserts that he was a legal migrant and that his wife's family was one of the earliest people to come to Canada. He thinks that most other immigrants, especially people of colour, are "riff-raff thugs who come with no passports, no visas, no papers … messing up the place … taking away our jobs, taking away our land, taking away our view" (124–5). Hunt represents the neo-colonial ideologies upheld by former colonizers, and his reference to Canadian land as "our" is an attempt to erase the colonial history. As Ojwang argues, food "acts as one of the most important ways of building bridges between hitherto hostile groups: to adapt to the culinary practices of others and to accept their food becomes a profound gesture of recognition."[29] However, Hunt shows no interest in recognizing fellow visitors at the café even as food offers him an opportunity to engage with people; he always sits alone in a corner, reads his newspaper, and vents loudly about any news pertaining to immigration. Thus, his love for Indian food seems to be driven by a "colonial thirst for adventure," to use Padoongpatt's words.[30] While Bibi-ji is perturbed by Hunt's colonial attitude, she empathizes with him, because she recognizes what he shares in common with all the patrons: he is "doing the splits between two cultures, just like the desis were," as he is "an Englishman transplanted to Canada" (58). She sees him as "a sad old man whose eyes and ears were so sealed by his skin that he could neither witness nor understand the changing world" (57). In dismissing Hunt's racist attitude and not responding to his outrages, Bibi-ji refuses to accord any power to the former colonizer and affirms her identity as a post-colonial subject. She sees Hunt's visits and his inability to resist her restaurant food as a sign of her success.

The Delhi Junction Café empowers Bibi-ji: not only is it her livelihood but it also allows her to create a space for herself and others in the new homeland. In opening the restaurant, Bibi-ji realizes "yet another of [her] ambitions" (56). The busy restaurant signals accomplishment as an entrepreneur and a manager: "A full restaurant was a good thing – yes, a very good thing indeed. She surveyed with satisfaction the crowded tables and the waiters running in and out of the kitchen carrying loaded trays" (57). As dishes are produced and consumed in the restaurant, India and Canada, and the memories associated with the two countries, become one. Mary Douglas, a British social anthropologist widely recognized for her work on human culture, in her pioneering 1972 essay on deciphering meal, has argued that food can indicate "different degrees of hierarchy, inclusion and exclusion, boundaries and transaction across boundaries."[31] South Asian food was considered messy and smelly for a long time. But the contributions of many South Asian restaurateurs, such as Vikram Vij with his multiple eateries and success as one of Canada's top chefs, have changed the global culinary landscape and led to the popularity of South Asian food. By the same token, in Badami's novel, restaurants such as the one run by Bibi-ji, and her success as an entrepreneur, serve as a reminder of the transforming Canadian national identity.

Female Friendship and Food

Likewise, cuisine is also a trope linking various female characters in the novel. Food-making and food-sharing among female characters – namely Bibi-ji and Leela, another important character – bring them closer and help build long-lasting friendships. Thus, not only does Bibi-ji connect communities through her restaurant but also her personal alliances grow through food. In fact, it is common for "immigrant women [to use] the culinary table as a site of connection between the old and the new."[32] At the same time, we see an interesting development of gastropolitics, "a conflict or competition over specific cultural or economic resources as it emerges in social transactions around food" as the two women exchange their respective regional cuisine.[33] Bibi-ji's friendship with Leela develops over the exchange of cuisines of north and south India. When Leela arrives in Canada, Bibi-ji sends food to her so that Leela does not have to cook after a long journey from India. Food is a gesture of welcome to the new "home" and a new community. When returning Bibi-ji's food containers, Leela refills them, as "it was rude to return empty boxes, and an admission of poverty" (131). For Leela, food is a medium through which she can uphold her class status in Canada. Bibi-ji and Leela grew up in different regions in India; Bibi-ji is from northern India and Leela from the south. Regional food differences, thus, are noticeable. When Bibi-ji smells the food that Leela has brought and confesses that she had never tasted South Indian food, Leela feels offended and thinks: "*As if it is from other country*" (133). Since Leela had had Punjabi food when growing up, she expects Bibi-ji to appreciate South Indian food. For Leela, it is important that just as she knew about Bibi-ji's regional cuisine, Bibi-ji should also know about hers. Nonetheless, the two women exchange food on a regular basis, initially out of a desire to show their cooking skills, but eventually these give-and-takes become a source of nostalgia. Both want to reclaim "the place left behind – Home – in food that [they] cooked" (135). Their memories of their homeland are tied to the food they prepare for themselves and each other. Badami provides a detailed description of the two women's cooking: "if one day Bibi-ji chopped onion-ginger-garlic to create a sauce for her famous chholey, leaning over the pot, stirring-stirring-stirring, adding a pinch of this or that and inhaling the aromas until she knew it was just exactly right, the next day saw Leela standing on tiptoe, using a long-handled ladle to draw forward a sealed packet of asafetida from the back of the kitchen cupboard, carried all the way from There to add to the pot of Venki's famous eggplant sambhar" (135). As Bibi-ji and Leela cook, their relations develop and they are no longer concerned about their differences of religion or class.[34] Bibi-ji becomes a mentor for Leela, advising her on where to buy vegetables, fruits, and spices. Furthermore, Bibi-ji's restaurant also eases Leela's arrival in Canada as she meets other members of the community at The Delhi Junction Café. Bibi-ji's relations with Leela, which develop via food sharing, are reminiscent of many female friendships and development of intersectional spaces.

The feminine connection between these two women of diverse circumstances, their exchange of food, and their desire to learn culinary creativity from each other, signal their embracing of their new environment.

Conclusion

In Badami's *Can You Hear the Nightbird Call?* diasporic identities of South Asian migrants to Canada are connected and built in culinary spaces. Food becomes a cross-cultural signifier through which Bibi-ji, the protagonist, links people, places, and communities. South Asian women are generally considered to be secondary to men, especially when they are expected to fulfill gendered roles in their households and in the kitchen. Bibi-ji, however, turns those gendered expectations around by taking control of the restaurant and making food a source of excitement and empowerment. Bibi-ji's kitchen, grocery store, and restaurant create a manifold space for invoking memories and building communities, while also affording her agency in her new homeland. These three venues, which serve as microcosms of multiracial, multilingual and multi-ethnic communities, are the only connection that many characters in the novel have with their homeland. It is through the consumption of food in these places that Bibi-ji, and the people in her family and community, are reminded of their Canadian identity and of the countries they have left behind. Although at times political tensions create momentary fissures, ultimately, food bonds people as they continue to thrive, and support each other, in the new intercultural spaces.

Notes

1 See Fleras, *The Politics of Multiculturalism*. It must also be noted here that just as chicken tikka masala was considered part of Britain's multicultural framework, butter chicken has taken on a similar position in Canada. Both serve as examples of celebrating multiculturalism through culinary delights.

2 For instance, Dulai in his review "Against Literary Confections" criticizes Badami and other diasporic writers for their "marinated nostalgia." He argues that food references seem to come mostly from authors of "established, upper-caste families" and suggests that many poor Punjabi authors are rarely published, perhaps because they lack "ghee-rich narratives" and come from a class of "manual labourers." Herein, Dulai simplifies the

question of publication of works of diasporic authors, a complex matter that is rooted not only in class-caste politics but also in issues of race and language. Nonetheless, his point about "food politics" is one that seems to resonate in Ruthnum's work as well.

3   For example, Sara Suleri's *Meatless Days* (Chicago: Chicago University Press, 1989), Uma Parameswaran's *Mangoes on a Maple Leaf* (Fredericton, NB: Broken Jaw, 2002), Anita Rau Badami's *Tamarind Mem* (Toronto: Penguin, 1996), Chitra Banerjee Divakaruni's *Mistress of Spices* (New York: Doubleday, 1997). Interestingly, Badami, in one of her interviews, notes that her US publishers of *Tamarind Mem* wanted her to change the title to *Sweet and Sour Woman*, but she found that title sounded Chinese and not Indian; see Tancock, "Interview with Author Anita Rau Badami."

4   Appadurai, "How to Make," 18.

5   See M.G. Vassanji's *The Gunny Sack* (London: Heinemann, 1989), Shani Mootoo's *Cereus Blooms at Night* (London: Granta, 1996), and Rohinton Mistry's *A Fine Balance* (Toronto: Emblem Editions, 1995).

6   Ruthnum, *Curry*, 9.

7   Ibid., 24.

8   Ibid., 53.

9   Maxey, *South Asian Atlantic Literature*, 163.

10   Ibid., 164.

11   Frank Chin wrote about food pornography in 1984; much has changed since then in terms of food landscape. In the current social-media-driven times, the term has different connotations as people post photos of their daily consumption on various social media platforms such as Twitter, Facebook, Instagram, Snapchat, etc. However, such change perhaps pushes the marketers further to include culinary images on book covers, especially in the context of works that are perceived as representing "exotic cultures."

12   Mannur, *Culinary Fictions*, 10.

13   Ibid., 12.

14   Ibid., 3.

15   The *Komagata Maru* was a steamship carrying more than 350 people, mostly Sikhs from India, which was denied entry to Canada under Continuous Passage regulation; many onboard died as the ship was sent back. Canadian prime minister Justin Trudeau apologized for the incident in the House of Commons on 18 May 2016. For further information on the *Komagata Maru*, see Johnston, *The Voyage of* Komagata Maru; Mawani, *Across Oceans of Law*; *Studies in Canadian Literature* 40.1, 2015, special issue on South Asian Canadian Literature; and Kazimi, *Continuous Journey* (documentary).

16   Khilnani, "Food and Identity," 77.

17 Badami, *Can You Hear*, 6. Subsequent quotations from Badami's novel have been cited parenthetically.
18 Michael, "On the Slipperiness," 261.
19 Ojwang, *Reading Migration and Culture*, 71.
20 Mehta, "Toronto's Multicultural Tongues," 156–7.
21 Ibid., 57.
22 Ojwang, *Reading Migration and Culture*, 64.
23 For further details, see Pazo, *Diasporic Tastescapes*; Heldke, *Exotic Appetites*; Fish, "Boutique Multiculturalism."
24 Gardaphé and Xu, "Introduction," 7.
25 Cho, *Eating Chinese*, 13.
26 Mehta, "Toronto's Multicultural Tongues," 164.
27 Appadurai, "How to Make," 10.
28 Appadurai, "Gastro-politics," 486.
29 Ojwang, *Reading Migration and Culture*, 64.
30 Padoongpatt, "Oriental Cookery," 192.
31 Douglas, "Deciphering a Meal," 36.
32 Iacovetta, Epp, and Korinek, eds., *Edible Histories, Cultural Politics*, 16.
33 Appadurai, "Gastro-politics," 495.
34 This situation changes later after Bibi-ji's husband is killed at the Golden Temple, which is raided by the Indian government looking for Khalistan separatists. Following the raid, Indian prime minister Indira Gandhi is killed by two of her bodyguards who are Sikh. Gandhi's assassination leads to riots in which many Sikhs are killed by angry Hindu mobs. After these events, although Bibi-ji has heard rumours of extremists' plans to plant a bomb in Air India flights, she does not stop Leela from travelling, and consequently, Leela dies as she is on the fatal Air India Flight 182 that kills 329 people.

Bibliography

Appadurai, Arjun. "Gastro-politics in Hindu South Asia." *American Ethnologist* 8, no. 3 (1981): 494–511.

– "How to Make a National Cuisine: Cookbooks in Contemporary India." *Comparative Studies in Society and History* 30, no. 1 (1988): 3–24.

Badami, Anita Rau. *Can You Hear the Nightbird Call?* Toronto: Alfred A. Knopf Canada, 2006.

Chin, Frank. *Chickencoop Chinaman and the Year of the Dragon*. Seattle: University of Washington Press, 1984.

Cho, Lily. *Eating Chinese: Culture on the Menu in Small Town Canada*. Toronto: University of Toronto Press, 2010.

Douglas, Mary. "Deciphering a Meal." In *Food and Culture: A Reader*, edited by Carole Counihan and Penny Van Esterik, 36–54. New York: Routledge, 1997.

Dulai, Phinder. "Against Literary Confections: Food for Naught: The Popular Indo-North American Novel Offers Chutney, Pickles, and Spice, but Not Enough Substance." *The Vancouver Sun*, 1 April 2000, E7.

Fish, Stanley. "Boutique Multiculturalism or Why Liberals Are Incapable of Thinking about Hate Speech." *Critical Inquiry* 23, no. 2 (1997): 378–95.

Fleras, Augie. *The Politics of Multiculturalism: Multicultural Governance in Comparative Perspective*. New York: Palgrave Macmillan, 2009.

Gardaphé, Fred L., and Wenying Xu. "Introduction: Food in Multi-Ethnic Literatures." *MELUS* 32, no. 4 (2007): 5–10.

Heldke, Lisa. *Exotic Appetites: Ruminations of a Food Adventurer*. New York: Routledge, 2003.

Iacovetta, Franca, Marlene Epp, and Valerie J Korinek, eds. *Edible Histories, Cultural Politics: Towards a Canadian Food History*. Toronto: University of Toronto Press, 2012.

Johnston, Hugh J.M. *The Voyage of Komagata Maru: The Sikh Challenge to Canada's Colour Bar*. Vancouver: University of British Columbia Press, 2014.

Kazimi, Ali, dir. *Continuous Journey*. 2004. TVOntario.

Khilnani, Shweta. "Food and Identity in Works of Jhumpa Lahiri and Bharati Mukherjee." *New Man International Journal of Multidisciplinary Studies* 2, no. 6 (2015): 75–81.

Mannur, Anita. *Culinary Fictions: Food in South Asian Diasporic Culture*. Philadelphia: Temple University Press, 2009.

Mawani, Renisa. *Across Oceans of Law: The* Komagata Maru *and Jurisdiction in the Time of Empire*. Durham: Duke University Press, 2018.

Maxey, Ruth. *South Asian Atlantic Literature, 1970–2010*. Edinburgh: Edinburgh University Press, 2011.

Mehta, Julie. "Toronto's Multicultural Tongues: Stores of South Asian Cuisines." In *Edible Histories, Cultural Politics: Towards a Canadian Food History*, edited by Franca Iacovetta, Marlene Epp, Valerie J. Korinek, 156–69. Toronto: University of Toronto Press, 2012.

Michael, Cheryl-Ann. "On the Slipperiness of Food." In *Beautiful/Ugly: African and Diaspora Aesthetics*, edited by Sarah Nuttall, 256–65. Durham: Duke University Press, 2006.

Ojwang, Dan. *Reading Migration and Culture: The World of East African Indian Literature*. New York: Palgrave Macmillan, 2013.

Padoongpatt, Mark. "Oriental Cookery: Devouring Asian and Pacific Cuisine during the

Cold War." In *Eating Asian American: A Food Studies Reader*, edited by Ka Robert Ji-Song, Manalansan Martin F.V., and Anita Mannur, 186–207. New York: New York University Press, 2013.

Pazo, Paula Torreiro: *Diasporic Tastescapes: Intersections of Food and Identity in Asian American Literature*. Zurich: Lit Verlag, 2016.

Ruthnum, Naben. *Curry: Eating, Reading, and Race*. Toronto: Coach House, 2017.

Tancock, Kat. "Interview with Author Anita Rau Badami." *Canadian Living*, 30 September 2006. www.canadianliving.com/life-and-relationships/.

Vij, Vikram. *Vij: A Chef's One-Way Ticket to Canada with Indian Spices in His Suitcase*. n.p.: Penguin, 2017.

Playing with Food

Jason Wright

Part One: The Appetizer

I Can Taste Memory

I am an artist who loves food; or rather I am an artist who loves to use food in his work. The culture of food is not merely the physical matter on one's fork, or in one's belly, but the stuff of grander encounters and exchanges. My work often examines these exchanges (our collective relationship to religion, gender, consumer culture, amongst others) through a lens of grotesque and absurdist comedy. Lard-covered barbecues, sugary donut crops, immaculately plated bones and offal, and fleshy sandwiches have all made their way into my artworks in an effort to provoke a wide range of senses in the viewer that extends beyond the visual. The work provides space in which to pause and consider, to reflect and laugh, as one may do while attending a lively and stimulating dinner party.

When I recall a moment from my past, it is often paired with a side of mashed potatoes. My recollections drip as gravy from my mouth, my life bracketed by the comforting sounds of loud and greasy laughs. *I can taste memory*. My tongue remembers the rites and ceremonies of my youth. These rituals of food and place remain with me, and set the table for my own creative practice.

In the Beginning There Were Pork Chops

As a thirteen-year-old boy living in the largely nondescript Vancouver suburb of North Delta (we are known for our large bog), I was given the task of cooking for my family every weekday for a year. There are three kids in my family and we all had our turn. I would often leave ball hockey games to go home and cook, to the jeers and taunts from other players: the kitchen was a place for moms and girls, not for me, not for busy boys. (Although my father did embody, perhaps reluctantly, the cliché of the manly summertime barbecue cook, often to smoky and charred effect.) Now in an age of ubiquitous celebrity chefs and Instagrammed dishes, I can sit back – far removed from 1980s North Delta, where boys did boy things and girls did girl things – and watch an episode of *Great Canadian Cookbook* with my young nephews, neither of them seeing the role of chef as being particularly gendered.[1]

A year of cooking did not mean I learned to be creative and inventive in the kitchen. Years down the road, I would learn to love being in the kitchen and cooking, but as a thirteen-year-old boy, I had 7-Eleven loitering to do, or a street hockey game to get back to, so I learned how to defrost, microwave, and boil with great speed and efficiency for a household that, frankly, was undiscerning and indifferent with what it put into its mouth. When I was younger, we would all meet at the kitchen table at the same time for dinner, our daily domestic ritual, but as teenagers, we were allowed to bring the food down to the basement where we would circle the wood-grained television, and plunk down my quickly made creations on rickety TV trays: boiled potatoes, creamed corn, and pork chops, slathered with Campbell's Cream of Mushroom soup.

We were five Anglo-European, Catholic, suburban Canadians, and in a way the quiet and flavourless environment of North Delta allowed me to think about ritual and place. North Delta, while not a neutral space by any means, did offer me a kind of tabula rasa upon which to draw and develop as a budding artist. The modest traditions of a bedroom community gain significance when there is little else to grab onto culturally. One may cultivate meaning in the most paltry of details within these spaces. Culture becomes simply anywhere people congregate. The overabundance of convenience stores where teens converge en masse, the ornate but beige church down the road, the dark and low-ceilinged local pub where I played darts with a neighbour's dad, and the plethora of uncannily similar family restaurants made an impact on me as sites of possibility and creative space.

Playing with My Food

My family didn't go out to dinner often but when we did, it was usually to the local Ricky's or Smitty's or The Pantry or other restaurants ending with a *Y*. My mom would hand me a pen out of her purse as soon as we would arrive. I would draw on the paper tablecloths, or whatever paper was available (even napkins would do the trick). I would often crawl underneath the table to draw, to create a dark and private studio for myself. Drawing in the restaurant was akin to playing with my food.

Drawing in these restaurants was about me creating my own worlds, peeking my head out only as the food arrived.

Every North Delta restaurant we would frequent had its own significance and appeal. We were allowed to order Shirley Temples at Shums. The Keg was for birthdays. Denny's has paper masks. White Spot's Pirate Packs came with a small chocolate coin and a cardboard pirate ship that floated unsuccessfully when you brought it to your bath. Muffin Break was for Sundays, if we were good.

The School of Drunk Chocolate

I was raised Catholic and being surrounded by the lavish spectacle of the Catholic Church sparked my burgeoning aesthetic sensibilities and my interest in performance, sculpture, and display. I loved the beauty and pageantry of it all, the excess, the silver and the gold, Jesus's protruding bones Lording over us, and then all of us lining up to eat his body and drink his blood. After church my family would go to Muffin Break and get five muffins the size of our heads, and us three kids would fight over who would get the Black Forest One, the One with the cream-cheese icing and cherry on top. This would be part of the ritual, part of the Catholic performance, The Fight for the Black Forest Muffin as Eucharist, The Chocolate and Cherry and Cream-Cheese Body of Christ.

When I inevitably went to art school, I learned other ways of displaying bones and blood, and after graduating, I travelled to Edinburgh, Scotland, and worked at a café and patisserie. In this ancient city, I learned even more about the staging of elaborate rituals. Edinburgh, unlike North Delta, was awash with art and history, and I loved the way art and history spurted onto you there, like the sloppy oozing out the backside of a late-night jelly donut. The past was a physical, moist, and viscous thing that stuck to your skin. The manager of the patisserie would often badly order the pastries, and I would bring home garbage bags full of leftover mille-feuilles and florentines and tarts and pain au chocolates to my eager flatmates. I would spend my days eating and working at this café, and I would volunteer at a local gallery stuffing envelopes, and I would drink and stuff my face with custards and pastries, and drink and work and stuff envelopes. I'd go drinking with my friends and maybe visit an old church and the history of Scotland would squirt all over us. We'd drink into the wee hours and a handful of us drunken twenty-somethings would go home and gorge ourselves on elaborate French pastries out of garbage bags while the sun came up. It was beautiful and cream-filled and a little gross.

JASON WRIGHT

Pink and Sugary Things

In 2007, I began my MFA in sculpture at the University of Regina and I entered the mouth right away. The objects I made were mucky and filled with sugar and lard. I shared my studio space with a sculptor who worked mainly with wood. His woodworking skills were virtuosic, and his side of the studio was filled with tools and blades, whereas mine was flush with pink icings and marshmallow, bubble gum, fake flowers, and strawberry Danishes. On many occasions it was remarked that the room appeared as a binary of sorts: his side was masculine and my side decidedly feminine. These comments were made in jest, yet the effects of such statements lingered. These studio remarks, while not purposefully pernicious, were not far removed from the mocking tone of my teenage friends as I made my way home to cook for my family; working with food, whether through cooking or art-making was seen by some as less than manly.

Within the scope of contemporary sculpture, traditional materials (metal, wood) and methods (welding, carving) have been challenged. One could even argue the non-traditional and contingent strategies of contemporary sculpture have become the dominant ideology, the dominant way of making. Yet, while there may be an embrace of the tentative, metaphorical language of contemporary sculpture, the term "sculptor" has remained relatively fixed and gendered as male. Despite the influx of equivocal and transient forms in new sculpture, the image of the stone-carving, welding master prevails. It is the disruption of this image of the master-sculptor, and the playful inquiry into the mythic binaries of masculine and feminine forms that inform the way in which I frame much of my art practice.

Part Two: The Main Course

The Soldier

In *Li'l Soldier (Phalanx)* (2008), a ring of metal bristles covered in dried barbeque sauce sits in a circular pattern on the top of a lard-covered barbeque. The legs are bare metal. The barbeque-body is pulled inside out: the lard, the fat of the barbequed meat, is layered on the outside, and is topped by the hairy, "bloody," grotesque bristles of an orifice or crown of thorns. The circular pattern of the bristles also resembles a host of spears, a phalanx of soldiers.

Li'l Soldier's companion piece, *Plating (I and II)*, consists of two identical posters from the film *300* (2006) that depict an absurdly muscular soldier screaming in de-

Figure 15.1
Jason Wright, *L'il Soldier (Phalanx)*, 2008; materials: barbeque, lard, steel bristles, barbeque sauce and *Plating (I and II)* posters, lard, icings, plastic and metal flowers.

fiance to an unknown enemy. The text reads "Tonight We Dine in Hell." The mouths of these hanging, beefy Jesus-like figures are filled with icings, chocolate, and fake flowers.

Both works are meant to play on the fantastical bodies of action films and the strangely macho barbeque, the fetishized armour of the suburban warrior. The figures in the posters are literally "ripped," a play on the musculature of the soldier form. The heroic bodies are decorated in icings and flowers, subverting their epic manliness. "Plating" acts as a pun on the armour of the soldiers and the presentation of food. As in much of my work, these pieces examine the male body as a site of desire, sacrifice, and futility in a way that complicates and parodies common narratives. The work echoes the aesthetics of my Catholic upbringing: an altar, flowers, and a hanging semi-nude man.

The precarious nature of my food-work may be seen as expressing my own difficulties in imagining myself as an artist, the work acting as a self-inflicted mark on my own falsely occupied body-as-sculptor. Perhaps playing with food is my own way of childishly snubbing my nose at what it means to be a sculptor before I am discovered to be inauthentic and unknowledgeable, or less than manly.

The Farmer

Regina, Saskatchewan, has a complex identity as a Prairie cultural hub, a capital city, and a tough farming town. Regina prides itself as an honest, hard-working, blue-collar Canadian town, and visitors may notice the tropes of a city that sees itself in these terms: oversized trucks, baseball caps, camouflage, and an abundance of curling and hockey rinks. Regina is also relatively economically stable and has seen a growth in population, and with this influx of new residents, comes a desire for more urbane cultural signifiers: health-food stores, craft breweries, boutique coffee shops, and upscale dining. Yet, despite these relatively new cultural signals, they have yet to usurp the devotion to what is seen as a Prairie institution: Tim Hortons.

Tim Hortons coffee and donuts seem to be the lifeblood of the Prairies, and one can only surmise the popularity of its products as being associated with a kind of working-man aesthetic. The Canadian brand of Tim Hortons (albeit owned by a multinational corporation) offers a manly regular cup of joe, a product that counters the decidedly American Starbucks chain and their brand of feminized, whip-creamed coffee smoothies.

In *Always Fresh (The Donut Farmer)* (2008), I planted a Timbit farm in a parking lot across from a farmers' market in downtown Regina. Part of a larger public art/performance initiated by Lane Level Projects (a Regina-based artist collective), the work was a response to the city's love of Tim Hortons and a nod to the local farming culture. I was thinking about the cycle of production, from wheat to flour, to mass-manufactured fried dough, and the contrast of the farmers' market, where products are available directly from the producer. I planted the Timbits in a large "field" of soil, and placed "growing" wheat stalks in each to suggest that the donuts were bulbs or roots. As soon as I completed the work, the skies opened up and it poured rain, knocking everything down. The photograph included here shows me sitting in a muddy mess, trying to reconstruct the work. The passers-by and the farmers from the market across the way laughed at my predicament and asked me if I bought crop insurance. The most enjoyable part of the day was talking to small children about where they thought their food came from. Parents took it upon themselves to use the work as a lighthearted way in which to explain what farmers do for a living, correcting me as I tried to convince the small ones that donuts had sprung from the earth fully formed.

I wrote the following for an accompanying booklet that was handed out during the day. The booklet was meant to resemble a pack of parking tickets: "Sometimes I wonder why I remain a donut farmer. It's a thankless job to be sure. There is such

Figure 15.2
Jason Wright, *Always Fresh (The Donut Farmer)*, 2008, photograph of the installation; materials: Timbits donuts, soil, wheat, plastic flowers.

a disconnect between people and their food. People see Timbits in their individual racks and they don't stop to think how they got there. The plowing, the planting, the spraying, the plucking, the glazing – these are all unseen acts to most. It's a shame, but I really think people have forgotten where their food comes from."

Vanitas and a Pile of Bones

I completed my studies and returned to Vancouver. A friend of mine was opening a restaurant and I came back to help serve and manage. After two years of art school, I felt this job created an opportunity to think of food in a new way, but frankly, as an artist with a new MFA, I really just needed to make a living.

While working at the restaurant, I started to think more about the presentation of foodstuffs in popular media. I am not immune to the sexy gloss of food photography and Netflix food-centred documentaries. Food culture in this regard represents a truly visible and accessible form of creativity for a wide audience. I began to research high-end restaurants around the world, including local Vancouver favourites (such as Wildebeest and L'Abattoir), paying close attention to each restaurant's particular food design and stylish table settings. Often dishes from these restaurants are served on what can only be described as industrial materials – slate, concrete, unfinished wood – in an attempt to accent (or even undermine) a cultivated and sensual dish (feminine, maybe) with a rustic, bucolic frame (masculine, maybe), a zeitgeist that mirrors the culinary ascendency of sweetbreads, offal, and bone, where the transgressive nature of the dishes are the source (the now edible heart) of its macho pleasure. I began to collect the grisly and meaty stuff this food most resembles. I began to collect dog chews.

In *Dogs' Dinner* (2015), I arranged an elaborate banquet showcasing dog treats. The dinner was inedible to humans, but meant to resemble the aesthetic of lavish contemporary dishes. These commercially available dog chews are cut, moulded, and stuffed to appear similar to human food. Abattoir floor remnants are cultivated and pressed into uncanny (yet poor) copies of bacon and steaks. Guests to the gallery thought appetizers were being served upon arrival, but they soon cringed and laughed at their error in responding to the presentation of this *almost-food*.

I designed this luxurious-looking table setting to resemble a kind of sixteenth-century Dutch vanitas painting – an opulent still life. Such paintings were meant to demonstrate the perils of an ostentatious living, a finger wag to the wrongs of a splashy lifestyle. Vanitas translates to *emptiness*, and paintings such as these coax us into remembering the shallowness of our lives and our inevitable death. The table

Figure 15.3
Jason Wright, *Dogs' Dinner* (detail), 2015; materials: dog treats, brick, plates, glassware, wood, tablecloth, grass.

is beautiful, but there is sadness here. After all, the table is filled with the remnants of gruesome deaths, and could be seen as a grim altar or gravesite to the sacrificed and unnamed dead figures lying before us, waiting to be consumed. For my humorous version of the vanitas, I was asking the audience to think of their own position as consumers, and more specifically, as consumers in foodie Vancouver. The work was ultimately destroyed (or donated to friends with dogs), but the photographs remain as sexy, slick remnants of the work.[2]

A Hero Sandwich

Tragedy of Open-Faced St Sebastians or The Sacrifice of Artisanal Sandwiches for the Redemption of the Ethical Glutton (2013) is a photograph series of collages that I created using images of Saint Sebastian and sandwiches from the restaurant where I work. Similar to *Dogs' Dinner*, I see this work as a kind of morality play and vanitas, where sacrificial bodies enter us as gruesome takeaway, where choosing the correct product, the correct foodstuff, simulates moral stance, simulates *doing good*.

The hundreds, if not thousands, of paintings depicting Saint Sebastian peppered by arrows have become icons of serene and noble sacrifice. What is not commonly known is that the oppressed Catholic Sebastian survives this attack. A woman named Irene rescues him and nurses him back to health, and when he recovers, he taunts the baffled emperor who is surprised to see him. Sebastian feels pretty good about his taunts (he got some real good ones in!) for about thirty seconds until the emperor's men beat him to death, and soon after Sebastian is awarded sainthood for being a cocky idiot. I quite enjoy the comic dimension of this oft-neglected part of the story – the juxtaposition of the elegant Sebastian's physical beauty and Heavenward-looking eyes in the paintings, and the forgotten tale of his subsequent foolhardy mocking of those-in-charge.

When I made the images in this series, I was thinking about being a server and how Sebastian's skyward glance reminds me of my own glance to the sky when I forget someone's ketchup, or when someone says something so horrifying that I can *only* look upwards, tied to the stake of servitude. And as with Sebastian's gibe, I think to myself how ultimately meaningless a sarcastic jab towards a rude guest can be, although I am certainly less likely to be clubbed to death by an emperor, and I would definitely be less likely to achieve sainthood for doing so.

There is always a whiff of class around serving, which is why I think people love restaurants so much, so they can appraise the wait staff and whisper about them, and they feel it's okay because the servers are paid to be looked at, they get paid to

Figure 15.4
Jason Wright, *Tragedy of Open-Faced St Sebastians or The Sacrifice of Artisanal Sandwiches for the Redemption of the Ethical Glutton* (detail), 2013, framed c-prints on paper.

do it. Servers are like Saint Sebastians, demure with sore feet, and instead of arrows piercing their sides, it's their feet in mandatory heels that are bloody and grisly, like pieces of bacon wrapped in leather. Saint Sebastian, like the noble server, looks as if he is in no pain, mustering only camp serenity, whereas in real life there would have been a lot more blood pouring out and squishing and bone-showing, and probably swearing.

The word "sacrifice" is at the heart of this work, but also the word "indulgence." The indulgence, in old Catholic days, was a means by which to pay your way into Heaven, like a tax on being a jerk while you were alive. And I was thinking how paying for expensive, artisanal, organic, local food has become the contemporary Indulgence, where one can feel good about being a good citizen, and a good capitalist. Where eating a sandwich can make you a hero. A hero sandwich.

Part Three: The Dessert

Hearts and Minds and Tongues

I see my work as playing with religion, gender roles, and consumer culture within a decidedly Canadian perspective, and with a decidedly Canadian sense of humour. Food and food culture act as the platform upon which I position myself as a self-deprecating joker and mild-mannered provocateur. My work may in part be associated with the *pleasure of being disgusted*, which is perhaps a wholly bourgeois perversion, and hence attached to a kind of educated distance and remove, a connoisseurship. "I love it because it almost made me throw up." This removed pleasure may only be the beginning. The next stages of culinary beauty may be even more extreme with abject horror appearing on our plates.

There is a battle for our hearts, minds, and tongues in Vancouver, and throughout Canada – a battle over food and *of* food. While I am not entirely suggesting such a divisive binary exists, there does seem to be a *taking-of-sides* by consumers who wish to portray and embody themselves within the discourse of Canadian food culture through class and gender. The sincere, unironic love of the North Delta family restaurant may be as abhorrent to the Vancouver foodie aesthete as the overpriced, organic quinoa and fermented blue algae cronut may be to the Costco-frequenting suburbanite. I have a stake in both, or rather my cultural consciousness and memory have a stake in both *spaces*. I often go to new and fashionable restaurants, yet I love family restaurants, their ludicrous portioning, all-day breakfasts, and utter lack of pretension. I am conflicted. I live and work in Vancouver, but I am from North Delta and have acquired certain values, tastes, and ways of being that have been cultivated within that particular space. This cultural *training* also includes my religious background, which has subsequently affected my aesthetic sensibility. My North Delta upbringing and my time studying in Regina have also led me to challenge my cultural role as a man, as an artist, and now as a server. When I work as a server, I am haunted by the classed and gendered ill-treatment I receive from ignorant guests, but I am also aware of my appearance as a bearded hipster dude working in a newly gentrified neighbourhood of Gastown. My art practice, in many ways, looks to examine the discourse surrounding these food-related social tensions. These tensions, which have been my perverse pleasure to document, may be seen as the true real-world grotesque of the contemporary Canadian culinary landscape.

Notes

1 *Great Canadian Cookbook* is a multi-platform, four-part television series and website created and developed by Food Network Canada in October 2015. Celebrity chefs travel throughout Canada to collect and compile favourite regional recipes and the stories that accompany them.
2 If I were to set up this piece again, I would invite a dozen friends' dogs to annihilate the banquet and film it. The thought of this now makes me smile, the dogs chomping down like furry little hedonists.

PART FOUR

Subverting Categories
Critical-Creative Re-interpretations of Food

The five essays in Part 4 turn to material and "messy" sources of inspiration, providing means of moving across expressive and disciplinary frameworks. Here, the topic of Canadian food cultures is examined from positions of critical and imaginative exchange, individual transformation, and challenges to societal norms. Whether in the contexts of popular culture, personal life experience, literature, or visual and performance art, food is experienced, shaped, examined, and consumed in ways that highlight and destabilize conceptual and physical boundaries, offering alternative ways of thinking about and relating to the world. In a piece of creative non-fiction that brings queer theory and object studies into conversation, Jes Battis opens this section by exploring the relationship between food and sexuality with "a queer twist." Through personal anecdote and analysis of popular television series, Battis poses an urgent and provocative question: what makes a meal queer? Moving from the queering of food to an examination of a "taste for the abject," artist Sandee Moore meditates on why food is a constant within her practice. Through public acts of consumption and food sharing, Moore highlights social bonds and power relations, demonstrating how uncomfortable encounters destabilize her audience's expectations and sense of intimacy. Turning to the intersections of literature and art, Heidi Tiedemann Darroch brings writer Alice Munro and painter Mary Pratt into conversation through paradoxical and sometimes mutually inspired depictions of gendered experience and violence via the domestic kitchen. Alexia Moyer then reveals how online communities have transformed her reading of Canadian literature through her cooking blog *Tableaux*. Theorizing her project as "an exercise in literary tourism," Moyer shares her favourite literary recipes. Closing the section is a conversation between Mi'kmaw artist Ursula Johnson and curators David Diviney and Melinda Spooner on the topic of Johnson's interrelated and award-winning multimedia performance artworks that provide a community-based examination of the natural and cultural ecologies and the foodways of Nova Scotia's Cape Breton Highlands National Park.

16

Breaking Bread

Queer Foodways and the Non-human

Jes Battis

Introduction: Cruising Food

A recent episode of the culinary program *Chopped* was ecstatic to focus on aphrodisiacs.[1] *Chopped* first aired in 2007, emerging from the "lifestyle" reality show boom of the early 2000s that also brought us *Queer Eye for the Straight Guy* (2003–07). Unlike *Iron Chef America* (2005–), which pits celebrity chefs against one another, *Chopped* focuses on unknown contestants who compete for prize money. The contestants come to the show with personal narratives, and the host, Ted Allen, plays the same neutral figure as he did on *Queer Eye for the Straight Guy*, with nary a raised eyebrow. In this episode, the menu included the usual suspects, like chocolate and oysters, as well as avocado, which I'd never thought of as a particularly sexy food. The contestants struggled to cook with ingredients that emerged from a mystery basket (not the easiest strategy for assembling a romantic meal). There is something decadent about *Chopped* as a show. It transforms cheap ingredients – often high in sodium or sugar – into aggrandizing works of art. This is an act of high camp, though the contestants are deadly earnest about it.

Before watching as the contestants try to combine chocolate with asparagus, we hear about their histories, their relationships, and – most importantly – why they need the prize money. Often, there is a recent marriage or death involved. This particular episode was playing with a number of well-worn Mediterranean stereotypes. The Spanish contestant gave provocative names to each of her dishes, while the chef from Sardinia was understood to value family above all else. The Jamaican chef, eliminated early, was accused of being "too spicy." By the halfway mark, it was clear that the white American chef, with his creepy fetish for Thailand, would be the winner. Inspired by the erotic undertones of the episode, the judges started to go off the rails. Amanda Freitag leaned across the table to proposition Aarón Sanchez, who looked decidedly uncomfortable. In spite of near-constant citations regarding the sexiness of the food, it was clear that nothing about this scene could actually be sexy.

I often watch *Chopped* with my mother, and that night was no exception. When they got to the oyster round, she said: "Your grandfather gave me a raw oyster once, and it came right back up." As a critique of the episode, it was incisive, as well as unsettling. The thought of my grandfather feeding people oysters was weird in itself, but her summary was what called the entire episode into question. What could be sexy about something that looks and feels the way that an oyster does? What could be sexy about the alimentary process in general? I thought about the Jamaican contestant, who had seemed queer to me. Perhaps it was his focus on brunch, or the fact that he didn't have a visible family. It made me wonder how the episode might have been different had all the contestants been queer. Would the menu have been the same? What does queer food look like, and does it share the same definition as pornography – that is, do we know it when we see it? The word "queer" supposes an orientation, but that's a relatively recent development. Sara Ahmed has argued that queerness might be no position after all, or a kind of productive vertigo. "It is not always obvious which places are the ones where we can feel at home."[2] If we unmoor sexuality from an experience that's either orientative or situational, what are we left with? I'm reminded of a Frank Zappa song, "Call Any Vegetable," in which we're asked to "think of a vegetable / lonely at home … Vegetables dream / of responding to you." I imagine the scene of a lonely avocado, watching *Chopped* with desperation. What kind of orientation would that be?

Food Studies and Object Studies: New Recipes for Subjectivity

I want to focus on the relationship between food and sexuality, with a queer twist. In addition to thinking about queer genres of food and the ways in which certain foods can signal sexuality, I also want to think about food as "vibrant matter," to use ecologist Jane Bennett's phrase, which might have a queer life of its own. In her book, Bennett describes the various relations between animate and (supposedly) inanimate matter, in order to challenge easy notions of what it means to have "agency" as a thing in the world. She asks whether a cascading power failure, a landfill, or molten steel might have a life of its own, especially at the contact point between human and object. Her work is part of the "materialist turn" within critical theory, inspired by Bruno Latour's theorization of "networks" among objects, as well as the idea of the "assemblage" (an organism composed of different parts/relations) popularized by Gilles Deleuze and Félix Guattari. The goal of much of this work has been to decentre the human within the world's larger narrative, as well as to extend some of the benefits of personhood to animals and objects.

Sara Ahmed's *Queer Phenomenology* debates the relationship between orientation and objects, but I'd like to expand this field to discuss the queerness of objects themselves: particularly, food objects. Could it be ecologically productive to think of food as something with agency, something that exists in a dynamic partnership with humans? Can the non-human have an orientation, a sexuality, and if so, how might this broaden the scope of queer studies? Through a mixture of cultural analysis and creative non-fiction, I'd like to spend some time blurring the boundaries of alimentary scholarship, parting sexuality from rigidly human properties. As I hope to argue, sexuality can resonate through meals just as clearly as it might through erotic encounters. The "love is love" tag privileges monogamous queer relationships, but what happens when our orientations drift towards the non-human? I'll touch upon queer meals, object studies, and Canadian popular culture in order to address these questions. My point is to query the value of implicating edibles in the study of queerness and, in particular, things that have a biological effect on us, which become us, as we become them.

It's one thing to say that meals can be queer in the sense of encoding a certain sensibility, a covert symbolism. It's different to say that food itself can have a queer orientation, like a sentient being with memories and agency. When I began writing this piece and would talk briefly about it with friends, they were all over the queer symbolism angle. "Cucumbers! Fruity drinks!" But the part about food *as queer* tended to provoke a raised eyebrow. Critical fields like object-oriented ontology suggest that vegetative life can form productive networks, even act upon human life, but can non-human life participate in sexuality? The more I was dissuaded from arguing this, the more I fell in love with the idea of a closeted avocado, a "vegetable ... lonely at home." Human beings certainly don't have a patent on sexuality. While it's true that we sex both plants and animals, this is a poor translation of how they experience the biological processes that we place under the umbrella of sexuality and reproduction.

My point is that the notion of queer orientation, which was more or less required to secure a framework of rights for queer people, is also a translation. Rock anthems like Lady Gaga's "Born This Way" suggest that sexuality is a recipe, encoded from birth and superimposed on the extraordinary chaos of desire. If we want this definition to remain livable, we need to extend it to the non-human; or we need to replace it with non-human patterns of sexuality, which offer fascinating, vegetative, non-prescriptive ways of being queer. We also need to query the life of the non-human, the desire of that which seems radically different from us, though sometimes familiar in its bonds, its alliances. Extending sexuality to things can be a way to look beyond the Anthropocene, to imagine the order of a world whose imperatives do not focus on us, the logical queers.

Food studies and object studies remain in a peripheral relationship with each other. In his edited volume on object studies, *Inhuman Nature*, Jeffrey Jerome Cohen thanks the "cheese [and] cherries … [that] fueled some of [the book's] thinking."[3] But the chapters that follow engage with noble objects, like ships and trees, even matter itself, rather than taking up questions of food. While we often think of eating as a relational act, it can also be solitary. Perhaps this boundary crossing is what makes it difficult to integrate food into critical theories such as object-oriented ontology. In a recent issue of *New Literary History*, Bennett notes the crisis within object studies between autonomy and community. We can point to symbiotic relationships between non-human life, or highlight the ways in which the human body works in co-operation with different organisms. But this doesn't necessarily work for what ecologist Timothy Morton calls hyper objects: "things that are massively distributed in time and space relative to humans."[4] Storms and glaciers may have agency, but they aren't team players. They don't belong to a system, nor do they require interlocutors. Bennett offers the following solution: "Perhaps there is no need to choose between objects or their relations … One would then understand 'objects' to be those swirls of matter, energy, and incipience that hold themselves together long enough to vie with the strivings of other objects, including the indeterminate momentum of the throbbing whole."[5] How might this erotic physics structure a conversation about non-human queerness? Bennett's language suggests that every object is an aphrodisiac, but to other objects, rather than to humans. It's starting to sound more like a queer orientation that goes on when we aren't looking, something as peculiar and necessary as gravitational waves. "Think of a vegetable, lonely at home." What do things want, without us?

Edible Orientations Part One: Wine

Television offers a variety of sex and food acts: to be consumed, critiqued, and, sometimes, feared. Whether we respond with desire or ambivalence, the popularity of reality food programs like *Chopped* and *Diners, Drive-Ins, and Dives* (meant to showcase family-owned restaurants in the United States and Canada) suggests that we devour food programming as if it were a form of visual erotica. Two Canadian comedies, *Schitt's Creek* and *The Kids in the Hall*, provide a queer fusion of food and sex that I'd like to explore. My treatment of *Schitt's Creek* focuses on wine as a queer orientation, and I then turn to coffee as a community-building substance in *Kids in the Hall*. Both programs address Canadian identity through scripted comedy, improvisation, and storytelling rooted in Canadian geography. *Schitt's Creek* explores what it means to have "taste" in a small Canadian town, while *Kids in the Hall* uses sketch comedy to deconstruct the urban gay rights movement in the 1990s.

In *Schitt's Creek*, the character David navigates sexuality through his deployment of taste. This implies not only Pierre Bourdieu's notion of taste that "classifies the classifier"[6] but also taste as one of the five senses. The show focuses on a wealthy family exiled to a small town that they once "bought" as a joke. It is David, in fact, who owns the town of Schitt's Creek, making his helplessness there all the more ironic. In the pilot episode, the Rose family visits a diner that serves as the town's gossip mill and community centre. David is particularly offended by the over-sized menus, which fold out accordion-style, unlike the chic prix-fixe menus to which he has become accustomed. They resemble the menus of a New York diner that calls itself a "New York diner," a kitchen masquerading as culture. David's frustration with the menu extends to the entire town as a surface that offends him. More than any other character on the show, he responds viscerally to the smells and textures of the aptly named town, which threaten to invade him at every turn.

Though coded as queer, David remains ambiguous. He has achieved a level of metrosexuality and critical shade that would qualify him as a success story on *Queer Eye for the Straight Guy*. He definitely has a queer eye, but his own desires remain private, until he drunkenly sleeps with his female friend Stevie. It's clear in previous episodes that Stevie has also coded David as queer. She repeatedly describes his clothes as "funky," and more than anything, it's his difference that she seems to value – the mystery of his taste, so unlike the town's usual fare. After they sleep together, Stevie delicately tries to broach the subject. They're at a liquor store, and she seizes upon wine as a suitable metaphor: "I *only* drink red wine," she says to him, "and until last night, I thought that *you* only drank red wine."[7] What's significant about David's response is how it refuses metaphor, while still using wine as a cipher for sexuality: "I do drink red wine. I also drink white wine. And I've been known occasionally to sample a rosé. And three summers back I tried a chardonnay that used to be a merlot ... I like the wine, not the label."[8] His monologue allows the audience to visualize sexuality through taste and colour, as a kind of mutable vintage, rather than a fixed orientation. This also recalls a famously deleted scene from the 1960 epic *Spartacus*, in which Laurence Olivier playfully tells Tony Curtis: "I prefer both oysters and snails."[9]

What's interesting here is not simply how food and wine become substitutes for sexuality, but how they become inseparable from sexuality, creating new orientations and anti-labels: rosé, snail. They are what Morton describes, in his work on ecology, as "strange strangers": matter both familiar and alien to us.[10] This might refer to the intestinal flora that make digestion possible, or the plant-based tannins that we absorb when we consume red wine, blending organisms. In *Schitt's Creek*, David's parents describe him as "pansexual," and Stevie, at first, views him as bisexual. David classifies himself simply as a wine drinker, a hater of labels. The very idea of "a chardonnay that used to be a merlot" suggests a liquid transition, from one taste to another. And what could a "rosé" be? I watched this episode with my roommate, and she wondered if David might be talking about intersexuality. Was his response politically inclusive, or simply a clever twist of gustatory language? I'd like to suggest that David's description is not figurative. Wine is an expression of his sexuality, and taste is a more accurate way to describe what he desires. Not orientation, but viniculture. In a later episode, he goes in search of a chocolate torte whose richness – and scarcity – perfectly defines how he feels about his mother.[11] Stevie fails to understand the significance of this torte, which precipitates their breakup. For David, food and wine are not metaphors, but life modes.

Wine was always a marker of queerness for me. I was supposed to like beer (and hockey), and I'll admit that I do appreciate a stout; however, like David from *Schitt's Creek*, my preference has always been wine. Red wine is to be savoured. White wine should be consumed to excess while slowly collapsing into a friend's couch. Before we'd come of age, my group of friends engaged in the tradition of ordering mixed drinks at a restaurant chain that was known to serve minors. Mostly we choked down Long Island Iced Teas, and when truly desperate, we raided liquor cabinets and watered down bottles of Malibu. When drinking was forbidden, it didn't matter what you actually drank, so long as there was alcohol in it. I could make a killer B-52, and my hockey-playing buds drank it without complaint. But after runs to the liquor store became possible, I found that my drinking choices were under scrutiny. Beer, not wine, was the correct response. Wine was for girls. At first, my trick was to buy insufficient beer, then shrug ruefully and drink the rest of the wine. Gradually, I found myself taking a vinicultural stand for the queerness that I felt. I defiantly brought red wine to backyard barbecues and after-game parties. I hung out with the girls in the kitchen, laughing easily, comparing notes on significant topics, like how many times we'd seen *Titanic*.

I grew up in the Fraser Valley, a rural and predominantly religious community in British Columbia that has become more culturally diverse in the last decade. Farms, corn stands, and berry picking were a part of my formative years. Another part was the hockey fundraiser: a "steak night" at a local pub, designed to generate funds for minor hockey. Chip in $15 and you help the team out, while scoring yourself a perfectly mediocre cut of meat, sandwiched between two dry pucks of garlic bread. One night, I found myself at a pub called Major League 2 (the first Major League had been such a success, they'd built a sequel in a nearby neighbourhood). A beer was included in the price of the steak, and I'd resigned myself to order a Corona, whose lime made it the fruitiest choice possible. As I was trying to summon up enthusiasm for this, a friend tapped me on the shoulder and pointed to the menu. "They've got a house red," he said. I can't describe the love I felt for him in that moment. When our drink order arrived, my cheap cabernet gleamed like a carbuncle among the drafts. Nobody said a word. I enjoyed a sense of belonging that can only come from a small town, dregs and all. A small place can make you bigger, even if it sometimes cuts you down. Nobody at the table would join me in a discussion of queer theory. Everyone at the table would defend me from harm at the slightest provocation. They considered me an equal, though slightly offside at times.

Edible Orientations Part Two: Coffee and Cheesecake

What *Schitt's Creek* does with wine, *The Kids in the Hall* does with coffee. This Canadian sketch comedy series features a recurring sketch called "Steps," in which a group of gay men hang out on the steps of a Church Street café in Toronto's gay village. *Kids in the Hall* was a transgressive program when it aired in the late 1980s, particularly because many of its sketches featured the male performers in drag.

Scott Thompson, part of the sketch troupe, was openly gay from the beginning of the show's run, even addressing his sexuality in multiple episodes. In Season 1, Episode 6 (1989), Thompson played a character called Running Faggot in a sketch of the same name. The brilliance of the sketch lies in its subversion of a horrific image – a gay man running from homophobic violence – and transformation of Thompson's character into a superhero who "runs" between locals, solving problems. In Season 3, Episode 2 (1991), Thompson plays a character who is repeatedly called "Fag" by a boy on a bike. The epithet is uttered cheerfully, as if the boy is saying "Good morning!" Thompson's character keeps changing outfits, cycling between Orientalist slippers and a lumberjack T-shirt, but the boy's cry of "Fag!" continues to haunt him. Finally, he dresses up as a bear and mauls the kid, knocking him off his bicycle, only to remove his bear head and say laconically: "Fag." This was a rare moment in which a queer actor was able to respond to hate speech on-air, while calling into question the very meaning of "Fag," since it seemed to apply in every situation.

As early as 1993, the characters on "Steps" were debating the necessity of gay marriage, while drinking coffee and cruising the boys who walked by – a practice combining sex, politics, and consumption.[12] The setting of this sketch was designed to mimic Timothy's café on Church Street in Toronto's gay village. For years, one of the cruisiest cafés in the village was Second Cup, a Canadian chain transformed, by virtue of its location, into what Gordon Brent Ingram calls "[an] explicit space of queer living."[13] In the early 1990s, there were no other shows that featured a group of queer characters, let alone a community of urban gay men like the one featured in "Steps." While it's true that the sketch trades in stereotypes, it also paves the way for more dramatic LGBT programming such as *Queer as Folk* and *The L Word*. Caffeine is the element that links this sketch to my previous discussion of wine. The characters gather on the steps of a café, installed as firmly middle-class citizens of Toronto, willing to overpay for espresso. Their queer money is, in fact, what keeps the café running, and coffee becomes symbolic of their politically charged discussion. The branded to-go cups turn their innocent gathering into a salon of sorts, designed to reflect on their urban status, while also physically claiming a space within downtown Toronto.

As the political spokesperson of the group, Smitty (who shares his name with a Canadian family restaurant chain) is most often worked up and over-caffeinated. Dressed in neutral khakis and a sweater vest, he's visually removed from the field of cruising that Butchy navigates so well. Yet in Season 5, Episode 17 (1993), both

Smitty and Butchy end up calling the same phone-sex line, proving that the former's politics don't make him any less sexual. In Season 4, Episode 16 (1992), Smitty scolds everyone for cruising: "Rome is burning, and all we do is cruise." Riley waves him away, responding: "I'd switch to decaf, Smitty." Here, coffee is political fuel, driving Smitty to decry their lack of engagement, though he can't quite look away from men passing by. It serves as a stimulant to discussion, as well as the source of their purpose-built community on the steps of the café. Electrified, sweaty, and talkative, the characters consume endless cups of coffee, which they can afford by virtue of having disposable income. The sketch comes to signal the rise of the Canadian queer middle class, who were becoming all the more visible in the 1990s as they engaged in politics of reconstruction near the close of the AIDS era. In Season 5, Episode 18 (1993), Smitty criticizes pharmaceutical industries for delaying a proper cure: "Because there's so much money in looking for a cure, they can't afford to find one." He does this while holding his coffee cup and raising an eyebrow at the camera, drawing further attention to the space shared by consumption and capital.

Cafés are unique queer spaces, especially in small towns that lack any kind of queer community organized around a bar. In the 1990s in Chilliwack, I spent a lot of time at a café called Afterthoughts, which today strikes me as the name of a thoroughly ambivalent gay bar (one step below Rumors). As a closeted high-school student, I would do my homework at the café, while unconsciously cruising the baristas. In spite of the success of shows like *Friends*, café culture was slow to catch on in the Fraser Valley, and Starbucks remained only semi-popular. Chilliwack was (and still is) a farming town, known for its overlapping Christian communities. Only a few hours from Vancouver, it felt like a different world. It was rare to see a teenager with a disposable coffee cup, and there was something Proustian about sipping expensive coffee while eating cheesecake from a glass plate. A part of me knew what I was doing. Afterthoughts was no bar, but it was the queerest place in Chilliwack, and I spent a lot of time there. After I came out, female friends would point out cute patrons, or gently encourage me to flirt with one of the baristas – anyone who looked like Duckie from *Sixteen Candles* was, in their mind, a potential boyfriend.

As a kid, I loved watching *The Golden Girls*, which transformed cheesecake into a symbol of both community and excess. The show, which ran from 1985–92, focused on the lives of four older women living in Miami, and had a large queer audience. I didn't see the episode featuring Blanche's gay brother, and Sophia's speech about love and tolerance, until I was an adult.[14] What impressed me most was its depiction of park cruising in 1988, addressed with a surprising lack of judgment. I remember the ways in which *The Golden Girls* celebrated the bodies of older women. They were always drinking, dancing, and eating food that was bad for you – especially cheesecake. Since I'm lactose-intolerant and have a number of food sensitivities, cheesecake is especially bad for me. Eating it is a queer act of rebellion against my own body. Part of what makes it good is that it's so very bad.

The Golden Girls were always eating cheesecake at the kitchen table, digging in with their forks while they talked about fears, loves, disappointments. It wasn't until I grew older that I began to suspect this particular dessert was coded as feminine. When the first posh café opened in Chilliwack, in the early nineties, they had a tremendous variety of cheesecakes. My female friends would often split a piece, or simply gaze at the perfect specimens under glass. My male friends never made cooing noises at the glazed cherries. Dessert wasn't part of their vocabulary, and cheesecake was the queen of desserts, which they wanted no part of.

When I think about coming out, I immediately smell coffee and taste cheesecake: both the sweet pleasure, and the inevitable damage. The shame in the bathroom later, as my body rebelled, would prepare me for the equally complex mechanics of shame that drove my sexuality. The danger of eating cheesecake in a town where boys ate burgers. Eating burgers at a backyard barbecue meant that you were an all-Canadian boy, en route to a hockey game somewhere. Eating cheesecake meant that your friend's car was nicknamed Madonna, that you drove around with a boom box in the backseat, burning out your *Little Mermaid* soundtrack, searching for a place to get your ear pierced on a Saturday night.

Eating In: Gay Neighbourhoods and the Politics of Food

Gay neighbourhoods have often organized themselves around bars and pubs, which serve as dual safe spaces and community centres. Buddy's, a gay bar in Edmonton that closed in 2015, served Christmas dinner to patrons who'd been kicked out of their homes for being gay. Since Edmonton doesn't have a discernible gay village, it was the task of bars like Buddy's and The Roost to create a sense of community across disparate neighbourhoods.[15] For decades in Vancouver's Davie Street Village, the two poles of queer nightlife were The Odyssey and Denny's. The Odyssey, formerly located on Davie and Howe streets, was a gay bar that opened in 1990 and closed in 2010 (reopening in 2015 as an entirely separate establishment in Vancouver's downtown business district). In its heyday, The Odyssey was a queer local that included dancing, drag shows, and male strippers (along with a healthy drug culture in the unisex bathrooms). The patio was the cruising epicentre, and also the place to go if you wanted cheap triples (when Joan-E was bartending). The bar was located along a high-traffic corridor and surrounded by 99-cent pizza places, which would fill up at closing time.

Although the intersection of Davie and Howe was slightly removed from the gay village proper, there was still the sense that it actually began with The Odyssey, that this ramshackle building marked the border between straight and gay Vancouver. For me, what symbolized being on Davie Street more than anything else was lining up at The Odyssey's back door. The bar had two entrances, and those in the know lined up at the rear, in a small lot where the owner's pink Cadillac had been parked forever. The line was long, but moved quickly, and you'd have the chance to catch up with friends and check out people's outfits. "Pre-cruising," as my then-boyfriend described it. The building itself resembled a crumbling villa, with the promise of old-world glamour and decadence (in addition to men dancing in raised showers, which offered a Canadian taste of Nero's flamboyant Rome). A night dancing at The Odyssey would always be followed by a semi-coherent meal at one of the surrounding late-night eateries: either pizza, twice-baked fries at Fritz, or Denny's.

Denny's on Davie is routinely described as "Gay Denny's," as if its Grand Slam Breakfast has some kind of queer quality. A cursory survey of Yelp reveals that Denny's restaurants all over Canada, when they happen to be in proximity to gay bars, are often called "Gay Denny's." In the Denny's on Davie, I'd often meet drag queens mingling with seniors late at night. I like to think that we transformed the restaurant into what J. Halberstam describes as "a queer time and place,"[16] subject to its own non-canonical laws. The restaurant itself had the veneer of a family place, but it was rare to see tourists there, and on weekends it became an unofficial after-hours club. You would slide unsteadily into a giant booth, already beginning to nod off but driven by the prospect of sugar and starch. The menus, like those featured at the diner on *Schitt's Creek*, were camp texts on their own: giant, full-colour images of skillet meals, and entrees with names like "Grand Slam," took on a sly subversion after you'd been dancing beneath a go-go boy for the last three hours. The wholesome baseball theme took on an ironic dimension when placed in the context of gay slang, like "pitcher" and "catcher," and the glossy pictures were reminiscent of gossip magazines like *Tiger Beat*.

Davie Street, located in Vancouver's wealthy West End, is replete with bars and restaurants. The street thrums with activity all night long, after more respectable neighbourhoods have gone to bed. You'll often encounter tourists who don't realize that they've wandered into the village, or suburban commuters who are looking for a spicy locale. Gentrification began in the 1980s, and was not a peaceful process.[17] In between the posh lounges and restaurants, however, you can make out food cultures of the past. There is Priscilla's, a Greek/Italian restaurant that has been open since the late-1970s, used to be a community space for drag culture and working-class queer folk. There are also coffee houses like Melriches, which I've been going to since I first arrived in Vancouver (2001). Part meeting place, part café, part lounge, the decor consists of scarred tables and community art, with the condiments stored on an antique chest of drawers.

On Davie Street, "eating in" is also a turn towards the safety of community. It means admitting that you don't want to leave the warm confines of a queer space where virtually anything goes. It also means having enough capital to pay for take-out, or to patronize an ultra-chic lounge (usually the former). Eating in comes to symbolize a particular urban identity, rooted in queer geography. When I wander around Davie Street, it sometimes feels like an extension of my apartment. Everything is familiar, everything is heavy with memories and the scent of meals past. But I also recognize that the gay village has never been wholly inclusive. While it serves as a centre of drag culture, it is not particularly encouraging of trans and non-binary people. Its population is largely gay, cisgender male, and white. As a particular nexus of sexuality and capital, Davie Street sometimes feels like a realm of gay bars and restaurants, with community activities under the surface. In reality, is a palimpsest: multiple neighbourhoods ghosting across each other, remembering the shifting borders that define the West End. Online culture has, perhaps, erased the materiality of the queer local: the bounce of the floorboards, the smell of the bathrooms, and the greasy food afterwards.

Bear Necessities: Devouring Queer Life

As I've grown older, I've found myself slipping more and more into the role of a bear. This term used to refer to gay men with body hair, those who carried extra pounds. In a culture obsessed with fit youth, the bear position was a forgiving one, a hirsute alternative that many of us fit into whether we wanted to or not. The culture of Instagram has mainstreamed the role of "bear" into a heavily muscled, younger man, locked in an endless bicep flex. What's lost in translation is the gut – the part that denotes appetite, comfort, and a wry shrug to genetics and body type. This version of the bear is incomplete: it streamlines the body while erasing its hungers, aches, and necessary curves. As a term, "bear" is decidedly visual, and has become a staple of online hookup apps, which depend upon the image to sell a specific persona. The bears that we see online are mediated by filters and camera angles, designed to distill an essence that borrows from pornography (poses), cultural cues (facial hair), and merchandising (bearish T-shirts, socks, dog tags, all of which you'll find at queer bookstores/emporia like Vancouver's Little Sister's). Food and drink are, in a way, the forces that invigorate bear identity, even as those forces are so often absent in online hookup culture.

There are a variety of hookup apps to choose from (especially when living in an urban centre), but Grindr and Scruff remain two of the most popular platforms. Grindr has been called out for its racism and lack of bodily inclusivity, with users able to filter out various body types and ethnic groups. Scruff is often billed as the more inclusive app, though it tends to put muscular bears at the forefront, privileging gym-toned bodies rather than bearish ones. Both platforms reduce the bear position to a strictly visual one, ignoring the impact of culture that might also fashion a bearish body: eating, drinking, reading, watching *RuPaul's Drag Race* on the couch (where the only six-pack is the one that you've just taken out of the fridge). As a counter-argument to gym culture, the bearish body type has often been a refusal of rigid social norms around what a queer body should look like. Part of the attraction of meeting someone on a bear site (such as Bear411, now fallen into disuse) was a kind of relief in knowing that your date would probably not spend the night talking about his gym routine. Apps like Scruff have streamlined "bearishness" into a sexual type, while ignoring the complex reasons why one might identify as a bear in the first place.

One antidote to the commodification of bear-identity lies in the survival of bear bars – gay pubs that cater to a particularly bearish aesthetic. These locales don't use an online filtering system or employ a rigid visual hierarchy. The patrons represent a number of different body types, and in effect, they are imagining the bear role into existence as a flexible category. An example of this occurs every night at PumpJack, Davie Street's bear and leather bar. While it does have a dance floor in the back, the centre of the PumpJack is the bar itself, where everyone shares pitchers by the open windows. Their laughter spills onto the street as they drink, share stories, and prepare for whatever the night holds. The bar also supplies nuts: for me, this has always been what makes it an ursine space, what separates it from the Vodka-fuelled dancing of other locations. At any point, you can hold out your hands – like a kid in the bulk section of a grocery store – and receive a cascade of salted peanuts and cashews. They absorb the alcohol, but they also signal that this is a place where snacking is encouraged. Fortified by salt, you then move on to business.

Bear culture is about more than food, of course: it emerges from a whole spectrum of body types that don't fit into the hookup ideal. But at its core, bearishness involves both fat-positive and sex-positive attitudes towards life. It acknowledges that a queer body might be implicated in various kinds of productive excess, that it might not fit within the visual frames that we apply to mainstream sexuality. This can be a fraught space, because larger bodies are often connected to narratives of shame: narratives that they refuse on a daily basis. Part of being a bear is saying a resounding *fuck you* to norms that are designed to make you feel unattractive, unhealthy. To be a bear is to know who you are, and how extraordinarily powerful that self-knowledge makes you. It allows you to find beauty in taste and texture, to admit that food, drink, and physical variation should be a cause for joy, rather than remorse. Some wariness comes with the package. When a guy says, "I like your belly," I'm skeptical, as if he's just complimented one of my degrees. What can't be faked is the pleasure of two imperfect bodies in colloquy, a hand on your stomach, tracing familiar contours. Your favourite table to eat at.

Queer Meals: A Personal History

What is a queer meal? Does it require fellowship, or can it admit solitude? I can think of various queer meals that I've had in my life, both shared with others and by myself. Some of them were queer in the literal sense, because everyone at the table (or on the steps, or the street corner) happened to be queer. Others deserved the name because of their singularity, their unrepentant strangeness or nearness to camp.

When I first moved to the prairies, I accepted a dinner invitation from a guy with whom I'd shared a few dates. We were excellent together on paper: both nerds, both introverts, both relatively unconcerned with appearances. The dinner party was at his friend's house, and when I arrived, I was struck by the odd group of people loosely gathered around the coffee table. Two couples, one in their early twenties, the other in their late fifties, shared spaghetti and garlic bread. Multiple generations were crammed into the living room, and none of them knew how to talk to each other. The older couple made bawdy jokes, often erupting into glorious laughter. They called each other bitch, and fanned themselves when someone mentioned a male celebrity. The twenty-somethings were primly embarrassed by this old-school faggotry, though they bore it with half-smiles of resignation. *Oh those queens*. The guy and I were both in our thirties, the middle queers, who remembered dial-up Internet but had not seen Bette Midler performing in bathhouses. I chewed my garlic bread in what I hoped was a thoughtful manner. As a new professor, I was feeling a class gap that warred with my small-town upbringing. The wine that I'd brought seemed hopelessly nouveau riche, a nervous gesture that made it look like I was trying to outclass the (delicious) spaghetti sauce. You couldn't ask for queerer messmates, yet I can't say that any of us connected that night on the level of community.

At eighteen, on Valentine's Day, I went out for dinner with a guy I'd met online. We'd chatted through ICQ, and made the – in retrospect – awful decision to meet on one of the most depressing days of the year. When we arrived at a local restaurant, we saw that there was a set Valentine's Day meal "for lovers." Since it was too late to back out, we awkwardly took a seat, trying not to stare too skeptically at the pink menu. It was Chilliwack in the nineties, and I fully expected the server to make a joke about two boys sharing a romantic meal together. I had prepared all kinds of excuses – *it's ironic, we're brothers, we just love lasagna* – but the server lit our candle without comment. We ate baked pasta surrounded by straight couples, and as I shovelled dangerous amounts of cheese into my mouth, I felt a rush of fear and excitement and something I couldn't quite name (later indigestion). It was stupid to plan a first date on Valentine's Day, but we were too young to realize that, too eager and open and exquisitely fragile. Years later, at the multi-generational spaghetti dinner, I recalled the sweetness of that marinara. The wry smile of the server as she lit our candle. Though I'd been on dates before, that ill-advised meal was one of the first times I was able to see myself as publically queer. We'd slipped unnoticed into a time-honoured straight ritual, half-expecting to be scoffed at or shown the door, when, ultimately, we dined by the same light.

Twenty years later, I remember meeting two friends at Club Q in Regina, where we ordered takeout. The delivery person was slightly baffled by the address, but offered no complaint as we met him at the door. The club wouldn't officially open for a few hours yet, but my friends were involved in its operation, so we could hang out early. The dance floor was dark, and the bartender was drinking a coffee while watching reruns of *Saved by the Bell*. We divvied up the naan and chana masala, washing it down with the finest red that we could find in the bar fridge. My friends were both community activists, who remembered Regina's first pride parade in 1990: everyone had worn masks to avoid being outed, fired, excommunicated. In those days, and before, the gay scene had revolved around clandestine house parties. It reminded me of the eighteenth-century molly houses, which, as Alan Bray observed, "must have seemed like a ghetto, at times claustrophobic and oppressive, at others warm and reassuring. It was a place to take off the mask."[18] Unlike that awkward spaghetti dinner, this was a moment when we also took off the mask, and shared stories with ease and humour. I was older and more comfortable with a sexuality that I sometimes described as "murky," like a bottle of wine that has turned (or is not yet complete). There was dancing later, but what I remember was the stained napkins, the laughter, the indigestion as an acceptable sacrifice.

Raw Food: A Spectrum of Desire

In *Vibrant Matter*, Bennett describes the ways in which we share relationships with food. Calling food "vagabond matter" for its ability to shift our own biological properties, she notes that "in the eating encounter, all bodies are shown to be but temporary congealments of a materiality that is a process of becoming."[19] We are transformed by what we eat, and vice versa. Cheesecake can make me feel something that no other food can, even as its operations on my body are violent. Food leaves its mark on us, and as we devour it, our bodies shift ever so slightly. Does food have rights? Would that matter? Bennett observes that the vitality of food is often "obscured by our conceptual habit of dividing the world into inorganic matter and organic life."[20] Thinking about the ways in which we coexist with food might galvanize us to treat non-human life in an ethical way. It might force us to think about sustainable modes of farming, which help not only people but also vegetables produce the needs of the landscape. Respecting things that don't think – at least not in the ways that we think – can only lead to a more expansive definition of the human. Admitting that we can be attracted to books, houses, and storms can only broaden our anthropocentric notions of sexuality to include alternative orientations. When we say, "love is love," there is no human caveat. Loving things, and perhaps feeling them love us back, can be as richly informative as any human relationship.

When we uncouple sexuality and allow it to spread among non-human life, it becomes a more inclusive force. As a bear, I can't help but acknowledge that my body type is connected to my sex life, and my body is implicated with food, wine, and other illicit substances. With this expansive framework in mind, an edible object need not simply *represent* queerness (as the symbolic cheesecake); instead, it might *embody* queerness, as a force of desire that so often remains untranslatable, insatiable. The late-night pizza, the beer quaffed to calm a nervous tremor, the unexpected handful of peanuts in a packed bar, the "moment on the lips" that brings with it a delicious lifetime: all of these edibles share in our experience of sexuality. They remind us that who we are, and what we desire, is a flux of random glances, tastes, and precious objects that go beyond a narrow definition of life. This includes the smell of your ex's breath, the stain on the tablecloth, and the blissful decay of a broken-down sweater. Objects have lives of their own, and they influence our desires in ways that we can't separate from our own intentions. They promise an orientation, to paraphrase Sara Ahmed, where what we love is so often close to hand.

Vancouver Pride and Queer Advertising

The pride parade always divides Vancouver into East and West. East Vancouver has traditionally been a space for diverse communities, although this now includes hipster enclaves. Vancouver's West End has tended to privilege those with disposable income. My East Van friends, particularly those living on Commercial Drive, find the whole spectacle to be vulgar, commercial, and discriminatory in its lack of trans and non-binary inclusion. The event is overwhelmingly cis, white, and middle class. But for residents of the city's West End, the parade is a community institution and raucous social gathering, including a week's worth of events. During Vancouver Pride Week in 2016, we wondered if Black Lives Matter would interrupt the parade, as they had so effectively in Toronto. Instead, the prime minister of Canada marched (for the first time in Canadian history), looking both sassy and vaguely imperial in white pants as he waved to the crowd.

I was preoccupied with thoughts of queer food, and how food and drink became associated with pride as affect/event. The most recognizable example was Absolut vodka in its rainbow bottle, encouraging queers of every stripe to get drunk on clear, tasteless liquid. Vodka is what you order when you want to pretend that you're drinking water. A friend remarked that the 2016 bottle was less gay than its 2015 predecessor. The earlier bottle displayed a rainbow flag, but the new bottle was covered in geometric shapes. "It's vague," he said. "Just colours." I compared it with the 2015 bottle, which we still had in our freezer, and had to agree. This slick new design was abstract, rather than political. It made me think how strange it was to impute queerness to this commodified bottle, and yet, how welcome the flag had been when it was clearly visible last year. Pride flags of every size and taxonomy were on sale at the street party, including the bear flag, which I already have on a pair of socks. It was impossible not to think that we were drinking queer vodka, touching queer fabric, in the midst of these unsettling corporate relations.

Two food examples stuck in my mind for their mixture of community outreach and bald capitalist desire. The first was a poster in the window of Denny's on Davie Street, which I've already described as an unlikely queer community centre. This poster depicted a stack of rainbow-coloured pancakes, along with the phrase: "Denny's has pride." I thought about the idea of a corporation having pride, and then remembered that corporations also possessed many of the same rights as humans. But it was the pancakes themselves that held my attention, oozing rainbow syrup like "pink blood," the title of historian Douglas Janoff's book on homophobic violence in Canada.[21] There was something macabre about the image, but it was also undeniably sexual, like the repartee of the late-night queens who unwound there after a long performance. Pancakes are not an especially queer dish, but they do have a desultory side when you eat them at night, while coming down. Something you eat the morning after, or the long night before. Something you can make when you can't make sense of any other recipe.

The second example was more surprising because of the way that it implicated "traditional" family values. While passing the A&W on Alberni Street – perhaps Vancouver's wealthiest shopping corridor – I saw a poster depicting the chain restaurant's "burger family," with a twist. In this version, there were three cartoon married couples: straight, gay, and lesbian. They were still the same iconic 1950s caricatures, but that somehow made it more transgressive to see two balding husbands with Eugene Levy eyebrows, cheek to cheek. Below them was a rainbow burger decal, similar to Denny's rainbow pancakes. I noticed that the poster didn't include queer kids, but then remembered that the kids in the original advertisement were supposed to be siblings. I couldn't help but smile as I imagined how this conversation must have gone down at the A&W corporate office. Had a well-meaning PR person dared to mouth the word "incest"? Had they brainstormed a way to queer the kids, only to abandon it for fear of category confusion? What pleased me most about the rainbow burger was how much meaning it held for me, a small-town kid raised on backyard barbecues. You were supposed to eat burgers to avoid suspicion, but here it was a suspicious burger. At the same time, I knew how sketchy it was for a fast-food company, already profiting on marginalized communities, to extend its profit to queers. Food participates in relays of sociability and capital flow, absorbing and conveying meaning. A&W was saying: *put down that pumpkin scone, have a Cheese n' Egger*. But I was also fascinated by the extent to which they were willing to debase their family values in order to court men like me, who bore a startling physical resemblance to those cartoon dads.

Conclusion: Who We Are/What We Eat

I've argued throughout this piece that food has always been involved in queer identity – mine included – and that thinking about the peculiar life of food may expand our concept of orientation in productive ways. Rather than fetishizing food as an erotic object, my goal has been to examine the ways in which we share our bodies with edible material, and how queering that material reminds us of how open we are as organisms. In "Cyborgs to Companion Species," biologist Donna Haraway notes that "organic beings [such as] rice, bees, tulips, and intestinal flora … [all] make human life what it is."[22] My aim has been to expand this permeability to include queer orientations, which may not take the kind of traditional objects that we'd expect. If sexual attraction is a murky honey of memories, physical features, smells, and tastes, then food becomes a necessary element within that process. This is the only way I can describe how eating Turkish Delight makes me feel, or how the smell of decayed book-binding glue and dust in a used bookstore can drive me over the edge. It smells of home, which orientation also signals: a sphere of belonging.

Too often, food and consumption are left out of the attraction when discussing queer desire. They are elided in favour of the immaterial, the staged image on the hookup app, with nothing but pixelated shadow in the background. An exception to this, surprisingly, is the OkCupid app, which asks users to list five things that they couldn't do without. Most people end up including a food or drink in that list, and sometimes that gustatory pleasure spills into their broader profile. To properly think of ourselves as desiring subjects, we must also think through what we crave, what we put in our bodies, what eventually transforms and quickens us. My initial question about the lonely avocado is tongue-in-cheek, but also partially serious. When we imagine food as part of our circulating desires, we have to acknowledge its value in making us human. Plus, there is the sobering thought that we are also food: we've fed animals in the past, just as they've fed us. The hunting metaphors that we use to describe sex and romance are not innocent: as we pursue things across the field of desire, we can't help but recall our own place in the shifting food chain.

When I initially sat down to write this, I thought about my first queer meal. Does one have to be gay to participate in a queer meal? I thought about the breakfast that I threw up before coming out for the first time, to a friend who understood what it was like to be judged by what she did with her own body. I thought of the mushroom caps that made me sick on my first date, and the schnitzel cooling on my plate when I realized that I was a third wheel. I thought of the buttered challah that I ate in front of my first boyfriend's parents, after reciting the Kiddush – a prayer that my goyish, teenage mind had memorized for love. I thought of the pancakes with dulce de leche that I'd learned to spin with the tips of my fingers. An exercise in not getting burnt that eventually failed. But the meal that I keep coming back to is the slice of pizza that I wolfed down at 2 a.m. standing in front of Luv Affair, a club on Richards Street in Vancouver that no longer exists. Not even a gay club, but somehow ours for that night. I danced to "Personal Jesus" with two friends, and we laughed about being stereotypes. We weren't incomplete. Just sweaty, hungry, and flammable. Tomato sauce stained a shirt immortalized in a photo from those days – a shirt that I have no hope of fitting into now. I remember thinking, as cheese seared the roof of my mouth, that I would grow older, that I would no longer have this effortless twenty-year-old body. Thankfully.

Notes

1 *Chopped*, Season 27, episode 7, "Love Bites." 2016.
2 Ahmed, *Queer Phenomenology*, 10.
3 Cohen, ed., *Inhuman Nature*, x.
4 Morton, Hyperobjects, 1.

5   Bennett, "Systems and Things," 227.
6   Bourdieu, *Distinction*, 6.
7   *Schitt's Creek*, Season 1, episode 10, "Honeymoon." Directed by Jennifer Ciccoritti. 2015.
8   Ibid.
9   *Spartacus*, directed by Stanley Kubrick. Hollywood, CA: Bryna Productions, 1960.
10 Morton, *The Ecological Thought*, 15.
11 *Schitt's Creek*, Season 1, episode 12, "Surprise Party," directed by Paul Fox. 2015.
12 *The Kids in the* Hall, Season 4, episode 16, directed by John Blanchard. 1993.
13 Ingram, *Queers in Space*, 23.
14 *The Golden Girls*, Season 4, episode 9, "Scared Straight," directed by Terry Hughes. 1988.
15 The Roost also had a late-night hot dog vendor, with a considerable lineup after hours.
16 Halberstam, *A Queer Time and Place*, 1.
17 Up until the late 1980s, Davie Street was one of the centres of Vancouver's sex trade, and served as a gathering space for queer and trans sex workers, as well as IV-drug users. The Vancouver Police Department gradually pushed these marginalized groups out of the West End, forcing them to concentrate in the embattled Downtown Eastside neighbourhood. This purge was what made Davie Street a destination for gay men with disposable income, but the gentrification process also pushed rents up steadily, making it an inaccessible space for many.
18 Bray, *Homosexuality in Renaissance England*, 84.
19 Bennett, *Vibrant Matter*, 49.
20 Ibid., 50.
21 Janoff, *Pink Blood*, 1.
22 Haraway, "Cyborgs," 302.

Bibliography

Ahmed, Sara. *Queer Phenomenology: Orientations, Objects, Others*. Durham: Duke University, 2006.

Bennett, Jane. "Systems and Things: A Response to Graham Harman and Timothy Morton." *New Literary History* 43, no. 2 (2012): 225–33.

– *Vibrant Matter: A Political Ecology of Things*. Durham: Duke University, 2010.

Bourdieu, Pierre. *Distinction: A Social Critique of the Judgment of Taste*. Cambridge: Harvard University Press, 1984.

Bray, Allan. *Homosexuality in Renaissance England*. New York: Columbia University, 1996 [1982].

Budgell, Jack, dir. *The Kids in the Hall*. Canadian Broadcasting Corporation. 1988–1994.

Ciccoritti, Jerry, dir. *Schitt's Creek*. Canadian Broadcasting Corporation. 2015–present.

Cohen, Jeffrey Jerome, ed. *Inhuman Nature*. n.p: Oliphaunt Books, 2014.

Halberstam, Judith. *A Queer Time and Place: Transgender Bodies, Subcultural Lives*. New York: New York University Press, 2005.

Haraway, Donna. "Cyborgs to Companion Species: Reconfiguring Kinship in Technoscience." In *The Haraway Reader*, edited by Donna Haraway, 295–320. New York: Routledge, 2004.

– *When Species Meet*. Minneapolis: University of Minnesota, 2008.

Hughes, Terry, dir. *The Golden Girls*. Witt/Thomas/Harris Productions. 1985–1992.

Ingram, Brent Gordon. *Queers in Space: Communities, Public Places, Sites of Resistance*. San Francisco: Bay Press, 1997.

Janoff, Douglas. *Pink Blood: Homophobic Violence in Canada*. Toronto: University of Toronto, 2005.

Morton, Timothy. *Hyperobjects: Philosophy and Ecology at the End of the World*. Minneapolis: University of Minnesota Press, 2013.

Ward, Ned. *The Second Part of the London Clubs*. London: J. Dutton, 1709. Eighteenth Century Collections Online.

A Taste for the Abject

Food in the Relational Artworks of Sandee Moore

Sandee Moore

This essay should start with a hot dog of a story. A hot dog story. When I was seventeen, my friends and I haunted the Royal Inland Hospital Thrift Cellar, where we found a copy of *The Aspic Cookbook*. Each turn of the page revealed yet another savoury concoction in moulded gelatin. Although vegetarians, we picked the most outrageous recipe – "Hot Dog Aspic" – to make ourselves. I didn't have a jelly mould, so substituted my mom's hexagonal salad bowl. The substitutions didn't stop there: angular tofu wieners and kanten – a seaweed thickening agent – replaced hot dogs and gelatin. We anticipated something magical – frankfurters suspended in a gleaming glob. Instead, the veggie dogs sank to the bottom of the semi-liquid ooze. We snapped a few photos with a disposable camera and left the failed hot dog aspic on the lawn to melt in the sun. While we were eager to abandon the disappointing result, the promise of hot dog aspic was too precious to throw away.

The authoritative voice is not my strong suit: the anecdote is. Anecdote is the ingredient that pulls everything together, like the gelatin in real aspic. Ideas central to this paper – the excess, The Real, and the impossible – are discretely suspended in its mucilage. In the introduction to her essay collection *Anecdotal Theory*, Jane Gallop writes of anecdote as a tool for cutting through binaries ("short vs. grand, trivial vs. overarching, specific vs. general") "to produce theory with a better sense of humor, theorizing which honors the uncanny detail of lived experience."[1] Anecdote's path is traced from excess to the impossible to The Real via Joel Fineman's "History of the Anecdote" and philosopher Jacques Derrida's *On Grammatology*. Fineman anoints anecdote as "the literary form or genre that uniquely refers to the real."[2] This view is bolstered by Gallop's reading of Derrida: "Derrida connects the exorbitant with the attempt to get outside the metaphysical closure that sequesters theory from the real."[3]

The notion of The Real, as expressed by psychoanalyst Jacques Lacan, further points to the impossible and the abject: The Real is "the state of nature from which we have been forever severed by our entrance into language … [The Real is] a state in which there is nothing but need. A baby needs and seeks to satisfy those needs with no sense for any separation between itself and the external world or the world of others."[4] Anecdote is not simply a way to illustrate theory or to spice up an academic tome; anecdote's proximity to The Real means that it is a way of accessing the inarticulable.

Anecdote makes a hole in what is orderly and allows access to The Real. This hole could be a mouth. A mouth that produces vomit and words; a mouth that consumes. A mouth that gives entrance to the abject. With the abject comes food. As Jim Drobnick notes in his essay "Recipes for the Cube: Aromatic and Edible Practices in Contemporary Art," "once the schism between art (visual) and life (multi-sensory) had been bridged, however, both the sensuous and the abject, aliment and excrement, were equally available as genres of work."[5]

I never realized how many of my artworks involve food – as a metaphor, material, or mere representation – until a colleague recently pointed it out to me. If I were to list the glut of food, food-related materials, and food refuse in my art practice, it

Figure 17.1
Sandee Moore, *It's Hard to Have an Original Idea without Just Regurgitating Other People's Art*, 2011, cast rubber sculpture.

would form a long and sordid shopping list. In the same way that I was unaware of food as a constant in my art practice, I was blind to the specifically Canadian context of my work. This context is illustrated by another anecdote, this time from Winnipeg, Manitoba: I made a special trip to The Bay basement on Portage Avenue to buy a hot dog.[6] Not just any hot dog. One that was shrivelled and blistered from countless rotations on a spit in a heated case, then laid between the snowy-white flaps of an ordinary hot dog bun. It is at once anti-foodie, pathetic, and innately desirable. It is the sort of thing I encountered often in one of the few places to buy groceries in the Exchange District, where my studio was located. It rarely failed to excite my curiosity: "Who would eat that?" I wondered. I would not eat that. I would make art with it. My other local shopping choices, both for art materials and food, included the astoundingly inclusive and random Giant Tiger, a chain primarily serving Northern communities, and several dollar stores in the underground mall that links the office towers of this winter-bound city.

I recently moved to (and from) the far reaches of suburban Surrey, British Columbia. Interestingly, my shopping habits differed little from Winnipeg to Surrey, perhaps because the suburban environment, though it offered up more options for fresh foods and bona fide art supplies, was still a landscape of discount supermarkets, food courts, and dollar stores. Food becomes shorthand for cultural identity, as in the foundational works of contemporary artist Rirkrit Tiravanija, in which he serves up Southeast Asian curries or soups to gallery-goers – inviting conviviality while providing an entry point to his identity. My locale no doubt informed my material choices: junk food, both desirable and repugnant, is emblematic of North American culture – industrialized, disposable, engineered, empty.[7]

My works use social conventions, shaped by local context and custom, to create relationships with and through artworks, and to provoke an examination of these structures at the same time. This sort of practice may be what curator, critic, and art theorist Nicolas Bourriaud termed "Relational Aesthetics": art practices that produce human interactions rather than symbolic representations – food and meals are key methods in relational aesthetics; food is innately desirable: mnemonic and communal.[8] Relational aesthetics are often used to engage participants/audiences in well-established, normative, and idealized social rituals of community and conviviality.[9] In such practices, meals tend to be invested with an almost magical power to unify people and to create positive action. The negative forces (debt, obligation, hatred) that create social bonds and give rise to community are often fearfully avoided.[10]

Instead of castigating practices that I feel engage with relational aesthetics or socially engaged practice in a shallow and naive fashion, I describe how, in my artworks, I acknowledge the role of power in fashioning community. In creating works that encourage relationships, I acknowledge that intimacy may not be appealing or positive for either the artist or the participant(s).[11] I strive to recognize and incorporate the disgusting, disappointing, and non-aesthetic in my artworks. Disappointment has the power to critically reveal normative structures that frame our expectations. An imperfect food experience often provokes a sudden, strong, and corporeal reaction.

Since 2000, I have staged relational projects that transform the mundane into absurd spectacle, encouraging viewers to question social conventions and expectations surrounding food, community, and exchange. In this chapter, I discuss four of my artworks that involve food.

In Sick & Hunger

I had moved back to Canada from Japan in 2000 and became obsessed with suburban residential construction: cookie-cutter houses in cupcake frosting hues. I began to make scale models of these supersize houses in gingerbread, eventually making a monstrous gingerbread model home that was big enough for me to stand inside, which I then consumed while trading stories about the gingerbread house with visitors. While it could house me, it could never contain the gingerbread house's multitude of meanings: normative family structures, colonialism, consumption, fairy tale as metaphor and dreams. The more I chewed, the more concepts and references emerged from the gingerbread house. I ate the house for six days, translating the cookie into words in my mouth.

The title of this work, *In Sick & Hunger* (2000), is the result of a garbled phone conversation. It means nothing, but hints at so much: a dangerous collision of food, purging, and insatiable need. This was my first foray into artworks that encouraged an exchange and potential collaboration with the audience. This early work relied heavily on spectacle: the spectacle of monstrous female appetite and an overabundance of food.

When I was invited to remount this performance at Montreal's Nuit Blanche in 2011 (a celebration of fine arts when gallery lights are kept on and doors and bars are left open all night), I decided to divest myself of the Gretel costume (from 2000)

Figure 17.2
Sandee Moore, *In Sick & Hunger*, 2000; materials: gingerbread sculpture; performance.

Figure 17.3
Sandee Moore, *In Sick & Hunger*, 2011; materials: gingerbread sculpture; performance.

that I felt was a fetishized figure of femininity. Braids and eyelet frills were traded in for the very symbol of out-of-control consumption in 2011: a blinged-out Juicy Couture velour tracksuit. I offered pieces of my suburban gingerbread palace in exchange for an item to add to the shopping list that I was reciting. I ate so much gingerbread that I threw up a few times. By the end of the night, my house was almost completely devoured. I ran to the washroom to vomit and later regretted that I hadn't prepared a prop, such as a wishing well, so that I could include the puke as an aspect of my performance. I also wondered how my cookie pig-out compared to the excesses of the Nuit Blanche audience.

I learned a lot from performing this piece back in 2000 and then re-enacting it in 2011. I learned that food was an incredibly flexible and appealing material, even as the symbolic weight of a material/subject, like the gingerbread house, can be unwieldy and unpredictable. I learned that I wanted to connect with audiences and to provide opportunities for them to be co-creators of their experience. I learned that it is not as important to eat the whole gingerbread house as to create the enticement of an incredible feat. I learned that failure could be wielded like a knife to deflate expectations.

Rather than optimistically model projects for convivial exchange that did nothing to recognize and destabilize power relations in our everyday lives, I decided to continue to directly address the repressed and negative emotions that create social bonds.

Imaginary Gift

Exchange, specifically gift giving, is a key strategy in my art practice. "The Gift" as a concept is fascinating because although it is generally perceived to be positive, giving a gift is a way of wielding power over another, binding them to you through the bonds of debt.[12] The impossibility of a (purely generous) gift is the topic of *Given Time* by Derrida: a gift given with no hope of profit or return is an imaginary gift. Social bonds are created by the time that separates the giving of a gift and its repayment; immediate repayment would simply be commodity exchange. Giving a gift with an eye to a return – even if the payback is merely self-congratulation on their own generosity – is a self-interested gift that serves to enhance the gift giver's power.[13]

Figure 17.4, 17.5
Sandee Moore, *Imaginary Gift*, 2011, interactive sculpture.

I was inspired to create *Imaginary Gift* (2011) by encounters with people who were asking for spare change as I was entering or leaving my downtown Winnipeg studio. I was irritated and befuddled by these requests. I would have to stop, take off my backpack, and rummage around for a suitable amount. What is a suitable amount? What amount is neither insulting nor self-congratulatory? Could I really afford to give anything away? Was it terrible of me to expect thanks? These questions boiled down to problems of power. The recipient of charity is in the giver's debt. It is this debt that binds people with bonds of mutual obligation to form a society.[14] However, were these bonds that I wanted to form and power that I wished to yield? My tactic was to give from a place of selfishness: *Imaginary Gift* is an interactive sculpture in which the push of a button produces a slightly assaulting gift of food from an unseen person above.

Imaginary Gift gives the sense of being automated, thus the necessity to recognize the giver with thanks is removed. From my fourth-floor studio, I dispensed gifts both useful and wonderful (coffee travelling at terminal velocity, a flurry of popcorn, a spray of water from a toy whale's mouth, a stream of bubbles, a note on a penny whistle, a peanut that travels to the ground through the body of a sock monkey) to people on my street, at my convenience, and without creating the bonds of debt a face-to-face transaction would create. The conventions around the gift – gratitude and indebtedness – were further disrupted by the annoyingly imperfect nature of the gifts that I dispensed. The hot coffee tended to splash one's hand; the popcorn was maddeningly difficult to catch in the provided bag. I always want to start from the impossible, to couple things that seem opposed. It then becomes possible to see that generosity is rooted in selfishness or that a kiss can be clinical.

The Taste of Someone Else's Mouth

The impossible start that I am dealing with now is the title for this essay: "A Taste for the Abject." "It is not lack of cleanliness or health that causes abjection but what disturbs identity, system, order. What does not respect borders, positions, rules. The in-between, the ambiguous, the composite."[15] Thank you, Julia Kristeva, for providing me with a quotation (and a whole body of theory!) that allows me to link my title with my practice of disturbing the established order, not with the classical figures of the abject that transgress selfhood – such as shit, blood, and pus – but the commonplace and pleasant made repugnant.[16]

Semiotician Roland Barthes notes that the gift disrespects borders and connects (self and other) with a "third skin."[17] While any artwork can easily be thought of as that third skin, I like to imagine something much more uncomfortably intimate. I had hoped to create an artwork in which people soaked their bodies in a pool of hot broth at the same time boiling morsels of food to consume and share in this communal tub; thus the soup would become a third skin uniting them, and one could metaphorically (and literally) become one with one's fellow bathers by ingesting particles of their person along with the food items. This project was rejected by the Banff Centre for Continuing Education. I was, however, invited to realize a different project at the Banff Centre in 2003. Leading up to my departure for Banff, I was inundated with cautionary tales of marriage breakups and wild sexual escapades. For instance, an artist I hardly knew whisked me away from a party to an all-night donut shop. There, he bought me a tea and warned me to be careful: "my marriage broke up in Banff," he told me seriously. In the end, I was terrified to attend the residency, which had been painted as a den of iniquity.

In response to this fear and also seeing an opportunity to examine the conventions of sexual relationships, I carried out the first stages of a project called *The Taste of Someone Else's Mouth* (2003). I tasted volunteers' mouths by kissing them, then created gum that replicated my experience of the taste of their mouth. The resulting artwork (a cast of my tongue made out of gum and flavoured like a remembered kiss) is an artifact of intimacy: atemporal and impersonal, it becomes unpalatable. Divorced from a person and from desire, the unwelcome aspect of the kiss – its flavour – becomes the focus of the experience. Seeking to chew the unwieldy lump of gum, the viewer will discover that there is a sickening parallel to the act of kissing, now tinged with violence. This is an apt snack to accompany the video component of *The Taste of Someone Else's Mouth*. The viewer sits on a carpet of flexible polyurethane foam tongues to view a close up of my tongue as it traces words onto a sheet of glass that detail my mouth-tasting research.

It's Hard to Have an Original Idea without Just Regurgitating Other People's Art

Food and its traces are taboo once they have entered our mouths. No one wants to know about other people's ingestion and (failed) digestion. In this way the abject – the unwelcome intimate knowledge – permeates the boundaries between individuals, creating a greater intimacy. A third skin that unites us. Coming back to Barthes

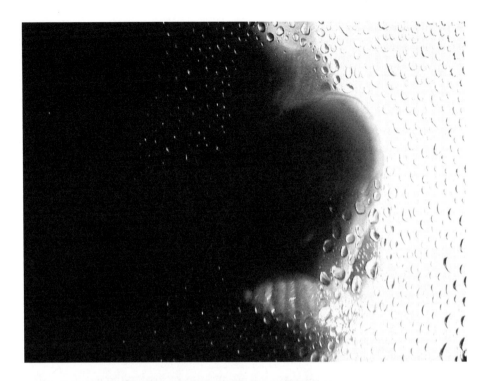

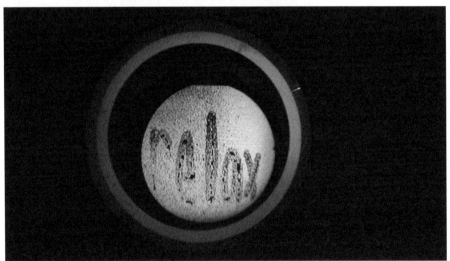

Figure 17.6 *Top*
Sandee Moore, *The Taste of Someone Else's Mouth*, 2003 [Version 1]; materials: cast gum, video, cast rubber sculpture.

Figure 17.7 *Bottom*
Sandee Moore, *The Taste of Someone Else's Mouth*, 2003 [Version 2]; materials: cast gum, video, cast rubber sculpture.

Figure 17.8
Sandee Moore, *It's Hard to Have an Original Idea without Just Regurgitating Other People's Art*, 2011, cast rubber sculpture.

again, he has said that "the gift is not necessarily excrement," meaning that it is a kind of unwanted excess.[18] Inspired by my experience at Montreal's Nuit Blanche and commissioned for Winnipeg's Nuit Blanche – events where there is an excess of art on display and art viewing is supplanted by drunken revelry – *It's Hard to Have an Original Idea without Just Regurgitating Other People's Art* (2011) is joke-store rubber barf on a heroic scale, featuring lifelike castings of food items (corn, gummy bears, beef jerky, hot dogs) and a unicorn vomiting glitter.

Vomiting and kissing have elements of Kristeva's definition of the abject – a breakdown of meaning caused by a loss of distinction between self and other, inside and outside – and some salty implications for my artworks that involve blurring of these boundaries.[19] The title of this piece is a parodic excess of frustration and futility and an uncomfortable admission of failure. It points to emotional abjection – the recognition that what one rejects and strives to separate from the self actually constitutes the self.[20] Referencing the eventual result of excessive drinking, the gigantic pool of rubber vomit demands attention, while a unicorn regurgitating glitter is merely gratuitous grandiosity. Is the unicorn the source of this impossibly large puddle of puke? Is it the failed and abject part of me that I have had to locate elsewhere and deem "not me"?[21]

Perhaps the unicorn is the excess, the accursed share. The enormous pool of puke and the unicorn nestled among its rivulets are examples of luxurious squandering – in the form of absolute waste and excessive and useless evolution – proposed by surrealist and sociologist Georges Bataille in *The Accursed Share*: "The history of life on earth is mainly the development of luxury, the production of increasingly burdensome forms of life," he asserts.[22] The unicorn exemplifies Bataille's evolutionary drive towards luxury. Like art making, the barf and the unicorn have no purpose beyond themselves. Bataille's insistence on excess and waste point to a radical view of economics, one in which waste rather than production is the engine of society.

I lose my toehold on authority in this landslide of possibilities. It had seemed possible that I could rightfully claim to be an expert and speak authoritatively on my own artwork. And yet, the unicorn presents me with many ideas simultaneously – none seems any better or more convincing than any other. This plurality is thrilling but also, I fear, exposes me as an impostor, one without an original idea.

The unicorn is a figure of the impossible.[23] (For one, horses can't vomit, so how could a unicorn do so?) To give without hope of profit or return is impossible. To seek to create relationships without exercising power over others is impossible. To permit all meanings to coexist is impossible. To know others without acknowledging the grossness of ourselves is impossible. To make this essay fit my title – "A Taste for the Abject" – (seems) impossible. I could simply forsake the notion of the abject and try another title: "Cooking Up the Impossible Gift," which would allow me to end with a positive statement: to cook up the impossible, that is the job of the artist.

Notes

1. Gallop, *Anecdotal Theory*, 1.
2. Joel Fineman, "The History of the Anecdote: Fiction and Friction," in *The Subjectivity Effect in Western Literary Tradition: Essays Toward the Release of Shakespeare's Will* (Cambridge, MA: MIT Press, 1991), 67, quoted in Gallop, *Anecdotal Theory*, 2.
3. Derrida, *De la grammatologie* (Paris: Minuit, 1967), 231, quoted in Gallop, *Anecdotal Theory*, 7.
4. Felluga, "The Real."
5. Drobnick, "Recipes for the Cube," 70.

6 The Bay, the Hudson's Bay Company, or the re-branded HBC is a national icon. The Bay is one of a handful of department stores to mythologize its brand as a part of a "common heritage" for Canadians, one that is untroubled by ethnic differences. This idea is discussed in Belisle's comprehensive *Retail Nation* and summed up in the following statement from the chapter "Creating Modern Canada": "Central to their publicity was the idea that department stores and their commodities helped Canadians attain social status and personal satisfaction. Department stores' notions of progress were thus middle-class and acquisitive" (60–1). In other words, to be able to shop is to be a member in the nation of Canada. My shopping choices are distinctly un-aspirational. Perhaps they are democratically so. As well, it seems that using food in art is seen as a "waste" and thus transgressive. By using food that is already closely associated with garbage, am I attempting to skirt this issue of "wasting" good food?

7 Brake makes the argument in *Comparative Youth Culture* that Canada's youth culture is merely a weak imitation of British, American and French identities due to historical associations coupled with a genuine Liberalism in Canada and lack of extremes of poverty, wealth and social strata that mark the United States and Britain. Brake further notes that long and severe winters tend to locate youth in shopping malls, where their gatherings and behaviour are easily controlled (144–8). I am tempted to extend his logic to Canadian cuisine or food culture. My experience of this food culture is one that is commercial, American/international in character, and affordable to nearly everyone.

8 Bourriaud, *Relational Aesthetics*.

9 Practices that take as their material and expression relationships to and through artworks, as well as co-creation, include social practice, community-based art, interventions, and participatory art. Each discipline is nuanced with regard to the extent of the collaborative nature of the projects, the artist's authorship (or lack of), and its engagement with the institutions of art. I tend to refer to my practice as relational or interactive.

10 Mauss, *The Gift*, 33.

11 Art historian Claire Bishop, in "The Social Turn" and "Antagonism," writes compellingly of a mistaken desire on the part of artists in socially engaged practices to extract art from the useless domain of the aesthetic, thereby robbing art of its unique power to disturb and contain the promise of a better world through its ambivalent blurring of the border between art and life, never fully autonomous nor integrated.

12 Derrida, *Given Time*, 15, 82, 146.

13 Ibid., 14.

14 Mauss, *The Gift*, 38.

15 Kristeva, *Powers of Horror*, 11.
16 I take Pheasant-Kelly's statements throughout *Abject Spaces in American Cinema* about Kristeva's theory of the abject as representative of the generally accepted reading of this concept: "Abjection, according to Kristeva, arises from the process of a child becoming autonomous of his or her mother. Rejection of the maternal body constitutes one form of abjection, but the child also begins to recognize and exclude various sources of body contamination. These include the detritus of the body, particularly bodily fluids and excrement, but they may extend to other forms of 'difference'" (5).
17 Barthes, *A Lover's Discourse*, 75.
18 Ibid., 76.
19 Kristeva, *Powers of Horror*, 11.
20 The abject is most often associated with encountering the body's corporeal reality in the form of a corpse and the unwelcome knowledge that the self and the corpse are the same, that one's body holds the promise of becoming a corpse. I propose that to be an unoriginal artist, in other words a failure, is as horrifying and destructive to the sense of self as physical death. Kristeva talks of "what I permanently thrust aside in order to live," meaning suppressing knowledge that disturbs one's sense of self (*Powers of Horror*, 3).
21 Kristeva, *Powers of Horror*, 2.
22 Bataille, *The Accursed Share*, 21.
23 According to Felluga's overview of "Terms Used by Psychoanalysis" in his online *Introductory Guide to Critical Theory* (updated 31 January 2011, Perdue University, https://cla.purdue.edu/academic/english/theory/psychoanalysis/psychterms.html), Lacan was fond of saying, "the real is impossible." (This is another anecdote.) Anecdote enables me to make a connection between The Real (the inarticulable), the impossible, and the abject (the unknowable, or that which we pretend not to know in order to preserve ourselves).

Bibliography

Barthes, Roland. *A Lover's Discourse*. Translated by Farrar, Straus and Giroux Inc. London: Vintage UK Random House, 2002.

Bataille, Georges. *The Accursed Share: An Essay on General Economy*, vol. 1: *Consumption*. Translated by Robert Hurley. New York: Zone Books, 1991.

Belisle, Donica. *Retail Nation: Department Stores and the Making of Modern Canada*. Vancouver: University of British Columbia Press, 2011.

Bishop, Claire. "Antagonism and Relational Aesthetics." *October* no. 110 (Fall 2004): 51–79.

– "The Social Turn: Collaboration and Its Discontents." *Artforum*, February 2006: 178–83.

Bourriaud, Nicolas. *Relational Aesthetics*. Translated by Simon Pleasance, Fronza Woods, and Mathieu Copeland. Dijon: Les Presses du Réel, 2010.

Brake, Michael. *Comparative Youth Culture: The Sociology of Youth Culture and Youth Subcultures in America, Britain and Canada*. London: Routledge & Kegan Paul PLC, 1985.

Delville, Michel. *Food, Poetry, and the Aesthetics of Consumption: Eating the Avant-Garde*. New York: Routledge, 2008.

Derrida, Jacques. *Given Time: I. Counterfeit Money*. Translated by Peggy Kamuf. Chicago: University of Chicago Press, 1992.

Drobnick, Jim. "Recipes for the Cube." In *FoodCultures*, edited by Barbara Fisher, 69–79. Toronto: YYZ Books, 1999.

Felluga, Dino. "The Real." *Introductory Guide to Critical Theory*. Last modified 31 January 2011. www.cla.purdue.edu/english/theory/psychoanalysis/definitions/real.html.

Gallop, Jane. *Anecdotal Theory*. Durham: Duke University Press Books, 2002. http://doi.org/10.215/9780822384021.

Kristeva, Julia. *Powers of Horror: An Essay on Abjection*. New York: Columbia University Press, 1982.

Mauss, Marcel. *The Gift: The Form and Reason for Exchange in Archaic Cultures*. Translated by W.D. Halls. New York: Norton, 1990.

Pheasant-Kelly, Frances. *Abject Spaces in American Cinema: Institutional Settings, Identity and Psychoanalysis in Film*. London: IB Taurus & Co., 2013.

Randolph, Jeanne. "Orality." Seminar notes, Banff, 2003.

"Viciousness in the Kitchen"

Women and Food in Alice Munro's Fiction and Mary Pratt's Visual Art

Heidi Tiedemann Darroch

Over their long careers, writer Alice Munro and painter Mary Pratt earned widespread acclaim for their portrayals of women's daily lives, including the particulars of "food, furnishings, and fashion" that literary critic Beverly Rasporich identifies as their shared subject matter.[1] Munro, who was born in Ontario in 1931, and Pratt, born four years later in New Brunswick (and who passed away in 2018), depict the home through an accumulation of careful details, using a strategy that approximates realism. Yet their writings and paintings repeatedly defamiliarize ordinary household items, intimating that just below a serene surface is a more disquieting story about how family life plays out. In their varied representations, food, in particular, offers the writer and artist a way to achieve complexity through surface-level, deceptive simplicity. Food provides an accessible idiom, readily understood by readers and viewers, but also one laden with extensive historical, mythological, social, and cultural meanings.

By paying sustained attention to food, a central source of both labour and pleasure in the home, Munro and Pratt consider the relationships between gender, sexuality, and power. Some of their textual and visual representations celebrate food as a feminized aesthetic achievement; more disquieting depictions link food to gendered and sexualized violence. Paradox characterizes the treatment of food and the kitchen in the works of both Munro and Pratt: they highlight the complexity of women's relationship to the home as simultaneously a site of creative freedom and accomplishment that enables self-discovery and a space of domestic confinement, predicated on hetero-patriarchal privilege that can erupt in violence.[2]

In Munro's fiction, the kitchen, while conventionally associated with comfort, often provides a mere simulacrum of safety. In "Royal Beatings," the opening story of *Who Do You Think You Are?* (1978), a young girl is chased and beaten by her father. She gazes at the familiar kitchen objects, recognizing that "none of them can rescue her ... Pots can show malice, the patterns of linoleum can leer up at you, treachery is the other side of dailiness."[3] Conversely, in a later story, "Vandals" (1994), a woman who endured childhood sexual abuse takes belated revenge in the perpetrator's home by pouring syrup and other sticky liquids she retrieves from his kitchen over his belongings. This emphasis on the kitchen as a volatile and potentially threatening space is echoed by Munro's literary peers, who similarly came of age during the post–Second World War elevation of domesticity for white, middle-class women. The opening lines of Sylvia Plath's poem "Lesbos" convey the literally simmering violence of the kitchen, the "viciousness" as the "potatoes hiss."[4] Overt gendered violence is even more evident in Canadian poet Pat Lowther's "Kitchen Murder": "Everything here's a weapon," she writes. "I pick up a meat fork, / imagine / plunging it in, / a heavy male / thrust."[5]

In Pratt's paintings, kitchen violence appears in images of animals, fish, and fowl at different stages of preparation for consumption, such as the raggedly severed and discarded *Fish Head in Steel Sink* (1983) and the roast presented on a silver platter in *Sunday Dinner* (1996). Pratt plays up contrasts in these two works, as pristine metallic surfaces are juxtaposed against vividly bloody flesh. In a video interview accompanying a recent retrospective of her work, Pratt describes life as a "very violent affair"; the kitchen, a reviewer of the exhibit remarks, "is where this violence plays out."[6] This observation echoes literary critic Sandra M. Gilbert's observation that "even, or perhaps especially, in fiction it's hard to forget that ... the kitchen is murderous and so is life that lives on life."[7]

Munro and Pratt use food to point to an essential tension between surfaces and essences, a contrast that is particularly marked when assessing the kitchen as alternately haven and abattoir. The recognition of submerged kitchen violence reflects Ajay Heble's observation that in Munro's fiction a "safe, recognizable, and knowable world ... presents itself as real and true" but is then undermined, as "ordinary objects in Munro's world can, at any moment, become sinister or threatening."[8] Joan Murray presents a similar insight about how surfaces and substantive meanings entwine in Pratt's work: "Her art is a way of organizing the surface of life, using what is 'palpable and mute.' The objects are silent witnesses. Through them, she apprehends the mystery of life."[9] By creating clashing representations of food, sometimes by juxtaposing images of comfort and beauty with a threat of violence, Pratt and Munro indicate that appearances can deceive, while senses can mislead and betray.

Some of their images of food seem entirely innocent: Pratt's celebrated still life depictions of fruit, notably, do not convey a sense of threat, and many of Munro's intricate descriptions of food are celebratory. Conversely, Pratt's paintings of beef, chicken, and fish arouse anxiety in part because they are eroticized. In a conversation with curator Sarah Milroy, Pratt describes her painting *Roast Beef* (1977) as "quite a sexy thing ... with that sort of drool coming out of it. I can remember when I first showed that in a gallery, I heard a woman say, 'Well, I guess she can paint, but do you think she can cook?'"[10] Pratt's anecdote illustrates the skepticism that she and Munro repeatedly encountered from interviewers who queried how they balanced their domestic responsibilities and artistic vocations, or even asked for their recipes: early profiles, while noting their obvious talents, characterized both as housewives with a creative bent.[11] This cozy approach is peculiarly at odds with the way violence is invoked in some Pratt images and Munro stories involving food.

Munro and Pratt have experienced a parallel trivialization of their chosen subjects and forms: women's domestic life, the short story rather than the novel, painting instead of more experimental art forms. Rather than defensively valorizing the domestic sphere's significance, they point to the ways it can be made startlingly new. Their formal choices, although they can be perceived as constraints, ultimately allowed both writer and artist to excel. Munro has described her choice to write short fiction rather than novels as a pragmatic decision shaped by the constant interruptions of a young family.[12] Pratt, living with her artist-spouse, Christopher Pratt, and their children in Newfoundland, was geographically and socially isolated from contact with the urban centres where feminist art of the 1960s and 1970s turned from painting and representational art; she remained tied to the tradition of the still life that was the foundation of her rigorous art studies at Mount Allison University.[13]

Munro and Pratt present the paradox of food and femininity: while the kitchen is a site of women's agency and achievement, it is also a place where vulnerability is exposed. To explore these aspects, I begin with their shared aesthetic and thematic concerns and then turn to three parallel portrayals. In the first example, I consider fruitcake as a representative image of baked goods, and one with especially strong associations to ritual and occasion. In the second instance, I consider how jelly, with its viscous properties, functions as a metonymic representation of women's bodies and sexuality in Munro's historical story "Meneseteung" (1990) and in Pratt's depictions of gelatinous substances, the paintings of jewel-toned jellies and moulded

Jell-O for which she is perhaps best known. Finally, turning to the depiction of animal flesh in relation to women's status as consumers and purveyors of flesh, and their potential for being perceived and treated *as* flesh, I compare Munro's "Wenlock Edge" (2010) to Pratt's unusually graphic *Service Station* (1978) and her noted work in portraiture.

Femininity and Food

Pratt's paintings are used as the cover art for editions of three of Munro's short story collections: *Friend of My Youth* (Pratt's *Wedding Dress*, 1986), *Runaway* (*The Bed*, 1968), and *No Love Lost* (a second wedding dress portrait, *Barby in the Dress She Made Herself*, 1986). Further, prior rights to *Wedding Dress* were ceded to a critic who had intended to reproduce the painting on the cover of her study of Munro's writing.[14] While none of these images are food-related, they point to the significance of domestic ceremony in women's lives: rituals of marriage and, more implicitly in the image of the bed, sexuality and childbearing. In other works by Munro and Pratt, this sense of women's lives as generational and cyclical is conveyed through attention to food rituals as part of the rhythm of life, the series of meals prepared, served, and then tidied away, with everyday meals punctuated by Anglo-Canadian ceremonial feasts – a Christmas or wedding cake, the holiday turkey, the Sunday roast.

Food depictions are particularly vivid because of the stylistic approaches taken by both writer and artist, which are sometimes discussed as a form of photo-realism. Pratt has worked extensively with photographic cues and visual vocabulary in her paintings, and Munro's fiction has been analyzed in terms of techniques of photography as well as painting.[15] This sense of photographic representation, particularly of food, can lend a sense of superficiality to their work, or even of commercialism, in the case of Pratt's images.[16] The crucial critical gesture, here, is that their version of "real" life is an artifice: food representations sustain the tension between the "real" and the work of art. "Real Life" was Munro's original title for her one novel, *Lives of Girls and Women* (1971), and she uses a culinary metaphor to describe how her writing depends on the "starter dough" of objects and places that she has seen, transmuted through invention and imagination.[17] Similarly, Pratt has described her need to ground her writing, which is autobiographical, and her visual art in reality:

"I was incapable of forming plots or making up characters ... I decided I might just as well face my dependence on real life and discuss it. My painting follows the same pattern."[18] In this embrace of the "real," there is some irony: a meal that is prepared, served, and eaten survives only in memory; in literary and visual representations, however, it is captured and preserved for posterity, eliminating the effects of time, including decay.

On the one hand, elaborate written and visual depictions of food create a heightened effect of verisimilitude by provoking readers' sense memories of sight, smell, and taste. Conversely, Munro constantly calls attention, via self-reflexivity and other meta-fictional strategies, to how her depiction of reality is an artful narrative construct, and she situates her depictions of domestic life within the transitions of her own historical era, from the uncritical acceptance of women's association with domesticity during the years immediately following the Second World War to the social upheavals of the late 1960s and 1970s Second Wave feminist movement that questioned gendered household roles. Pratt's paintings of food, in turn, beguile viewers with cozy, homespun domestic scenes of lace doilies and silver trays, artfully arranged vases of flowers, jars of homemade jam, and freshly baked iced cakes. Munro and Pratt memorialize home cooking; fast, frozen, and canned foods are only occasionally represented in their work. This emphasis is anachronistic, a point that can be seen especially clearly in a Pratt painting of a glass jar labelled "Red Crabapple Jelly" and sealed within a small plastic bag. Pratt titles the work, wryly, *Specimen from Another Time* (2001), presenting it as a kind of archaeological find. Misao Dean suggests that Pratt's "paintings signify *as* ordinary a particular kind of domestic life: heterosexual, with happy well-fed children, clean crocheted tablecloths, ceremonial marriages, food cooked in traditional ways and served on beautiful china – a domestic life which exists, for most of us, more as nostalgia than reality."[19]

Pratt and Munro invite viewers and readers to lean in, to pay close attention, and then to step back, startled and discomfited by what now appears peculiar and threatening. In the phrase coined by literary critic W.R. Martin, "the strange and the familiar" are brought together in Munro's fiction, and this is particularly notable in how both Pratt and Munro convey the paradoxical qualities of food.[20] In her own medium, Pratt, like Munro, invites a closer attention to the details of food and rewards the viewer's scrutiny with an unsettling recognition that ordinary, familiar food items have acquired additional layers of significance. A 1976 review by journalist Robert Fulford suggested that Pratt "wants to grasp the visual aspect of everyday objects and elevate them into art," acting as "the visual poet of the kitchen."²¹ This gesture, though, does not merely "elevate" but actively deconstructs, calling attention to the web of familial and social relationships implied by the presentation of the domestic space. In turn, Rasporich argues that "food in Munro is charged with feminine value,"²² while Redekop characterizes her stories as "culinary," a term, Redekop notes, "often used to deride women's fiction,"²³ but amenable to reclamation.

From Fruit to Fruitcake: Symbolism and Allegory in Food Depictions

Many food portrayals in Munro's fiction and Pratt's paintings can be appreciated as pleasurable aesthetic achievements, "labour[s] of love," as the title of Canadian fiction writer and former art student Lisa Moore's assessment of Pratt's work suggests.²⁴ Pratt's jam jars and still-life fruit depictions have analogies in Munro's fiction, and many of these celebrate the visual appeal of foods that have been artfully prepared and carefully presented. A culinary category that the writer and artist both treat extensively is sweet baked goods and desserts. Pratt's paintings feature trifle in a glass bowl (*Trifle in a Dark Room*, 1995) and cakes elevated on pedestals (*Poppyseed Cake, Glazed for Calypso*, 2002), set on silver trays (*Fruit Cake – Very Dark, Very Rich*, 1993), or domed under glass (*Marble Cake*, 1998). Munro's female characters agonize over elaborate creations, like the raspberry bombe in "Labour Day Dinner" or the Gateau St Honoré, a "monstrosity" of "cream and custard and butterscotch" that a character tosses into the sea so that she will not "gorge" and "purge" on it.²⁵

Would Pratt and Munro acknowledge an affinity? While Pratt admires Munro, including her in a listing of the "Great Writers," she contrasts these august authors with her preference for cookbooks and Lucy Maud Montgomery: "The straightforward, blunt and simple observations and instructions found within these unpretentious books smooth the way for me and allow me to go alone into personal observations that the Great Writers of Great Books insist on dominating," Pratt explains, before offering a food analogy that condemns serious literature even as it appears to celebrate its merits. "Perhaps they are like Christmas cakes – so full of rich and wonderful stuff that they are dense and heavy and fill you up so completely that they just put you to sleep. Whereas a sponge cake or an angel food cake is so full of air that after eating a piece of one of these it is still possible to float around and imagine and dream while still awake."[26]

The fruitcake simile is particularly striking because it is a dessert portrayed by both Pratt and Munro, and one that is associated, crucially, with the celebratory rituals of weddings and Christmas. Pratt's *Fruitcake – Very Dark, Very Rich* depicts the remaining portion of a cake resting on a doily set atop a round silver tray, the cake partially reflected in the tray's rim. The interior shows candied fruits against a dark binding. The cake is iced with a white, thick frosting, and a small portion lies flat in front of the rest of the loaf. The effect is both rich and feminine: the small slice appears dainty, a delicate morsel that hints at self-restraint. The fork and knife lying neatly to the side of the cake slice reinforce this sense of control, but as in *Chocolate Birthday Cake* (1997), the presence of the knife implies a hand that not only bakes and ices but also slices, a more threatening gesture.

Fruitcake is a key wedding ritual in Munro's "A Real Life," from *Open Secrets* (1994), where female neighbours are determined to transform an independent woman into an unlikely middle-aged bride.[27] Wedding dress and reception preparations irritate the bride-to-be, Dorrie; only in the wedding-cake making does she derive pleasure, using her "strong arms," "stirring and stirring a mixture so stiff it appeared to be all candied fruit and raisins and currants, with a little gingery batter holding it together like glue."[28] Dorrie's response to the physicality of stirring, unlike her more diffident response to her intended groom, is eroticized: "When Dorrie got the big bowl against her stomach and took up the beating spoon" there is the "first satisfied sigh to come out of her in a long while."[29] She wants to cancel the wedding to retain her autonomy, but is persuaded by a neighbour to go through with the event. While this neighbour alleges that marriage confers on women a "real life," her actual concern is that the elaborate preparations not be wasted: "the wedding cake is made," so the ceremony must take place.[30]

This insistence is part of the compulsory transformation of women into wives, a process in which other women collude even if they are not particularly happy in their own marriages, as Munro's story makes clear. The cake is held together "like glue": resistant women like Dorrie must be held especially close. Wedding cakes are, of course, overdetermined symbols, linked to evolving ideas of gender and class. In the nineteenth century, ornate, multi-tiered cakes featured thick white frosting that came to be known as "royal" icing after Queen Victoria's wedding cake.[31] As anthropologist Simon Charsley describes, during this era the traditional white icing acquired symbolic meaning, as "it came to be felt that the whiteness of the cake was an appropriate reference to the purity of the bride coming to her marriage."[32] Pratt and Munro, who frequently depict bridal apparel, demonstrate an acute consciousness of how each element, including the cake, supports the symbolic weight of weddings as a loss of women's autonomy once their identities are subsumed by their married state.

Jellies, Jams, and the Female Body

In an interview, Pratt described women as "leaky creature[s]."[33] A preoccupation with the female body's fluidity is taken up in Munro's historical story "Meneseteung," where the apparent tranquility of a mid-nineteenth-century domestic space is shattered by violence just outside the home. The consequence is that a "poetess" who had been contemplating marriage replaces her hope with an artistic vision of an ambitious poem about the local river – one, sadly, that the gendered constraints of the era prevents her from achieving. Almeda prepares a batch of grape jelly, leaving the fruit pulp to drip through cloth overnight. She is awakened by a noisy altercation. The next morning, Almeda discovers a woman prostrate against a fence, one breast bared and a "haunch showing a bruise as big as a sunflower. The unbruised skin is grayish, like a plucked, raw drumstick."[34] Her neighbour, with whom she has engaged in a tentative courtship, prods the woman's leg "with the toe of his boot, just as you'd nudge a dog or a sow."[35] While his romantic ardour is aroused by Almeda's display of "indiscretion … agitation … foolishness" and "need," she is sickened by his conduct.[36] Left untended, the grape juice overflows its basin, creating a permanent stain on the kitchen floor that attests to the enduring effects of violence. Almeda "walks upstairs leaving purple footprints and smelling her escaping blood and the sweat of her body."[37] As Katrine Raymond's insightful reading of the story points out, the jelly imagery "demonstrates how female flow can exist not just as uncontrollable leakage but also as viscous resistance" to male assertions of authority.[38]

A similar gelatinous, not-quite-liquid state is captured in Pratt's paintings of vividly coloured jams and jellies, many in shades of red that suggest, according to Lisa Moore, "sacrificial blood, or menstruation." And it is not just the colour, Moore indicates, that fosters this association: "There is something extra, a fullness that threatens to brim over."[39] In a representative Pratt work, *Red Currant Jelly*

(1972), several glass containers are set on silver foil and filled to the top, the colour and light reflecting off the foil, the transparent glasses barely containing their contents. A later work, *Jello on Silver Platter* (2001), features a startling deep-crimson moulded dessert that has been turned out onto a platter, the wobbly Jell-O retaining (just barely) the shape of its previous container. These are among Pratt's best-known and most frequently reproduced works: one painting, *Jelly Shelf* (1999), was even adapted as a postage stamp. Yet, alongside her startling rendering of colour and light in these images of gelled substances, Pratt is also conveying the containment of potential overflow, a disciplining of feminine excess.[40]

Food and Violence: Animal-Woman Analogies

Women produce food, but as Rasporich notes in writing about Munro, in many portrayals "she *is* also food."[41] In *The Sexual Politics of Meat*, feminist theorist Carol Adams argues that "sexual violence and meat eating, which appear to be discrete forms of violence," are intimately linked.[42] Munro and Pratt get at the visceral reality of slaughter through divergent approaches to representing animal bodies, including as analogies for sexualized violence. In one of Pratt's most famous paintings, *Service Station*, she depicts the partial carcass of a moose suspended from a truck in a garage, an image recreated from a photograph she took at a neighbour's home, and at his urging. She told interviewer Mireille Eagan that she was initially "offended" and horrified, "almost sick to look at it" because to her it was "significant of rape and, I hate to say it but, everything that man does to women."[43] Art critic Sarah Milroy assesses the artwork as "the most violently charged painting Pratt has ever made."[44] An explicit analogizing of gendered violence and animal slaughter is also evident in Munro's "Vandals" (1994), which features a sexually abusive man who is a skilled taxidermist, a juxtaposition explored in detail by critic Carrie Dawson.[45]

Unflinching depictions of animal carcasses appear frequently in Munro's work, reflecting her rural upbringing. In "Nettles" (2001), the narrator describes "the meat-house in the barnyard" where the "pale horse carcasses hung from brutal hooks."[46] "Characters" (1978), a Flo and Rose story excluded from *Who Do You Think You Are?*, opens with a detailed description of how to kill and pluck a chicken: "go in with your knife. Slit the roof of the mouth and the upper part of the beak. Go for the veins that cross each other at the back of the throat … That's when you hit the brain."[47] Munro's fiction takes a more grisly approach than is evident in Pratt's bloodless *Eviscerated Chickens* (1971), a painting of two raw, plucked chickens nestled together in paper, or in the glistening golden roast bird that is being basted in her *Christmas Turkey* (1980).

Munro is often explicit in portraying a woman's status as a potential comestible.[48] In "Wenlock Edge," first published in *The New Yorker*, a university student is asked to remove her clothing before sharing a lavish dinner with her elderly (and fully dressed) host.[49] The meal is a torment, the narrator hyper-aware of her skin sticking to her chair. After dinner, at her host's request, she reads from the A.E. Housman *Shropshire Lad* segment used in the story's title; absorbed in her reading, she briefly forgets to be self-conscious. Days later, however, when she sees a sign advertising a talk about Housman, she recognizes belatedly that she has been permanently marked by her experience: "Had he known that I would never think of those lines again without feeling the prickle of the upholstery on my bare haunches? The sticky prickly shame. A far greater shame it seemed now than at the time."[50] Here the paragraph published in *The New Yorker* diverges in a crucial way from the same passage in the collection *Too Much Happiness* (2009). The earlier version notes: "He had got me, in spite of myself."[51] In the book publication, this phrase becomes: "He had done something to me, after all."[52] In the first version it is more apparent that the narrator's shame stems from having been "had," a parallel to sexual violation.

In her exploration of how nudity is related to power and agency in "Wenlock Edge," Munro considers, as she does in many of her works, how women feel about displaying their bodies to observers. Munro's female characters are warily appreciative of aspects of the female body – their own and others – and, alternately, disgusted by the body's aging or excesses. A woman's gaze cast on the female body creates a complicated relationship: women can self-objectify, but they may shy away from looking closely at other women, as Pratt suggests in explaining why she did not initially paint women extensively. The nude, in particular, was a genre Pratt resisted: "I thought that if you didn't have an erotic reaction to a nude, you probably shouldn't paint it, because wasn't that what it was all about? … then, I began to think about it, and thought, 'How ridiculous. If anybody has the right to paint the naked female, it's another woman.'"[53] Some critics see a sharp departure from genre conventions and artistic intent in Pratt's portraits, with Wendy Schissel proposing that Pratt is able to "challenge … the specularized nudes of male art," offering images of women as subjects rather than objects.[54] In several portraits, this is evident through the direct, even confrontational gaze of the model who looks steadily out at the viewer in portraits like *Girl in Glitz* (1987), *Girl in My Dressing Gown* (1981), or the self-possessed and apparently nude *Girl in Wicker Chair* (1978), which was featured on the cover of *Saturday Night* magazine, prompting, Pratt recalls, cancelled subscriptions by puritanical readers.[55] In resisting objectification while presenting women's bodies, Pratt points the way to treating women as self-possessing subjects who can resist the appropriative male gaze, such as the one cast on the young narrator of "Wenlock Edge."

In their food depictions, Pratt and Munro evoke a particular historical moment's construction of femininity and domesticity, but from an ideological stance that is not always transparent. For example, Marjorie Garson wonders whether detailed passages that describe women's culinary labour in *Lives of Girls and Women* represent, for Munro, "a celebration of ... energy and skills, or an indictment of a culture that defines real work as masculine, abstract, and cerebral, while imposing a kind of domestic slavery upon women?"[56] A similar ambivalence can be discerned in Pratt's paintings, where the domestic realm is aestheticized while the work to produce the household meals is largely concealed. Munro and Pratt problematize women's association with the kitchen and the food it produces by teasing out relationships between objectification, labour, and the simmering threat of violence. In doing so, they contribute to an evolving understanding of how autonomy as well as submission, freedom as well as subjugation, can be negotiated in the fraught site of the kitchen. Pratt's paintings and Munro's stories are linked not only through their shared thematic preoccupations of gender, labour, and food but also through their intense scrutiny. By attending to the more subtly insinuating and suggestive nuances of Pratt's work, we can return to Munro's fiction with greater acuity, noting the parallels in their evocations of the domestic sphere. The visual artist and writer invite us to look and then consider anew what can be perceived in women's long and emotionally charged association with food.

Notes

1 Rasporich, "Locating the Artist's Muse," 127.
2 Murray, "Mary Pratt," n.p.
3 Munro, "Royal Beatings," 19.
4 Plath, "Lesbos," 227.
5 Lowther, "Kitchen Murder," 237.
6 Stoffman, "Commonplace Treasures," 6–7.

7 Gilbert, *Culinary Imagination*, 240.
8 Heble, *The Tumble of Reason*, 4.
9 Murray, "Mary Pratt," n.p.
10 Milroy, "A Woman's Life," 73.
11 Thacker's biography of Munro cites "Housewife Finds Time to Write Short Stories" as authored by Moira Farrow, but provides no further bibliographic details. The date is identified more specifically as 1951 in Gessell, "A Delicate Balance," A11.
12 Feeney, "Why Alice Munro Is a Short Story Writer, Not a Novelist."
13 A perceptive discussion is provided in Judith E. Buzzell, "Media Orientations of Four Women Artists," MA thesis, Concordia University, 1989, https://spectrum.library.concordia.ca/3661/.
14 Redekop, *Mothers and Other Clowns*, 233.
15 Cooke, *The Influence of Painting on Five Canadian Writers*.
16 Moray, *Mary Pratt*, 23.
17 Munro, "What Is Real?," 225.
18 Pratt, *A Personal Calligraphy*, 12.
19 Dean, *Practising Femininity*, 4–5.
20 Martin, "The Strange and the Familiar in Alice Munro."
21 Quoted in Smart, *The Art of Mary Pratt*, 81.
22 Rasporich, *Dance of the Sexes*, 95.
23 Redekop, *Mothers and Other Clowns*, 30.
24 Moore, "A Labour of Love."
25 Munro, "Hard-Luck Stories," 187.
26 Pratt, *A Personal Calligraphy*, 137.
27 Garson characterizes Dorrie as one of several "alien bride" portrayals in Munro's fiction, women who lack conventional bridal attributes, such as youth, beauty, or overt femininity. As these characters are ill-suited to a wedding gown, the wedding cake may be even more crucial in conveying a sense of occasion. See "Alice Munro and Charlotte Brontë," 793.
28 Munro, "A Real Life," 70.
29 Ibid., 70.
30 Ibid., 75.
31 Wilson, "Wedding Cake," 70.
32 Charsley, "The Wedding Cake," 237.
33 Eagan and Pratt, "In Conversation: Mary Pratt and Mireille Eagan."
34 Munro, "Meneseteung," 65.
35 Ibid., 66.

36 Ibid., 67.
37 Ibid., 71.
38 Raymond, "'Deep Deep into the River of Her Mind,'" 108.
39 Moore, "A Labour of Love."
40 Many thanks to Shelley Boyd and Dorothy Barenscott for their thoughtful comments about Pratt's paintings of jelly.
41 Rasporich, *Dance of the Sexes*, 95.
42 Adams, *The Sexual Politics of Meat*, 43.
43 Eagan and Pratt, "In Conversation: Mary Pratt and Mireille Eagan."
44 Milroy, "A Woman's Life," 85.
45 Dawson, "Skinned."
46 Munro, "Nettles," 159.
47 Munro, "Characters," 72.
48 Rasporich, *Dance of the Sexes*, 95–8.
49 Munro, "Wenlock Edge," *The New Yorker*.
50 Munro, "Wenlock Edge," 88.
51 Munro, "Wenlock Edge," *The New Yorker*.
52 Munro, "Wenlock Edge," 88.
53 Quoted in Sandals, "Mary Pratt."
54 Schissel, "Her Own Frame of Reference," 80.
55 This incident is described in Smart, *The Art of Mary Pratt*, 91, and in Pratt's interview with Mireille Eagan.
56 Garson, "'I Would Try to Make Lists,'" 53.

Bibliography

Adams, Carol J. *The Sexual Politics of Meat: A Feminist-Vegetarian Critical Theory*. New York: Continuum, 1990.

Carrington de Papp, Ildiko. *Controlling the Uncontrollable: The Fiction of Alice Munro*. DeKalb: Northern Illinois University Press, 1989.

Charsley, Simon. "The Wedding Cake: History and Meanings, *Folklore* 99, no. 2 (1988): 232–41.

Cooke, John. *The Influence of Painting on Five Canadian Writers: Alice Munro, Hugh Hood, Timothy Findley, Margaret Atwood, and Michael Ondaatje*. Lewiston, NY: Edwin Mellen Press, 1996.

Dawson, Carrie. "Skinned: Taxidermy and Pedophilia in Alice Munro's 'Vandals.'" *Canadian Literature* 184 (2005): 69–83.

Dean, Misao. *Practising Femininity: Domestic Realism and the Performance of Gender in Early Canadian Fiction*. Toronto: University of Toronto Press, 1998.

Eagan, Mireille. "Look, Here." In *Mary Pratt*, 17–39. Fredericton, NB: Goose Lane Editions/The Rooms Corporation of Newfoundland and Labrador, 2013.

Eagan, Mireille, and Mary Pratt. "In Conversation: Mary Pratt and Mireille Eagan." Accessed 12 August 2016. www.mcmichael.com/video-transcripts/In_Conversation_Mary_Pratt_and_Mireille_Eagan_January_18_2014.pdf.

Feeney, Nolan. "Why Alice Munro Is a Short Story Writer, Not a Novelist." *The Atlantic*, 10 October 2013. www.theatlantic.com/entertainment/archive/2013/10/why-alice-munro-is-a-short-story-writer-not-a-novelist/280463/.

Garson, Marjorie. "Alice Munro and Charlotte Brontë." *University of Toronto Quarterly* 69, no. 4 (2000): 783–825.

– "'I Would Try to Make Lists': The Catalogue in *Lives of Girls and Women*." *Canadian Literature* 150 (1996): 45–63.

Gessell, Paul. "A Delicate Balance: Motherhood, Writing: Alice Munro's Daughter Writes about Life with the Celebrated Author." *Vancouver Sun*, 7 April 2001, A11. http://search.proquest.com.ezproxy.library.uvic.ca/docview/242575368?accountid=14846.

Gilbert, Sandra M. *The Culinary Imagination: From Myth to Modernity*. New York: Norton, 2014.

Heble, Ajay. *The Tumble of Reason: Alice Munro's Discourse of Absence*. Toronto: University of Toronto Press, 1994.

Howells, Coral Ann. *Alice Munro*. Manchester: Manchester University Press, 1998.

Lowther, Pat. "Kitchen Murder." In *Collected Works*, edited by Christine Wiesenthal, 237. Edmonton, AB: NeWest Press, 2010.

Martin, W.R. "The Strange and the Familiar in Alice Munro." *Studies in Canadian Literature* 7, no. 2 (1982): 214–26.

Milroy, Sarah. "A Woman's Life." In *Mary Pratt*, 67–91. Fredericton, NB: Goose Lane Editions/The Rooms Corporation of Newfoundland and Labrador, 2013.

Moore, Lisa. "A Labour of Love." *Canadian Art* 30, nò. 4 (2014): 114–19. http://canadianart.ca/features/mary-pratt-a-labour-of-love/.

Moray, Gerta. *Mary Pratt*. Toronto: McGraw-Hill Ryerson, 1989.

Munro, Alice. "Characters." *Ploughshares* 14 (Fall 1978): 72–82.

– "Dimensions." *Too Much Happiness*. Toronto: McClelland and Stewart, 2009.

– "Free Radicals." *Too Much Happiness*. Toronto: McClelland and Stewart, 2009.

– "Hard-Luck Stories." *The Moons of Jupiter*. Toronto: Macmillan, 1982.

– *Lives of Girls and Women*. New York: Vintage Books, [1971] 2001.

– "The Love of a Good Woman." *The Love of a Good Woman*. Toronto: McClelland and Stewart, 1998.
– "Meneseteung." *Friend of My Youth*. Toronto: McClelland and Stewart, 1990.
– "Nettles." *Hateship, Friendship, Courtship, Loveship, Marriage*. Toronto: Penguin Canada, 2001.
– "Open Secrets." *Open Secrets*. Toronto: McClelland and Stewart, 1994.
– "A Real Life." *Open Secrets*. Toronto: McClelland and Stewart, 1994.
– "Royal Beatings." *Who Do You Think You Are?* Toronto: Penguin Canada, [1978] 2006.
– "Vandals." *Open Secrets*. Toronto: McClelland and Stewart, 1994.
"Wenlock Edge." *The New Yorker*, 5 December 2005. www.newyorker.com/magazine/2005/12/05/wenlock-edge.
– "Wenlock Edge." *Too Much Happiness*. Toronto: McClelland and Stewart, 2009.
– "What Is Real?" In *Making It New: Contemporary Canadian Stories*, edited by John Metcalf, 223–6. Toronto: Methuen, 1982.

Murray, Joan. *Confessions of a Curator*. Toronto: Dundurn, 1996.
– "Mary Pratt: The Skin of Things." In *Mary Pratt: June 19–August 16, 1981*. London, ON: London Regional Art Gallery, 1981.

Plath, Sylvia. "Lesbos." In *The Collected Poems*, 227–30. New York: HarperPerennial, 1992.

Pratt, Mary. *A Personal Calligraphy*. Fredericton, NB: Goose Lane Editions, 2000.

Rasporich, Beverly J. *Dance of the Sexes: Art and Gender in the Fiction of Alice Munro*. Edmonton: University of Alberta Press, 1990.
– "Locating the Artist's Muse: The Paradox of Femininity in Mary Pratt and Alice Munro." In *Woman as Artist: Papers in Honor of Marsha Hanen*, edited by Christine Mason Sutherland and Beverly Jean Rasporich, 121–44. Calgary: University of Calgary Press, 1993.

Raymond, Katrine. "'Deep Deep into the River of Her Mind': 'Meneseteung' and the Archival Hysteric," *English Studies in Canada* 40, no. 1 (2014): 95–122.

Redekop, Magdalene. *Mothers and Other Clowns: The Stories of Alice Munro*. London: Routledge, 1992.

Sandals, Leah. "Mary Pratt: On the Labours of Love." *Canadian Art* (12 October 2013): N.p. http://canadianart.ca/reviews/mary-pratt/.

Schissel, Wendy. "Her Own Frame of Reference: A Feminist Reading of Mary Pratt's Painting," *Atlantis* 17, no. 2 (1991): 77–89.

Smart, Tom. *The Art of Mary Pratt: The Substance of Light*. N.p: Beaverbrook Art Gallery and Goose Lane Editions, 1995, 1996.

Stoffman, Judy. "Commonplace Treasures." *Literary Review of Canada* 22, no. 1 (1 January 2014): 6–7. [Review of *Mary Pratt*, edited by Ray Cronin, Mireille Eagan, Sarah Fillmore,

Sarah Milroy, Catharine Mastin, and Caroline Stone] http://reviewcanada.ca/magazine/2014/01/commonplace-treasures/.

Thacker, Robert. *Alice Munro: Writing Her Lives*. Toronto: McClelland and Stewart, 2005.

Wilson, Carol. "Wedding Cake: A Slice of History." *Gastronomica* 5, no. 2 (Spring 2005): 69–72.

York, Lorraine. *"The Other Side of Dailiness": Photography in the Works of Alice Munro, Timothy Findley, Michael Ondaatje, and Margaret Laurence*. Toronto: ECW Press, 1988.

19

Table of Contents
Reading, Cooking, Eating Canadian Literature

Alexia Moyer

Canadian Literary Fare is the web platform of a group of scholars interested in food narratives.[1] The site was conceived as a repository of primary and secondary materials on the subject of literary cookery, to be used by anyone who happened upon it or followed it. In other words, making the contents available to as wide a public as possible was a priority. Five years into the project, our readership includes scholars, teachers, food bloggers, writers, artists, Canadian literature enthusiasts, and cooks from seventy-one countries, some using the site for course planning or as a means of showcasing student work, some for the writing of research articles or the preparation of exhibitions. Many are looking for a recipe. After all, a portion of the site is given over to an experiment in CanLit cooking: *The Tableaux Blog*, wherein each dish is sourced from works of Canadian literature, cooked, and photographed, its culinary merit and literary functions then weighed and discussed. During a post-doctoral fellowship devoted to the study of food in literature, *The Tableaux Blog* was certainly the most visual and indeed visceral part of my work. That is to say, much of the content is image- rather than text-based. Before the writing part comes the work of sourcing ingredients, making the meal, setting the scene, taking the photographs, and then, of course, eating the final product. Unless the final product is sardines. Too many little bones to contend with. The cheese-and-chutney sandwiches that accompany the central characters on that lakeside lunch in Margaret Atwood's "Wilderness Tips," however, get more than a passing grade. This simple sandwich has earned itself a spot – next to Michel Tremblay's *chapeaux de baloney* – in the easy-lunch-eaten-alone-while-reading-a-novel segment of my culinary arsenal. Some of the more practical considerations of the blog: Is there enough description or instruction to go on? Is the recipe – for there is sometimes an actual recipe – plausible or accurate? What, if any, culinary concessions have to be made in producing the dish? Consider Fred Wah's description of

Figure 19.1
Traversée des Sentiments, for *The Tableaux Blog*, Canadian Literary Fare.

tomato beef in *Diamond Grill*. There are measurements, some (1 tsp sugar) more precise than others (a ladle full). It is written in the imperative mood. Those who have never made tomato beef before can follow along with relative ease, as Wah adheres to some of the more conventional forms of cooking instruction. This process of recreating mostly fictional meals is not without difficulty. There is sometimes a bit of fudging going on in these cooking experiments: shortfalls in skill or accuracy, imposter ingredients. Savoy cabbage is swapped for kale to pleasing results in Dede Crane's recipe for kale and apple soup from the food-writing anthology *Apples under the Bed: Recipes and Recollections from B.C. Writers and Artists*. A photograph of the fish soup from George Elliott Clarke's *Whylah Falls* shows off the brilliant orange roe of the scallop while, perhaps mercifully, concealing the grit not wholly purged from the clams. Georgian Bay, Ontario – patently devoid of seals and whales as it is – stands in for the Pacific Ocean in a photo essay of Audrey Thomas's *Intertidal Life*. A plane ticket for a photography session is not in the offing, but a borrowed family cottage will do in a pinch. Such is my budget. Initially equipped with a digital camera and little knowledge of how to use it, an espresso-stained pine table in a furnished rental apartment (this to serve as background), a limited collection of dishes, and access to the varied foodscape that is Marseille, France,[2] I set out to translate food-filled passages to photographs. Their aesthetic sensibilities have undoubtedly been informed by such conditions, together with the emerging conventions and visual vocabulary of foodie photography encountered on Instagram, other food blogs, and the food stylist trends of today's cookbooks. The look is spare with very few props. The dishes are often shot from above, with the clutter of everyday family life just beyond the frame. The photographs certainly refer to the stories, but they also say something about the neophyte photographer, looking at food for the first time through a camera lens, marvelling at the shapes, textures, and colours of the raw materials: marbled steak, ruffled cabbage leaves, fish scales. References to the original literary scenes are subtle: here, a bit of lace hints at the turn-of-the-century table upon which the *chapeaux de baloney* would have been served; there, the picnic table's surface is grey and weathered, much like driftwood and appropriate for a seaside meal. Without actually replicating the scenes, I seek rather to capture the care with which these authors select, stage, and frame their cheese-and-chutney sandwiches. There is nothing incidental about food as narrated by Margaret Atwood, Audrey Thomas, or Phyllis Brett Young. Similarly, there is nothing entirely incidental about the photographs. These are not casual snapshots, but more intentionally composed scenes of culinary narratives, as the blog's title, *Tableaux*, suggests.

The project is not without reward, of the gustatory, sensory, emotional, and intellectual kind. Often the food is good. The ingredients in Carmine Starnino's recipe for *pasta con alice*, delivered in sonnet form, are few: three cloves of garlic, three anchovy fillets, olive oil. Add spaghetti al dente. Serve with wine. The result is, as with so many simple recipes, more than the sum of its parts. There is something interesting about the idea, as expressed by Jennifer Conrad-Black and Melissa Goldthwaite, of ingesting a story, of "incorporat[ing it] … at the cellular level."[3] Mostly though, I like the kind of reading this project necessitates. Reading food for its literary functions, figuring out, as Diane McGee states, what it says about "characters, their world, and their relationship to that world" is one part of the process.[4] And yet, I now also find myself reading these same books while standing at the kitchen counter, following along with my index finger as I would with a cookbook. Checking once, twice, for hints about cooking times and ingredient lists embedded in the text. Reading slowly, with repetition in other words, opening up the spaces between the descriptions, seeking instruction. This is close reading of a different kind, one that yields a tangible, edible result.

Cooking CanLit is an exercise in literary tourism. Rather than trek around the Lake District with map in hand, one has merely to seek out the kitchen. Both trips require a sense of adventure. But, as Nicola Watson writes, this practice of visiting authors' homes, haunts, and graves as well as their literary settings and of bringing home souvenirs in the form of flower pressings, grave rubbings, bookmarks, and postcards – or, I would add, taking cooking lessons from Fred Wah – are all, in some sense, "a deeply counter-intuitive response to the pleasures and possibilities of imaginative reading."[5] On the one hand, making tomato beef and then photographing it extends the text from whence it comes, giving the original meaning of the work new dimensions, visibility, and many potential modes of circulation, sharing, and consumption. On the other hand, the exercise is often necessarily restricted by that which can be materially replicated or visualized. As in the case of Michael Ondaatje's "rat jelly" or Jeni Couzyn's "The Preparation of Human Pie," where replication is neither possible nor desirable. I have yet to find a workable recipe for Gwendolyn MacEwen's "boiled chimera / and apocalyptic tea" and "arcane salad of spiced bibles, / tossed dictionaries,"[6] though I did fry up some of her "Kanadian Eggs" featured in Margaret Atwood's *The CanLit Foodbook*. For Watson, particular modes of writing induce particular modes of tourism. In this vein, food-laden literature sends readers into the kitchen, some more insistently than others. There is, Adam Gopnik and Anne LeCroy each propose, a recognizable gradient of cookable books, from those in which dishes are "mere stops on the ribbon of narrative"[7] to others that present "not just the result but the whole process – not just what people eat but how they make it, exactly how much garlic is chopped, and how, and when it is placed in the pan. Sometimes entire recipes are included."[8] To push this taxonomy of literary cookery a bit further, there are some for which the literary is almost entirely at the service of the cookery. Not only are readers encouraged to put the text into practice, there is documented evidence of them having done so. Originally published as a series in *Good Housekeeping* from 1885 to 1887 and later released in novel form, *Ten Dollars Enough: Keeping House Well on Ten Dollars a Week* regales readers with tales of newlyweds Molly and Harry Bishop's second year of marriage with such recipe-centred chapter titles as "Veal and Ham Pie – Beefsteak Pudding – Trifle" and "What to do with a Soup-Bone." In her preface, Catherine Owen expresses her pleasure at hearing from those readers who "have tried [protagonist] Molly's recipes with such success."[9] *Tableaux* then keeps company with those readers who sought to work their way through *Ten Dollars Enough* with both spectacles and spatula. It is also a nod to more recent experiments: Dinah Fried's *Fictitious Dishes* and Kate Young's *The Little Library Café*, the first, a book of fifty photographic interpretations of literary meals, and the second, a blog and now literary cookbook – each with *Moby Dick*–related clam chowder and afternoon tea à la *Alice in Wonderland*, with Young providing actual recipes.

Posting

Every term – and I say term because I habitually organize my year according to an academic calendar – Shelley Boyd from the sister blog *CanLitFare* and I decide on a theme, be it Canada's capital cities, outdoor meals, turning-point meals, drink, literary breakfasts, fish and seafood, and so on. Every two weeks or so, one or the other of us uploads a post related to that theme. Below is a cross-section of writings

Figure 19.2
"Kanadian Eggs," *The CanLit Foodbook*, for *The Tableaux Blog*, Canadian Literary Fare.

to the tune of butter tarts and cucumber-shaped boats, containing even a recipe for good measure. The focus here is intentionally broad, from investigations of Canada's regional and/or national foodways to evaluations of cucumbers as receptacles for other foods to an invitation to the social event of the summer season: a barbecue – all from old, new, nearly forgotten, or recently recovered food writings.

Post # 1: Edmonton Butter Tarts, 26 February 2015

These are *Edmonton* Butter Tarts, submitted by historian Lynne Bowen to *The Great Canadian Literary Cookbook*. It stands to reason that they should be made and eaten this very week in honour of the latest stop on our tour of Canada's capital cities. The recipe is not overly time consuming and the ingredients are easily obtained. You might even omit the raisins. Or keep them in. Either choice has its risks in butter tart circles. The raisin debate remains heated.

Is there anything particularly Edmonton-y about this recipe? How might one determine this? Extensive comparative taste-testing may yield some result. Sweet teeth aside, Elizabeth Driver's *Culinary Landmarks: A Bibliography of Canadian Cookbooks 1825–1949* is invaluable as far as resources go. Driver will help you to establish your field of inquiry. For instance, she has not found any printed examples of butter tarts in nineteenth-century cookbooks.[10] In her introduction, she refers to the tart as a *Canadian* specialty from the turn of the twentieth century.[11] This bit of information both narrows and widens your sample. You have only just over a century's worth of cookbooks from which to draw your conclusions. But Butter Tart territory is nationwide (and then some, if you take into account its pecan, treacle, and shoofly pie relatives). Peruse the dessert section of a handful of cookbooks and you'll begin to see commonalities in their Butter Tart selection (should they have one): eggs … brown sugar … cooked in pastry. As for the variables – milk, butter, dates, raisins, currants, vanilla, nutmeg, rum flavouring – there are several. And these variables do not seem to originate from, or adhere to, specific regions or cities. I found all of the above in The United Farmers of Canada, Saskatchewan Section Limited recipe book, boasting at least five recipes for butter tarts (if you count the suspiciously familiar Banbury tart). In her article, "Regional Differences in the Canadian Meal? Cookbooks Answer the Question," Driver warns us against "reading too much meaning into recipes with a Canadian place-name." These connections can be slight. "'Manitoba Pudding' in the Quebec City book," she discovered, "is very similar to the 'Montreal Pudding' in the Toronto book; 'Muskoka Chocolate

Cake' in the Toronto book is not the same as 'Muskoka Cake' in the Victoria book, which contains no chocolate!"[12] The Nanaimo Bar and Montreal Smoked Meat may launch a protest.

What then makes this an Edmonton Butter Tart? Beyond the title, there is little textual evidence to suggest that *this particular recipe* is … well … particular. Though it is sweet and rich and all you would want in a butter tart. And you can enjoy the result from city to city and province to province.

Adapted from Lynne Bowen's Edmonton Butter Tart Recipe[13]
Ingredients:
- Pastry for eight tarts
- 1 cup Sultana raisins
- 1 cup brown sugar
- 1 egg
- ½ tsp vanilla
- ice cream

Instructions:
- Preheat oven to 400°F.
- Line eight muffin tin depressions with your favourite pastry.
- Pour boiling water over 1 cup raisins, let sit for five minutes and then drain.
- In a bowl mix the raisins, 1 cup brown sugar, and 1 beaten egg. Beat for as long as you can, advises Bowen (or five minutes, whichever comes first).
- Add ½ tsp vanilla.
- Fill pastry shells with the mixture and bake 20 minutes.
- Bowen suggests you serve tarts warm with ice cream. I found that cooled in the refrigerator overnight, they developed a better, that is to say creamier, texture. This is a matter of personal preference I would say.

Post #2: Cowcumber Boats, 14 May 2015

Cucumber … concummer … cowcummer … cowcumber. All are variants of "cucumber."[14] Or so says the *Oxford English Dictionary*. What the OED does not discuss are cucumbers in relation to boats. Is this vegetable sufficiently seaworthy? I, who have read at least twelve books in Patrick O'Brian's Jack Aubrey/Stephen Maturin series – and can therefore tell a luff from a lubber's hole – would not venture to sail in one. The cucumber is, however, an excellent vessel for tuna salad. Or so says *The Anne of Green Gables Cookbook* from which this recipe is drawn.

Figure 19.3
"Edmonton Butter Tarts," *The Great Canadian Literary Cookbook*, for *The Tableaux Blog*, Canadian Literary Fare.

L.M. Montgomery's Anne books are chock full of fare. At least two people have noticed this. The person who borrowed the *Anne of Green Gables* omnibus before me from the Bibliothèque et Archives nationales du Québec had discreetly (in pencil) underlined any and all mentions of food. I couldn't help but feel a certain kinship with this unknown reader, vandal though s/he might be. The second person is Kate McDonald, granddaughter of Montgomery and author of this literary cookbook. Within, you will find recipes for raspberry cordial (sans alcohol), plum pudding (sans mouse), and the cowcumber boats tested below.

This recipe is simple and good and belongs on one's potluck/summer picnic menu. Next time I will make smaller boats (bite-sized), nix the pasta and carrots, switch out the tuna for crab, and add fresh herbs … and diced shallots. My version is perhaps for the parents of this text's intended reader.

Figure 19.4
"Cowcumber Boats," *The Anne of Green Gables Cookbook*, for *The Tableaux Blog*, Canadian Literary Fare.

Figure 19.5
The Torontonians, for *The Tableaux Blog*, Canadian Literary Fare.

Post # 3: Barbecue, 4 September 2015

You are cordially invited to a cookout at the Whitney residence in Rowanwood, Toronto (roughly late 1950s). That this event is privately referred to by hosts Karen and Rick Whitney as "that bloody barbecue" should not deter you from enjoying a menu of steaks (the best that can be had), special rolls (only from the Patisserie Française), tossed salad with oil and vinegar dressing. And for dessert, "marvelous little rum cakes."[15]

Location: The fictional world of Phyllis B. Young's novel, *The Torontonians*.

Dress: "sports clothes." The lady of the house will be wearing "dark blue slim gabardine jeans and a full-sleeved blue silk shirt,"[16] and for her husband, nothing but a Jaeger shirt will do. If you're unsure, might we propose a slacks suit?

Please do not use the guest bedroom for intimate encounters with other peoples' husbands. Even if such other people are insufferable. It musses the sheets. Also, you will not find the packaging for the little rum cakes (ordered by mail from that store in Stratford) in the kitchen garbage. It has been cleverly hidden elsewhere.

Do, however, enjoy your taste of "Gracious Outdoor Living."[17] And be sure to mark the yearly winter tea on your calendars. There might well be cucumber sandwiches and little ice cakes.

....

What distinguishes *Tableaux* from its counterparts and contemporaries is its strictly Canadian content as well as the fact that this blogger is neither food stylist nor cook but reader *of* and writer *about* literature. In the end, it's necessarily about the stories.

Notes

1. Canadian Literary Fare is located at https://canadianliteraryfare.org/. Members of the research team hail from McGill University, Kwantlen Polytechnic University, and the University of British Columbia. Guest contributors to the website have also come from beyond these institutions.
2. And later, Montreal.
3. Cognard-Black and Goldthwaite, *Books That Cook*, 425.
4. McGee, *Writing the Meal*, 3.
5. Watson, *The Literary Tourist*, 13.

6 MacEwen, *A Breakfast for Barbarians*, 1.
7 Gopnik, *The Table Comes First*, 197.
8 Ibid., 198.
9 Owen, *Ten Dollars Enough*, iii.
10 Driver, *Culinary Landmarks*, 452.
11 Ibid., xxvi.
12 Driver, "Regional Differences in the Canadian Meal?," 202.
13 Bowen, "Edmonton Butter Tarts," 27.
14 *Oxford English Dictionary*, s.v. "cucumber." Accessed 3 November 2016. www.oed.com/.
15 Young, *The Torontonians*, 159.
16 Ibid., 157.
17 Ibid., 170.

Bibliography

Atwood, Margaret. *The Canlit Foodbook: From Pen to Palate: A Collection of Tasty Literary Fare*. Toronto: Totem Books, 1987.

– "Wilderness Tips." *Wilderness Tips*. New York: Doubleday, 1991.

Bowen, Lynne. "Edmonton Butter Tarts." In *The Great Canadian Literary Cookbook*, edited by Gwendolyn Southin and Betty Keller, 27. Sechelt, BC: Festival of the Written Arts, 1994.

Clarke, George Elliott. *Whylah Falls*. 10th anniversary ed. Vancouver: Polestar Book Publishers, 2000.

Cognard-Black, Jennifer, and Melissa A. Goldthwaite. *Books That Cook: The Making of a Literary Meal*. New York: New York University Press, 2014.

Coldwell, Joan. *Apples under the Bed: Recollections and Recipes from B.C. Writers and Artists*. Sidney, BC: Hedgerow Press, 2007.

Cook Book. Saskatoon: Women's Section, United Farmers of Canada Saskatchewan Section Ltd, 1940.

Couzyn, Jeni. "Preparation of Human Pie." *Life by Drowning: Selected Poems*. Toronto and Buffalo: House of Anansi Press, 1983.

Driver, Elizabeth. *Culinary Landmarks: A Bibliography of Canadian Cookbooks, 1825–1949*. Toronto: University of Toronto Press, 2008.

– "Regional Differences in the Canadian Meal? Cookbooks Answer the Question." In *What's to Eat? Entrées in Canadian Food History*, edited by Nathalie Cooke, 197–212. Montreal and Kingston: McGill-Queen's University Press, 2009.

Fried, Dinah. *Fictitious Dishes: An Album of Literature's Most Memorable Meals.* New York: Harper Design, an Imprint of HarperCollins, 2014.

Gopnik, Adam. *The Table Comes First: Family, France, and the Meaning of Food.* New York: Knopf, 2011.

LeCroy, Anne. "Cookery Literature or Literary Cookery." In *Cooking by the Book: Food in Literature and Culture,* edited by Mary A. Schofield. Bowling Green, OH: Bowling Green State University Popular Press, 1989.

Macdonald, Kate, and Barbara DiLella. *The Anne of Green Gables Cookbook.* Toronto: Oxford University Press, 1985.

MacEwen, Gwendolyn. *A Breakfast for Barbarians.* Toronto: Ryerson Press, 1966.

McGee, Diane E. *Writing the Meal: Dinner in the Fiction of Early Twentieth-Century Women Writers.* Toronto: University of Toronto Press, 2002.

Ondaatje, Michael. "Rat Jelly." *Rat Jelly.* Toronto: Coach House Press, 1973.

Owen, Catherine. *Ten Dollars Enough: Keeping House Well on Ten Dollars a Week; How It Has Been Done; How It May Be Done Again.* Boston: Houghton, Mifflin and Co., 1893.

Starnino, Carmen. "What My Mother's Hands Smell Like." *Credo.* Montreal and Kingston: McGill-Queen's University Press, 2000.

Thomas, Audrey Callahan. *Intertidal Life: A Novel.* New York: Beaufort Books, 1984.

Tremblay, Michel. *La traversee des sentiments: Roman.* Montreal: Lemeac, 2009.

Wah, Fred. *Diamond Grill.* 1st ed. Edmonton: NeWest, 1996.

Watson, Nicola J. *The Literary Tourist: Readers and Places in Romantic & Victorian Britain* Houndmills: Palgrave MacMillan, 2007.

Young, Kate. *The Little Library Cookbook: 100 Recipes from Your Favorite Books.* New York: Sterling Epicure, 2018.

Young, Phyllis B. *The Torontonians: A Novel.* Montreal and Kingston: McGill-Queen's University Press, 2007.

A ~~MEAT~~/MEETing in the Park

Ursula Johnson's *(re)al-location* and The Festival of Stewards

David Diviney and Melinda Spooner
(in conversation with Ursula Johnson)

On a cool, overcast day early in the summer of 2017, three hundred or so people gather beneath a large tent in MacIntosh Brook Campground on Cape Breton Island, Nova Scotia, to share a locally sourced meal and enjoy the varied stories and sounds of Unama'ki – loosely translated as the "Land of Fog" – the Mi'kmaq peoples' ancestral name for the island. Dozens of children wearing wildly coloured capes and masks run about the surrounding grassy fields, jumping through mud puddles, climbing trees, and blowing soap bubbles. Visitors of all ages and backgrounds wear patterned jumpsuits, aprons, and kerchiefs of similar fashion, adding an air of continuity, the appearance of a united culinary community in the buildup to the festivities. While waiting to eat, some take part in a nature walk to a nearby stream and waterfall where they learn about native aquatic life and play Waltes, an ancient Mi'kmaw dice game. Others sit patiently – listening to the tunes, catching up on old times, and meeting new friends. The aromas of barbequed moose kebabs, stir-fried field greens, and fish cakes waft across the grounds from a nearby tent where cooks and caterers huddle over their pots and busily tend to the fire pit. In these fleeting moments, born from a recipe of equal parts music, food, and fun, artist Ursula Johnson's *(re)al-location* begins to take shape.[1]

Ursula Johnson's feast, titled "The Festival of Stewards," functions as both a contemporary performance and a socially engaged artwork. As the culminating event of her year-long *(re)al-location* project (which, itself, was part of *Landmarks2017/Repères2017*, a network of contemporary art projects staged in Canada's national parks), The Festival of Stewards invites the audience to become socially involved through sharing in a meal and talking with one another.[2] A commonality is ignited and interpersonal connections emerge through this communal participation. This is representative of relational aesthetics – a contemporary artwork that invites viewers not only to look at a work of art but also to be a part of it, to actually experience it.

Figure 20.1 *Above*
Children playing at MacIntosh Brook Campground, 2017.

Figure 20.2 *Left*
Preparing stir-fried field greens for the communal meal, 2017.

Figure 20.3
Artist Ursula Johnson welcoming guests to The Festival of Stewards, 2017.

By eating food from the surrounding land and water, the viewer becomes an active participant in *(re)al-location*, sharing in relations with ecosystems, cultures, and traditions. The meal stands as metaphor for building a sustainable relationship with the environment and with one another.

A performance and installation artist of Mi'kmaw First Nation ancestry, Johnson has explored various mediums throughout her young career, including performance art, sculpture, music, and printmaking while utilizing delegated performers as well as collaborative processes in the making of new works. In 2017, she won the Sobey Art Award, Canada's pre-eminent prize for contemporary art, in recognition of her practice that was praised by the award's selection committee for redefining traditional materials while re-imagining colonized histories.[3] Her performances are often place-based and employ co-operative, didactic intervention. Within this, Johnson's ongoing interest in sustainability and consumption has led her to use food as an artistic medium and subject matter.[4]

In *(re)al-location*, Johnson engages the Mi'kmaw philosophy of *Netukulimk*, or self-sustainability, in a community-based examination of the natural and cultural ecologies of Nova Scotia's Cape Breton Highlands National Park past, present, and future. Having created several projects on memory, Johnson reflects, for this multimedia performance artwork, upon the memories that the forest carries of interactions between species and interactions between people. *(re)al-location* is rooted in an investigation of the historical relationships between the communities around Cape Breton Highlands National Park, including the Acadian (descendants of French colonists) and Scottish Gaelic peoples. This project also considers these relationships with respect to more difficult and recent histories, such as the tensions arising from the moose cull that took place on North Mountain only a few years earlier.[5] Johnson is particularly interested in understanding how these relationships have changed since the park was established in 1936, in part through the expropriation of land from the communities themselves. She is also curious to see whether those communities might be re-engaged with the park through a framework centred on the idea of stewardship.

Through community engagement and self-directed research, Johnson has sought through the multiple and interconnected components of *(re)al-location* to make visible the links between Cape Breton Highlands National Park, its natural resources, and the people living in the surrounding area. Over the course of a year, for example, she photographed the boreal forest and its seasonal changes. Her creative process for *(re)al-location* also involved several interactive community-based forums to promote more sustainable relationships with the environment and the people who live there. The resulting dialogue and photo documentation led to the development of a camouflage pattern – a gift to the community[6] – based upon the unique forest ecosystem of the Cape Breton Highlands. Project partners and audience members wore garments featuring this new pattern during the subsequent participatory performance event, The Festival of Stewards. At this celebratory feast, the wearing of the clothing and the consumption of food served as further physical embodiments of *(re)al-location*. In the sharing of a meal, a commonality was ignited and interpersonal relationships emerged.

A direct offshoot of *(re)al-location*, then, The Festival of Stewards was a cooperative intervention designed by Johnson in collaboration with students from Cabot Junior-Senior High School in Neil's Harbour. The daylong event was comprised of commissioned performances and contributions by local musicians, storytellers, visual artists, craftspeople, and chefs that engaged the area's natural and cultural histories. Project partners included Angie Arsenault (Sydney),[7] Adrianne Chapman-Gorey and Mike Gorey (Cape North), Maxim Cormier (Chéticamp), Chrissy Crowley (Margaree Forks), Grant Haverstock (Whycocomagh), Rebecca-Lynne MacDonald May and Geoffrey May (Dunvegan), Kyle Mischiek (Sydney), Jenessa Paul (Membertou), and Jason Roach (Chéticamp). The menu for the feast featured regional cuisine prepared by Salty Rose's & the Periwinkle Café (Ingonish) and moose meat provided by Kwilmu'kw Maw-klusuaqn, also known as the Mi'kmaq Rights Initiative.

By working in conversation with and across diverse communities, Johnson aims to (re)locate local knowledge and traditions to collectively address concerns related to natural resources and stewardship of the land. Thus, *(re)al-location* and The Festival of Stewards may be viewed as catalysts for discourse and social change.

The following dialogue with Ursula Johnson unfolded over approximately two years, beginning during the earliest stages of the development of *(re)al-location* and continuing through to the spring of 2018. The interview includes excerpts of pre-existing audio and video footage from Johnson's Banff Centre residency in November and December 2016 that have been reframed within a Q & A format and merged with a more recent conversation between the artist and curators David Diviney and Melinda Spooner. The resulting text reveals the layers of meaning in and between Johnson's *(re)al-location* and The Festival of Stewards.

MELINDA: *Perhaps we should start with this term "Netukulimk" as this is where things really stem from.*

DAVID: *According to the Unama'ki Institute of Natural Resources,* Netukulimk *is defined as "achieving adequate standards of community nutrition and economic well-being without jeopardizing the integrity, diversity, or productivity of our environment. As Mi'kmaq, we have an inherent right to access and use our resources and we have a responsibility to use those resources in a sustainable way."*[8]

MELINDA: *Ursula, could you briefly explain how this philosophy is so closely linked to notions of conservation and responsibility?*

Figure 20.4
Group portrait of The Festival of Stewards partners and collaborators, 2017.

URSULA: When someone has gone to practice *Netukulimk*, it is said that this person has gone into the forest to sustain themselves by living. But they are not going into the forest simply to live. They are entering into the forest to obtain resources in order to survive. These resources can be of a physical nature, including animal, plant, or mineral matter. But these resources can also be of a metaphysical nature. The intention of entering into *Netukulimk* means that the utmost care is taken in ensuring that your responsibility in the acknowledgement of these resources comes from the most sincere place possible … as well as understanding your intention … for obtaining these resources and doing so in a respectful way.

DAVID: *This philosophy was integrated into your examination of the site, Cape Breton Highlands National Park, and the resulting dialogue that you had with members of the surrounding communities.*

MELINDA: *This dialogue was centred on notions of responsibility and stewardship. As with much of your work, there's a sense of agency here. Could you touch upon this as it relates to the history of land expropriation?*

URSULA: Within the Cape Breton Highlands, one thing that is really interesting to me was this whole idea of expropriation, because a lot of national park systems in Canada were based upon expropriation. People had settled on that land and they were asked to move. Then a lot of the communities felt displaced. So, I am really interested in [the] intangible cultural history of these settlement groups that live around the area ... I am hoping to incite a conversation about how you use the land in the present day and what is your responsibility today with the land.

MELINDA: *So, what did your creative process look like? I'm thinking about the steps you took in producing the camouflage pattern based on the forest ecosystem.*

URSULA: The project started with a survey of the ecology of Cape Breton Highlands National Park. From that survey, I collected a number of different images and I took the photographs and turned them into drawings, abstracted a number of the drawings and the elements that were based upon the ecology of the Cape Breton Highlands, and I created this design. The Cape Breton Highlands is very foggy and often you can see the fog into the forest but the forest has a blue tinge to it, almost like a bluish-grey. And so, when you're looking at these photographs, what I did was I took a number of different elements from the different plants I was drawing. From those plants, I turned them into a number of different stencils. I kind of played with the idea of pattern creation. I took a map of Cape Breton Island and I was really interested in the negative space ... as positive space ... So, I took the drawing that I made tracing the Bras d'Or Lakes and kind of moved it around a number of different ways. I flipped it ... turned it around and reversed it and then kind of mixed it all up and then I ended up with this emblem ... this bright [letter] S and this kind of long bright-yellow emblem on it, and that was my starting point.

There's also a really great obsession in regards to superheroes, superhero movies. You know, comics, colouring books. So, I thought, keep it playful ... the design

Figure 20.5
Ursula Johnson's *(re)al-location* design pattern, 2017.

[has] a little of this superhero element, and I thought this was something that we could potentially market to the people who are interested in the superhero aspect of it. But it is also an *S*, kind of like "Stewards of the Environment." ... [This *S* emblem sparks] this idea of responsibility with regards to our own consumption and engage[s] people in conversation about ... where ... you play a role in ... conservation, ecological practices, [and] as a consumer within the market.

DAVID: *I also appreciate how this strategy intervenes in consumer culture. In using the trending Pantone colours for the spring 2017 season – Primrose Yellow, Pale Dogwood, Hazelnut, Island Paradise, Greenery, Flame, Pink Yarrow, Niagara, Kale, and Lapis Blue – you've created something that co-opts yet contests the influence of major brands over youth culture.*

MELINDA: *The new pattern was unveiled at The Festival of Stewards on apparel worn by project participants and given to community members. You conceptualized this event in collaboration with students from the Cabot Junior-Senior High School in*

Neil's Harbour, Nova Scotia. You also connected with the children who attended the feast through the playful superhero costumes designed with the "Stewards" emblem. Why is it important for you to work with and empower youth?

URSULA: In the past one hundred years, we've gone so far in technological advances. But, by the time you're in your forties ... when you're talking to a seven-year-old ... you say, "when you're in your forties, I can't even begin to think to tell you what your future is going to be like because we can't think that far ahead." Because today's the day we need to engage people in this conversation so that the people who are going to lead the way – ... the children who are being born at North Dakota right now, at Standing Rock – they're the ones who are going to lead the way [in which] we interact with our resources that nature provides.

DAVID: *The topic of consumption played a big role in your conversations with the students. Could you talk a bit about the multiple readings of this word and how this manifested in the work?*

URSULA: Well, consumption was something that was really important for me from the beginning of this project because we are looking at the natural ecology of the Cape Breton Highlands being changed due to the consumption of the forest by the moose.[9] So, I looked at a number of different ecological plans found throughout the world with regards to conservation, and oftentimes it seemed like when there was an invasive species, the best way to control that invasive species was with another invasive species ... And, normally what would happen in the ecology of the Cape Breton Highlands ... the wolves ... would have been the natural predators. But since the wolf population is no longer there, then I thought, well, what if we look at the next predator, which would be ... humans.

So, if we use the idea of consumption by humans consuming the moose then that would hopefully create a balance. And, this is also in line with what the Cape Breton Highlands National Park was thinking with regards to creating a moose cull harvest in certain areas as a pilot project. I was looking at ... things that were already in play and how we could play with it, and then when I talked to the kids from the Cabot School, we talked about consumption and how that could also tie into different things with regards to the moose consuming the forest and humans consuming the moose, but then it also brought us back to ideas of people getting together.

URSULA JOHNSON'S *(RE)AL-LOCATION* AND THE FESTIVAL OF STEWARDS

DAVID: *This kind of leads into the next question. In developing The Festival of Stewards, you talked about music, food, and fun being key ingredients – how so?*

URSULA: In the conversations that I had with the kids from Cabot School, we talked about that recipe of food, fun, and music, which has always brought people together for millennia. It doesn't matter what their cultural background is. If there is music, food, and some kind of fun activity, then it brings people together. And so, we started looking at this idea of creating a festival to celebrate consumption and … the resources that are there, but also the histories and heritages. We started talking about what type of heritages or different community groups were there and looked at the ideas of traditional foods.

DAVID: *And then there are the community collaborators and local vendors who, among other contributions, provided the food for the event.*

URSULA: We were looking at what type of traditional foods … came from the communities of the Acadian, the Mi'kmaq, and the Gaelic. The kids created a menu thinking about different traditional foods that they either tried or heard their families talking about. And so we created this menu that we sent to Salty Rose's & the Periwinkle Café in Ingonish and asked them if they were familiar with the food and if they could make it. And they were all, of course, very familiar with the food, and they were very happy to provide that food.

So, we figured we would serve local dishes made by local people and try to tie it in as much as possible with local resources that didn't come from too far away. We were looking at … sustainability and local harvesting within this topic of consumption.

MELINDA: *While the feast featured regional dishes like grilled chard and fish cakes, the barbequed moose was certainly the highlight. In this context, what was the significance of the moose?*

URSULA: Everybody in the Highlands area for hundreds of years has sustained themselves on moose meat, and so it was very important for me to look at those types of sustenance … [and] to be able to access moose that was harvested directly in that area because of the moose management project … I wanted to use the moose as … the main staple with regards to the meal and have it really kind of in a flashy way, have it shown and cooked.

DAVID: *You made special arrangements to serve moose meat. What were those? And why did it matter to you to have moose meat?*

URSULA: The moose was provided by Kwilmu'kw Maw-klusuaqn, or KMKNO,[10] which is working with the Department of Natural Resources and the park on the moose management project. And so, it all sort of ties in. It was really important for me to have the moose that was harvested from that cull and that project to be served to the people who maybe didn't have the opportunity to have a taste of that moose while that project was happening.

MELINDA: *As with the moose meat, every detail around the event was considered right down to the commissioning of a custom barbeque dubbed the "~~MEAT~~/MEET swing." This is an interesting play on words.*

URSULA: It was really important for me to work with the local artists in the Highlands, not only to have the musicians … or the caterers from the local area, but I had always had this dream of creating a custom spit or a barbeque grill. So, when I found Grant Haverstock, who is from Whycocomagh … I had several meetings with him … I think I made three or four trips down before we actually started to hash out the design. One of the things I brought to him was this idea of the community groups, being the Mi'kmaq, the Acadian, the Gaelic, and the Anglo communities, about how we could create something that tied everyone together. We were looking at ideas of different designs and maybe having cultural symbols or something, but I asked Grant to think of it in a bit more of a conceptual way with regards to the actual structure that we would be cooking the meat on. Instead of having ornamentation built into the design, what was something conceptually that could tie everyone in? And so, he thought about it for a bit and he came up with the concept of the "~~MEAT~~/MEET swing," which I thought was perfect because every household in the Cape Breton Highlands – it doesn't matter their ethnographic background – you know, everybody has a porch swing. And so, that's something that would tie them all in together, this idea of having a porch swing. It doesn't matter what your cultural group is … in Cape Breton you're always sitting on the porch swing waiting for the sunset while you're cooking your dinner.

Figure 20.6
Artist Ursula Johnson working the "MEAT/MEET swing" grill, 2017.

Notes

1 Descriptions of Johnson's *(re)al-location* found throughout this chapter appeared previously on the *Landmarks2017/Repères2017* website: www.landmarks2017.ca.

2 Johnson's *(re)al-location* and, in turn, The Festival of Stewards was part of *Landmarks2017/Repères2017*, a network of contemporary art projects staged in Canada's national parks that was a forum for collaboration, knowledge-sharing, negotiation of differing perspectives, Indigenous epistemologies, and the creation of new frameworks of understanding through a coordinated art curriculum in sixteen universities.

3 See "Nova Scotia Artist Ursula Johnson Wins $50K Sobey Art Award." Johnson graduated from the Nova Scotia College of Art and Design University (NSCAD) in 2006 and has since participated in over fifty exhibitions.

4 *Fine Dine* (2016–17), a collaboration between Johnson and her spouse and fellow artist Angella Parsons as the duo Kinuk, consists of a series of photographs that depict the artists in the act of eating. *Fine Dine* is made using an iPhone camera at a time when "food selfies" were just becoming a phenomenon on social media platforms. The artists are interested in exploring food consumption while subverting gendered stereotypes and notions of public and private space.

5 The conversation around the moose cull began in 2014 when Parks Canada engaged in a four-year project with the Unama'ki Institute of Natural Resources and other partners in an attempt to restore the boreal forest in Cape Breton Highlands National Park. This followed a 2012 interim arrangement between Parks Canada and the Mi'kmaq of Nova Scotia to collaborate on areas of mutual interest including cultural and natural resources, consultation, access/park entry, gathering of plants and other natural objects, and the establishment of advisory committees. The first moose cull was held in Cape Breton Highlands National Park in fall/winter 2015 and was marked by conflict between various communities, sparking the largest RCMP operation undertaken within the boundaries of a Canadian national park to date.

6 Barber, "The Gift in Littoral Art Practice."

7 For example, artist Angie Arsenault's contribution was titled *Haunting the Valley* and took the form of a commemorative garden installed on the grounds of the Keltic Lodge in Ingonish, Nova Scotia. This garden referenced crops grown by her ancestral family when it farmed the Clyburn Valley (pre–Cape Breton Highlands National Park) and was accompanied by a narrative relating local historical and familial information. See Arsenault, *Haunting the Valley*.

8 According to the website for Unama'ki Institute of Natural Resources in Cape Breton, Nova Scotia. UINR represents the five Mi'kmaw communities of Unama'ki–Eskasoni,

Membertou, Potlotek, Wagmatcook, and We'koqma'q, and was formed to address concerns regarding natural resources and their sustainability. See Unama'ki Institute of Natural Resources (UINR).

9 The maturation of the boreal forest has stalled due to over-browsing by an overabundant moose population (a subspecies that was reintroduced to Cape Breton Highlands National Park from Alberta in the 1940s) that eats approximately 50 to 60 per cent of the new growth. Over fifteen years of monitoring by staff and outside researchers has shown that the boreal forest is not recovering; rather it is quickly being converted to grasslands. These grasslands have now increased in size to the point where they have replaced nearly a third of what was once a boreal forest. These open areas are poor habitat for species that rely on boreal ecosystems, including species-at-risk like Bicknell's thrush, Canada lynx, and the American marten. See Government of Canada.

10 The mission of Kwilmu'kw Maw-klusuaqn Negotiation Office is to address the historic and current imbalances in the relationship between Mi'kmaq and non-Mi'kmaq people in Nova Scotia and secure the basis for an improved quality of Mi'kmaq life. See Mi'kmaq Rights Initiative.

Bibliography

Arsenault, Angie. *Haunting the Valley – A Commemorative Garden Installation* (blog), 22 June 2017. https://haunting-the-valley.tumblr.com.

Barber, Bruce. "The Gift in Littoral Art Practice." Conference paper presented at Symposium 2000, Christchurch, New Zealand, 10–13 November 2000. http://brucebarber.ca/index.php/the-gift.

[Diviney, David, Ariella Pahlke, and Melinda Spooner: a collective known as ACT]. "Ursula Johnson: Re(al)-location." *Landmarks2017/Repères2017*, Partners in Art, Toronto Dominion Bank, Government of Canada: A Canada 150 Signature Project. Accessed 31 January 2019. https://landmarks2017.ca/info/ursula-johnson/real-location/.

Government of Canada. "Cape Breton Highlands National Park." Parks Canada. Accessed 6 June 2018. www.pc.gc.ca/en/pn-np/ns/cbreton/decouvrir-discover/conservation/foret-forest/orignaux-moose.

Mi'kmaq Rights Initiative. "About Us." 2018. Accessed 6 June 2018. http://mikmaqrights.com/about-us.

"Nova Scotia Artist Ursula Johnson Wins $50K Sobey Art Award." *CBC News*, 25 October 2017. www.cbc.ca/news/entertainment/sobey-art-award-winner-1.4371486.

Unama'ki Institute of Natural Resources (UINR). "Netukulimk." 2018. Accessed 6 June 2018. www.uinr.ca/programs/netukulimk.

Figures

0.1 "Good Morning!" reprinted in Marshall McLuhan and Quentin Fiore, *The Medium Is the Massage*, produced by Jerome Agel. Corte Madera, CA: Gingko Press, 2001. With kind permission of Gingko Press and Mrs Jerome Agel. | 5

0.2 Douglas Coupland, *Gumhead*, 2014–15. Photograph courtesy of Dorothy Barenscott. | 11

0.3 Jay Cabalu, *De Los Reyes*, 2018. Photograph courtesy of David Koppe. | 12

0.4 Jay Cabalu, detail from *De Los Reyes*, 2018. Photograph courtesy of David Koppe. | 13

0.5 Lawrence Paul Yuxweluptun, *Haida Hot Dog*, 1984, acrylic on canvas. Courtesy of UBC Museum of Anthropology, Vancouver, Canada. Photograph courtesy of Paul Ohler. | 16

0.6 Maddy Shaw, *#remain*, 2016. Also known as *Brexit, a Still Life*. With permission of Maddy Shaw. | 17

0.7 Aislin [Terry Mosher], "Canadian No More? Get Serious." Editorial cartoon published in *The Ottawa Citizen*, 2014. With kind permission of Terry Mosher. | 19

1.1 Barry Pottle, *Starting the Feast*, 2012. Digital photograph courtesy of artist. | 33

1.2 Barry Pottle, *From the Community Freezer 1*, 2012. Digital photograph courtesy of artist. | 33

1.3 Barry Pottle, *Cutting Tuktu (Caribou)*, 2012. Digital photograph courtesy of artist. | 34

1.4 Barry Pottle, *Setting the Table*, 2012. Digital photograph courtesy of artist. | 34

FIGURES

1.5 Barry Pottle, *Mamaqtut (Delicious)*, 2012. Digital photograph courtesy of artist. | 35

1.6 Barry Pottle, *Kanon-ized*, 2012. Digital photograph courtesy of artist. | 36

3.1 Canadian Native Haute Cuisine team at the 1992 World Culinary Olympics. Robert Grains and Robert St-Onge, screenshot from *Going for the Gold* promotional film, 1993. | 60

3.2 Canadian Native Haute Cuisine entry from 1992 World Culinary Olympics: Impression of table display. Verband der Köche Deutschlands e.V., 1992. Reprinted with permission of photographer. | 62

3.3 Canadian Native Haute Cuisine entry from 1992 World Culinary Olympics: "Menu of the day from sea and forest." Wolfgang Usbeck, 1993, photograph. Reprinted in Verband der Köche Deutschlands e.V. *Kochkunst in Bilder*. Vol. 4. Stuttgart: Matthaes, 1993. | 63

3.4 Berta Skye with Danielle Medina at the award ceremony. Verband der Köche Deutschlands e.V., 1992. Reprinted with permission of photographer. | 65

5.1 Michael Farnan, *Beaver Candy*, and Leah Decter, *oh-oh canada*, 1 July 2016. Laura Margita, photographer. Courtesy of Gallery 101 archives. | 95

6.1 [Bear Pit illustration] Charles McKiernan, ca 1835–1889, *Joe Beef of Montreal, the Son of the People*, 1879 or 1880, Montreal. Courtesy of McGill Rare Books and Special Collections. | 123

6.2 Feeding the piglet at Au Lutin qui Bouffe, 18 October 1947. Courtesy of Ariel Buckley and her mother, Sarah Compton. (See http://time.com/13883/playing-with-food-posing-with-piglets-at-dinner/.) | 125

7.1 Sylvia Grace Borda, *Viskaalin Farm, Muhos, Oulu* from *Mise en Scene: Farm Tableaux*. Finland Google Street View Project, 2015. Courtesy of artist. | 147

7.2 Sylvia Grace Borda in collaboration with John M. Lynch, *Farm Tableaux*, 2013, photograph profiling Kevin Bose at Medomist Farm, Surrey, BC. Courtesy of artist. | 149

7.3 Sylvia Grace Borda in collaboration with John M. Lynch, *Farm Tableaux*, 2013, photograph profiling Pam Tamis at Rondriso Farms, Surrey, BC. Courtesy of artist. | 150

7.4 Sylvia Grace Borda in collaboration with John M. Lynch, *Farm Tableaux*, 2013, still image profiling the Zaklan Heritage Farms, Surrey, BC. Courtesy of artist. | 153

7.5 Sylvia Grace Borda in collaboration with John M. Lynch, *Farm Tableaux*, 2013, portrait taken at Medomist Farm, Surrey, BC. Courtesy of artist. | 154

FIGURES

8.1 Joachim Bueckelaer, *The Well-Stocked Kitchen*, 1566, oil on canvas. Courtesy of Rijksmuseum, Amsterdam. | 166
8.2 Carel Fabritius, *The Beheading of John the Baptist*, ca 1640–45, oil on canvas. Courtesy of Rijksmuseum, Amsterdam. | 167
8.3 Jan Asselijn, *The Threatened Swan*, ca 1650, oil on canvas. Courtesy of Rijksmuseum, Amsterdam. | 167
9.1 People's Food Security Bureau (Don and Cora Li-Leger), *Encyclopedia House*, 2015. Photograph courtesy of Don Li-Leger. | 185
9.2 PLOT planning, 2016. Photograph courtesy of Don Li-Leger. | 187
9.3 A family explores the garden, 2016. Photograph courtesy of Don Li-Leger. | 189
9.4 PLOT aerial view, June 2016. Larry Smith, photographer, 2016. Courtesy of Golden Eagle Aerial Photography. | 190
9.5 The free fruit stand, 2016. Photograph courtesy of Cora Li-Leger. | 193
9.6 PLOT garden beds, spring 2016. Photograph courtesy of Don Li-Leger. | 195
9.7 Sunday potluck lunch, 2016. Photograph courtesy of Don Li-Leger. | 195
10.1 Ghost River Theatre tasting, 2015. Photograph courtesy of Chris Malloy. | 202
10.2 Ghost River Theatre tasting with actor Joe Perry, 2015. Photograph courtesy of Chris Malloy. | 207
11.1 Douglas Coupland, File 177-17: Chewed Paper Samples, Douglas Coupland Fonds, Rare Books and Special Collections, University of British Columbia. | 220
11.2 Pieter van der Heyden, after Pieter Bruegel the Elder, *The Land of Cockaigne*, after 1570, engraving. Harris Brisbane Dick Fund, 1926. Metropolitan Museum of Art (www.metmuseum.org/art/collection/search/338703). | 223
12.1 Front cover of Janice Wong's *Chow*. Permission to reprint courtesy of Janice Wong. | 242
12.2 Original cover of the unpublished family version of *Chow*. Photograph courtesy of Janice Wong. | 253
12.3 Original photograph of Dennis Wong that appears in cropped form in Janice Wong's *Chow*. Photograph courtesy of Janice Wong. | 255
12.4 The Lotus Café neon sign. Photograph courtesy of Janice Wong. | 256
12.5 The Lotus Café matchbook cover. Photograph courtesy of Janice Wong. | 256
13.1 Elyse Bouvier, *Royal Cafe* installation, outside view, 2016. Photograph courtesy of artist. | 264

FIGURES

13.2 Elyse Bouvier, *Royal Cafe* installation, inside view, 2016. Photograph courtesy of artist. | 264

13.3 Elyse Bouvier, *Vulcan Royal Cafe*, 2010, instant photograph. Courtesy of artist. | 267

13.4 Elyse Bouvier, *Plate #2 – Peking Cafe*, 2015, digital photograph. Courtesy of artist. | 268

13.5 Elyse Bouvier, *Coffee at Chin's,* 2016, digital photograph. Courtesy of artist. | 269

13.6 Elyse Bouvier, *Lan in the Dragon Room*, 2015, digital photograph. Courtesy of artist. | 271

13.7 Elyse Bouvier, *Booth with Cups*, 2015, digital photograph. Courtesy of artist. | 271

13.8 Elyse Bouvier, *The Diana*, 2015, digital photograph. Courtesy of artist. | 272

13.9 Elyse Bouvier, *Lucky Cat Lucky Dragon*, 2015, digital photograph. Courtesy of artist. | 273

15.1 Jason Wright, *L'il Soldier (Phalanx)* and *Plating (I and II)*, 2008. Photograph courtesy of artist. | 299

15.2 Jason Wright, *Always Fresh (The Donut Farmer)*, 2008. Photograph courtesy of artist. | 301

15.3 Jason Wright, *Dogs' Dinner* (detail), 2015. Photograph courtesy of artist. | 303

15.4 Jason Wright, *Tragedy of Open-Faced St Sebastians or The Sacrifice of Artisanal Sandwiches for the Redemption of the Ethical Glutton* (detail), 2013. Photograph courtesy of artist. | 304

17.1 Sandee Moore, *It's Hard to Have an Original Idea without Just Regurgitating Other People's Art*, 2011; collection of the artist. Photograph courtesy of Dunlop Art Gallery. | 334

17.2 Sandee Moore, *In Sick & Hunger*, 2000; collection of the artist. Photograph courtesy of Sean Whalley. | 337

17.3 Sandee Moore, *In Sick & Hunger*, 2011; collection of the artist. Photograph courtesy of Audrey-Anne Ross. | 337

17.4 Sandee Moore, *Imaginary Gift*, 2011; collection of the artist. Photograph courtesy of William Eakin. | 339

17.5 Sandee Moore, *Imaginary Gift*, 2011; collection of the artist. Photograph courtesy of William Eakin. | 339

17.6 Sandee Moore, *The Taste of Someone Else's Mouth*, 2003 [Version 1]; collection of the artist. Photograph courtesy of artist. | 342

17.7 Sandee Moore, *The Taste of Someone Else's Mouth*, 2003 [Version 2]; collection of the artist. Photograph courtesy of artist. | 342

17.8 Sandee Moore, *It's Hard to Have an Original Idea without Just Regurgitating Other People's Art*, 2011; collection of the artist. Photograph courtesy of Dunlop Art Gallery. | 343

19.1 *Traversée des Sentiments*, food and photograph by Alexia Moyer for *The Tableaux Blog*, Canadian Literary Fare. Courtesy of photographer. | 365

19.2 "Kanadian Eggs," *The CanLit Foodbook*, food and photograph by Alexia Moyer for *The Tableaux Blog*, Canadian Literary Fare. Courtesy of photographer. | 368

19.3 "Edmonton Butter Tarts," *The Great Canadian Literary Cookbook,* food and photograph by Alexia Moyer for *The Tableaux Blog*, Canadian Literary Fare. Courtesy of photographer. | 371

19.4 "Cowcumber Boats," *The Anne of Green Gables Cookbook*, food and photograph by Alexia Moyer for *The Tableaux Blog*, Canadian Literary Fare. Courtesy of photographer. | 372

19.5 *The Torontonians*, food and photograph by Alexia Moyer for *The Tableaux Blog*, Canadian Literary Fare. Courtesy of photographer. | 372

20.1 Children playing at MacIntosh Brook Campground, 2017. Photograph courtesy of Jaron Felix. | 377

20.2 Preparing stir-fried field greens for the communal meal, 2017. Photograph courtesy of Jaron Felix. | 377

20.3 Artist Ursula Johnson welcoming guests to The Festival of Stewards, 2017. Photograph courtesy of Jaron Felix. | 378

20.4 Group portrait of The Festival of Stewards partners and collaborators, 2017. Photograph courtesy of Jaron Felix. | 381

20.5 Ursula Johnson's *(re)al-location* design pattern, 2017. Image courtesy of artist. | 383

20.6 Artist Ursula Johnson working the "~~MEAT~~/MEET swing" grill, 2017. Photograph courtesy of Jaron Felix. | 387

Contributors

DOROTHY BARENSCOTT is an art historian whose research relates to the interplay between urban space and emerging technology and media forms in the articulation of a range of identities. She teaches modern and contemporary art history and theory in Kwantlen Polytechnic University's Fine Arts Department. Her essays have appeared in journals such as *Postmodern Culture Journal*, *Invisible Culture*, *History and Memory*, and *Mediascape*, with examinations of painted panoramas, experimental and mainstream cinema, architecture, and conceptual photography. She regularly contributes art writing to exhibition catalogues and leads interdisciplinary student groups on field schools to global art cities. (www.dorothybarenscott.com)

JES BATTIS teaches literature and creative writing at the University of Regina. Areas of research and teaching include medieval and eighteenth-century literature, LGBTQ studies, and neurodiversity. Work-in-progress includes a monograph on wizardry and medievalism in YA texts, and a mystery novel that focuses on Arthurian mythology. He/they is also the author of the Occult Special Investigator series and Parallel Parks series, both with Ace/Penguin.

SYLVIA GRACE BORDA is an artist-lecturer. She has exhibited internationally for over fifteen years and presented her work at Northern Ireland and Scottish collateral Venice architectural events. She received the Lumen Prize for Digital Art (2016) and was the recipient of the EU-funded "Frontiers in Retreat" Arts Fellowship (2013–17) for which she created ecological artworks in Finland, Latvia, and Scotland. She was the inaugural artist-in-residence at Kwantlen Polytechnic University (2018) and is founder of CARE – Climate Arts for Resilient Environments (2019). (www.sylviagborda.com)

CONTRIBUTORS

ELYSE BOUVIER is a Western-Canadian artist based in Calgary with an MFA in documentary media from Ryerson University (2016) and a BCom from Mount Royal University (2010). Her practice explores ideas around Albertan and Canadian identity, particularly through the lens of food culture, such as in her project *Royal Cafe: Chinese-Western in Alberta*. Recently, she launched *Independent Study* (ongoing), a pop-up art bookstore that seeks to foster a culture of art books in the city. When not participating in the arts community in Calgary, she can be found exploring rural roads in her trusty Volvo. (elysebouvier.com)

SHELLEY BOYD is a Canadian literature specialist in the Department of English and an associate dean of the Faculty of Arts at Kwantlen Polytechnic University. She is the author of *Garden Plots: Canadian Women Writers and Their Literary Gardens* (2013). Her food-related research has touched on a variety of topics – from Thanksgiving traditions (in *What's to Eat? Entrées in Canadian Food History*) to experiential learning in the literature classroom (in *CuiZine*). Her more recent publications examine food scares in Canadian drama (in *Studies in Canadian Literature*) and utopian/dystopian meals in Margaret Atwood's fiction (in *Utopian Studies* and *The Good Gardener? Nature, Humanity, and the Garden*).

NATHALIE COOKE is professor of English and associate dean of the Library (Rare and Special Collections) at McGill University. Her publications focus on the shaping of Canadian culinary and literary taste. She is founding editor of *CuiZine: The Journal of Canadian Food Cultures* (2008–) and editor of *What's to Eat? Entrées in Canadian Food History* (2009). Most recently, she is co-editor of *Catharine Parr Traill's "The Female Emigrant's Guide": Cooking with a Canadian Classic* (Carleton Library Series 2017).

HEIDI TIEDEMANN DARROCH holds a PhD from the University of Toronto and teaches at Camosun College in Victoria. She has published on Atwood, Munro, trauma, Canadian theatre, and teaching-stream faculty roles. She has work forthcoming on reconciliation discourse and Canadian writing instruction.

GLENN DEER teaches Canadian literature, Asian North American literature, and cultural studies in the Department of English Language and Literatures at the University of British Columbia, Vancouver. He is the author of *Postmodern Canadian*

Fiction and the Rhetoric of Authority (McGill-Queen's University Press) and is currently an associate editor for *Canadian Literature*. Along with Chris Lee and Marissa Largo, he guest edited a special issue of *Asian Diasporic Visual Cultures and the Americas*: *Beyond Canada 150: Asian Canadian Visual Cultures* (2018). His teaching has included several graduate seminars on "Eating the Text," and culinary interests run in his family: "My father was a chef at one of Edmonton's most popular Chinese Canadian restaurants: The Seven Seas."

DAVID DIVINEY is the senior curator at the Art Gallery of Nova Scotia. He previously held the positions of assistant curator at the Southern Alberta Art Gallery and director of the artist-run centre Eye Level Gallery. He has also taught courses at the Alberta College of Art and Design, University of Lethbridge, Thompson Rivers University, and Sheridan College Institute of Technology and Advanced Learning. He participated in the Canada Council for the Arts Asia-Pacific Visual Arts Delegation in 2014 and is a three-time curatorial panelist for the Sobey Art Award.

MARGERY FEE, PHD, FRSC, is a professor emerita of English at the University of British Columbia. Her recent publications are *Literary Land Claims: The "Indian Land Question" from Pontiac's War to Attawapiskat* (Wilfrid Laurier University Press, 2015), *Tekahionwake: E. Pauline Johnson's Writings on Native North America* (Broadview, 2016), co-edited with Dory Nason, and *Polar Bear* (Reaktion, 2019). With Daniel Heath Justice, she is co-investigator on the SSHRC-funded project The People and the Text, led by Deanna Reder.

ANGELA FERREIRA is a PhD performance studies student at the University of Alberta with a focus on post-dictatorship Portuguese theatre and female representation on stage. She holds a BA (theatre/French) from the University of British Columbia and MFA (interdisciplinary studies) from Simon Fraser University. She has presented papers in Canada, United States, and Europe. She is a theatre director, playwright, and co-founder of the theatre company Theatre Elsewhere. (www.theatreelsewhere.com)

L. SASHA GORA is a cultural historian with a focus on food studies. Since 2015 she has taught North American history at Ludwig Maximilian University of Munich.

CONTRIBUTORS

She completed her doctoral studies at the Rachel Carson Center and is currently working on her first manuscript titled *Culinary Claims: A Cultural History of Indigenous Restaurants in Canada*. As a writer, her work has been featured in publications such as *Gather*, *C Magazine*, VICE, BBC *Travel*, and *Chickpea*, and she has given lectures at art institutions such as Haus der Kulturen der Welt, Berlin, and the Centre for Contemporary Arts, Glasgow. (www.lsashagora.com)

Founded in 2015 by artists and avid gardeners CORA LI-LEGER and her late husband DON LI-LEGER, the People's Food Security Bureau (PFSB) strives to integrate art and life through food. With art at the centre of all aspects, PFSB advocates artisanal agriculture, home cooking, and living in the oneness of all things. Other projects include *Encyclopedia House* and participation in *Window Dressing, Cabinets of Curiosity*, both staged in the Newton Town Centre of Surrey, BC. Well known as a painter and printmaker, Don's work also involved sound and moving image. A retired art therapist, Cora's art is informed by an ongoing interest in human behaviour and close observations of the natural world. (www.corali-leger.com)

SANDEE MOORE proposes to animate social relationships through personal exchange via artwork in media such as performance, video, installation, and interactive electronic sculpture. She has screened and exhibited across Canada and in Japan. She earned her BFA (Honours) from the University of Victoria and MFA in intermedia from the University of Regina. Following her education, she has worked variously as an arts administrator, writer, and university instructor in Winnipeg, Surrey, and, currently, Regina.

ALEXIA MOYER holds a PhD in *études anglaises* from Université de Montréal. Having completed an FQRSC post-doctoral fellowship with McGill's Department of English and McGill's Institute for the Study of Canada, she now runs a collective of scholarly editors called redline-lignerouge. She is a member of Editors Canada. (www.redline-lignerouge.ca)

BARRY POTTLE is an Inuk artist originally from Nunatsiavut in Labrador (Rigolet), now living in Ottawa, Ontario. He has worked with the Indigenous arts community for many years, particularly in the city of Ottawa. He has always been interested in photography as a medium of artistic expression and as a way of exploring the world around him. Living in Ottawa, which has the largest urban population of

Inuit outside the North, he has been able to stay connected to the greater Inuit community. Through the camera's lens, he showcases the uniqueness of this community. (www.barrypottle.com)

WENDY ROY is a professor of Canadian literature at the University of Saskatchewan. Her books include *The Next Instalment: Serials, Sequels, and Adaptations of Nellie L. McClung, L.M. Montgomery, and Mazo de la Roche* (2019), *Maps of Difference: Canada, Women, and Travel* (2005), and the co-edited collection *Listening Up, Writing Down, and Looking Beyond: Interfaces of the Oral, Written, and Visual* (2012). She has published essays on writers, including Margaret Atwood, Margaret Laurence, and Carol Shields, and her current research is on dystopian and apocalyptic fiction by Canadian women. She is past president of the Association for Canadian and Quebec Literatures/ l'Association des littératures canadienne et québécoise.

ASMA SAYED is a Canada Research Chair in South Asian Literary and Cultural Studies at Kwantlen Polytechnic University. Her numerous articles have appeared in various academic anthologies and journals such as *Canadian Review of Comparative Literature* and *South Asian Review*. She has edited or co-edited five books, which include *The Transnational Imaginaries of M.G. Vassanji* (2018); *Screening Motherhood in World Cinema* (2016); *M.G. Vassanji: Essays on His Works* (2014); and *Writing Disapora: Transnational Memories, Identities, and Cultures* (2014).

SEBASTIAN SCHELLHAAS studied ethnology, philosophy, and art history at Goethe University Frankfurt where he specialized in the anthropology of food. After graduating in 2011, he curated The World in a Spoon at the Weltkulturen Museum in Frankfurt and edited the subsequent volume *Die Welt im Löffel. Kochen – Kunst – Kultur*. He has been a scholarship holder and research fellow at Goethe University Frankfurt where he also wrote his dissertation on Indigenous gastronomy in Canada. Alongside his academic career, he is part of the gastronomic-art project Freitagsküche (freitagskueche.de) where he worked as a chef.

MELINDA SPOONER is a part-time faculty member at NSCAD University. Previously, she taught at the University of Lethbridge and Thompson Rivers University. She teaches courses in the master's of art education, fine art, and foundation studies departments. For more than two decades, she has been active in socially engaged practice, collaboration, and site-specificity. She was a co-curator for the national project *LandMarks* (https://partnersinart.ca/projects/landmarks2017-reperes2017/). Her recent projects include The REgeneration Project (2020) and Shorelines – Creating Community (2016) (www.shorelines.prospectcommunities.com/). She recently presented at the 2019 Conference on the Arts in Society, Lisbon, and the 2017 Culture, Sustainability, and Place Conference, University of the Azores.

ZOE TENNANT is an award-winning producer, writer, and journalist. Her work has been published and broadcast by the Canadian Broadcasting Corporation, *Granta*, *The Walrus, Monocle,* and *The Globe and Mail*, among others. She was the founding associate editor of the Canadian edition of the scholarly journalism site *The Conversation*. She's an alumna of the University of British Columbia's Graduate School of Journalism, and the Reporting in Indigenous Communities program. She works at CBC and teaches at the Ryerson School of Journalism. She sees food as a lens for exploring questions that lie at the intersection of identity, colonialism, place, and power. (www.zoetennant.com)

JASON WRIGHT is an artist and educator based in Vancouver. He received a BFA in visual arts from Simon Fraser University, an MFA in sculpture from the University of Regina, and a BEd in art education from the University of British Columbia. His current work focuses on art-educational practice, and he has presented his research at the most recent NAEA and INSEA conferences. He is currently an instructor for Arts Umbrella, the Vancouver School Board, and Kwantlen Polytechnic University. (www.jasonwright.ca)

Index

A&W (restaurant), 328–9
abject (the): and the body, 346n20; and food, 334, 341; and horror, 306; theory of, 340, 343, 346n16, 346n23
Aboriginal Culinary Arts Class, 67
Aboriginal Culinary Team Canada (ACTC), 68
Aboriginal Peoples Television Network (APTN), 96
Acadian, 379, 385–6
Adrià, Ferran, 204
African Asian literature, 282–3
agri-art, 115, 146–57
agriculture, 102, 146–7, 151–3, 156–61. *See also* farming
Air India bombing, 281, 292n34
Aislin. *See* Mosher, Terry
Alberta, 7, 20, 106, 200–10, 244, 259n8, 263–76
alphabet: and Coupland, 226, 228–30, 235n65; as a form, 225
American consumerism, 214, 221–3, 228
American popular culture, 99–100
anecdote, 309, 335; in culinary memoir, 243; and food history, 121, 125–6, 128; as literary form, 118, 333–4, 346n23; Pratt and, 350
Anglo-American culinary influence, 13–14, 82–8, 175, 196, 226–30, 279, 300, 311, 345n7
Anishinaabe food, 83
Anthropocene, 314
Appadurai, Arjun, 86–7n15, 278, 285–6
Aristotle: on rhetoric, 246–7, 260n16; on tragedy, 207
Artaud, Antonin, 206
Ashkenazi Jews, 127–8, 138n56; matzoh ball soup, 131
Asian Canadian, 243–4, 259n8, 268, 274. *See also* Chinese restaurants
Asselijn, Jan: *The Threatened Swan*, 165–7, 173

Atwood, Margaret: *The CanLit Foodbook*, 367; *The Edible Woman*, 15, 138–9n62; "Wilderness Tips," 364, 366
Au Lutin qui Bouffe (restaurant), 124–5
Au Petit Poucet (restaurant), 124
Au Pied de Cochon (restaurant), 104, 120, 124
Au Pied de Cochon Sugar Shack, 104–5
avant-garde, 16, 21, 156, 157n7; and the alphabet form, 225; *Generation X*, 214, 221, 233–4n49; the Vancouver School, 158–9n13

baking: bannock, 81; in a beaver tail, 107n1; butter tarts, 370; *The Great Canadian Baking Show*, 7–8; Munro and, 350, 353–4; Pratt and, 352–4
Banff Centre, 341, 380
barbeque (or barbecue): beaver, 105; Johnson and, 376, 385–7; moose, 104; PLOT and, 186; in small towns, 317, 320, 329; in *The Torontonians*, 373; Wright and, 295–6, 298–9
Barthes, Roland: on death and the image, 154; on food and communication, 9–10, 247; on the gift, 341, 343; on myth, 222, 225, 227; on "nutritional consciousness," 223; on "totem foods," 226
Barton, Bruce, 200, 209
bear: behaviour, 41; in *Canada Picture No. 6*, 216; as chocolate centrepiece, 64; in Indigenous stories, 29, 37–50; in Joe Beef canteen, 123–4; in *The Kids in the Hall*, 318; in queer culture, 322–4, 327–8
beaver: as fish, 98; and fur trade, 109n46; as Indigenous food, 95–7; meat, 29, 41, 63, 93–4, 106–7; as national symbol, 18, 93–4, 99–101; in political cartoons, 18; recipes for, 51n18, 103–5; and restaurants, 102–3; in soup, 64, 73n27, 95; in *Stanley Park*, 180n31

INDEX

BeaverTails, 93, 105
beer: as accompaniment to ginger beef, 275n5; as Canadian, 19, 122, 226; and desire, 327; as masculine, 316–17; Molson Canadian advertisements, 99; Montreal's craft beer scene, 120; stubby bottles, 227. *See also* Molson Canadian
Bellerose, Pierre, 126–7
Bennett, Jane, 312–13
Ben Wong Restaurant, 265
berry picking, 40, 42, 317
Black Lives Matter, 327
blogs: *CanLitFare*, 368; food and, 366, 368; *Tableaux*, 309, 364–5; 366, 368, 371–3; tourism and, 126, 136n21
Bonavista Biennale, 31
Bose, Kevin, 149–50
Bourdain, Anthony, 244, 23n19; on beaver meat, 93; *Parts Unknown*, 8, 23n18, 104
Bourdieu, Pierre, 82, 214, 217, 232n23, 315
Brexit, 17–18, 25n51
Brillat-Savarin, Jean Anthelme, 6, 77, 244, 248, 260n18
British Columbia, 17, 40–7, 51n17, 64, 69-70, 81–2, 96, 102, 163, 183–98, 224, 317
bubble gum: as artistic material, 298, 341; on Coupland's *Gumhead*, 11–12
Bueckelaer, Joachim, 174; *The Well-Stocked Kitchen*, 164, 166, 179–80n21
Bunn-O-Matic, 269
Burger King (restaurant): poutine, 236n84; and Tim Hortons, 18–19
Burke, Kenneth, 246
Burry, Hans, 134
butter tart, 119, 369–71

Cabalu, Jay, 10; *De Los Reyes*, 12–14
Campbell's Cream of Mushroom soup, 296
Canada Day: and Canada 150, 58, 214; the Centennial, 119; *Landmarks2017/Repères2017*, 376; *oh-oh canada*, 93, 95, 100; *Souvenir of Canada*, 213–14
Canadian Broadcasting Corporation (CBC): 102, 277
Canadian Literary Fare, 364–5, 368, 371–2
Canadian literature, 162, 309, 364, 367–8
Canadian Native Haute Cuisine, 60–3, 66–7, 70
Canadian Tourism Commission (CTC), 61
Cape Breton Highlands National Park, 309, 379, 382, 384, 388n5, 388n7, 389n9

Cape Breton Island (NS), 376, 382, 386
Carl, James: *Spring Collection*, 216, 232n19
Catholic Church, 296; and beaver, 98; mass, 37; and Montrealers, 126, 132; *Plating I and II*, 299; and spectacle, 297; St Sebastian, 304–5
Caudron, Remi, 81
Cayuga foodways, 65
Certificate of Head Tax Exemption, 253
Cézanne, Paul, 259n6
Charles, Jeremy, 8
Chauvet, George, 60, 62
cheese: as Canadian, 226–7, 263, 266; cheesecake, 319–20, 326–7; poutine, 133
Chicago School of Media Theory, 3
Child, Julia, 244,
Chilliwack (BC), 147, 319–20, 325
Chin, Frank, 279–80, 291n11
Chinatown: Montreal, 125–6, 128, 133, 136n20; Toronto, 263; Vancouver, 175
Chinese Canadian. *See* Asian Canadian
Chinese restaurants: 211, 241, 244–5, 254–7; 259n8; Chinese-Western, 259n8, 263, 265–70, 273–4, 275n2, 275n5, 284; and Christmas, 128; Jewish community and, 128, 137n39; Montreal, 133
Chinook Wawa, 69, 176
Cho, Lily, 244–5, 266, 274, 284
Chopped (TV series), 58, 311–12, 315
Chopped Canada (TV series), 58
Chrétien, Jean, 127
Christmas: Anglo-Canadian, 351; Buddy's gay bar, 320; and Chinese food, 128, 257; and country food, 35; fruitcake, 353–4; and Pratt's *Christmas Turkey*, 357; in *Stanley Park*, 171
Citrus (restaurant), 133–4
City of Surrey, 159n17, 183
Clover Valley Organic Farm, 151–2, 157
Coast Salish, 16, 68, 81, 163
Cockaigne, 222–4, 234n57
cod: Atlantic, 229; as Canadian, 226; fishing moratorium, 8; threatened, 229. *See also* fish
coffee: Chinese cafés, 257, 269, 273–4; and community building, 194, 315, 326; as gift, 340; on Indigenous restaurant menus, 85; *The Kids in the Hall*, 317–20; small towns and, 319–20; Starbucks, 300; Tim Hortons, 18–19, 25n54, 300
coffee shop: 254, 317–20, 322. *See also* coffee

coffee-table book, 211; Coupland, 213, 216–17, 219, 221, 224, 226, 229–31; as genre, 214–15, 218, 227, 231n8, 246
community building: and contemporary performance, 376, 379, 383, 385–6; and Inuit, 31, 35–6; and queer, 315, 318–19, 320, 322, 325–8; and relational aesthetics, 335–6; and South Asians, 277–8, 282–4, 287, 289–90
community engagement: and Johnson, 379; and PLOT, 183–4, 192–7; and restaurateurs, 122–4
conceptual art, 10, 12, 25n51, 158n13, 218, 386
Confederation: 135th anniversary, 213n4; 150th anniversary, 58, 214; "Confederation Beaver" recipe, 104–6
consumerism, 14–15, 129, 204, 213–31, 233n49, 304, 306, 351, 383–4
Cook, Inez, 81
cookbooks, 7, 29, 139n63, 215, 246, 333, 353; beaver, 94–7, 99, 101–6; blogs, 366; culinary memoir, 242–4, 247–50, 258; Indigenous, 51n18, 57–8, 60, 70, 73n28, 79–80, 94–5, 97, 102, 105; as literature, 366–72; of Montreal, 115, 118–19, 131; of South Asian diaspora, 278–9; and television, 296, 307n1
Cook It Raw Alberta: The Shaping of a Culinary Frontier, 58, 106
Coulthard, Glen, 79, 82, 86n3
counter-cuisine, 211, 219, 221; in *Generation X*, 222–4; in *Souvenir of Canada*, 224–5, 227–31
counter-environment: Canada as, 221; Coupland and, 219; and food, 14–15; McLuhan and, 4, 22n6
country food: beaver as, 94, 97, 107; Indigenous food as, 94; and Indigenous peoples, 9, 29, 31–6
Coupland, Douglas, 10, 14; book sculptures, 213, 218–19; *Generation X*, 213–14, 219–24, 228; *Gumhead*, 10–13; as restaurant reviewer, 217–18, 230; *Souvenir of Canada* series, 211, 213–17, 224–31
Couzyn, Jeni, 367
cowcumber boats, 370–2
culinary memoir, 211, 242–5, 247–50, 256, 259n8, 259–60n9
Culinary Olympics, 29, 58–71, 97
culinary tourism, 61, 115, 245; in Montreal, 120–2, 125–8. *See also* tourism
Cunningham, Imogen, 252

Dammann, Derek, 103–5
Davie Street Village (Vancouver, BC), 320–3, 328, 331n17
Deleuze, Gilles, 313
Demers, Pierre, 134
Denny's (restaurant), 297; "Gay Denny's," 320–1, 328
Derrida, Jacques: on anecdote, 333; on the gift, 338
Dhalwala, Meeru, 243
Diamond, Albert, 61
Diana camera, 265, 267
diaspora, 17, 211; culinary art, 259n8, 277–8, 280, 286, 290; displacement, 243; farmers, 155; food, 277; space, 270. *See also* South Asian
diet: Canadian 94, 226–7; Inuit country food, 31; locavore, 80–1; 100-mile, 9, 43, 80–1; Paleolithic, 43; religious prohibitions, 98, 285
Diners, Drive-Ins, and Dives (TV series), 315
dinner party: Chilean, 230; moose spaghetti sauce, 228; as queer meal, 324; reflection on, 295
Dion, Céline, 8, 127
domesticity, 20, 139n63, 296, 348–53, 358
Douglas, Mary, 247, 288
Dreyfuss, Richard, 128–9
Dryden, Ken, 127
Duncan, Dorothy, 99, 101

Eagleton, Terry, 17, 218
ecocriticism, 115, 163, 176
ekphrasis, 165–7, 178n3, 179n13, 180n28, 256–7
encyclopedia: as artistic form, 225, 228; *The Encyclopedia House*, 184–5, 194
Escoffier, Auguste, 59
excess: consumer culture, 221, 316, 319, 338, 343–4; feminine, 356–7; queer body, 324
Expo 67: Canadian culinary culture, 95–6, 119; world's chefs, 133–4

Fabritius, Carel: *The Beheading of John the Baptist*, 165, 167
Facebook: food pornography, 291n11; Shaw's #remain, 17, 25n51
family restaurant, 248, 270, 296–7, 306, 318. *See also* individual restaurants by name
farmers' markets: in culinary memoir, 244; Newton, BC, 184, 197; Regina, 300–1; Vancouver, 168

INDEX

farming, 81–3, 102, 146–59, 183–4, 201, 224, 265, 300–2, 319, 326, 369. *See also* agriculture
FarmVille, 155
Farnan, Michael, 100, 107n4; *Beaver Candy*, 93–5
fast food, 18–19, 329
Feast Café Bistro, 78
female body: 15, 355–8
Ferri, Raymond, 134
Finley's Rhododendrons, 152, 157
Fiore, Quentin, 4–5
fish: fish farms, 17, 170, 229; Indigenous foodways and, 9, 31, 35, 64, 81; in Indigenous stories, 41, 44, 46; in literature, 365–6, 368; in painting, 16–17, 349–50; in performance, 385. *See also* cod; salmon
Fisher, M.F.K., 244, 260n18
Fong, Matthias, 201, 209
food: as comfort, 216, 224, 250, 266, 278, 285, 295, 348–9; as human need, 162, 183, 193–4; as language, 7, 9–10, 15–18, 131–2, 218, 316; in literature, 129–31, 364; as multimodal media 4, 9–12, 14–20, 211, 242, 249, 255–6
foodie: anti-foodie, 335; culture, 215; photography, 366; as restaurant patron, 58, 71; as traveller, 120; trends, 29; Vancouver, 304, 306
food photography, 4, 17–18, 226, 241, 244–6, 252–5, 302, 356, 364–73
food pornography, 291n11, 312; absence from online queer culture, 323; and South Asian writers, 279–80
foodscape: Canada, 18, 68, 211; definition of, 78, 86–7n15; of France, 366; as related to restaurants, 78, 85; across time, 115
food security, 8–9, 31–2, 58, 151–2, 158n8, 187, 196
foodways: Canadian, 7–9, 22n12, 99, 242–3; in literary genres, 243, 245, 247, 278, 369; Montreal, 117–35; Newfoundland, 8–9; Quebec, 133; regional, 95, 102; Western world, 140n78. *See also* immigrant foodways; Indigenous foodways
Forage (restaurant), 81–2
Freitag, Amanda, 312
Fritz (restaurant), 321
Fussell, Betty, 17

Gairns, Robert, 61
Gallop, Jane, 333

Gandhi, Indira, 281, 286, 292n34
gardening, 185, 194; guerrilla gardening, 183
gastro-politics, 286
Genaille, Ben, 68, 71
gender: conventions, 15, 20, 226, 298, 352–5, 388n4; and food, 162, 165–8, 172, 177, 244, 277–9, 290, 295–6; 306; and power, 79, 322, 348; and space, 164, 177, 211; violence, 309, 349, 356–8
George Jr, Andrew, 60–4, 66–7, 69 70, 72n2, 79–80, 86n4, 97, 105
Ghost River Theatre, 115, 200–2, 206–7, 209
gift theory, 338, 340–1, 343
Gilbert, Sandra M., 4–6, 15, 17, 119, 244, 259n6, 349
ginger beef: Alberta, 20, 266–8; Bouvier and, 263, 267–8, 274; Calgary, 275
gingerbread, 336–8
Gitk'san Nation, 97
glossary, 217; relationship to tongue, 221–2
The Golden Girls (TV series), 319–20
Goldsworthy, Andy, 190, 198n3
Google Street View, 115, 146–57; Trusted Photographer, 147–8, 157
Google Trekker, 148
Goya, Francisco, 244, 259n6
The Great Canadian Baking Show (TV series), 7–8
Great Canadian Cookbook, 296
Green, Laurel, 203, 209
Greenberg, Clement, 219
Griffith, Colwyn: *Eye Candy 3*, 216, 232n19; *Inglis Manitoba*, 232n19; *Northern Lights*, 232n19
Grindr, 323
grocery store: in art, 216; in the imagination, 324; in literature, 281–3, 290. *See also* supermarket
grotesque, 211; Cabalu and, 14; Coupland and, 12, 222–4; Wright and, 295, 297–9, 302–6
Group of Seven, 16, 224, 235n64
Guattari, Félix, 313
gum. *See* bubble gum
gummy bears, 37, 343

Haida, 101
Harnett, William Michael, 216
Hayes, Dan, 96, 102
health: bear identity, 324; country food, 29, 32,

35, 95; dietary choices, 38; impact of settler-colonialism on, 58; of land, 229; and poverty, 130; and restaurant regulations, 174
Historic Collishaw Farm, 157
Hitz, Christian, 134
home cook, 104, 249–50; home cooking, 20, 352
Howell, Sal, 201, 209
Hudson's Bay Company: Canadian department store, 100, 335, 344–5n6; fur trade, 100
human-animal interaction, 39–47

immigrant communities, 14, 126, 183, 196, 241–58, 268, 274, 278
immigrant foodways, 13, 126–7, 137n38, 268, 277, 280–90
impossible (the), 333–4, 340, 344, 346n23
Indigeneity in literature, 173–7, 228, 243
Indigenous chefs, 57–71, 106
Indigenous foodways 29, 31–6, 77–8, 80–5, 86n3, 94–6, 99, 107, 163, 176–7, 228–9
Indigenous gastronomy, 58, 68–71, 72n2, 96–7, 173, 385–6
Indigenous restaurants, 69–70, 78–9, 81–3, 103
Indigenous worldviews, 9, 16–17, 29, 37–50, 50n1, 52n42, 96, 101, 186, 192, 196, 198n5, 376–86
Indo-Canadian, 243, 277, 283, 287. *See also* South Asian
Indo-Pakistani War, 285–6
Instagram, 231, 291n11, 296, 323
International Exhibition of Culinary Art (Internationale Kochkunst-Ausstellung, IKA), 59, 72n8
Inuit, 78; anthropology, 39; art, 31; country food, 31–6; Health Canada food guide, 95; stories, 42–3
Inuit Day, 35
Inuit Nunangat (Inuit homeland), 31

Jacobs, W.W.: "The Monkey's Paw," 170, 178–9n10
James Bay hydroelectric project, 99
Jarvis, Dale, 8–9
Jell-O, 350–1, 356
Jewish Montreal: culinary traditions, 118, 120–1, 125–8, 137n38; recipes, 131, 133
Joe Beef: as Charles McKiernan, 121–4; the restaurant, 8, 120–2, 124, 133–4, 136n22–n23

Johnson, Ursula, 309, 376, 378–87
Jolie, Angelina, 127
junk food, 21, 216, 335

The Keg (restaurant), 297
Kennedy, Jamie, 106
Khalistan separatist movement, 285, 292n34
The Kids in the Hall (TV series), 315, 317–19
Kinder Morgan Trans Mountain expansion, 46
Kirshenblatt-Gimblett, Barbara: on "edible chronotopes," 245; on food as performance medium, 171, 218–19
kitchen, 6, 22; in art, 165–6, 168, 216, 228–9, 348–58; and childhood, 295–6; communal, 197; in diner, 315; *The Golden Girls*, 320; in literature, 129, 172–4, 180n28, 247–8, 257–8, 282–4, 288–90, 348–58, 366–7; in names of culinary competitions, 72n16; professional, 59–60, 63, 83; and professional chefs, 70, 96; and women, 139n63, 309, 317, 348–58
Kjeldsen, Niels, 62
Kleinzahler, August: "Christmas in Chinatown," 128
Koch, Anton, 134
Komagata Maru (ocean liner), 280–1, 283, 291n15
Kozak, Brayden, 106
Kraft Dinner: as Canadian, 20, 226–7, 231; and socio-economic class, 222, 227, 235n79
Kū-kūm (restaurant), 78, 85
Kwantlen Polytechnic University (KPU), 135, 157, 373

L'Abattoir (restaurant), 302
Lady Gaga, 314
Lakoff, George, 247
land art, 189–91, 198n3–n4
Landmarks2017/Repères2017, 376, 388n1
landscape: in art, 16, 18, 117; Canadian, 101, 216–17, 306; digital, 7; food-producing, 8, 102–3, 115, 155, 326; global culinary, 288; Indigenous views of, 48; of local foods, 80; in photography, 216, 263, 291n11; of restaurants, 78, 80–1, 84, 236n87; urban, 12, 335
Lane Level Projects, 300
language: in advertising, 221–2; bilingual packaging, 230; and biocultural diversity, 43–4; and culinary memoir, 244–7, 250; as

embodied, 218; in Montreal, 118, 126, 128, 131–2; multilingualism, 196–7; and place, 163; restaurant menus, 82–5, 118, 132
Laprise, Normand, 134
Latham, John, 218–19, 233n39
La Toundra (restaurant), 95–9
Latour, Bruno, 48–9, 313
Lévi-Strauss, Claude: 4, 10, 247
Liên-Worrall, Brandy, 243
Liliget Feast House (restaurant), 69, 97, 102
Lippard, Lucy, 10
literature: and cookery, 364, 367; and decolonizing food in, 115, 163, 177; and tourism, 309, 367
local food, 9, 43, 80, 305; Indigenous food as, 80–4, 87n27, 105; producers, 146, 151; *Stanley Park*, 171, 173
Lotus Café, 241, 254–7
Lowther, Pat: "Kitchen Murder," 349
Lucky Cat (*maneki neko*), 263, 273
Lukacs, Attila Richard, 172, 180n28
Lynch, John M., 147–50, 153–4, 157

MacIntosh Brook Campground (NS), 376–7
MacLennan, Hugh, 117
Manitoba, 335
Mannur, Anita, 244, 280, 286
maple syrup: as Canadian, 93, 226; from Quebec, 119; served on pork, 124
Mar (Mah), Mary, 253–4
mash-up, 18–19, 85
mass market: Coupland and, 221; food rituals of, 4; 21, 300; forces of, 19; literary genres of, 217; and marketing, 127
Mayer, Ken, 216
McLuhan, Marshall: Barthes and, 10; counter-environments, 4, 15, 22n6, 219, 221, 224; food metaphors, 3–4; global village, 3, 6; media, 4–5, 14–15
McMillan, David, 8, 122, 133–4
McNeil, Gemma, 149, 153
medicine wheel, 115, 186, 188, 190–2, 194, 196, 198n5
Medina, Danielle, 61, 65, 67
Medina Foods, 61, 70
Medomist Farms, 149–51, 154, 157
memory: Badami and, 277–8, 282; Cho and, 270; Coupland and, 230; *Diamond Grill*, 245; and eating, 200, 352; and human survival,

45; Johnson and, 379; photographic albums, 257–8; phototextual, 245–6; Proust and, 246; of restaurants, 306; rhetoric, 248; roti, 283; Wong and, 242, 254
meta-fictional, 352
Mi'kmaq peoples, 376, 380–6, 388n5
Molnar's Taber Corn & Pumpkin Farm, 201
Molson Canadian, 99, 122. *See also* beer
Montgomery, Lucy Maud (L.M.), 353, 370–1
Montreal: and cuisine, 117, 132, 134; foodways, 117–35. *See also* Jewish Montreal
Moore, Brian, 117
moose: as Canadian, 8, 104, 228; dishes, 40, 51n18, 104, 228, 376, 386–7; Nova Scotia, 20, 379–80, 384–6, 388n5, 389n9; Pratt and, 356; Quebec restaurant regulations, 104
Moosemeat & Marmalade (TV series), 96–8
Morin, Frédéric, 8, 122
Morris, Carolyn, 77, 82–3, 86–7n15
Mosher, Terry (Aislin), 18–19
Mowachaht-Muchalaht First Nation, 57
Muckamuck (restaurant), 69
Mueller, Peter, 133–4
Muk^{w}ina, 57
multiculturalism, 211, 284; culinary, 286, 290n1
multi-sensory experience, 203, 243, 245–6, 248, 252–3, 273–4, 334
Mulvihill, Bryan, 189, 197–8n2
Munro, Alice, 138–9n62, 309, 348–58
Muskrat Falls hydroelectric dam, 9
Musqueam, 176
Myers, Lisa, 79–80

Napoleon, Art, 96–7, 102–3
National Household Survey, 126, 138n56
Natrall, Paul Roy, 68
Netukulimk, 379–81
New Brunswick, 348
Newfoundland and Labrador, 8–9, 23n18, 23n19, 23n20, 31, 35, 119, 350
Newton (in Surrey, BC), 183–4, 186–7, 196–7
NishDish (restaurant), 78, 83, 85
Nixon, Rob, 48
Noble Savage, 49
North Delta (BC), 295–7, 306
nostalgia: Coupland and, 230, 236–7n101; culinary memoirs, 250; domestic life, 352; food imagery, 278–80, 289, 290–1n2; in photographs, 270–3; *Taste*, 201; Tim Hortons, 18

Nova Scotia, 20, 78, 83, 104, 376–89
Nuit Blanche (Montreal), 336–8, 343
Nunavut, 35
Nuu-chah-nulth nations, 46, 82
Nuxalk Nation, 81
Nyce, Samantha, 68

object-oriented ontology, 313–14
The Odyssey (bar), 320–1
Oka Crisis, 61
Okanagan, 16, 39, 44–5
Oliver, Jamie, 103–4
Olson, Arnold, 60, 62
Olympic Games: Montreal, 99; Vancouver, 69, 97, 197–8n2
Ondaatje, Michael, 367
Ontario, 32, 35–6, 64–5, 102, 105, 348, 365
orality: Coupland and, 218–19; Wong and, 242–3, 245, 247, 251–4, 256–8
oral stories: Indigenous, 38–40, 47; local histories, 119–20; and women, 139n64
Oudeheemin Foods, 61, 67, 70
Owen, Catherine, 367–8

Painted Pony Café, 78
painting, 16, 165–72, 216, 224, 244, 302, 304, 348–58
Pakistan, 286; Muslims, 284; Indo-Pakistani War, 285
Parts Unknown (TV series), 8–9, 23n19, 104
performance: as theatre, 174, 201, 200–9
performance art, 10, 166, 171, 204, 206, 218, 274, 300, 336–8, 376, 376–87
photography: as art, 31, 35, 147, 149, 151, 252, 267, 274
photo-realism, 351
phototextual, 245
Picard, Martin, 103–6, 124
picnic: Generation X, 223–4, 228; PLOT, 186; *Souvenir of Canada 2*, 228; *Tableaux Blog*, 366, 371
Plath, Sylvia: "Lesbos," 349
pop art, 10, 16, 226
Porcelli, Alessandro, 106
portrait: and death, 154; food memoir as, 244; of food producers, 146–9; of livestock, 150; Lukacs and, 172; of Montreal, 130. *See also* self-portrait
post-colonial, 163, 176, 288

postmodern, 221
Prairies, 119, 211, 324; Chinese restaurants, 266, 268, 270, 273, 274; rural towns, 275; Tim Hortons, 300
Pratt, Christopher, 350
Pratt, Mary, 309, 348–58
Pratt, Mary Louise, 127
Prince Edward Island, 119
processed food: as Canadian, 15, 217, 226; as Filipino, 13; and Inuit, 31
public art, 12, 93–4, 152–7, 192–7, 300
Punjab: cuisine, 281–4, 289; writers from, 290

Quebec, 7, 23n18, 64, 67, 78, 84, 98, 104, 117–40, 228, 233n27, 369, 371
Queer as Folk (TV series), 318
Queer Eye for the Straight Guy (TV series), 311, 315
queer food, 312, 327–9
Quilicum (restaurant), 69

Ray, Krishnendu, 77
Real (the), 333–4, 346n23
(re)al-location, 376, 378–80, 388n2; design pattern, 383
recipes: beaver, 95, 97–8, 104–6; butter tarts, 370; communal sharing of, 194, 256; and contemporary art, 334, 376, 385; in culinary memoirs, 139n64, 241–3, 247, 250–4, 258; from the French, 59; Hot Dog Aspic, 333; Indigenous, 51n18, 62, 65, 79–80; on the Internet, 246; Jewish, 131; in literature 309, 364–73; from Montreal restaurants, 133; *pasta con alice*, 366; regional, 307; Schwartz's smoked meat, 127; in South Asian literature, 280; in *Stanley Park*, 162,165, 169; for subjectivity, 312–14, 328; wild game, 102, 104; and women, 350
Redzepi, René, 80
Regina (SK), 298–302, 306; Club Q bar, 325–6; farmers' market, 300–1; pride parade, 326; University of Regina, 298
relational aesthetics, 189, 335–6, 345n9, 376, 378
restaurant, 6, 20, 96, 117–18; *Can You Hear the Nightbird Call?*, 277–8, 281–90; *Chow*, 254–8; culture, 29, 78, 80; decor, 124, 127, 170, 270–3, 286, 322; family, 296–7, 306, 315, 318, 321; high-end, 302, 304; in Montreal, 120–8,

132–5; and racism, 67, 69; reviews, 217–18, 233n32; and *Stanley Park*, 164–5, 168–75. *See also* Chinese restaurants; Indigenous restaurants; *individual restaurants by name*
restaurantscape, 78, 80, 84
rhetoric: Aristotle and, 246–8, 260n16; and culinary memoir, 211, 247–50; and metaphor, 246
Richler, Mordecai, 117, 125, 128–9
Richler, Noah, 117
River Café, 201, 203–4, 209
Robin Hood flour, 14, 216
Robinson, Harry, 39, 51n16
Robinson, Henry Peach, 151, 157–8n7
Rondriso Farms, 150–1, 157
The Roost (bar), 320, 331n15
Rose, Eric, 200, 203–9
'Round Table Tours, 120–1, 136n20
Roy, Gabrielle, 117; *Bonheur d'occasion* (*The Tin Flute*), 118, 129–30, 139–40n67
Royal Café, 263–7, 274, 275n1
Rubens, Paul, 244, 259n6
Ruthnum, Naben, 278–9, 290–1n2
Ryerson Artspace gallery, 263–5

Saint Henri (in Montreal, QC), 129–30, 139–40n67
salmon: as Canadian, 231; Chilean, 170; Culinary Olympics, 64–5, 68; farmed Atlantic, 229; as pan-Aboriginal cuisine, 79; as restaurant entrée, 81; smoked, 84; in stories, 41–2; threatened, 16; from West Coast, 20, 119. *See also* fish
Salmon n' Bannock (restaurant), 69, 78, 81–2
Salty Rose's & the Periwinkle Café, 380, 385
Sappier, Bryan, 62
Saskatchewan, 64, 119, 254, 300, 369
Save On Meats (restaurant), 168
Schitt's Creek (TV series), 315–17, 321
Schnell, Albert, 134
Schwartz's (deli), 126–7, 137n38, 138n47; *Schwartz's Hebrew Delicatessen: The Story*, 129
Scott, F.R., 117–18; "Bonne Entente," 132
sculpture, 12, 198n4, 213, 298, 334–43
seals, 31–2, 39–40; served in restaurants, 104; smoked, 74n54
Second World War: Britain's food security, 18; Montreal, 129–30; Philippines, 13–14

self-portrait: Borda and, 153–4, 159n14; Cabalu and, 10, 12–14; Coupland and, 10–12
Sephardic Jews, 128, 138n56
server. *See* wait staff
settler colonialism, 16–17, 77, 79–81, 85–6, 94, 107
7-Eleven, 224, 296
sexuality: bear culture, 324; Davie Street, 322; and drink, 316; and food, 309, 312–14, 320, 326–7, 350; *The Kids in the Hall*, 318; *Schitt's Creek*, 315–16; *Stanley Park*, 180n29; women, 350–1
Shaw, Maddy, 17, 25n51; *#remain*, 17–18
Shore, Stephen, 273
Simard, Melissa, 121, 125–6, 136n20
Sisika Nation, 79
Sitar Restaurant, 218
Siwash Rock, 175–7, 181n37
Six Nations Reserve, 64–5, 67
Skye, Bertha, 60, 62, 64–5, 67
slow food movement, 9, 38. *See also* diet
small town: childhood, 317, 319, 325, 329; Chinese restaurants, 259n8, 263–75
Smithson, Robert, 191, 198n4
Smitty's (restaurant), 296; as inspiration for Smitty on *The Kids in the Hall*, 318–19
social practice art, 183, 187–9, 336, 338, 345n9, 345n11
Société des Cuisiniers Française, 59
South Asian: diaspora, 211, 277–90, 290–1n2; film, 244; gastronomy, 277–80; heritage, 7–8
Southeast Asian, 13, 335
South Indian, 289
space: as designed, 170, 172; digital, 148–9, 152, 155–6; green, 183–97; intercultural, 285, 290; language's relationship to, 163; and Montreal, 117–18; production of, 9; public, 6, 10, 12, 13–14, 58
Spam, 13–14
Spartacus, 316
Spivak, Gayatri, 49–50
Squamish Nation, 68, 81, 176
Starnino, Carmine, 366
Statistics Canada, 78, 120
still life: Brexit, 17–18, 25n51; cookbooks, 246; Coupland and, 216–17, 226, 228, 229, 232n17; Dutch vanitas painting, 302; Lukacs and, 172; Pratt and, 350, 353; Wong and, 252
Stoney Nakoda Haudenosaunee, 79

St Sebastian, 304–5
St Viateur Bagel Shop, 126, 129
suburban: culture, 296, 299, 306, 322, 335, 338; farms, 151–3
supermarket: Indigenous foodways, 43; local food, 146; processed food, 23n20; Steinbergs, 137n39; waste, 208. *See also* grocery store
Surrey Art Gallery, 147, 157
sustainability: Coupland and, 229; farming, 146, 326; Forage (restaurant), 81; Indigenous worldviews, 39–40, 43–5, 380–1, 388n8; Johnson and, 378–81, 385; Newfoundland, 8; and performance, 115, 206, 208; River Café, 201, 207; *Taste*, 200, 207
Syilx, 39, 44, 45

Tableaux Blog, 309, 364, 366, 371–3
tableaux vivants, 152–3
takeout, 69, 269, 325
Tallbear, Kim, 39, 42, 49
techno-food, 12
teepee, 63; as smoker, 96
television: food messaging 22n12. *See also television series by name*
tenderloin: beaver, 105; El Chaco Angus beef, 174; raccoon, 173; venison, 64
terra nullius, 78, 84–5
Terroir Symposium, 58
Thanksgiving, 257
theatre, 200–9; restaurant opening as, 174; Theatre of Cruelty, 206; Yiddish, 126
Thiebaud, Wayne, 244; *Girl with Ice Cream Cone*, 259n6
Thomas, Audrey, 366; *Intertidal Life*, 365
Thomas, Jacqui, 252
300 (film), 298–9
Thrush, Coll, 57, 84–5, 87n27
Tim Hortons (restaurant): *Always Fresh (The Donut Farmer)*, 300–2; and Burger King, 18–19; as Canadian, 20, 25n54; the Prairies, 300; Timbits, 300–2
Timothy's (café), 317–18
Tlingit, 42
tomato beef, 365, 367
tongue: cast of, 341; and glossary, 221–2; and memory, 295; as mother tongue, 56, 176; slip of the, 254, 259–60n28; and taste, 200, 206, 306; *The Taste of Someone Else's Mouth*, 341–2; as in tongue-in-cheek humour, 133, 227, 330

Toody-Ni Grill and Catering Company, 61, 69
Top Chef, 58
Toqué! (restaurant), 120, 133–4
tourism: as literary, 309, 367; Montreal, 126. *See also* culinary tourism
Traditional Ecological Knowledge (TEK), 47
Tremblay, Michel, 117; *chapeaux de baloney*, 364–5
Tsimshian, 39, 41, 51n20, 68
Turkish Delight, 329
Turner, Mark, 247
Turner, Nancy, 39

ulu, 36
Unama'ki, 376
Unama'ki Institute of Natural Resources (UINR), 380, 388n5, 388–9n8

Vancouver Community College (VCC), 67–8
Vancouver Pride Week, 327–8
vanitas painting, 216, 230; *Dogs' Dinner*, 302–4
Vegreville (AB), 268–71
Vickers, Faith, 68
Vij, Vikram, 243, 278–9, 288
violence: depicted in art, 168; in the domestic kitchen, 309, 349; gender, 165, 348–50, 355–8; homophobic, 318, 328; and kissing, 341
visual elements, 242–3, 245–7, 250
vomit, 228, 334, 338 343, 344
Vulcan (AB), 259n8, 265, 267, 275n2

Wah, Fred, 367; *Diamond Grill*, 243–5, 364–5, 259n3; "faking it," 254, 260–1n28
Wainwright Steak House (restaurant), 265, 275n3
wait staff, 81, 130, 172, 201, 205, 209, 287–8, 304–6, 325
Watts, Dolly and Annie, 97
Weston, Edward, 252
Wet'suwet'en, 60, 79–80, 86n4, 97
White Spot (restaurant), 297
Wildebeest (restaurant), 302
Wildlife Act, 102
Wild Salmon (restaurant), 68
Wilensky, Moe, 125, 137n38
Wilensky's (restaurant), 125, 127, 129, 138n47
William Tell Restaurant, 134
wine: as Canadian, 19; communion, 175; as feminine, 317; and food, 201, 366; as

Indigenous, 69; as queer, 315–16; river of, 222; and sexuality, 326–7; and socio-economic class, 325
Winfield, Andrew, 201, 209
Wolastoqiyik, 62
Wolfman, David, 60, 62, 67
Wong, Dennis, 252, 254–6, 258
Wong, Janice, 211, 241–3, 245–7, 250–8
Woodland Cultural Centre, 67
World Association of Chefs Society (WACS), 61
World Tea Party, 189–90, 197–8n2

Yellowknives Dene, 79
Yelp, 321
Young, Phyllis B., 366, 373; *The Torontonians*, 372–3
Yukon, 40, 42
Yuxweluptun, Lawrence Paul, 16–17; *Haida Hot Dog*, 16; "hot-dogging," 25n46

Zaklan, Doug, 149, 153
Zaklan Heritage Farm, 149, 151, 153, 157